gilbert

LAW SUMMARIES

CORPORATIONS

Fourteenth Edition

Jesse H. Choper
Professor of Law
University of California, Berkeley

Melvin A. Eisenberg
Professor of Law
University of California, Berkeley

THE
barbri
GROUP

HARCOURT BRACE LEGAL AND PROFESSIONAL PUBLICATIONS, INC.
EDITORIAL OFFICES: 111 W. Jackson Blvd., 7th Floor, Chicago, IL 60604

gilbert
LAW SUMMARIES

REGIONAL OFFICES: Chicago, Dallas, Los Angeles, New York, Washington, D.C.
Distributed by: **Harcourt Brace & Company** 6277 Sea Harbor Drive, Orlando, FL 32887 (800)787-8717

SERIES EDITOR
Elizabeth L. Snyder, B.A., J.D.
Attorney At Law

PROJECT EDITOR
Maureen A. Mitchell, B.A., J.D.
Attorney At Law

QUALITY CONTROL EDITOR
Blythe C. Smith, B.A.

gilbert
LAW SUMMARIES

Titles Available

Administrative Law
Agency & Partnership
Antitrust
Bankruptcy
Basic Accounting for Lawyers
Business Law
California Bar Performance Test Skills
Civil Procedure
Civil Procedure & Practice
Commercial Paper & Payment Law
Community Property
Conflict of Laws
Constitutional Law
Contracts
Corporations
Criminal Law
Criminal Procedure
Dictionary of Legal Terms
Estate and Gift Tax
Evidence

Family Law
Federal Courts
First Year Questions & Answers
Future Interests
Income Tax I (Individual)
Income Tax II (Corporate)
Labor Law
Legal Ethics
Legal Research & Writing
Multistate Bar Exam
Personal Property
Property
Remedies
Sales & Lease of Goods
Securities Regulation
Secured Transactions
Torts
Trusts
Wills

Also Available:

First Year Program
Pocket Size Law Dictionary
Success in Law School Handbook

Gilbert Law Audio Tapes
"The Law School Legends Series"

Bankruptcy
Civil Procedure
Commercial Paper
Constitutional Law
Contracts
Corporations
Criminal Law

Criminal Procedure
Evidence
Family Law
Federal Income Taxation
Future Interests
Law School ABC's
Law School Exam Writing

Professional Responsibility
Real Property
Remedies
Sales & Lease of Goods
Secured Transactions
Torts
Wills & Trusts

All Titles Available at Your Law School Bookstore,
or Call to Order: 1-800-787-8717

Harcourt Brace Legal and Professional Publications, Inc.
176 West Adams, Suite 2100
Chicago, IL 60603

There are two things BAR/BRI will do for you:

1 Get you through LAW SCHOOL

2 Get you through the BAR EXAM

O.K. we'll throw in a highlighter*

*Available at your local BAR/BRI office.

Over 4 Million Copies Sold!

- Gilbert Law Summaries
- Legalines
- Law School Legends Audio Tapes
- Employment Guides
- Casebriefs Interactive Software

Relied On By Over 600,000 Students!

- Lectures, Outlines & Mini Review
- Innovative Computer Software
- Multistate, Essay & Performance Workshops
- Complete MPRE Preparation
- First Year Review Program

Our Only Mission Is Test Preparation

BAR/BRI Bar Review 1-888-3BARBRI

GILBERT LAW SUMMARIES 1-800-787-8717

SUMMARY OF CONTENTS

Page

CORPORATIONS CAPSULE SUMMARY I

TEXT CORRELATION CHART i

APPROACH TO EXAMS . . . . (i)

I. CHARACTERISTICS OF THE CORPORATION 1
    Chapter Approach 1
    A. Principal Characteristics 1
    B. Corporations Distinguished from Other Forms of Business Associations 2
    C. Disregard of Corporate Entity 10
    D. Subordination of Shareholder Debts—"Deep Rock" Doctrine 13

II. ORGANIZING THE CORPORATION 15
    Chapter Approach 15
    A. General Corporation Laws 15
    B. Formalities in Organizing Corporation 15
    C. Defects in Formation Process—"De Jure" and "De Facto" Corporations 17

III. LIABILITIES FOR TRANSACTIONS BEFORE INCORPORATION 21
    Chapter Approach 21
    A. Promoters 21
    B. Contracts Made by Promoters on Corporation's Behalf 21
    C. Obligations of Predecessor Business 24

IV. POWERS OF THE CORPORATION 26
    Chapter Approach 26
    A. Corporate Powers 26
    B. Ultra Vires Transactions 29

V. MANAGEMENT AND CONTROL 32
    Chapter Approach 32
    A. Allocation of Powers Between Directors and Shareholders 33
    B. Directors 38
    C. Officers 47
    D. Conflicts of Interest in Corporate Transactions 48

VI. INSIDER TRADING 61
    Chapter Approach 61
    A. Introduction 62
    B. Common Law 62
    C. Securities Exchange Act of 1934—In General 62
    D. Section 10(b) and Rule 10b-5 63
    E. Section 16 of the 1934 Act 82
    F. Section 16(b) Compared to Rule 10b-5 90
    G. Common Law Liability for Insider Trading 91

VII. RIGHTS OF SHAREHOLDERS 92
    Chapter Approach 92

	A.	Voting Rights	94
	B.	Restrictions on Transfer of Shares	112
	C.	Shareholders' Informational Rights	116
	D.	Fiduciary Obligations of Controlling Shareholders	119
	E.	Shareholder Suits	126

VIII.	CAPITALIZATION OF THE CORPORATION		145
	Chapter Approach		145
	A.	Shares—In General	146
	B.	Classes of Shares—Preferences	146
	C.	Authorization and Issuance of Shares	148
	D.	Stock Subscriptions	148
	E.	Consideration Required To Be Paid for Shares	149
	F.	Fiduciary Duties of Promoters	152
	G.	Preemptive Rights	153
	H.	Underwriting	155
	I.	Statutes Regulating Issuance of Shares	156

IX.	DISTRIBUTIONS TO SHAREHOLDERS		167
	Chapter Approach		167
	A.	Dividends	168
	B.	Redemption and Repurchase of Shares	173

X.	FUNDAMENTAL CHANGES IN CORPORATE STRUCTURE		177
	Chapter Approach		177
	A.	Introduction	179
	B.	Appraisal Rights	179
	C.	Statutory Mergers	183
	D.	De Facto Mergers	186
	E.	Triangular Mergers	188
	F.	Sale of Substantially All Assets	189
	G.	Amendment of Articles	190
	H.	Dissolution and Liquidation	194
	I.	Limitations on Power of Controlling Shareholders to Effect Fundamental Changes in Corporate Structure	198
	J.	Tender Offers	202

XI.	CONFLICT OF LAWS PRINCIPLES		217
	Chapter Approach		217
	A.	General Rule	217
	B.	Limitations	217

REVIEW QUESTIONS AND ANSWERS	219
SAMPLE EXAM QUESTIONS AND ANSWERS	251
TABLE OF CASES	265
INDEX	273

TEXT CORRELATION CHART

Gilbert Law Summary Corporations	Cary, Eisenberg Corporations 1995 (7th ed.—Unabridged)	Cary, Eisenberg Corporations 1995 (7th ed.—Concise)	Choper, Coffee, Gilson Corporations 1995 (4th ed.)	Hamilton Corporations 1994 (5th ed.)	Henn Corporations 1986 (2nd ed.)	Vagts Corporations 1989 (3rd ed.)
I. CHARACTERISTICS OF THE CORPORATION						
A. Principal Characteristics	117-120	74-77	1-10	5-6, 12-18, 143-145, 162-174	24-26	1-17
B. Corporations Distinguished From Other Forms of Business Associations	31-116, 120-124, 389-391	25-73, 77-82, 269-271	671-696	7-174	49-80	18-34
C. Disregard of Corporate Entity	163-200, 204-212	111-135	260-288	273-322	38-48, 176-227	82-98
D. Subordination of Shareholder Debts—"Deep Rock" Doctrine	200-204	136-137	284-288	318-322	215-219	159-167
II. ORGANIZING THE CORPORATION						
A. General Corporation Laws	125-139	137-138	11-34	2-7, 12-18, 175-206	1-23	1-17
B. Formalities in Organizing Corporation		83-85, 88-89, 90	66-67, 245-249	209-228	137-154	76-78
C. Defects in Formation Process—"De Jure" and "De Facto" Corporations	149-163	99-111	249-260	256-272	155-175	78-87
III. LIABILITIES FOR TRANSACTIONS BEFORE INCORPORATION						
A. Promoters	139-140	90-92	296-297	238-239	118-121	98-100
B. Contracts Made by Promoters on Corporation's Behalf	140-149	92-98	296-309	239-255	121-136	
C. Obligations of Predecessor Business			289-296	1258-1260	878-883	
IV. POWERS OF THE CORPORATION						
A. Corporate Powers	213-240	145-165	34-49, 53-65	215-216, 237, 1261-1262	143-146, 275-279	101-130
B. Ultra Vires Transactions	185-197, 204-212	138-145	66-73	228-238	278-279, 386-387, 399	104-130, 435-438
V. MANAGEMENT AND CONTROL						
A. Allocation of Powers Between Directors and Shareholders	220-284, 305-306, 391-413, 424-444	166-190, 207-208, 269-285, 297-308, 315-326, 342-362	34-49, 53-65, 166-168, 532-539, 632-656, 696-721, 730-755	223-224, 428-439, 450-484, 527-529, 536-537, 554-555	265-274	385-403
B. Directors	137, 261-262, 287-298, 524-527, 557-643, 647-651, 689-711	88-89, 178-179, 193-201, 297-308, 364, 379-440, 474-478	6-9, 34-49, 53-57, 73-115, 142-168, 578-583, 607-608, 749-755	538-541, 564-571, 587-604, 627-656, 735-821, 886-895	332-365, 384-442, 521-541	196-224, 290-296, 362-403
C. Officers	298-304, 557-634, 634-643	201-206, 379-440	57-65, 582-583	275-281, 298, 571-586	366-442, 521-541	287-361
D. Conflicts of Interest in Corporate Transactions	647-737, 1177-1184	437-496	115-183	821-895	442-520	224-276
VI. INSIDER TRADING	325-329, 810-995	546-652	340-342, 349-520	896-1074	464-471, 681-698, 713-720	543-616
VII. RIGHTS OF SHAREHOLDERS						
A. Voting Rights	245-252, 285-286, 305-309, 330-388, 405-453	206-211, 227-268, 285-314	521-529, 608-669, 710-740	476-538, 604-626, 656-734, 1271-1289	285-321, 610-625, 698-713	362-443, 757-776

Gilbert Law Summary Corporations	Cary, Eisenberg Corporations 1995 (7th ed.—Unabridged)	Cary, Eisenberg Corporations 1995 (7th ed.—Concise)	Choper, Coffee, Gilson Corporations 1995 (4th ed.)	Hamilton Corporations 1994 (5th ed.)	Henn Corporations 1986 (2nd ed.)	Vagts Corporations 1989 (3rd ed.)
B. Restrictions on Transfer of Shares	491-522	342-361	700-708, 745-746	527-538, 842	632-649	753, 777-786
C. Shareholders' Informational Rights	310-329	212-227	317, 322, 595-608, 618, 624	666-674, 969-970, 1220-1239	321-330	405, 480
D. Fiduciary Obligations of Controlling Shareholders	453-475, 737-809	314-326, 496-545	134-142, 740-777, 977-997, 1033-1053	318-322, 425-429, 547-563, 844-867, 886-890, 1074-1101	471-508	443-454, 616-636, 739-747
E. Shareholder Suits	996-1129	653-747	775-885	205, 693, 695, 734, 780-821, 1094, 1102-1132	974-1138	455-535
VIII. CAPITALIZATION OF THE CORPORATION						
A. Shares—In General	1403	84-85, 166-174	9-10, 206, 521-530	364-368	236-245	131-136
B. Classes of Shares—Preferences	135-137, 422-424	84-88	207-211, 571-578	324-331	236-240, 774-779, 799-808	131-136, 652-656, 748-749
C. Authorization and Issuance of Shares	133, 1403-1404	84, 89-90, 902	206-235, 314-316	332-333	236-245	131-167
D. Stock Subscriptions	137-138	89-90	296-309	331-332	125-126, 263-264	135-136
E. Consideration Required To Be Paid for Shares	1328-1332	879-882	17-20, 218-239	331, 333-350	245-251	135-167
F. Fiduciary Duties of Promoters	139-140	90-99	301-309, 314-316, 827-829	238-255	118-136	40-54
G. Preemptive Rights	133	84-85	533, 535-550, 850-855	391-402	561-567	642-652
H. Underwriting	1404, 1410-1416, 1483-1495	903, 908-913	314-316, 318-320	375	672-674	167, 176-187, 561-562
I. Statutes Regulating Issuance of Shares	1403-1409, 1416-1530	904-964	314-316, 318-349, 872	368-391	671-743	167-195
IX. DISTRIBUTIONS TO SHAREHOLDERS						
A. Dividends	1332-1382	882-901	215-216, 228-235, 895-899, 1025-1026, 1057	326-327, 349, 402-449	744-793, 806-829	665-676
B. Redemption and Repurchase of Shares	1383-1402	899-901		425-439, 443, 447-448	793-799, 823-825	446-454, 676-683
X. FUNDAMENTAL CHANGES IN CORPORATE STRUCTURE						
A. Introduction	1130-1132	748-749	533-534	548-557, 863-867, 1240-1250, 1256-1257	830-844	684-687
B. Appraisal Rights	213-217, 475-491, 1136-1147, 1167, 1176-1187	327-342, 753-756, 780-781	187-218, 1042-1044		892-911	688-693, 743-748
C. Statutory Mergers	306, 1147-1152, 1167-1169	756-761, 780-781	533-534, 577	850-867, 1240-1250	852-873	698-701, 718-749
D. De Facto Mergers	776-780, 1153-1169, 1176-1184	761-773	537-538, 577, 1055	1250-1260	896-898	688-698
E. Triangular Mergers	1169-1176	773-780				
F. Sale of Substantially All Assets	1132-1136, 1153-1169	749-753	889, 1055	1250-1260	874-892	385-389, 443-446, 688-697
G. Amendment of Articles	306	208	533	16-18, 477-484, 1240-1250	844-852	684-685, 748-749
H. Dissolution and Liquidation	306, 522-524, 527-552, 1366, 1379-1380	362-378	760-773	538-557	654-670, 799-806, 911-919	698-699, 786-793, 796

TEXT CORRELATION CHART—continued

Gilbert Law Summary Corporations	Cary, Eisenberg Corporations 1995 (7th ed.—Unabridged)	Cary, Eisenberg Corporations 1995 (7th ed.—Concise)	Choper, Coffee, Gilson Corporations 1995 (4th ed.)	Hamilton Corporations 1994 (5th ed.)	Henn Corporations 1986 (2nd ed.)	Vagts Corporations 1989 (3rd ed.)
I. Limitations on Power of Controlling Shareholders to Effect Fundamental Changes in Corporate Structure	776-809, 1177-1212, 1219-1231, 1386-1387	375-376, 522-545, 782-803	134-142, 977-997, 1025-1026	850-867, 936-944, 1074-1101	471-508, 862-871	717-718, 725-750
J. Tender Offers	1213-1327	803-878	892-894, 899-977, 997-1030, 1053-1079	1133-1219	924-973	704-717
XI. CONFLICT OF LAW PRINCIPLES	125-132	82-83			81-117, 975-980	76-79

gilbert
capsule summary
corporations

Text Section

I. CHARACTERISTICS OF THE CORPORATION

A. PRINCIPAL CHARACTERISTICS
1. **Entity Status:** A corporation is a legal entity created under the authority of the legislature . . . . [1]
2. **Limited Liability:** As a legal entity, a corporation is responsible for its own debts; its shareholders' liability is limited to their investment . . . . [2]
3. **Free Transferability of Interests:** Shares, representing ownership interests, are freely transferable . . . . [3]
4. **Centralized Management and Control:** A corporation's management is centralized in a board of directors and officers. Shareholders have no direct control over the board's activities . . . . [4]
5. **Duration—Continuity of Existence:** A corporation is capable of perpetual existence . . . . [5]
6. **Taxation:** A corporation, as an entity, pays taxes on its own income; shareholders are taxed only on dividends . . . . [6]

B. CORPORATIONS DISTINGUISHED FROM OTHER FORMS OF BUSINESS ASSOCIATIONS
1. **General Partnerships:** In most states, partnerships are governed by the Uniform Partnership Act ("UPA"). However, the Revised Uniform Partnership Act ("RUPA") has been adopted by a few states and more states will probably follow . . . . [8]
   a. **Aggregate status:** A partnership is an aggregation of two or more persons who are engaged in business as co-owners. Although not a legal entity, a partnership is treated as one for certain purposes, *e.g.*, ownership and transfer of property. RUPA confers entity status on partnerships . . . . . [9]
   b. **Unlimited liability:** Every partner is subject to unlimited personal liability on partnership debts . . . . [11]
   c. **Transferability of interests:** A partner cannot make a transferee a *member* of the partnership. She can, however, *assign* her interest in the partnership, thus permitting the assignee to receive distributions of profits. Because the assignee does *not* become a member of the partnership, he is not entitled to participate in partnership business or management . . . . . [12]
   d. **Duration and dissolution:** A partnership cannot have perpetual existence. It is terminable at will unless a definite term is expressed or implied, and is also dissolved by the death, incapacity, or withdrawal of any partner . . . . . [14]
      (1) **Wrongful dissolution:** Partnerships can also be dissolved in contravention of the partnership agreement, by the express will of any partner, by a court, or by a partner's conduct. Upon wrongful dissolution, nonbreaching partners may seek damages for breach and, if they choose to do so, may continue the partnership upon payment to the breaching partner of the value of his interest . . . . [16]
      (2) **Compare—dissociation under RUPA:** Termination of partnership status under RUPA results in either the winding up of the partnership or the buyout of the dissociating partner, depending on the event triggering the termination. A buyout of a dissociating partner may

      be reduced by damages if the dissociation was wrongful . . . . [18]

  e. **Management and control:** Absent a contrary agreement, every partner has a right to participate equally in the partnership management . . . . [22]

  f. **Authority:** Each partner, as an agent of the firm, may bind the partnership by acts done for the carrying on, in the usual way, the business of the partnership . . . . [24]

    (1) **RUPA:** RUPA makes clear that a partnership is bound by a partner's act for carrying on in the usual way either the ***actual*** partnership business or a ***business of the kind*** carried on by the partnership. Further, RUPA provides for the filing of a Statement of Partnership Authority, which is conclusive in favor of third persons even if they are unaware of the statement. However, limitations on a partner's authority contained in such a statement, other than those regarding real estate transfers, are ineffective unless the third party knows of them or a statement was delivered to him . . . . [25]

  g. **Ownership of property:** Title may be held in the name of the partnership, but the property is ***owned*** by the individual partners as tenants in partnership. There is no tenancy in partnership under RUPA, which provides that property acquired by the partnership is owned by the partnership, not by individual partners . . . . [28]

  h. **Capacity to sue and be sued:** Under the UPA, a lawsuit must be brought by or against individual partners, rather than the partnership. Partners are jointly and severally liable for wrongful acts and breaches of trust; they are only jointly liable for debts and obligations of the partnership . . . . [30]

    (1) **Statutory reforms:** Many state statutes specifically allow a partnership to be sued in its own name. Other states make all partnership liabilities joint and several. Other reforms provide that not all joint obligors need be joined in a suit . . . . [32]

    (2) **RUPA:** Under RUPA, a partnership may sue and be sued in its own name, and partners are jointly and severally liable for ***all*** partnership obligations. A claim against the partnership cannot be satisfied from a partner's personal assets unless partnership assets have been exhausted . . . . [33]

2. **Joint Venture:** A joint venture is essentially a partnership formed for some ***limited*** investment or operation, as opposed to a continuing business enterprise. Joint ventures are governed by most, if not all, of the rules applicable to partnerships . . . . [34]

3. **Limited Partnership:** This is a partnership consisting of two classes of partners: general partners (with rights and obligations as in an ordinary partnership) and limited partners (with no control and limited liability). There are three versions of the Uniform Limited Partnership Act, each with different provisions regarding a limited partner's liability to third parties . . . . [35]

4. **Limited Liability Partnerships:** In a limited liability partnership ("LLP"), a general partner is ***not*** personally liable for ***all*** partnership obligations arising from negligence, wrongful acts, and misconduct absent her involvement in the conduct. There is no exclusion for liability for contractual obligations . . . . [41]

5. **Limited Liability Companies:** A limited liability company ("LLC") is a non-corporate business entity whose owners (members) have limited liability and can participate actively in its management. An LLC may be either for a term or at will. It can be managed either by its members or nonmember managers. Depending on the statute, distributions are made either equally to each member or in proportion to each member's contribution . . . . [45]

  a. **Withdrawal and dissolution:** Some statutes provide that any event that terminates a member's membership (*e.g.*, death, resignation) causes dissolution. Other statutes distinguish between fault events (*e.g.*, member misconduct) and nonfault events (*e.g.*, death, bankruptcy), and some

II—Corporations

provide that dissolution can be avoided by paying the withdrawing member fair value for his interest . . . . [52]

    b.   **Advantages of LLCs:** An LLC for a business association, not publicly held, has strong advantages: partnership taxation; virtually no restrictions in structuring ownership interests and management; limited liability for owners and managers; and no limitations on the number or nature of owners . . . . [57]

C. DISREGARD OF CORPORATE ENTITY

    1.   **In General:** Since a corporation is a distinct legal entity, shareholders are normally shielded from corporate obligations. In certain instances, however, the corporate entity will be disregarded . . . . [60]

    2.   **Suits by Corporate Creditors Against Shareholders:** This is the most common situation for disregarding the corporate entity, and it is called "piercing the corporate veil." The following are the most important elements considered by the courts: . . . . [61]

        a.   **Commingling of assets:** Commingling of corporate assets and personal assets of shareholders (*e.g.*, paying private debts with corporate funds) may lead to piercing of the corporate veil . . . . [62]

        b.   **Lack of corporate formalities:** Whether basic corporate formalities (*e.g.*, regular meetings, corporate records maintained, issuance of stock) were followed is also relevant. Note that ***statutory close corporations*** are permitted more flexibility regarding corporate formalities . . . . [63]

        c.   **Undercapitalization:** If the corporation was organized without sufficient capital or liability insurance to meet obligations reasonably expected to arise, the corporate veil may be pierced . . . . [65]

        d.   **Domination and control by shareholder:** The corporate veil is often pierced when an individual or other corporation owns most or all of the stock so that it completely dominates policy or business decisions . . . . . . [66]

        e.   **"Alter ego"; "instrumentality"; "unity of interest":** When no separate entity exists and the corporation is merely the alter ego or instrumentality of its shareholders, or when there is a unity of interest between the corporation and its shareholders, the corporate veil is often pierced. Note that these terms are usually applied only if other grounds (*see* above) are present . . . . [67]

        f.   **Fraud, wrong, dishonesty, or injustice:** Generally, the veil will be pierced only if one of these elements is available, *e.g.*, no piercing of veil if there is a lack of corporate formalities without resultant injustice. Piercing the veil usually involves corporations with a small number of shareholders . . . . . . [68]

    3.   **Piercing the Wall Between Affiliated Corporations:** This occurs when a plaintiff with a claim against one corporation attempts to satisfy the claim against the assets of an affiliated corporation under common ownership. This type of aggregation is permitted only when each affiliated corporation is not a free-standing enterprise but is merely a fragment of an entity composed of affiliated corporations . . . . [70]

    4.   **Use of Corporate Form to Evade Statutory or Contract Obligations:** The corporate form may be ignored when it is used to evade a statutory or contractual obligation. The issue is whether the contract or statute was intended to apply to the shareholders as well as the corporation . . . . [71]

    5.   **Disregard of Corporate Entity in Favor of Corporation or Its Shareholders:** Only ***third parties***, not the corporation or its shareholders, are generally allowed to disregard the corporate entity . . . . [72]

D. SUBORDINATION OF SHAREHOLDER DEBTS—"DEEP ROCK" DOCTRINE

If a corporation goes into bankruptcy, debts to its controlling shareholders may be subordinated to claims of other creditors. When subordination occurs, shareholder loans are treated as if they were ***invested capital*** (stock) . . . . [73]

1. **Grounds:** Major factors in determining whether to subordinate include fraud, mismanagement, undercapitalization, commingling, excessive control, and other equitable reasons . . . . [76]

II. **ORGANIZING THE CORPORATION**

A. **GENERAL CORPORATION LAWS**
Generally, corporations are created under and according to statutory provisions of the state in which formation is sought . . . . [77]

B. **FORMALITIES IN ORGANIZING CORPORATION**
1. **Certificate or Articles of Incorporation:** State law governs the content of the articles, which are filed with the secretary of state. Usually, the articles *must* specify the corporate name, number of shares authorized, address of the corporation's initial registered office and name of initial registered agent, and the name and address of each incorporator. Optional provisions may include provisions concerning the purpose, management and powers of the corporation, par value of shares, shareholder liability for corporate debt, and any provision that is required or permitted in the bylaws . . . . [78]
   a. **Purpose clause:** Under most statutes, no elaborate purpose clause is needed. It is sufficient to state that the purpose of the corporation is to engage in any lawful business activity . . . . [81]
2. **Organizational Meeting:** Filing the articles in proper form creates the corporation, after which an organizational meeting is held by either the incorporators or the initial board of directors named in the articles . . . . [82]
   a. **Matters determined at meeting:** If no directors are named in the articles, directors are elected and bylaws are adopted at the meeting of the incorporators. Matters determined at the meeting of the initial directors include adoption of bylaws (if necessary), election of officers, adoption of corporate seal and form of stock certificate, authorization of share issuance at designated prices, and designation of corporate bank . . . . [83]

C. **DEFECTS IN FORMATION PROCESS—"DE JURE" AND "DE FACTO" CORPORATIONS**
1. **In General:** When there is a defect or irregularity in formation, the question is whether the corporation exists "de jure," "de facto," "by estoppel," or not at all. This issue usually arises when a third party seeks to impose personal liability on would-be shareholders. Another method for challenging corporate status, used only by the state, is a *quo warranto proceeding* . . . . [85]
2. **De Jure Corporation:** This exists when the corporation is organized *in compliance with the statute*. Its status cannot be attacked by anyone—not even the state. Most courts require only "substantial compliance"; others require exact compliance with the *mandatory requirements* . . . . [88]
3. **De Facto Corporation:** This exists when there is insufficient compliance as to the state (*i.e.,* state can attack in quo warranto proceeding), but the steps taken are sufficient to treat the enterprise as a corporation with respect to its *dealings with third parties*. A colorable attempt to incorporate and some actual use of the corporate existence is required . . . . [91]
4. **Corporation by Estoppel:** Certain parties are estopped from asserting defective incorporation when they have dealt with the corporation as though properly formed. For example, shareholders who claimed corporate status in an earlier transaction are estopped to deny that status in a suit brought against the corporation. The estoppel theory normally does *not* apply to bar suit against would-be shareholders by tort claimants or other involuntary creditors . . . . [94]
5. **Who May Be Held Liable:** When a would-be corporation is not a de jure or de facto corporation or a corporation by estoppel, the modern trend imposes

personal liability against only those owners who ***actively participated*** in management of the enterprise . . . .   [99]

6. **Effect of Statutes**
   a. **On de facto doctrine:** States following the prior version of the Model Act have abolished the de facto doctrine, thus making all purported "shareholders" jointly and severally liable for all liabilities incurred as a result of the purported "corporation." However, statues based on the Revised Model Business Corporation Act require a person acting on behalf of the enterprise to ***know*** that there was no incorporation before liability attaches . . . .   [103]
   b. **On estoppel doctrine:** The effect of both Acts is an unsettled issue . . . .   [105]
   c. **On liability:** Under the prior Model Act, liability extends to investors who also exercise control or actively participate in policy and operational decisions. It is expected that the Revised Model Act will be interpreted in the same manner . . . .   [106]

III. LIABILITIES FOR TRANSACTIONS BEFORE INCORPORATION

A. PROMOTERS
1. **Definition:** A promoter participates in the formation of the corporation, usually arranging compliance with the legal requirements of formation, securing initial capital, and entering into necessary contracts on behalf of the corporation during the time it is being formed . . . .   [107]
2. **Fiduciary Duties to Each Other:** ***Full disclosure*** and ***fair dealing*** are required between the promoters and the corporation and among the promoters themselves . . . .   [108]

B. CONTRACTS MADE BY PROMOTERS ON CORPORATION'S BEHALF
1. **Rights and Liabilities of Corporation**
   a. **English rule:** The corporation is ***not directly liable*** on pre-incorporation contracts even if later ratified. *Rationale:* The corporation was not yet in existence at the time the promoter was acting . . . .   [110]
   b. **American rule:** The corporation is ***liable if it later ratifies or adopts*** such contracts . . . .   [113]
   c. **Corporation's right to enforce contract:** Under either rule, the corporation may enforce the contract against the party with whom the promoter contracted, if it chooses to do so . . . .   [116]
2. **Rights and Liabilities of Promoters**
   a. **Liability on pre-incorporation contract:** Generally, promoters are liable if the corporation rejects the pre-incorporation contract, fails to incorporate, or adopts the contract but fails to perform, ***unless*** the contracting party ***clearly intended*** to contract with the corporation only and not with the promoters individually . . . .   [117]
   b. **Right to enforce against other party:** If a corporation is not formed, the promoter may still enforce the contract . . . .   [120]

C. OBLIGATIONS OF PREDECESSOR BUSINESS
A corporation that acquires all of the assets of a predecessor business does not ordinarily succeed to its liabilities, with some exceptions . . . .   [122]
1. **Exceptions to Rule:** The successor corporation may be liable for its predecessor's liabilities if: (i) the new corporation expressly or impliedly assumes the predecessor's obligations (the creditors of the old business may hold the new corporation liable as ***third-party beneficiaries***); (ii) the sale was an attempted ***fraud*** on the creditors; or (iii) the predecessor is merged into or absorbed by the successor. Some courts have held that a successor corporation ***may*** be liable for a predecessor's debts on a theory that it is a ***continuation*** of the predecessor . . . .   [123]

IV. POWERS OF THE CORPORATION

A. CORPORATE POWERS

Generally, corporate purposes and powers are those **expressly** set forth in the corporation's articles, those conferred by statute, and the **implied** powers necessary to carry out the express powers. Transactions beyond the purposes and powers of the corporation are **ultra vires** . . . . [128]

1. **Traditional Problem Areas:** The following three powers are particularly significant express powers since older statutes did not specifically confer them . . . [130]

    a. **Guaranties:** Modern statutes confer the power to guarantee the debts of others if it is in furtherance of the corporate business . . . . [131]

    b. **Participation in a partnership:** Present-day statutes explicitly allow the corporation to participate with others in any corporation, partnership, or other association . . . . [132]

    c. **Donations:** Because the general rule is that the objective of a business corporation is to conduct business activity with a view to profit, early cases held that charitable contributions were ultra vires; the modern view permits **reasonable** donations for public welfare, humanitarian, educational, or philanthropic purposes without showing the probability of a direct benefit to the corporation . . . . [133]

B. ULTRA VIRES TRANSACTIONS

1. **In General:** Ultra vires transactions are those beyond the purposes and powers, express **and** implied, of the corporation. Under common law, **shareholder ratification** of an ultra vires transaction nullified the use of an ultra vires defense by the corporation . . . . [140]

2. **Tort Actions:** Ultra vires is **no defense to tort liability** . . . . [143]

3. **Criminal Actions:** Claims that a corporate act was beyond the corporation's authorized powers are **no defense** to criminal liability . . . . [144]

4. **Contract Actions:** At common law, a purely **executory** ultra vires contract was not enforceable against **either party**, **fully performed contracts** could not be rescinded by either party; and, under the majority rule, **partially performed contracts** were generally enforceable by the performing party since the nonperforming party was estopped to assert an ultra vires defense . . . . [145]

5. **Statutes:** Most states now have statutes that preclude the use of ultra vires as a defense in a suit between the contracting parties, but permit ultra vires to be raised in certain other contexts . . . . [151]

    a. **Suit against officers or directors:** If performance of an ultra vires contract results in a loss to the corporation, it can sue the officers or directors for **damages** for exceeding their authority . . . . [153]

    b. **Suit by state:** These limiting statutes do not bar the state from suing to **enjoin** a corporation from transacting unauthorized business . . . . [154]

    c. **Broad certificate provisions:** When the certificate of incorporation states that the purpose is to engage in any lawful act or activity for which corporations may be organized, ultra vires issues are unlikely to arise . . . . [158]

V. MANAGEMENT AND CONTROL

A. ALLOCATION OF POWERS BETWEEN DIRECTORS AND SHAREHOLDERS

1. **Management of Corporation's Business:** Corporate statutes vest the power to manage in the **board of directors**, except as provided by valid agreement in a close corporation. The board's power is limited to **proper purposes** . . . . . [159]

2. **Shareholder Approval of Fundamental Changes:** Shareholders must approve certain fundamental changes in the corporation, *e.g.*, amendment of articles, merger, sale of substantially all assets, and dissolution . . . . [161]

3. **Power to Elect and Remove Directors:** Shareholders have the power to elect directors and to remove them **for cause**, absent provisions for removal without

cause in the certificate, bylaws, or in statutes. Some statutes also permit the board or the courts to remove a director for certain specified reasons (*e.g.*, conviction of a felony) . . . . [162]

4. **Power to Ratify Management Transactions:** Shareholders have the power to ratify certain management transactions and insulate the transactions against a claim that managers lacked authority or shift the burden on the issue of self-interest . . . . [166]

5. **Power to Adopt Precatory Resolutions:** Shareholders may also adopt advisory but nonbinding (precatory) resolutions on proper subjects of their concern . . . . [167]

6. **Bylaws:** Shareholders usually have the power to adopt and amend bylaws, although some statutes give the board of directors the concurrent power to do this . . . . [168]

7. **Close Corporation:** This is a corporation owned by a small number of shareholders who may actively manage, it has no general market for its stock, and it has some limitations regarding transferability of stock . . . . [169]

8. **Statutory Close Corporation Status:** Although they may vary in different jurisdictions, the basic requirements to qualify for special treatment under these statutes are that, in its certificate of incorporation, a statutory close corporation must identify itself as such (sometimes, this must also be stated in its share certificates) and must include certain limitations as to the number of shareholders, transferability of shares, or both . . . . [173]

   a. **Functioning as a close corporation:** Once qualified as a statutory close corporation, a corporation has great flexibility in its management methods. There may be shareholder agreements relating to any phase of the corporation's affairs (some statutes require *all* shareholders to join in such agreements). Under some statutes, the shareholders, rather than the directors, directly manage the corporation's affairs and thereby become personally liable for managerial acts or omissions to the same extent as managing directors . . . . [176]

      (1) **Rights and liabilities of transferees:** Restrictions (*e.g.*, number of shareholders, transfer restrictions) are often required to be conspicuously noted on the stock certificates. Statutes vary as to the problem of transfers to ineligible or unknowing transferees. For example, Delaware law provides that if a transferee has actual notice or is conclusively presumed to have notice that (i) he is ineligible to be a shareholder, (ii) the transfer will cause the number of shareholders to exceed that permitted in the certificate of incorporation, or (iii) the transfer violates a valid restriction, the corporation may refuse to register the transfer . . . . [180]

B. **DIRECTORS**

1. **Appointment of Directors:** Initial directors are either designated in the articles of incorporation or elected at a meeting of the incorporators. Subsequent elections are by the shareholders at their annual meetings. The board may fill vacancies occurring between shareholders' meetings. The *number* of directors is usually set by the articles or bylaws . . . . [186]

   a. **Qualifications:** Absent a contrary provision in the articles or bylaws, directors need not be shareholders of the corporation or residents of the state of incorporation . . . . [188]

   b. **Vacancies:** Statutes vary, but under the Revised Model Business Corporation Act ("Model Act"), a vacancy may be filled by either the shareholders *or* the directors . . . . [189]

      (1) **Compare—removal:** Some statutes require that vacancies created by removal of a director be filled by the shareholders unless the articles or bylaws provide otherwise . . . . [190]

2. **Tenure of Office**
    a. **Term of appointment:** Under most statutes, office is held until the next annual meeting, although on a classified board, directors may serve staggered multiyear terms . . . . [191]
    b. **Power to bind corporation beyond term:** Unless limited by the articles, the board has the power to make contracts binding the corporation beyond the directors' terms of office . . . . [193]
    c. **Removal of director during term:** At common law, shareholders can remove a director only for *cause* (*e.g.*, fraud, incompetence, dishonesty) unless an article or bylaw provision permits removal without cause. A director being removed for cause is entitled to a *hearing* by shareholders before a vote to remove. Note that a number of statutes permit removal *without cause* . . . . [194]
        (1) **Removal by board:** The board can never remove a director, unless authorized by statute . . . . [197]
        (2) **Removal by court:** There is a split of authority as to whether a court can remove a director for cause . . . . [198]
            (a) **Statutes:** Some statutes permit courts to remove a director for specified reasons (*e.g.*, fraudulent or dishonest acts). Usually, a petition for removal can be brought only by a certain percentage of shareholders or the attorney general . . . . [199]
3. **Functioning of Board**
    a. **Meetings:** Absent a statute, directors can act only at a duly convened meeting consisting of a quorum. In most jurisdictions, a meeting can be conducted by telephone or other means whereby all participants can hear each other simultaneously. Most statutes also permit board action by unanimous written consent without a meeting . . . . [200]
        (1) **Notice:** Although formal notice is unnecessary for a regular meeting, special meetings require notice to every director of date, time, and place. Usually, notice can be waived in writing before or after a meeting. Attendance waives notice unless the director attends only to protest the meeting . . . . [201]
        (2) **Quorum:** A majority of the *authorized* number of directors constitutes a quorum. Many statutes permit the articles or bylaws to require more than a majority; some statutes permit the setting of a lower number . . . . [202]
        (3) **Voting:** Absent a contrary provision, an affirmative vote of a majority of those *present*, not a majority of those voting, is required for board action . . . . [203]
    b. **Effect of noncompliance with formalities:** Today, most courts hold that *informal but unanimous* approval of a transaction is *effective*, as is a matter receiving the explicit approval by a majority of directors without a meeting, plus acquiescence by the remaining directors . . . . [204]
    c. **Delegation of authority:** The board has the power to appoint committees of its own members to act for it either in particular matters or to handle day-to-day management between board meetings. Typically, these committees *cannot* amend the articles or bylaws, adopt or recommend major corporate changes (*e.g.*, merger), recommend dissolution, or declare a dividend or authorize issuance of stock unless permitted by the articles or bylaws. Note that while the board may delegate operation of the business to an officer or management company, the ultimate control must be retained by the board . . . . [207]
    d. **Provisional directors:** A growing number of statutes (some apply only to close corporations) provide for provisional directors to be appointed by court if the board is deadlocked and corporate business is endangered. A provisional director serves until the deadlock is broken or until removed by

a court order or the majority of shareholders . . . . [211]

    e. **Voting agreements:** An agreement in advance among directors as to how they will vote as directors is void as contrary to public policy. There are certain exceptions for statutory close corporations . . . . [214]

4. **Compensation:** Directors are *not* entitled to compensation unless they render extraordinary services or such compensation is otherwise provided for. Officers are entitled to reasonable compensation for services . . . . [215]

5. **Directors' Rights, Duties, and Liabilities**

    a. **Right to inspect corporate records:** If done in *good faith* for purposes germane to his position as director, this right is absolute . . . . [220]

    b. **Duty of care:** Directors must exercise the care of an *ordinarily prudent and diligent person* in a like position, under similar circumstances. There is no liability (absent a conflict of interest, bad faith, illegality, or gross negligence and, in some cases, ordinary negligence) for errors of judgment (*"business judgment rule"*), but the director must have been reasonably diligent before the rule can be invoked . . . . [223]

        (1) **Extent of liability:** Directors are personally liable for corporate losses directly resulting from their breach of duty or negligence in failing to discover wrongdoing. A director may seek to avoid being held personally liable for acts of the board by recording his *dissent* . . . . [230]

            (a) **Note:** Many statutes permit the articles to *abolish or limit* directors' liability for breach of the duty of care absent bad faith, intentional misconduct, or knowing violation of law . . . . [232]

        (2) **Defenses to liability:** These include good faith reliance on management or experts' reports. Disabilities may be considered in determining whether the director has met the standard of care . . . . [233]

    c. **Duty of loyalty:** Directors have a duty of loyalty in all dealings with the corporation . . . . [238]

    d. **Statutory duties and liabilities:** In addition to the general duty of care, federal and state laws also impose certain duties and liabilities, *e.g.*, registration requirements under the Securities Act of 1933, liability for rule 10b-5 violations, liability for illegal dividends. Some statutes also impose criminal liability on corporate managers for unlawful corporate actions . . . . [239]

C. OFFICERS

1. **Election:** Officers are generally elected by the board of directors and hold office at its pleasure. Some statutes permit election of officers by shareholders . . [244]

2. **Authority of Corporate Officers—Liability of Corporation to Outsiders:** Only authorized officers can bind the corporation. Authority may be: *actual* (expressed in bylaws or by valid board resolution), *apparent* (corporation gives third parties reason to believe authority exists), or *power of position* (inherent to position). If *ratified* by the board, even unauthorized acts may bind the corporation . [245]

    a. **Authority of president:** The majority rule is that the president has power to bind the corporation in transactions arising in *regular course of business* . . . . [250]

3. **Duties of Corporate Officers:** The duty of care owed by an officer is similar to that owed by directors (and sometimes higher) . . . . [255]

D. CONFLICTS OF INTEREST IN CORPORATE TRANSACTIONS

1. **Duty of Loyalty:** Because of their fiduciary relationship with the corporation, officers and directors have the duty to promote the interests of the corporation without regard for personal gain . . . . [256]

2. **Business Dealings with Corporations:** Conflict of interest issues arise when a corporation transacts business with one of its officers or directors, or with a company in which an officer or director is financially interested . . . . [257]

    a. **Effect of self-interest on right to participate in meeting:** Most statutes permit an "interested" director to be counted toward a quorum, and interested director transactions are not automatically voidable by the corporation because the interested director's vote was necessary for approval . . .   [258]

    b.   **Voidability because of director's self-interest:** Today, such transactions are voidable only if *unfair* to the corporation. The burden of establishing fairness is on the interested director. Note that a director's failure to *fully disclose* material facts may be per se unfair . . . .   [260]

        (1) **Unanimous shareholder ratification:** If, after *full disclosure*, shareholder ratification is unanimous, the corporation will be *estopped* from challenging the transaction with the interested director (except as to creditors) . . . .   [268]

            (a) **Less-than-unanimous ratification:** If there is less-than-unanimous ratification, courts will look at whether the majority shares were owned or controlled by the interested director. Courts are more likely to uphold ratification by a disinterested majority so as to preclude the transaction from being attacked by the corporation or by a shareholder in a derivative suit . . . .   [269]

        (2) **Statutes:** Most statutes provide that such transactions are *not* voidable if: (i) approved, after *full disclosure*, by a *disinterested board majority or by a majority of shareholders*, or (ii) the transaction is *fair* to the corporation. The transaction must be fair notwithstanding disclosure . . . .   [277]

            (a) **"Interested":** An "interested" director or officer is one who has a business, financial, or familial relationship with a party to the transaction that would reasonably affect the person's judgment so as to adversely affect the corporation . . . .   [282]

    c.   **Remedies:** The corporation may rescind, or affirm and sue for damages .   [283]

  3. **Interlocking Directorates:** Generally, transactions between corporations with common directors are subject to the same rules of interested director transactions. There is no conflict of interest if one corporation is the wholly-owned subsidiary of the other. However, the question of fairness arises where the parent owns only a majority of the subsidiary's shares . . . .   [289]

  4. **Corporate Opportunity Doctrine:** This bars directors from usurping any business opportunity belonging to the corporation without first offering it to the corporation. If the corporation is *unable* to take advantage of the opportunity, then the director generally may take advantage of it. If the corporation is *unwilling* to pursue an opportunity (after an independent board is fully informed of the opportunity), the director may pursue it . . . .   [296]

    a.   **Remedies:** Remedies for usurping a corporate opportunity include a constructive trust or damages . . . .   [306]

  5. **Competing with Corporation:** Such competition by a director or officer may be a breach of fiduciary duty even when the competing business is *not* a corporate opportunity . . . .   [309]

  6. **Compensation for Services to the Corporation:** The compensation plan must be *duly authorized* by the board and its terms *reasonable*. Good faith and the business judgment rule ordinarily protect disinterested directors from liability to the corporation for approving compensation . . . .   [310]

    a.   **Publicly held corporations:** The SEC has increased the type and amount of information about executive compensation that must be disclosed by large corporations, and has authorized shareholders to make proposals about executive pay in management's proxy materials. Further, the tax code now limits expense deductions for executive pay over $1 million unless it is tied to the corporation's performance . . . .   [316]

    b.   **Past and future services:** Compensation for *past services* is generally invalid; compensation for *future services* is proper if there is reasonable assurance that the corporation will receive the benefit of the services . . . .   [324]

VI. INSIDER TRADING

A. INTRODUCTION
The purchase and sale of corporate stock by a director, officer, or other insider raises issues of fiduciary responsibility . . . . [333]

B. COMMON LAW
Under the majority rule, there was *no* duty to disclose to the shareholders inside information affecting the value of shares (the minority rule imposed a duty to disclose) . . . . [334]

C. SECURITIES EXCHANGE ACT OF 1934—IN GENERAL
The common law rules governing insider trading have been largely superseded by the Act. Section 12 of the Act requires *registration* of any security traded on a national exchange, or any equity security (held by 500 or more persons) of a corporation with assets exceeding $5 million . . . . [338]

D. SECTION 10(b) AND RULE 10b-5
Section 10(b) prohibits any manipulation or deception in the purchase or sale of any security, whether or not registered; rule 10b-5 prohibits the use of the mails or other instrumentality of interstate commerce to defraud, misrepresent, or omit a material fact in connection with a purchase or sale of *any* security . . . . [339]

1. **Covered Conduct:** Rule 10b-5 applies to *nondisclosure* by directors or officers, as well as to *misrepresentations*. It applies not only to insider trading but also to *any* person who makes a misrepresentation in connection with a purchase or sale of stock . . . . [340]

2. **Covered Securities:** Rule 10b-5 applies to the purchase or sale of *any* security, registered or unregistered. A jurisdictional limitation requires that the violation must involve the use of some *instrumentality of interstate commerce* . . [342]

3. **Who Can Bring Suit under Rule 10b-5:** Suits for violation of rule 10b-5 can be brought by the SEC and by private plaintiffs. However, private plaintiffs must be either purchasers or sellers of securities . . . . [343]

4. **Materiality:** For rule 10b-5 to apply, the information misrepresented or omitted must be material (*i.e.*, a reasonable shareholder would consider it important in deciding whether to buy or sell) . . . . [345]

5. **Fault Required—Scienter:** A defendant is not liable under rule 10b-5 for a misrepresentation or omission if he was without fault or merely negligent. The scienter requirement is satisfied by *recklessness* or an intent to deceive, mislead, or convey a false impression. Scienter is also required for injunctive relief . [346]

6. **Causation and Reliance:** A plaintiff must prove the violation caused a *loss* (*i.e.*, she must establish reliance on the wrongful statement or omission). However, in *omissions* cases, there is a rebuttable *presumption* of reliance once materiality is established . . . . [349]

   a. **"Fraud on the market":** Where securities are traded on a well-developed market (rather than in a face-to-face transaction), reliance on a *misrepresentation* may be shown by alleging reliance on the integrity of the market . . . . [351]

   b. **Face-to-face misrepresentations:** A plaintiff can show actual reliance in these cases by showing that the misrepresentation was material, testifying that she relied upon it, and showing that she traded soon after the misrepresentation . . . . [352]

7. **When Nondisclosure Constitutes a Violation**

   a. **Mere possession of material information:** Generally, nondisclosure of material, nonpublic information violates rule 10b-5 *only* when there is a duty, independent of rule 10b-5, to disclose . . . . [354]

   b. **Trading by insiders:** Insiders (directors, officers, controlling shareholders, and corporate employees) violate rule 10b-5 by trading on the basis of material, nonpublic information obtained through their positions. They have a duty to disclose before trading . . . . [355]

   c. **Misappropriation:** The liability of noninsiders who wrongfully acquire (misappropriate) material nonpublic information has not been ruled upon by the U.S. Supreme Court, although some lower federal courts have imposed criminal liability . . . . [356]

      (1) **Duty to employer:** Using the misappropriation theory, *criminal liability* under rule 10b-5 has been imposed where an employee trades on information used in violation of that employee's fiduciary duty to his employer. An employee's duty to "abstain or disclose" with respect to his employer does *not* extend to the general public. However, the Insider Trading and Securities Fraud Enforcement Act of 1988 makes any person who violates rule 10b-5 by trading while in possession of material, nonpublic information liable to *any person* who, contemporaneously to the transaction, purchased or sold securities of the same class. Liability is limited to the defendant's profit or avoided loss . . . . [359]

      (2) **Mail and wire fraud:** The application of the federal mail and wire fraud statute to this situation lessens the importance of the misappropriation theory in imposing *criminal liability* under rule 10b-5 . . . [363]

      (3) **Special rule for tender offers:** Once substantial steps toward making a tender offer have begun, it is a fraudulent, deceptive, or manipulative act for a person possessing material information about the tender offer to purchase or sell any of the target's stock if that person knows that the information is nonpublic and has been acquired from the bidder, the target, or someone acting on the bidder's or target's behalf . . . . [364]

   d. **"Disclose or abstain":** Nondisclosure by a person with a duty to disclose violates rule 10b-5 *only* if she trades . . . . [365]

8. **Liability of Nontrading Persons for Misrepresentations:** A nontrading corporation or person who makes a misrepresentation that could cause reasonable investors to rely thereon in the purchase or sale of securities is liable under rule 10b-5, provided the scienter requirement is satisfied . . . . [366]

9. **Liability of Nontrading Corporation for Nondisclosure:** The basic principle is "*disclose or abstain.*" Thus, a nontrading corporation is generally not liable under rule 10b-5 for nondisclosure of material facts . . . . [368]

   a. **Exceptions:** A corporation has a duty to: (i) *correct* misleading statements (even if unintentional); (ii) *update* statements that have become materially misleading by subsequent events; (iii) correct material errors in statements by others (*e.g.,* analyst's reports) about the corporation—if the corporation was involved in the preparation of the statements; and (iv) correct *inaccurate rumors* resulting from leaks by the corporation or its agents . [369]

10. **Tippee and Tipper Liability:** A person, not an insider, who trades on information received from an insider is a tippee and may be liable under rule 10b-5 if (i) she received information through an insider who breached a fiduciary duty in giving the information, and (ii) the tippee knew or should have known of the breach . . . . [373]

   a. **Breach of insider's fiduciary duty:** Whether an insider's fiduciary duty was breached depends largely on whether the insider communicated the information to realize a gain or advantage. Accordingly, tips to friends or relatives and tips that are a quid pro quo for a past or future benefit from the tippee result in a fiduciary breach. Note that if a tippee is liable, so too is the tipper . . . . [376]

11. **"Temporary Insiders":** Corporate information legitimately revealed to a professional or consultant (*e.g.,* accountant) working for the corporation may make that person a fiduciary of the company . . . . [380]

12. **Aiders and Abettors:** These are people who aid and abet *another person* who improperly trades. Liability cannot be imposed solely because that person aided and abetted a violation of the rule . . . . [381]

13. **Application of Rule 10b-5 to Breach of Fiduciary Duties by Directors, Officers, or Controlling Shareholders**
   a. **"Ordinary mismanagement":** A breach of fiduciary duty not involving misrepresentation, nondisclosure, or manipulation *does not violate rule 10b-5* . . . . [382]
   b. **Misrepresentation or nondisclosure:** If this is the basis of a purchase from or sale to the corporation by a director or officer, the corporation can sue the fiduciary under rule 10b-5 *and* also for breach of fiduciary duty. If the corporation does not sue, a minority shareholder can maintain a *derivative* suit on the corporation's behalf . . . . [383]
   c. **Purchase or sale by controlling shareholder:** Where a corporation purchases stock from or sells stock to a controlling shareholder at an unfair price, and material facts are not disclosed to minority shareholders, a derivative action may lie if the nondisclosure *caused a loss* to the minority shareholders. The plaintiffs must establish *causation* by showing that an effective state remedy (*e.g.*, injunction) was forgone because of the nondisclosure . . . . [385]

14. *Blue Chip* **Rule—Private Plaintiff:** A plaintiff can bring a private cause of action only if she actually purchased or sold the relevant securities. "Sale" includes an exchange of stock for assets, mergers and liquidations, contracts to sell stock, and pledges. The SEC can bring actions under rule 10b-5 even though it has neither purchased nor sold securities . . . . [390]

15. **Defenses**
   a. **Due diligence:** If a plaintiff's reliance on a misrepresentation or omitted fact could have been prevented by his exercise of due diligence, recovery may be barred. Mere negligence does not constitute a lack of due diligence, although a plaintiff's intentional misconduct and his own recklessness (if defendant was merely reckless) will bar recovery . . . . [398]
   b. **In pari delicto:** A private suit for damages under rule 10b-5 will be barred if: (i) the plaintiff bears *substantially equal responsibility* for the violations, and (ii) preclusion of the suit would not *significantly interfere* with the enforcement of securities laws . . . . [399]

16. **Remedies**
   a. **Out-of-pocket damages:** This is the difference between the price paid for stock and its actual value . . . . [402]
      (1) **Compare—benefit-of-the-bargain damages:** These are measured by the value of the stock as it really is and the value it would have had if a misrepresentation had been true . . . . [403]
      (2) **Standard measure of conventional damages:** *Out-of-pocket damages* is the standard measure in private actions under rule 10b-5; benefit-of-the-bargain damages are generally not granted . . . . [404]
   b. **Restitutionary relief:** This may be sought instead of conventional damages . . . . [405]
      (1) **Rescission:** The most common form of restitutionary relief is rescission, which returns the parties to their status quo before the transaction, *e.g.*, seller returns purchase price and gets back stock she sold . . . . [406]
      (2) **Rescissionary or restitutionary damages:** These damages are the money equivalent of rescission. They are measured by the difference between the value of what plaintiff gave up and the value of what the defendant received . . . . [407]
      (3) **Difference between conventional damages and restitutionary relief:** Out-of-pocket damages are based on the plaintiff's loss while

restitutionary relief is based on the defendant's wrongful gain. Rescission or rescissionary damages may be attractive remedies when the value of the stock changed radically after the transaction. However, restitutionary relief is usually **unavailable** in cases involving **publicly** held stock . . . . [408]

    c. **Remedies available to the government:** Although the SEC cannot sue for damages, it can pursue several remedies including special monetary remedies . . . . [426]

        (1) **Injunctive relief:** The SEC often seeks injunctive relief accompanied with a request for disgorgement of profits or other payments that can be used as a fund for injured private parties . . . . [427]

        (2) **Other remedies:** A person who violates rule 10b-5 can be subject to **criminal sanctions** (fines and jail sentences) and **civil penalties** (up to three times the profit gained or loss avoided) . . . . [428]

17. **Jurisdiction, Venue, and Service of Process:** Suits under rule 10b-5 are based on the 1934 Act, and exclusive jurisdiction is in the **federal district courts**. **State claims** arising out of the same transactions may be joined with the federal claim under the **supplemental jurisdiction** doctrine. Venue can be wherever any act or transaction constituting a violation occurred, or where the defendant is found or transacts business. Process can be served where the defendant can be found or where he lives . . . . [430]

18. **Statute of Limitations:** The 1934 Act contains no statute of limitations; however, the Supreme Court has held that **private** actions must be brought within **one year** after discovery of the relevant facts and within **three years** following accrual of the cause of action. The tolling doctrine is inapplicable . . . . [433]

    a. **Exceptions:** The time limitations do not apply to all rule 10b-5 private actions, *e.g.*, SEC limitations period of five years for private suits by contemporaneous traders against purchasers or sellers who violate rules regarding trades while in possession of material, nonpublic information. Further, the SEC is not subject to any limitations period in civil enforcement actions . . [437]

E. SECTION 16 OF THE 1934 ACT
Section 16 concerns purchases followed by sales, or sales followed by purchases, by certain insiders, within a six-month period; *i.e.*, "short-swing trading" . . . . [438]

1. **Securities Affected Under Section 16:** Section 16 applies to those securities that must be registered under section 12 of the 1934 Act . . . . [439]

    a. **Note:** Trading in **all** of a corporation's equity securities is subject to section 16 if **any class** of its securities is registered under section 12.

2. **Disclosure Requirement:** Section 16(a) requires every **beneficial owner** of **more than 10%** of registered stock **and directors and officers** of the issuing corporation to file periodic reports with the SEC showing their holdings and any changes in their holdings . . . . [440]

3. **Liability:** To prevent the unfair use of information, section 16(b) allows a corporation to recover profits made by an officer, director, or more-than-10% beneficial owner on the purchase and sale **or** sale and purchase of its securities within a **six-month period** . . . . [443]

    a. **Coverage:** Section 16(b) does not cover all insider trading and is not limited to trades based on inside information. The critical element is short-swing trading by officers, directors, and more-than-10% beneficial owners . [444]

    b. **Calculation of short-swing profit:** The profit recoverable is the difference between the price of the stock sold and the price of the stock purchased within six months **before or after** the sale . . . . [445]

        (1) **Multiple transactions:** If there is more than one purchase or sale transaction within the six-month period, the transactions are paired by matching the highest sale price with the lowest purchase price, the next highest sale price with the next lowest purchase price, etc. A

court can look six months forward or backward from any sale (to find a purchase) or from any purchase (to find a sale). *Any pair* of transactions within that period must be accounted for . . . . [446]

   c. **Who may recover:** The profit belongs to the corporation alone. Although not a typical derivative action, if the corporation fails to sue after a demand by a shareholder, the shareholder may sue on the corporation's behalf. The cause of action is federal so there is no posting of security requirement, and no contemporaneous shareholder requirement . . . . [448]

   d. **"Insiders":** Insiders are officers (named officers and those persons who function as officers), directors (actually serving or who authorized deputization of another), and beneficial owners of more than 10% of the shares (ownership determinable by control over stock). Insider status for officers and directors is determined at the time they made a purchase *or* sale. Transactions made before taking office are not within section 16(b), but those made after leaving office are subject to the statute if they can be matched with a transaction made while in office. Liability is imposed on a beneficial owner only if she owned more than 10% of the shares at the time of *both* the purchase and sale . . . . [451]

   e. **"Purchase or sale":** This includes any garden-variety purchase or sale of stock (*e.g.*, exchange of stock for cash). Unorthodox transactions that result in the acquisition or disposition of stock (*e.g.*, merger for stock, redemption of stock) are also purchases and sales . . . . [466]

F. SECTION 16(b) COMPARED TO RULE 10b-5

   1. **Covered Securities:** Section 16(b) applies to securities *registered* under the 1934 Act; rule 10b-5 applies to *all* securities . . . . [472]

   2. **Inside Information:** Section 16(b) allows recovery for short-swing profits *regardless* of whether they are attributable to misrepresentations or inside information; rule 10b-5 recovery is available *only* where there was a misrepresentation or a trade based on inside information . . . . [473]

   3. **Plaintiff:** Recovery under section 16(b) belongs to the corporation, while rule 10b-5 recovery belongs to the injured purchaser or seller . . . . [474]

   4. **Overlapping Liability:** It is possible that insiders who make short-swing profits by use of inside information could be liable under both section 16(b) and rule 10b-5 . . . . [475]

G. COMMON LAW LIABILITY FOR INSIDER TRADING

Insider trading constitutes a breach of fiduciary duties owed to the corporation, so the *corporation* can recover profits made from insider trading . . . . [476]

   1. **Common Law Liability Compared to Section 16(b) Liability:** Both common law and section 16(b) liability run against insiders and in favor of the corporation. However, unlike section 16(b), the common law theory applies to *all* corporations (not just those with registered securities), recovery can be had against *any* corporate insider, the purchase and sale is not limited by a six-month period, and the transaction *must* be based on inside information . . . . [477]

   2. **Common Law Liability Compared to Rule 10b-5 Liability:** The theories of recovery are similar except that under the common law recovery runs to the corporation (not the injured purchaser or seller), there is no purchaser or seller requirement, and noninsiders (*e.g.*, tippees) have not yet been held liable . . . . [482]

VII. RIGHTS OF SHAREHOLDERS

A. VOTING RIGHTS

   1. **Right to Vote—In General:** Shareholders may generally vote for the *election and removal of directors*, to *amend the articles or bylaws*, and on *major corporate action* or *fundamental changes* . . . . [485]

a. **Who may vote:** The right to vote is held by shareholders of record as of the record date . . . . [486]

b. **Restrictions on right:** Shares may be either voting or nonvoting, or have multiple votes per share. Similarly, restriction on the number of votes any shareholder may have has been upheld . . . . [488]

2. **Shareholders' Meetings:** Generally, shareholders can act only at meetings duly called and noticed at which a quorum is present . . . . [491]

a. **Compare—informal action:** Statutes permit shareholder action without a meeting if there is *unanimous written consent* of all shareholders entitled to vote . . . . [496]

3. **Shareholder Voting**

a. **Straight voting:** This system of voting allows *one vote for each share* held and applies to all matters other than director elections, which may be subject to cumulative voting. Certain fundamental changes (*e.g.*, merger) frequently require higher shareholder approval . . . . [497]

b. **Cumulative voting for directors:** This system *allows each share one vote for each director* to be elected, and the votes may be cast all for one candidate or divided among candidates, as the shareholder chooses, thereby helping minority shareholders to elect a director. Cumulative voting may be mandatory or permissive . . . . [499]

(1) **Devices to avoid cumulative voting:** These include staggering the terms of directors, removing directors elected by the minority (but statutes impose limitations on such removal), and reducing the size of the board . . . . [503]

4. **Voting by Proxy:** A proxy authorizes another person to vote a shareholder's shares. The proxy usually must be *in writing*, and its effective period is statutorily limited (*e.g.*, 11 months) unless it is validly irrevocable . . . . [511]

a. **Revocability:** A proxy is normally revocable by the shareholder at any time, although it may be made irrevocable if *expressly* stated and *coupled with an interest* in the shares themselves (or in some states, an interest in the corporation). Absent written notice to the corporation, the death or incapacity of a shareholder does *not* revoke a proxy. A shareholder may revoke a proxy by notifying the proxy holder, giving a new proxy to someone else, or by personally attending the meeting and voting . . . . [513]

b. **Proxy solicitation:** Almost all shareholders of publicly held corporations vote by proxy. Solicitations of proxies are regulated by the Securities Exchange Act of 1934 (section 14(a)), federal proxy rules and, in some cases, state law. Federal proxy rules apply to the solicitation of all proxies of registered securities, but not to nonmanagement solicitation of 10 or fewer shareholders. The term "solicitation" is broadly interpreted by the SEC to include any part of a plan leading to a formal solicitation, *e.g.*, inspection of shareholder list . . . . [519]

(1) **1992 amendments:** The SEC revised the proxy rules to make it easier for shareholders (especially institutional shareholders) to communicate with each other. Significant changes include: a safe harbor for communications between shareholders that do not involve solicitation of voting authority; relaxation of requirements involving broadcast or published communications; relaxed preliminary filing requirements for solicitations; and removing communications between shareholders concerning proxy voting from the definition of "solicitation" . . . . [526]

(2) **Requirement of full disclosure:** The proxy rules require full and accurate disclosure of all pertinent facts and the identities of all proxy participants, disclosure of compensation paid to certain officers and directors, and disclosure of conflict-of-interest transactions involving more than $60,000 . . . . [531]

(3) **Inclusion of shareholder proposal:** Shareholder proposals must be included in corporate proxy materials if the proponent is a record or beneficial owner of *at least 1% or $1,000* worth of securities entitled to vote on the matter. The proposal must not exceed 500 words . . . . [533]

    (a) **Exceptions:** A proposal need *not* be included if it: is not a proper subject for shareholder action, would be illegal, is false or misleading, seeks redress of a personal claim, relates to operations accounting for less than 5% of the corporation's total assets and is not otherwise significantly related to the corporation's business, concerns a matter beyond the corporation's power to effectuate, relates to ordinary business operations, relates to an election to office, is counter to a proposal submitted by the corporation at the same meeting, is moot or duplicative, deals with the same subject matter as a very unsuccessful prior proposal, or relates to specific amounts of cash or stock dividends . . . . [540]

    (b) **Private right of action:** A private right of action is available to a shareholder whose proposal was rejected by the corporation on the ground that it falls within one of the proposal exceptions . [541]

    (c) **Providing shareholder lists:** A shareholder has the right to obtain a list of shareholders or to have her communication included with the corporate proxy materials . . . . [542]

(4) **Remedies for violation of proxy rules:** These include suit by the SEC to enjoin violations or to set aside an election and individual suits, class actions, or derivative suits by the shareholders. (In a private suit, the plaintiff must show *materiality and causation*, but causation is normally presumed from materiality. Fairness to the corporation is not a defense to a violation of proxy rules.) The court may rescind corporate action resulting from a misleading proxy solicitation or award damages . . . . [543]

c. **Expenses incurred in proxy contests:** Corporate funds may be used by management with respect to reasonable proxy solicitation expenses incurred in order to obtain a quorum for the annual meeting or regarding a controversy over *corporate policy* (as opposed to a personnel controversy). The corporation may, with shareholder approval, *voluntarily* pay the reasonable expenses of insurgents who win a proxy contest involving policy . . . . [559]

5. **Other Methods to Combine Votes for Control—Close Corporations:** Other methods include shareholder voting agreements (*e.g.*, pooling and self-executing agreements), which may be enforced by specific performance; agreements requiring greater-than-majority approval; shareholder agreements binding the discretion of the directors; and voting trusts . . . . [562]

B. RESTRICTIONS ON TRANSFER OF SHARES

1. **Restrictions Imposed by Articles, Bylaws, or Shareholder Agreement:** Although most frequently used in close corporations, stock transfer restrictions may also be imposed by larger corporations (*e.g.*, to restrict ownership to employees). The two most common types of restrictions are a *right of first refusal* and a *mandatory buy-sell provision*. Restrictions must be reasonable and will be strictly construed . . . . [590]

a. **Notice requirements:** A lawful stock transfer restriction is of no effect unless *noted conspicuously* on the stock certificate. If there is no such notice, an innocent transferee is entitled to have the shares transferred to him . . . . [610]

C. SHAREHOLDERS' INFORMATIONAL RIGHTS

1. **Types of Books and Records:** These include shareholder lists, minutes, financial records, and business documents . . . . [614]

			Text Section

2. **Common Law:** At common law, a shareholder has a qualified right to inspect records for a *proper purpose* . . . . [615]

3. **Statutes:** Statutes govern these rights in most states. Many statutes apply only to certain shareholders (*e.g.*, those who own 5% or those who have been record holders for six months), but are usually interpreted to supplement the common law. Most statutes preserve the proper purpose test, but place the burden on the corporation to prove improper purpose . . . . [616]

4. **Proper vs. Improper Purposes:** The test is whether the shareholder is seeking *to protect his shareholder interest*. Multiple purposes that include a proper one usually will not preclude inspection. Generally, a shareholder can inspect the shareholder list because it is often necessary to the exercise of other rights, *e.g.*, proxy fights, shareholder litigation. Inspection of shareholder lists for a proxy contest is a proper purpose. However, it has been held that corporate records cannot be examined solely for the purpose of advancing political or social views or to aid a shareholder as a litigant on a personal, non-shareholder claim . . . . . [618]

5. **Compare—Mandatory Disclosure of Information:** A shareholder's inspection right is separate and distinct from the statutory requirements governing the affirmative disclosure of certain information by corporations (*e.g.*, section 12 of Securities Exchange Act of 1934, proxy rules, state statutes) . . . . [625]

D. **FIDUCIARY OBLIGATIONS OF CONTROLLING SHAREHOLDERS**

1. **Introduction:** A controlling shareholder owes a fiduciary duty in his *business dealings with the corporation*, in taking advantage of corporate opportunities (rules more lenient than those applied to officers and directors), and in *causing fundamental changes* . . . . [633]

2. **Actions Entirely in Shareholder Capacity:** A controlling shareholder must not act to benefit himself at the expense of the minority shareholders; *i.e.*, in a transaction where control of the corporation is material, he must act with good faith and inherent fairness toward the minority . . . . [644]

3. **Obligations of Shareholders in Close Corporations:** Both majority and minority shareholders owe each other an even stricter duty (utmost good faith and loyalty) than is owed by controlling shareholders in publicly held corporations. This duty has been interpreted to mean that there must be *equal treatment* of all shareholders, *i.e.*, they must be afforded equal opportunities . . . . . . [645]

4. **Disclosure:** A controlling shareholder must make full disclosure when dealing with minority shareholders . . . . [651]

5. **Sale of Control:** In most jurisdictions, a controlling shareholder is permitted to sell his stock at a premium, *i.e.*, a price not available to other shareholders. Exceptions to this rule include a bare sale of office (invalid), the corporate action theory, sales involving fraud or nondisclosure, and knowing sales to transferees who plan to loot or deal unfairly with the corporation . . . . [652]

E. **SHAREHOLDER SUITS**

1. **Direct (Individual) Suits:** A direct suit may be brought by a shareholder *on his own behalf* for injuries to shareholder interests. If the injury affects a number of shareholders, the suit may be brought as a *class action* . . . . [673]

2. **Derivative Suits:** If a duty owed to the corporation has been abridged, suit may be brought by a shareholder *on behalf of the corporation* . . . . [675]

   a. **Distinguish direct from derivative suits:** The test is whether the injury was suffered by the *corporation* directly or by the shareholder, and to whom the defendant's *duty* was owed . . . . [678]

     (1) **Close corporations:** In some cases, minority shareholders have been allowed to bring a direct action against controlling shareholders for breach of fiduciary duty . . . . [681]

   b. **Prerequisite to suit—exhaustion of corporate remedies:** The plaintiff-shareholder must specifically *plead and prove* that he exhausted his remedies within the corporate structure . . . . [683]

    (1) **Demand on directors:** The plaintiff-shareholder must make a demand on the directors to remedy the wrong, unless such demand would have been futile. Note that in the absence of negligence, self-interest, or bias, the fact that a majority of directors approved the transaction does not itself excuse the demand . . . . [684]

        (a) **Model states:** Under both model statutes, demand should be excused only if it is shown that irreparable injury to the corporation would result . . . . [687]

        (b) **Effect of rejection of demand:** If the matter complained of does not involve wrongdoing by the directors, the board's good faith refusal to sue bars the action, unless the plaintiff-shareholders can raise a reasonable doubt that the board exercised reasonable business judgment in declining to sue. If the suit alleges wrongdoing by a majority of the directors, the board's decision not to sue will not prevent the derivative suit . . . . [689]

    (2) **Demand on shareholders:** In most states, the plaintiff-shareholder must also make a demand on shareholders unless excused (*e.g.*, the alleged wrongdoing is beyond the power of the shareholders to ratify). Where demand on shareholders is required, a good faith refusal to sue by the majority of disinterested shareholders will preclude the suit . [702]

  c. **Qualifications of plaintiff:** A few states require the plaintiff to be a registered shareholder; most states also allow a beneficial owner of shares to bring suit. (Also, a shareholder of a parent corporation can bring a derivative suit on a subsidiary's cause of action.) Shareholders cannot complain of wrongs committed before they purchased their shares except: (i) where the plaintiff acquires the shares by operation of law, (ii) in section 16(b) violations, (iii) where serious injustice will result, or (iv) where the wrong is continuing in nature. The plaintiff must fairly and adequately represent the interests of the shareholders . . . . [712]

  d. **Security for expenses:** In a number of states, the plaintiff, under certain circumstances, must post a bond to indemnify the corporation against certain of its litigation expenses, including attorneys' fees, in the event the plaintiff loses the suit. A plaintiff-shareholder who loses may also be liable for the court costs incurred by the parties . . . . [729]

  e. **Defenses:** Defenses to the derivative suit include the statute of limitations and equitable defenses (*e.g.*, laches, unclean hands, etc.) . . . . [742]

  f. **Settlement and recovery:** Any settlement or judgment belongs to the corporation, absent special circumstances. Settlement or dismissal of the suit is generally subject to court approval after notice to all shareholders . [745]

  g. **Reimbursement to plaintiff:** A victorious plaintiff may be entitled to reimbursement from the corporation for litigation expenses . . . . [754]

  h. **Indemnification of officers and directors:** Indemnification issues arise when officers and directors are sued for conduct undertaken in their official capacity. If the officer or director wins on the merits, she may be indemnified. Most statutes also authorize the corporation to *advance* (not pay) expenses in defending against the claim. Statutes vary where the officer or director settles or loses; they are more liberal concerning indemnification in a third-party suit as opposed to a derivative suit . . . . [760]

  i. **Liability insurance:** In most states, a corporation can obtain liability insurance for its indemnification costs and for any liability incurred by its officers and directors in serving the corporation . . . . [775]

VIII. CAPITALIZATION OF THE CORPORATION

A. SHARES—IN GENERAL

A "share" represents the shareholder's proprietary interest in a corporation; specifically, it represents a right to dividends as declared, a right to share in corporate assets upon liquidation, and if voting shares, the right to vote . . . .   [779]

B. CLASSES OF SHARES—PREFERENCES
1. **Common Stock:** Common shares generally entitle the owner to pro rata dividends, voting rights, and rights to liquidated assets—without any preferences .   [783]
2. **Preferred Stock:** This is a class of stock having some preference over other classes of stock—generally as to dividends or liquidation rights. Preferred shares may be given redemption rights (right to compel the corporation to repurchase shares) . . . .   [785]
    a. **Particular preferences**
      (1) **Preference in receipt of dividends:** Preferred shares are entitled to a specified rate before dividends are paid to other classes. The dividend rights may be cumulative or noncumulative . . . .   [789]
      (2) **Participation rights:** The preferred shares may be entitled to participate with common shares in the funds available for distribution *after the preferred dividend* is paid . . . .   [792]

C. AUTHORIZATION AND ISSUANCE OF SHARES
Subject to detailed regulations, shares must be authorized by the articles and issued by the board of directors; share certificates are issued for consideration . . . . .   [793]

D. STOCK SUBSCRIPTIONS
1. **Definition:** Stock subscriptions are agreements by subscribers to purchase stock to be issued . . . .   [800]
2. **Offer and Acceptance Problems:** *If the agreement is post-incorporation*, both parties are bound. *If the agreement is pre-incorporation*, at common law, it was *not* enforceable since the corporation did not yet exist; the subscription is merely a *continuing offer* to purchase shares and can be revoked prior to acceptance by the corporation. By statute in most states today, pre-incorporation subscriptions are irrevocable for a designated period, absent contrary agreement . . . .   [801]

E. CONSIDERATION REQUIRED TO BE PAID FOR SHARES
1. **Form of Consideration:** In most states, consideration is limited to "money paid, labor done, or property acquired" . . . .   [806]
    a. **Executory promises:** Unless adequately secured, these are generally *not* legal consideration . . . .   [807]
2. **Amount of Consideration:** The price the corporation must receive for shares depends on whether shares have a par value . . . .   [810]
    a. **Par value shares:** These must be sold at least at "par" (with some exceptions—*e.g.*, to remedy impairment of capital) . . . .   [811]
      (1) **"Watered stock":** If sold for less than par, the stock is "watered" . . .   [813]
        (a) **Remedies for creditors:** If the corporation becomes insolvent, creditors may recover from the shareholders the amount by which their shares were watered . . . .   [817]
         1) **Which creditors may sue:** Under the majority view, only those extending credit *after* watered stock is issued can recover. Some courts require creditor reliance on the corporation's having received par value for its shares. Under the minority view, all creditors can recover; the capital stock of the corporation constitutes a trust fund for all of its creditors . . . .   [818]
         2) **Extent of liability:** Under the majority view, watered stock liability exists only where there is *intentional overvaluation* of the assets being received by the corporation . . . .   [822]

b. **No-par value shares:** These may be sold at any price deemed *reasonable* by the directors. Most states require that assets of the corporation be actually worth the "stated value" .... [823]

F. FIDUCIARY DUTIES OF PROMOTERS
1. **Duty to Corporation:** A promoter owes the corporation fiduciary duties. Typical problems occur when a promoter sells property he owns to the corporation ... [827]
    a. **Duty of disclosure:** A promoter owes the corporation a duty of *full disclosure* as to dealings with it in which the promoter has a personal interest. This requires a full revelation of *all material facts* that might affect the corporation's decision .... [828]
    b. **Effect of no plan to issue additional shares:** If the promoters are the *sole* shareholders of the corporation and there is no plan to issue additional shares, a failure to disclose their adverse financial interest does *not* violate their fiduciary duty to the corporation. (*But note:* The **corporation** may have a cause of action under rule 10b-5 for nondisclosure) .... [829]
    c. **Effect of plan to issue additional shares:** Under the majority ("Massachusetts") rule, the corporation can maintain an action for nondisclosure against promoters who were the only original shareholders if a further issue to innocent subscribers was contemplated as part of the original capitalization .... [830]
2. **Effect of Securities Laws:** Promoters' fiduciary duties are now governed by comprehensive state and federal laws mandating disclosure (*e.g.,* Securities Act of 1933), violations of which may result in penal sanctions and/or civil damages .... [833]

G. PREEMPTIVE RIGHTS
1. **Definition:** Preemptive rights are shareholder rights, regulated by statute, to subscribe to a new issue of shares in proportion to the shareholder's interest in a corporation .... [835]
2. **When More Than One Class of Shares Exists:** When there is more than one class of shares, states are split on whether the rights are granted to all shares or only to shares that are the same as the new issue (unless the articles expressly provide) .... [841]
3. **Authorized But Unissued Shares:** There is also a split of authority as to whether preemptive rights apply to previously authorized but unissued shares . [843]
4. **Shares Issued for Other Than Cash:** Absent a contrary provision in the articles, only shares issued for cash give rise to preemptive rights in most states . [845]
5. **Remedies:** Where recognized, preemptive rights may be enforced by *specific performance* to compel issuance of authorized shares to retain a proportionate interest, *damages*, and an *injunction* preventing the corporation from issuing shares in violation of preemptive rights .... [847]
6. **Equitable Limitations on Issuance of New Shares:** Regardless of preemptive rights, courts generally do not permit majority shareholders or directors to cause an *unfair dilution* of the minority's interest by issuing shares to themselves at less than fair value .... [848]

H. UNDERWRITING
Underwriting is the process whereby a securities dealer takes stock issued by a corporation and arranges a sale to the public. In *"firm commitment"* underwriting, the underwriters purchase the entire issue. In *"best efforts"* underwriting, the underwriters are not responsible for unsold stock. Underwriting is *strictly regulated* by statutes .... [852]

I. STATUTES REGULATING ISSUANCE OF SHARES
A corporate issuer must often comply with *both* state and federal regulations ..... [856]

1. **State "Blue Sky" Laws:** Under *fraud type* blue sky laws, civil or criminal sanctions are imposed for misrepresentation. Under *license type* blue sky laws, sellers of securities must register with the state and submit certain information. Under *registration type* blue sky laws, stock must be registered with an appropriate state officer prior to issuance. Registration may be by notification (description of issuer, shares, etc.), qualification (substantive review of the proposed issuance), or coordination with the federal scheme . . . . [857]

2. **Federal Regulations:** The 1933 Securities Act requires registration (*full disclosure*) of certain securities when using interstate facilities to "offer to sell" (this includes any type of solicitation or stirring of interest) a "security" (stocks, bonds, some promissory notes, etc.) . . . . [864]

    a. **Exempt securities:** The 1933 Act lists a number of securities exempted from registration requirements. Such securities are still subject to the Act's anti-fraud rules . . . . [879]

    b. **Exempt transactions:** These include the following types of transactions: [880]

        (1) *Ordinary trading transactions* between individual investors *not* underwriters, issuers, or dealers;

        (2) *Dealer transactions*, unless the dealer is acting as an underwriter or during the initial distribution of the securities;

        (3) *Private placements*—*i.e.*, offerings to a small number of private subscribers who are *sufficiently experienced or informed* that disclosure requirements are unnecessary and who are acquiring the shares *as an investment* rather than for resale to the public;

        (4) *Intrastate offerings* where the offering and sale is made entirely to residents of the same state in which the issuer resides and does business; and

        (5) *Other exemptions*—for a public offering not exceeding $5 million in any 12-month period, the SEC permits an abbreviated offering circular (*Regulation A*); limited registration is available for securities issued pursuant to certain shareholder approved transactions, *e.g.*, mergers; and a simplified system of offerings by small business issuers (under $25 million in revenue in last fiscal year and no more than $25 million of outstanding public securities) is permitted.

    c. **Remedies**

        (1) **False registration statement:** There are *civil and criminal* sanctions for *material misstatements or omissions* in the registration statement. Any person acquiring securities without knowledge of a violation may sue. No privity is required between the plaintiff and the parties sought to be held liable . . . . [905]

            (a) **Elements of plaintiff's action:** Generally, the plaintiff need only show that a *material* fact was omitted or misrepresented. The plaintiff need *not* prove reliance or that the misrepresentation or omission caused the loss in value of the security (unless the plaintiff acquired the shares *after* the corporation published an earnings statement for the 12-month period following the effective date of the registration) . . . . [909]

            (b) **Who may be held liable:** Parties potentially liable include the corporation, its directors, all persons signing the registration statement, the underwriter, and experts (including lawyers and accountants) . . . . [913]

            (c) **Defenses:** The issuer is *absolutely liable* unless it can show the plaintiff knew of the untruth or omission at the time she acquired the shares. All other persons may avoid liability under a "due diligence" defense (they must show they reasonably investigated the corporation's affairs personally) . . . . [916]

            (d) **Measure of recovery:** The plaintiff is entitled to actual damages (purchase price minus resale price) . . . . [921]

(2) **General civil liability:** This is imposed on any person who offers or sells a security violating section 5 (registration, delivery of a prospectus), or through means of interstate commerce or the mails by use of material misstatements or omissions (public offerings). There must be *privity* with the seller, and only the issuer and other sellers can be held liable . . . . [923]

(3) **Criminal liability:** It is unlawful for any person to offer or sell securities through the mails or in interstate commerce by means of fraud or of any misstatement or omission of material fact. Some courts also *imply a civil remedy* under this section . . . . [929]

(4) **Indemnification agreements:** If the underwriter (or other indemnified party) has knowledge of the violation, the indemnification agreement is unenforceable . . . . [933]

IX. **DISTRIBUTIONS TO SHAREHOLDERS**

A. **DIVIDENDS**
1. **Definition:** A dividend is any distribution of *cash or property* paid to shareholders on account of share ownership . . . . [939]
2. **Right to Dividends:** Payment of dividends is within the *business judgment of the board*, unless bad faith or abuse of discretion is shown . . . . [940]
3. **Source of Lawful Dividends:** Restrictions on dividend sources protect corporate creditors and often preferred shareholders . . . . [943]
   a. **When capital account is impaired:** Under traditional statutes, cash or property dividends are payable only when the corporation has a surplus. Thus, such dividends cannot be paid out of stated capital. If the corporation's capital account has become impaired, it cannot declare dividends ("nimble dividends") even though it has current net profits . . . . [944]
      (1) **Model Act:** The Revised Model Act authorizes dividends as long as the corporation's total assets are at least equal to its total liabilities . . [952]
   b. **Type of surplus account from which dividends may be paid:** Earned surplus (all states), paid-in surplus (most states), and capital reduction surplus (most states) are proper sources of dividends. (The two latter sources may be subject to restrictions.) In most states, reappraisal surplus is not a proper source . . . . [956]
   c. **Insolvency or endangerment of liquidation preference:** If a corporation is insolvent or a dividend would render it insolvent, it may not legally pay a dividend. Similarly, a corporation cannot pay a dividend that would endanger the liquidation preference of preferred shares . . . . [967]
   d. **Contractual restrictions:** Some lending institutions may insert a provision in a loan agreement with a corporation limiting payment of dividends until the loan is repaid . . . . [970]
4. **Remedies for Illegal Dividends:** *Directors* who declare an illegal dividend are jointly and severally liable to the corporation. Most states limit recovery to the amount of injury suffered by the creditors and preferred shareholders. Directors held liable may compel contributions from other directors who could be held liable and from shareholders who received the unlawful dividend with knowledge of the illegality. *Shareholder* liability is absolute when illegal dividends are declared and the corporation is insolvent . . . . [971]

B. **REDEMPTION AND REPURCHASE OF SHARES**
1. **Redemption:** This is a corporation's acquisition of some or all outstanding shares at a stipulated price. Redeemed shares are usually canceled . . . . [979]
   a. **Source of funds:** In most states, a corporation is permitted to redeem out of any available funds unless it would prejudice the rights of creditors . [980]

2. **Repurchase of Shares:** "Repurchase" is generally authorized by statute. Usually shares are not canceled but remain issued, held by the corporation as *treasury stock* until resold. Generally, any accounts available for payment of dividends may be used to repurchase outstanding shares . . . . [981]

3. **Further Limitations on Repurchase and Redemption:** No redemption or repurchase is permitted where the corporation (i) is insolvent or would be rendered insolvent, or (ii) would be unable to cover the liquidation preferences of outstanding shares. A corporation's solvency is determined at the time of payment on the redemption or when repurchase is made . . . . [987]

   a. **Note:** Any discretionary redemption or repurchase must serve some bona fide *corporate purpose* rather than the personal interests of the directors or insiders . . . . [993]

4. **Remedies:** The same remedies available for illegal dividends are available against directors and shareholders for unlawful redemptions or repurchase of shares . . . . [997]

X. FUNDAMENTAL CHANGES IN CORPORATE STRUCTURE

A. INTRODUCTION
Fundamental changes in a corporation's structure (*i.e.*, mergers, sales of substantially all assets, article amendments, and dissolution) are subject to special statutory requirements. Special rules also apply to tender offers . . . . [998]

B. APPRAISAL RIGHTS OF SHAREHOLDERS
1. **In General:** Usually, shareholders who *dissent* from certain fundamental corporate changes are entitled to have the corporation purchase their shares at "fair value" (determined by either the Delaware block method or a modern finance method) or "fair market value" . . . . [999]

2. **Procedure:** The procedural requirements for exercising appraisal rights vary widely. Under a typical statute, before a vote is taken, a shareholder must give *written notice* of her intent to demand payment for her shares *and* must not vote for the proposed action. If the action is approved, the corporation must deliver *notice to the dissenters* within 10 days of the approval vote after which the shareholder must *demand payment*. The corporation must then pay each dissenter who followed the proper procedure and must include certain information with payment (*e.g.*, financial statements, corporation's estimate of fair value, etc.) . . . . [1014]

   a. **Appraisal proceedings:** If a dissenting shareholder is unwilling to accept the corporation's fair value estimate, the corporation must petition the court to determine fair value. The corporation is liable for costs unless the dissenters acted arbitrarily, vexatiously, or in bad faith . . . . [1019]

C. STATUTORY MERGERS
1. **In General:** A statutory merger occurs when one corporation is legally absorbed into another. The surviving corporation issues its shares to shareholders of the disappearing corporation . . . . [1021]

   a. **Consolidation:** A consolidation occurs when two or more corporations combine to form a wholly new corporation. Requirements are virtually identical to those for mergers . . . . [1022]

2. **Effect of Merger:** The surviving corporation, by operation of law, succeeds to all of the disappearing corporation's rights, assets, and liabilities, including its contracts . . . . [1023]

3. **Board Approval:** The board of each corporation must adopt a plan of merger . [1026]

4. **Shareholder Approval:** After board approval, the plan of merger must be approved by that majority of shareholders (of each corporation) as is required by

statute (usually a majority or two-thirds of the *outstanding stock*). Furthermore, some statutes require approval by each class . . . .   [1027]

    a. **When no shareholder approval required**

       (1) **Short-form mergers:** Mergers between a parent (owning 90% of
stock) and its subsidiary usually require only the approval of the two
boards (or of the parent board alone). However, the *subsidiary's
shareholders* do have *appraisal rights* . . . .   [1032]

       (2) **Small-scale mergers:** Some statutes do not require approval by the
shareholders of the *survivor* corporation if: (i) the voting stock of the
survivor issued to effect the merger does not constitute more than a
certain percentage (usually one-sixth) of the outstanding shares after
the merger, *and* (ii) the merger does not make any change in the
survivor's articles. *Note:* Approval by shareholders of the disappearing corporation *is* still necessary and these shareholders (unlike those
of the survivor) have appraisal rights . . . .   [1035]

    b. **No appraisal rights:** Appraisal rights are denied under certain circum-
stances based on (i) the nature of the merger (*e.g.*, short-form merger), or
(ii) the nature of the stock (*e.g.*, listed on a national stock exchange, stock
held by more than 2,000 shareholders). These exceptions vary according
to statutes . . . .   [1038]

    c. **Exclusive remedy:** Some statutes make assertion of appraisal rights an
exclusive remedy . . . .   [1043]

D. DE FACTO MERGERS

Many courts hold that transactions having the effect of a merger are subject to the
procedural requirements of merger (*e.g.*, rules for voting and appraisal rights). Examples of a de facto merger are sale of substantially all assets in exchange for stock
and sale of a majority of stock for the stock of the acquiring corporation. The issue
turns on whether the transaction has the "*indicia*" or "*all the characteristics and
consequences*" of a merger. Some courts reject the de facto doctrine, applying
instead the *equal dignity rule*—various combination forms have equal dignity—and
the label used by management is determinative. Several jurisdictions have *statutes*
that treat each corporate combination on the basis of *substance* rather than form . .   [1044]

E. TRIANGULAR MERGERS

    1. **Conventional Triangular Merger:** A and X plan to merge but instead of A (the
survivor corporation) issuing its shares to X's shareholders, A creates a subsidiary (B) and transfers a certain number of shares to B in exchange for all of B's
stock. X is then merged into B, whereupon B issues its shares of A stock. Thus,
A now owns X indirectly, through its wholly owned subsidiary. The major pur-
pose for this procedure is to avoid assuming X's liabilities . . . .   [1058]

    2. **Reverse Triangular Merger:** The same procedure as above is followed ex-
cept that B is merged into X. B disappears and X becomes a wholly owned
subsidiary of A. This form of merger may insulate A from X's liabilities, and X's
legal status as a corporation is preserved, allowing it to retain valuable rights
(*e.g.*, leases, licenses, franchises, etc.) that may have been lost in a merger . .   [1059]

    3. **Voting and Appraisal Rights in Triangular Mergers:** Triangular mergers may
be used to erode voting and appraisal rights. At least one court has refused to
apply the de facto merger doctrine to such a transaction . . . .   [1060]

F. SALE OF SUBSTANTIALLY ALL ASSETS

    1. **Shareholder Approval:** Approval by a certain percentage is normally required
for sale of substantially all the assets of the corporation . . . .   [1061]

       a. **Exception—sales in ordinary course of business:** If the sale is made
in the ordinary course of business of the corporation, shareholder approval
is generally not required . . . .   [1062]

b.   **Other exceptions:** Other exceptions to shareholder approval may include sales when the corporation is in failing circumstances and execution of mortgage . . . . [1063]

2.   **Appraisal Rights:** Most statutes provide dissenting shareholders with appraisal rights . . . . [1065]

3.   **What Constitutes "Substantially All Assets":** The percentage of assets sold is not determinative. The issue is whether the assets constitute substantially all of the corporation's operating assets, account for most of the corporation's revenues, or are vital to the operation of the business . . . . [1067]

G.   **AMENDMENT OF ARTICLES**

1.   **Vote Required:** An amendment must normally be approved by the board and a majority (or two-thirds) of outstanding shares . . . . [1069]

a.   **Class voting:** Amendments affecting a certain class, *e.g.*, change of preference, may require approval by all shareholders and by the class voting separately . . . . [1070]

b.   **Special provisions:** The certificate (or shareholder agreement) may require a higher (but not lower) percentage of shareholder approval for any proposed amendment than would otherwise be required by statute. By statute, other changes may require special procedures, *e.g.*, reducing number of directors . . . . [1071]

2.   **Appraisal Rights:** Many states give appraisal rights in connection with certain kinds of article amendments, *e.g.*, abolishment of a preferential right . . . . [1073]

3.   **Constitutional Issues:** Because a certificate of incorporation is a contract—between the state and corporation **and** also among the shareholders—the Contract Clause limited the state's power to regulate corporations and also limited shareholders' power, absent unanimity, to amend the articles or make fundamental changes. Thus, today most statutes contain **reserved power clauses** permitting a state to alter, amend, or repeal its corporation laws; statutes were also amended to allow fundamental changes or amendments with a **less than unanimous shareholder** vote. These clauses are given effect because they are deemed to be part of every contract (*i.e.*, certificate of incorporation) . . . . . [1074]

a.   **Remaining problems:** A **state** today may enact laws restricting or prohibiting certain business activities that were proper when organized. However, under the Due Process Clause, it cannot eliminate vested property rights or impair the obligations of contracts with third persons. **Shareholders** are limited in amending by the **fairness** requirement . . . . [1080]

H.   **DISSOLUTION AND LIQUIDATION**

1.   **Introduction:** Dissolution is the termination of a corporation's status as a **legal entity**. Liquidation is the termination of the corporation's business . . . . [1085]

2.   **Voluntary Dissolution:** This generally requires board approval and approval by a majority of the outstanding shares . . . . [1086]

3.   **Involuntary Dissolution:** In an action by shareholders or directors, **absent statutory authority**, courts will seldom grant dissolution and then, only for fraud, dissension, deadlock, gross mismanagement, or abuse of minority shareholders. More commonly, statutes give directors or shareholders the right to petition a court for dissolution on various grounds: deadlock among management or shareholders, oppressive or fraudulent management, and waste of assets. In practice, involuntary dissolution is rarely ordered for any corporation other than a **close corporation** . . . . [1087]

4.   **Dissolution Under Shareholder Agreement:** Agreements among shareholders (usually of a close corporation) to dissolve upon the occurrence of a specified event are valid even if not statutorily authorized . . . . [1095]

5. **Action by Directors:** Some statutes permit directors to petition for involuntary dissolution on specified grounds . . . . [1096]

6. **Action by State:** The state may bring a dissolution action in *quo warranto* where the corporation has abused its authority or when a particular requirement in which the state has an important interest is not met . . . . [1097]

7. **Liquidation:** After dissolution, the corporate business continues only to wind up its affairs, *e.g.*, pay debts, distribute assets, etc. The winding up period must be reasonable or the directors may be personally liable for corporate debts . . . [1098]

    a. **Rights of shareholders:** If only one class of shares is outstanding, each shareholder receives a pro rata share of the assets after the creditors are satisfied. If there are several classes, preferred shareholders are paid off before a pro rata distribution among common stock . . . . [1100]

    b. **Rights of creditors:** A corporation remains liable on its debts after dissolution. Statutes govern the manner in which creditors must be given *notice* of the dissolution and the time within which they must file their claims . . . . [1103]

I. **LIMITATIONS ON POWER OF CONTROLLING SHAREHOLDERS TO EFFECT FUNDAMENTAL CHANGES IN CORPORATE STRUCTURE**

    1. **Fiduciary Duty to Minority Shareholders:** The fiduciary duty owed by controlling shareholders to the minority exists when any fundamental change in which the controlling shareholder is interested occurs . . . . [1107]

    2. **Freeze-outs**

        a. **Sale of substantially all assets:** A controlling shareholder normally may not freeze out the minority by a sale of substantially all the corporation's assets to a corporation that he controls . . . . [1109]

        b. **Merger:** Freeze-out occurs in mergers when a surviving corporation issues cash, rather than stock, in exchange for the stock of the disappearing corporation. The minority shareholders end up with stock in a corporation that holds only cash, while the survivor owns all of the corporate business . . . . [1111]

        c. **Reverse stock splits:** Most statutes allow the corporation to eliminate fractional (less than one full share) shares . . . . [1112]

        d. **When permissible:** A freeze-out may be permissible *if* effected for a *legitimate business purpose*, *e.g.*, operating efficiency. This requirement does not apply in Delaware, but Delaware does require "entire fairness" . . [1114]

    3. **Effect of Securities Acts:** In addition to rights under state law (*e.g.*, appraisal rights), a shareholder dissenting to a fundamental change may sue under rule 10b-5 or the federal proxy rules if the controlling shareholders engaged in deceptive conduct . . . . [1119]

    4. **Self-Tender:** A corporation may make a tender offer for its minority shares. This is *not* technically a freeze-out since shareholders are not legally required to accept the offer, although it may be the only economically feasible alternative . . . . [1120]

    5. **Going-Private Transactions:** Transactions eliminating public ownership are governed by rule 13e-3 of the Securities Exchange Act, which defines such transactions to include: (i) *a purchase* of any equity security by the issuer; (ii) *a tender offer* for any equity security by the issuer; and (iii) *a solicitation of proxies* in connection with a fundamental corporate change under defined circumstances that tend to devalue the remaining securities . . . . [1121]

        a. **Other factors:** In going-private actions, the issuer is required to *file and disseminate* certain information. The transaction is also subject to an *antifraud rule* similar to that of rule 10b-5 (minus the "purchase and sale" requirement) . . . . [1123]

    6. **Effect of Appraisal Rights:** Even under statutes making appraisal an exclusive remedy, usually a dissenting shareholder can attack the transaction on the

basis of lack of authorization, improper procedures, and fraudulent misrepresentation. Generally, the shareholder can request injunctive relief or rescission, but not money damages .... [1125]

J. TENDER OFFERS
1. **Terminology:** Terms frequently used in tender offers include the following:
   a. **Raider:** More accurately called a *bidder*, this is a person (or corporation) who makes a tender offer for the shares of a corporation (*target*) she is seeking to acquire .... [1130]
   b. **White knight:** To prevent a takeover by a certain corporation, the target management may solicit competing offers from more friendly corporations (white knights) .... [1132]
   c. **Lock-up; crown jewels:** A "lock-up" is a device that gives a friendly bidder an option to acquire certain assets or shares to defeat less friendly bidders. "Crown jewels" refers to the target's most desirable business, which the target may give or sell to a white knight .... [1133]
   d. **Standstill:** A target may reach agreement with a shareholder holding a significant amount of stock under which the shareholder agrees to limit her stock purchases .... [1135]
   e. **Junk bonds:** These are bonds that carry an unusually high risk and an unusually high yield .... [1136]
   f. **Greenmail:** This occurs when a potential target pays a potential bidder in order to buy back its shares already owned by the bidder in exchange for the bidder's agreement not to pursue a takeover bid .... [1138]
   g. **Fair price provision:** This requires a supermajority (usually 80%) shareholder approval of any merger with an acquiror who owns a specified interest (usually 20%) in the corporation .... [1139]
   h. **Poison pill:** This is a device adopted by a target to make its stock less attractive to a bidder, *e.g.*, issuance of new series of preferred stock ..... [1140]
   i. **Leveraged buyout:** This is a combination of a management buyout and a high degree of leverage (use of debt to increase the return on equity) .. [1141]
2. **In General:** A tender offer is an offer to shareholders of a target corporation asking them to tender their shares in exchange for cash or securities. A *friendly offer* is supported by the target's board, whereas a *hostile offer* is not ..... [1143]
   a. **Approval:** Since neither type of tender offer is a *corporate* transaction from the target's perspective (it is an offer to individual shareholders), a vote by the target's shareholders is *not* required absent a statute .... [1148]
   b. **Defensive tactics:** Defensive actions that may be taken by target boards include: combination with an alternative corporation ("white knight"), sale of business to management, or giving a third party or management an option ("lock-up") on a key division of the corporation ("the crown jewel"). Defensive actions will probably be judged by a standard between the strict duty of loyalty rule and the liberal business judgment rule. Courts focus on, among other things, the best interests of the corporation and shareholders and enhanced scrutiny of the reasonableness of the corporation's defensive tactics .... [1149]
3. **Federal Securities Law—The Williams Act:** This Act regulates *tender offers* and the preceding *toehold share acquisitions* .... [1165]
   a. **Notice of five percent ownership:** This requires filing of a schedule 13D within 10 days of acquiring beneficial ownership of 5% of any class of registered securities .... [1166]
   b. **Tender offers:** Although not completely settled, what constitutes a tender offer is sometimes determined using an eight-part test. It is clear that purchases made anonymously on the open market do not constitute a tender offer within the meaning of the Act .... [1170]
   c. **Information statement:** Any person making a tender offer for a class of

registered securities that would result in his owning 5% or more of such class must file a schedule containing extensive disclosures . . . . [1174]

    d.   **Regulation of terms:** The terms of a tender offer are governed by section 14(d) of the Securities Exchange Act, and rules 14d and 14e. There are also provisions regulating the obligations of the target's management and tender offers by corporations for their own stock . . . . [1176]

    e.   **Anti-fraud provision:** Section 14(e) prohibits material misstatements, misleading omissions, and fraudulent or manipulative acts in connection with a tender offer or any solicitation for or against it . . . . [1179]

        (1)   **Damages suit by offeror:** No damages for false statements by the target are available since the Act was designed to protect target shareholders. However, *injunctive relief* may be possible . . . . [1180]

        (2)   **Damages suit by target:** The corporation cannot sue for damages (injury is to shareholders) but can sue for an *injunction* for violation of the Act by the bidder . . . . [1182]

        (3)   **Target's shareholders:** *Tendering* shareholders can sue for *both* damages and injunctive relief if they tender on the basis of false and misleading information. *Nontendering* shareholders can probably sue under section 14(e) if they can show resultant damages . . . . [1184]

  4.   **State Statutes Regulating Tender Offers:** Many of the "first-generation" statutes strictly regulating takeovers were held unconstitutional based on the Commerce Clause (and possibly the Supremacy Clause). Most *second-generation statutes* fall into two categories: (i) *fair price statutes* (acquiror must pay all shareholders the best price paid to any one of them) and (ii) *control share acquisition* statutes. A control share acquisition statute has been ruled constitutional. Some statutes ("third-generation statutes") regulating takeovers do not fall into either category, *e.g.,* five-year delay required between tender offer and merger with bidder absent target board's prior approval . . . . [1186]

XI. CONFLICT OF LAWS PRINCIPLES
As a general rule, all questions concerning the organization or internal affairs of a corporation are decided according to the law of the state in which it was incorporated. A few states have statutes subjecting foreign corporations having substantial local contacts to local regulations intended to protect shareholders and creditors. Corporations listed on a national securities exchange may be exempt from the statutes . . . . [1204]

approach to exams

Corporations problems may require a determination either of the rights and liabilities of parties within the corporate structure (shareholders, officers, directors); parties outside the corporate structure (creditors, underwriters, promoters, etc.); and/or of the corporation itself.

Such rights and liabilities may arise under three separate bodies of law: First, the traditional *common law* rules governing corporations; second, *state statutes*, as most states today have enacted comprehensive codes that have altered or displaced the common law rules; and third, *federal securities laws* which, in various areas, have engrafted totally new doctrines into the law of corporations.

Analysis of corporations problems may be facilitated by considering the following factors:

A. HAS THE STATUS OF A CORPORATION BEEN ATTAINED?

1. Has the entity been organized in *sufficient compliance* with statutory requirements governing the formation of a corporation?

2. If not, should the case be decided *as if* a corporation has been validly formed?

   a. Has the entity attained at least a *"de facto"* status?

   b. Or, are the facts such that a particular party may be *estopped* from challenging the corporate status?

3. If there is still no basis for treating the entity as a corporation, what are the *liabilities of the members*? Are the members *individually liable* for the debts incurred in the entity's name?

4. Assuming that a corporation has been formed, are the circumstances such that the *corporate entity should be disregarded*? That is, should the case be decided *as if there were no corporation*?

5. Is there any issue as to *consequence of the corporate status*? The fact that a valid corporation has been formed may in itself be determinative of various issues involved (*e.g.*, the corporation's right to hold title to property, or to sue in the corporate name). More frequently, however, the fact that the entity has attained corporate status is merely a stepping-stone to a determination of some issue as to the validity of a corporate act or the rights and liabilities of individuals involved with the corporation.

B. IS THERE ANY ISSUE AS TO THE VALIDITY OF A CORPORATE ACT?

Examine each act undertaken by the corporation, and each act for which the corporation is sought to be held liable (*e.g.*, each contract, conveyance, distribution to shareholders), with the following in mind:

1. Was the act within the *express or implied powers* of the corporation?

   a. *What is the source of the power*? Remember that a corporation, by its very nature, has only the powers conferred upon it by its articles, bylaws, or applicable statutes or case law.

b. ***Are any limitations or prohibitions*** applicable?

    (1) Consider whether the act would violate any ***statutory or certificate restriction*** (*e.g.*, unlawful dividend; unlawful redemption or purchase of shares).

    (2) Of at least equal importance, consider whether the act would violate any ***equitable limitation*** on corporate powers—*i.e.*, limitations implied by courts for the protection of minority shareholders, creditors, or the public (*e.g.*, interested director transactions; inadequate capitalization).

2. Was there a ***valid exercise*** of such power by the corporation?

    a. If the corporation is sought to be held liable for the act of some ***individual*** (promoter, officer, director, etc.), the issue is basically one of authority—was the individual the authorized agent of the corporation with respect to the particular act?

    b. As to corporate resolutions or other direct acts by the entity, the issue is whether the necessary ***internal procedures*** specified in the articles, bylaws, statutes, etc., have been complied with:

        (1) Was there a valid ***adoption or ratification by the board*** of directors?

        (2) Was ***shareholder approval*** required, and if so, was it obtained?

        (3) Did the ***personal interest*** of directors or shareholders disqualify their vote?

3. ***Who may challenge*** the validity of the corporate act?

    a. Are the parties to the transaction (including the corporation) ***estopped*** to challenge it?

    b. Will a shareholders' ***derivative suit*** lie?

    c. What about ***quo warranto*** proceedings by the state?

C. WHAT ARE THE RIGHTS AND LIABILITIES OF THE PARTICULAR INDIVIDUALS INVOLVED?

1. **Characterization:** The first step in analyzing the rights and liabilities of the various individuals involved in a corporations problem is to determine their status—*e.g.*, shareholders, officers, directors, creditors, contracting parties, etc.

    a. This may require a determination of the ***validity of some prior corporate act or other event*** (*supra*) upon which their status depends. For example as to a claimed shareholder, were the shares validly issued in the first place? Were the shares validly transferred to this individual? What is the effect of any restriction on the transfer of the shares? Of failure to deliver the certificate to the transferee, etc.?

        (1) In characterizing corporate acts or events, remember that ***de facto doctrines*** may be employed to avoid injustice (*e.g.*, a sale of corporate assets

that has the effect of a merger may be treated as such, with appropriate requirements for shareholder approval, etc.).

    b.   It may not be enough merely to categorize an individual as "shareholder," "creditor," etc. ***Distinctions*** may have to be drawn between the rights and liabilities of ***persons in the same category***, *e.g.*, as a shareholder (controlling vs. minority); as a creditor (prior vs. subsequent); as a director (dissenting vs. approving, present vs. absent, interested vs. noninterested).

    c.   Keep in mind that ***the same person may play multiple roles*** in the problem—the person may be both a director and a shareholder, or both an officer and creditor of the corporation, etc. In such cases, consider whether that person owes any duties to the corporation in one capacity (*e.g.*, as officer or director) that might impair or limit her rights in the other capacity (*e.g.* as creditor or shareholder).

2.   **Rights:** Once the status of each individual is ascertained, the next step is to determine the nature and extent of his rights with respect to whatever issues are raised in the problem. For example, as to a shareholder, the problem may require an analysis of the "right" to dividends, voting rights, the right to protection against majority action, etc.

3.   **Liabilities:** The determination of liability usually flows from the determination of status; *e.g.*, a person who is shown to be a promoter, director, or controlling shareholder may owe various duties to the corporation, to the shareholders, to creditors, or to others.

    a.   Consider first what duties are prescribed by the ***articles or bylaws*** of the corporation itself.

    b.   Next consider what duties are prescribed by statute—with attention both to state corporations statutes and ***federal securities laws***.

    c.   If there are no statutory duties, consider whether any ***common law fiduciary duty*** is owed by such person ***to the corporation*** (full disclosure regarding transactions in which she has an interest, right of first refusal as to corporation opportunities, etc.) and/or to ***any other aggrieved party*** (minority shareholders, creditors, etc.).

    d.   The rules may vary somewhat where ***close corporations*** are involved. By statute or case law, fewer formalities are required in the corporate structure, but stricter fiduciary duties are usually imposed among the shareholders.

4.   **Remedies:** Consider what remedies should be made available to each possible plaintiff (including the corporation), as against each possible defendant (including the corporation):

    a.   **Form of action:** Federal or state court? Law or equity? Individual suit or class action? Suit by corporation or derivative action by shareholder?

    b.   **Form of relief:** Appraisal, injunction, rescission, constructive trust, specific performance, or damages? What is the measure of damages (secret profits measure, penalty measure, restitutionary measure)?

I. CHARACTERISTICS OF THE CORPORATION

chapter approach

This chapter describes the principal characteristics of corporations and compares those characteristics with the characteristics of other business associations. You may find a question on your exam asking you to determine which form of business association would best meet particular clients' needs. In such a case, you would need to consider the advantages and disadvantages of the various forms.

A fairly common exam question involves the disregard of the corporate entity (_i.e._, piercing the corporate veil). For suits seeking to impose liability on **shareholders**, you should determine whether elements such as undercapitalization or commingling of funds were present. In suits to pierce the wall between **affiliated corporations**, you should determine whether each affiliated corporation is a free-standing enterprise. Remember too that the corporate entity may also be disregarded where it is used to evade statutory or contractual obligations. Finally, in questions involving an insolvent corporation, keep in mind that a shareholder-creditor's claim may be subordinated to other creditors' claims on equitable grounds.

A. PRINCIPAL CHARACTERISTICS

1. **Entity Status:** [§1]   A corporation is a legal entity, separate from its shareholders, created under the authority of the legislature.

2. **Limited Liability:** [§2]   As a legal entity, a corporation is responsible for its own debts. A corporation's shareholders normally are not responsible for its debts. Their liability—or more accurately, their risk—is **limited** to the amount of their investment.

3. **Free Transferability of Interests:** [§3]   Ownership interests in a corporation are represented by shares, which are freely transferable.

4. **Centralized Management and Control:** [§4]   The management and control of a corporation's affairs are centralized in a board of directors and officers acting under the board's authority. Although the shareholders elect the board, they cannot directly control its activities. Shareholders, as such, have no power to either participate in management or determine questions within the scope of the corporation's business. These matters are for the board. [Charlestown Boot & Shoe Co. v. Dunsmore, 60 N.H. 85 (1880)] Correspondingly, shareholders, as such, have no authority to act on the corporation's behalf.

5. **Duration—Continuity of Existence:** [§5]   As a legal entity, the corporation's existence continues notwithstanding the death or incapacity of its shareholders or a transfer of its shares. Therefore, a corporation is capable of perpetual duration.

6. **Taxation:** [§6]   The general principle is that a corporation is treated as an entity for tax purposes, so that it is taxed on its own income. (If the corporation pays a

dividend to its shareholders, the shareholders are taxed on the dividend.) However, corporations that have 35 or fewer shareholders, only one class of stock, and no foreign shareholders can elect to become "S" Corporations. S Corporations are not treated as entities for tax purposes. Instead, the shareholders are taxed on their pro rata share of the corporation's income (and can claim a pro rata share of the corporation's losses).

B. CORPORATIONS DISTINGUISHED FROM OTHER FORMS OF BUSINESS ASSOCIATIONS [§7]

A useful way to understand the principal characteristics of the corporation is to contrast those characteristics with the characteristics of other forms of business associations, such as general partnerships, limited partnerships, and limited liability companies.

1. **General Partnerships:** [§8]   In most states, general partnerships (or "partnerships") are governed by the Uniform Partnership Act ("UPA"). The Revised Uniform Partnership Act (1994) ("RUPA") was recently promulgated. As of 1995, RUPA had been adopted by only a few states, but it seems highly likely that other states will follow. A partnership has the following characteristics:

    a. **Aggregate status:** [§9]   In contrast to a corporation, a partnership under the UPA is not a legal entity. Rather, it is an **aggregation** of two or more persons who are engaged in business as co-owners. [UPA §6] If strictly pursued, the theory that a partnership is not an entity would lead to highly impracticable results. For example, the partnership could not hold property in its own name. In practice, therefore, certain rules of the UPA treat a partnership *as if* it were a legal entity. For example, under UPA section 8, a partnership can hold and convey title to property in its own name.

        (1) **RUPA:** [§10]   In contrast to the UPA, RUPA confers entity status on partnerships: RUPA section 201 expressly provides that "a partnership is an entity."

    b. **Unlimited liability:** [§11]   In contrast to the corporation, in which the liability (or risk) to shareholders is limited to their investment, every partner of a general partnership is subject to unlimited personal liability for all debts of the partnership.

    c. **Transferability of interests:** [§12]   In contrast to corporate stock, which is freely transferable unless transferability is limited by contract, a partner *cannot* (unless otherwise agreed) transfer his partnership interest in such a way as to make the transferee a *member* of the partnership, except with the consent of all remaining partners. [UPA §8]

        (1) **Compare—interest in partnership profits:** [§13]   Although a partner cannot make a transferee a *member* of the partnership, a partner can assign his *interest* in the partnership. Such an assignment does not entitle the assignee, during the continuance of the partnership, to interfere in the management or administration of the partnership business or affairs, to require any information or account of partnership transactions, or to inspect the partnership books. It merely entitles the assignee to receive, in accordance with his contract, the profits to which the assigning partner

would otherwise be entitled. In case of a dissolution of the partnership, the assignee is entitled to receive his assignor's interest. [UPA §27; Rapoport v. 55 Perry Co., 50 A.D.2d 54 (1975)]

d. **Duration and dissolution:** [§14]   In contrast to a corporation, which has perpetual existence, under the UPA a partnership is not capable of perpetual existence. Instead, a number of circumstances will result in dissolution.

(1) **Rightful dissolution:** [§15]   A partnership is terminable at will unless a definite term is specified or can be implied. [UPA §31(1)(a); Page v. Page, 55 Cal. 2d 192 (1961)] Furthermore, because a partnership is not an entity, but only an aggregation of the individual partners, under the UPA a partnership is normally dissolved—even before the expiration of any stated term—by the death, incapacity, or withdrawal of any partner.

(2) **Wrongful dissolution:** [§16]   Under the UPA, dissolution can also be caused, *in contravention of the agreement between the partners*, by the express will of any partner at any time, or by a court, where a partner has: (i) been guilty of conduct that tends to prejudicially affect the carrying on of the business, (ii) willfully or persistently committed a breach of the partnership agreement, or (iii) otherwise so conducted himself, in matters relating to the partnership business, that it is not reasonably practicable to carry on the business in partnership with him. [UPA §§31, 32]

(a) **Consequences of wrongful dissolution:** [§17]   Under the UPA, when dissolution is caused in contravention of the partnership agreement, each partner who has not wrongfully caused the dissolution has the right to damages for breach of the agreement from the partner who wrongfully caused the dissolution. If all the partners who have not wrongfully caused the dissolution desire to continue the business in the same name, they may do so during the agreed term of the partnership, provided they pay to the partner who has wrongfully caused the dissolution the value of his interest in the partnership at the dissolution, less any damages, or give a bond for such payment. However, in ascertaining the value of that interest, the value of the goodwill of the business is not considered. [UPA §38]

(3) **Dissociation under RUPA:** [§18]   RUPA uses the term "dissociation" to describe the termination of a person's status as a partner. Although the term "dissociation" is new, the concept is not. For example, RUPA continues the rule of the UPA that every partner has the right to dissociate (withdraw) from the partnership at any time, rightfully or wrongfully, by express will. [RUPA §602(a)] Under RUPA, a partner who wrongfully dissociates is liable to the partnership and to the other partners for damages caused by the dissociation. Furthermore, if a partner wrongfully dissociates, the partnership can continue without him. [RUPA §602(c)]

(a) **Effect of dissociation:** [§19]   Under RUPA, a dissociation normally leads to one of two forks: winding up (Article 8), or mandatory buyout of the dissociated partner (Article 7). Which fork must be taken depends on the nature of the event of dissociation.

1) **Winding up:** [§20]   The events of dissociation that require the partnership to be wound up under RUPA are described in

section 801. These events include: the express will of a partner in an at-will partnership to withdraw, the express will of all of the partners to wind up the partnership business, the expiration of the term or the completion of the undertaking, a judicial determination that the economic purpose of the partnership is likely to be unreasonably frustrated, a partner has engaged in conduct relating to the partnership business that makes it not reasonably practicable to carry on the business in partnership with that partner, or it is not otherwise reasonably practicable to carry on the partnership business in conformity with the partnership agreement.

2) **Mandatory buyout:** [§21] If, upon the dissociation of a partner, winding up is not required under section 801, a buyout of the dissociated partner's interest by the partnership is required. However, if the dissociation was wrongfully caused by the dissociated partner, the buyout price is reduced by damages for the wrongful dissociation. Furthermore, a partner who wrongfully dissociates before the expiration of a definite or implied term is not entitled to payment of the buyout price until the expiration of the term, unless the partner establishes to the satisfaction of the court that earlier payment will not cause undue hardship to the business of the partnership. [RUPA §701]

e. **Management and control:** [§22] In contrast to shareholders, who have no right to participate in the corporation's business, under the UPA *unless otherwise provided in the partnership agreement*:

(i) Every partner has a *right to participate* in the management of the partnership business.

(ii) Any *difference* arising as to ordinary matters connected with the partnership business may be decided by a *majority* of the partners, with each partner having one vote regardless of the relative amount of his capital contribution.

(iii) *Extraordinary* matters require approval by *all* the partners.

[UPA §18; Summers v. Dooley, 481 P.2d 318 (Idaho 1971)]

(1) **Comment:** The right of a partner to participate in the management of the partnership's business is one reason that partners have unlimited liability. In contrast, the fact that a shareholder has no right to participate in the management of a corporation's business is one reason that shareholders have limited liability.

(2) **RUPA:** [§23] RUPA basically continues the rules of the UPA concerning the management and control of a partnership's business, with only minor, technical variations.

f. **Authority:** [§24] In contrast to a corporate shareholder, who has no authority to bind the corporation, every partner is an agent of the partnership for the purpose of its business. Accordingly, under the UPA, the act of every partner for carrying on, in the usual way, the business of the partnership binds the partnership—unless the partner so acting in fact has no actual authority to act for the partnership in the particular matter, and the person with whom he is dealing knows that he has no such authority. However, an act of a partner that is not for the carrying on of the business of the partnership in the usual way does not bind the partnership unless the act is actually authorized by the other partners. [UPA §9; Owens v. Palos Verdes Monaco, 142 Cal. App. 3d 855 (1983)]

(1) **RUPA:** [§25]   RUPA takes the same general approach to a partner's authority as the UPA, but there are several differences in important details.

    (a) **Business of the same kind:** [§26]   Under the UPA, it was unclear whether a partner's apparent authority extended to acts for carrying on business of the *kind* carried on by the partnership, or was limited to acts for carrying on the *actual* business of the partnership. [*See* Burns v. Gonzalez, 439 S.W.2d 131 (Tex. 1969)] RUPA makes clear that a partnership is bound by an act of the partner for carrying on in the usual way either the actual partnership business or a business of the kind carried on by the partnership.

    (b) **Statement of authority:** [§27]   Also, RUPA provides for the filing of a "Statement of Partnership Authority." A *grant* of authority set forth in such a statement is normally conclusive in favor of third persons, even if they have no actual knowledge of the statement, unless they have actual knowledge that the partner has *no* such authority. However, a *limitation* on a partner's authority that is contained in such a statement—other than a limitation on the partner's authority to transfer real property—will not be effective unless the third party knows of the limitation or the statement has been delivered to him. A limitation on a partner's authority to transfer *real property* will be effective if properly filed, even if the third party does not know of the statement and it has not been delivered to him. [RUPA §303]

g. **Ownership of property:** [§28]   Like a corporation, a partnership can hold and convey title to property in its own name. [UPA §8] But under the aggregate theory of the UPA, even though title to assets may be held in the name of the partnership, the property is said to be "owned" by the partners in a unique form of ownership known as "tenancy in partnership." [UPA §25(1)] However, the partners' "ownership" interest in partnership property under the UPA's tenancy in partnership is largely theoretical, because UPA section 25(2) strips away from the partners all the usual incidents of ownership, such as the right to assign and the right to bequeath.

(1) **RUPA:** [§29]   RUPA abolishes the tenancy-in-partnership apparatus of the UPA. Under RUPA, a partnership is an entity, and property acquired by the partnership is owned by the partnership, not by the individual partners. [RUPA §203]

h. **Capacity to sue and be sued:** [§30]   Unlike a corporation, which as an entity can sue and be sued in its own name, under the UPA a partnership cannot sue or be sued in its own name, because it is an aggregation rather than an entity. Rather, under the UPA, suit on a partnership obligation must be brought by or against individual partners.

(1) **Type of liability:** [§31]   Under general law, if an obligation is "joint and several," the obligors can be sued either jointly or separately. If, however, an obligation is only "joint," the obligee normally must join all the obligors. Under the UPA, partners are *jointly and severally* liable for wrongful acts and omissions (*e.g.*, torts) of the partnership and breaches of trust. [UPA §15(a)] However, partners are only *jointly* liable "for all other debts and obligations of the partnership." [UPA §15(b)] Therefore, under the UPA, a contract creditor of the partnership not only is barred from suing the partnership as such, but also must join *all* the individual partners in her suit.

(2) **Statutory reforms:** [§32]   The inability of a partnership contract creditor to sue a partnership in its own name under the UPA is obviously undesirable, and many states have statutorily patched up the UPA rule by adopting "common name statutes," which explicitly allow a partnership to be sued in its own name. Also, some states address this issue by making *all* partnership liabilities joint and several, so that not all the partners need to be joined in a suit. Other states have adopted "joint debtor statutes," which provide that a suit against joint obligors can proceed even if some of the obligors are not joined.

(3) **RUPA:** [§33]   Unlike the UPA, RUPA specifically provides that a partnership may both *sue and be sued* in its own name [RUPA §307(a)], and that partners are jointly and severally liable for all obligations of the partnership [RUPA §306]. However, RUPA adds a new barrier to *collecting* against an individual partner on such a *liability*. A judgment against a partner, based on a claim against the partnership, normally cannot be satisfied against the partner's individual assets unless and until a judgment on the same claim has been rendered against the partnership and a writ of execution on the judgment has been returned unsatisfied. [RUPA §307] To put this differently, RUPA adopts an exhaustion rule, under which partnership assets must be exhausted before a partner's individual assets can be reached.

2. **Joint Venture:** [§34]   A joint venture is essentially a species of partnership, except that a joint venture is formed for some *limited investment or operation*, such as the construction of a single building, while a partnership is generally formed as a continuing business enterprise. There is a split of authority on the extent to which joint ventures are governed by partnership law. Some commentators argue that joint ventures are governed by all the rules applicable to partnerships, while other commentators argue that joint ventures are not entirely subject to partnership rules. The same split is found in the cases. Even under the concept that joint ventures are not subject to *all* the rules of partnership law, however, it is clear that they are subject to most of those rules.

3. **Limited Partnerships:** [§35]   In a limited partnership, the partners are divided into two classes: *general partners*, who essentially have the rights and obligations of partners in an ordinary partnership, and *limited partners*, who do not participate in the management of the partnership's business and are subject to only limited liability.

a. **General partners:** [§36]   A limited partnership must have one or more general partners. The general partners have unlimited liability for partnership obligations, as in an ordinary partnership. (However, a corporation can be a general partner. If a corporation is the sole general partner, as a practical matter no individual will have unlimited liability.)

b. **Limited partners:** [§37]   Generally, the liability of a limited partner for partnership debts is limited to the capital she contributes to the partnership. Under certain circumstances, however, a limited partner may have the liability of a general partner. There have been three versions of the Uniform Limited Partnership Act ("ULPA"). Each version has a different provision concerning the liability of limited partners to third parties, and each version is in force in at least some states.

(1) **Uniform Limited Partnership Act (1916):** [§38]   Under the ULPA, a limited partner is not liable as a general partner unless, in addition to the exercise of her rights and powers as a limited partner, she takes part in the control of the business. [Holzman v. de Escamilla, 86 Cal. App. 2d 858 (1948)]

(2) **Revised Uniform Limited Partnership Act (1976):** [§39]   Under the original version of the Revised Uniform Limited Partnership Act ("RULPA"), a limited partner is not liable for the obligations of a limited partnership unless she is also a general partner or, in addition to the exercise of her rights and powers as a limited partner, she takes part in the control of the business. However, if the limited partner's participation in the control of the business is not *substantially the same as the exercise of the powers of a general partner*, she is liable only to persons who transact business with the limited partnership with actual knowledge of her participation in control.

(3) **Revised Uniform Limited Partnership Act (1985):** [§40]   Under the current (1985) version of RULPA, a limited partner is not liable for the obligations of a limited partnership unless, in addition to the exercise of her rights and powers as a limited partner, she participates in the control of the business. However, even if the limited partner participates in the control of the business she is liable only to persons who transact business with the limited partnership *reasonably believing, based upon the limited partner's conduct, that the limited partner is a general partner*. [RULPA §303]

4. **Limited Liability Partnerships:** [§41]   An important new form of business organization is the limited liability partnership ("LLP"). Essentially, LLPs are partnerships, but the liability of a general partner in an LLP is less extensive than the ordinary liability of a general partner.

a. **Liability for negligence, wrongful acts, and misconduct:** [§42]   Although the statutes vary, generally speaking, a general partner in an LLP is *not* personally liable for *all* partnership obligations arising from negligence, wrongful acts, and misconduct. Instead, a partner is liable only for obligations arising from: (i) the partner's own negligence or wrongful acts; (ii) the acts of persons under the partner's supervision and control; and (iii) under some statutes, the negligence, wrongful acts, or misconduct of those engaged in a specific activity (as opposed to the general partnership business) in which the partner was involved. This core idea is articulated differently under different LLP statutes, and the precise liability of a partner in an LLP will depend on the statute.

b. **Contractual liability:** [§43]   The LLP statutes apparently do not appear to exclude a partner's liability for contractual obligations. Furthermore, under the statutes the liability of a partner in an LLP is "limited" only in the sense that the partner is not personally liable for *all* of the LLP's obligations. A partner in an LLP is personally liable for certain obligations, and as to those obligations a partner's liability is unlimited—*i.e.*, a partner is personally liable for those obligations to the entire extent of her wealth.

c. **Insurance and registration:** [§44]   Under some statutes, an LLP is required to have a designated minimum amount of liability insurance or segregated funds. Under all statutes, an LLP, like a limited partnership, must be registered.

5. **Limited Liability Companies:** [§45]   Limited liability companies ("LLCs") are a relatively new form of business organization. An LLC is a non-corporate business entity whose owners ("members") have limited liability and can participate actively in the entity's management. Some characteristics of the LLC resemble those of partnerships; other characteristics resemble those of corporations. Most states have now adopted LLC statutes. The statutes differ very considerably in detail. The Commissioners on Uniform State Law have adopted a Uniform Limited Liability Company Act ("Uniform Act"), but the statute is very new and has not yet been enacted by any state. Delaware has become an important state for LLCs, as it is for corporations. The LLC statutes generally allow wide scope to agreements concerning internal matters, like management and entitlement to distributions, and provide default rules where the organizational documents do not specify a rule to govern a specific issue.

a. **Organization:** [§46]   An LLC can be organized only by filing papers with the state. The statutes generally provide for two kinds of basic organizational documents: one usually called "articles," and another usually called an "operating agreement" or "limited liability company agreement." The articles are equivalent to a corporation's certificate of incorporation. The articles must be filed with the state, but can be relatively brief. The operating agreement is the equivalent of corporate bylaws, a shareholders' agreement, or a partnership agreement. It need not be filed.

b. **Duration:** [§47]   Under most statutes, an LLC may be either for a term or at will. A few statutes limit the term of an LLC to 30 years. A few, including Delaware, permit an LLC to have perpetual duration.

c. **Ownership:** [§48]   Owners of an LLC are usually referred to as "members." Ownership interests are usually referred to as "membership interests" or "limited liability company interests." The financial characteristics of membership interests, including the rights to distributions, can be structured in any way the members desire, and can differ from member to member.

d. **Transferability of interests:** [§49]   A transferee of a membership interest is entitled to receive the distributions that her transferor was entitled to receive.

Some statutes require unanimous consent for the admission of a member's transferee as a member. Under other statutes, a transferee cannot become a member of the LLC unless the organizational documents otherwise provide or all members consent.

e. **Management:** [§50] Under most statutes, management can be structured in any way the organizational documents provide. In particular, an LLC can be managed either by its members or by nonmember managers. Under some statutes, in the absence of a contrary provision in the organizational documents, an LLC is managed by its members, with each member having an equal vote. Under other statutes, in the absence of a contrary provision in the organizational documents, an LLC is managed by its members, with voting rights based on the members' interests in profits. [Del. Code Ann. tit. 6, §18-402]

f. **Distributions:** [§51] Under some statutes, in the absence of a contrary provision in the organizational documents, distributions must be made equally to each member. Under others, in the absence of a contrary provision in the organizational documents, profits are allocated on the basis of the value of each member's contributions, and distributions are made on the same basis.

g. **Withdrawal and dissolution:** [§52] Some statutes provide that the death, retirement, resignation, expulsion, bankruptcy, or dissolution of a member, or the occurrence of any other event that terminates the member's continued membership, will cause dissolution, although the members may choose to continue the business of the LLC after dissolution. Other statutes take a more flexible position on dissolution.

(1) **Uniform Act:** [§53] Under the Uniform Act, a member has power to withdraw ("dissociate") at any time, rightfully or wrongfully, and can be expelled on various grounds. Dissolution may be triggered by a variety of events that, very broadly speaking, fall into three basic classes:

(i) Events (including votes by a designated percentage of members) that are *specified* to cause dissolution in the operating agreement;

(ii) Events that involve *fault*, such as conduct by a member that makes it not reasonably practicable to carry on the company's business with that member; and

(iii) Events that *do not involve fault*, such as the *death or bankruptcy* of a member. (Dissolution for non-fault events can be avoided by a provision in the operating agreement that confers a right to continue the business on the remaining members, or by a vote of a majority of the remaining members to continue the business.)

(a) **Purchase of shares on withdrawal:** [§54] If a member withdraws or is expelled, and dissolution does not result, the LLC *must purchase* the member's interest at its fair value.

(b) **Modification by agreement:** [§55] Most, although not all, of the Uniform Act's provisions on withdrawal and dissolution can be varied by a provision of the operating agreement.

(2) **Compare—California statute:** [§56]   Under the California statute, in the absence of a provision to the contrary in the organizational documents, a member may withdraw on six months' notice. Within a reasonable time after withdrawal, the member is entitled to be paid the fair market value of his interest "based upon his right to share in distributions." The provisions governing dissolution for non-fault events, like the death of a member, are similar to the provisions of the Uniform Act. Dissolution on the basis of fault can be avoided by a purchase of the complaining member's interest at fair value. [Cal. Corp. Code §§17252, 17350, 17351; *and see* Del. Code Ann. tit. 6, §§18-603, -604, -801, -802—similar provisions except grounds for dissolution for fault more limited]

h. **Advantages of LLCs:** [§57]   For a business association that is not to be publicly held, an LLC offers strong advantages over competitive forms, because LLCs can combine partnership taxation, virtually complete freedom in structuring ownership interests and management, limited liability for both owners and managers, and no limits on the number or nature of the owners.

(1) **Compare—limited liability partnerships and limited partnerships:** [§58]   In contrast to LLCs, in limited liability partnerships, the partners may have *personal liability for contractual obligations* of the firm and for actions that a partner takes or supervises. In limited partnerships, in contrast to LLCs, at least one partner *must be a general partner* with personal liability (although that requirement can be alleviated by making that partner a corporation), and limited partners may have personal liability under certain circumstances.

(2) **Compare—close and subchapter S corporations:** [§59]   Unlike LLCs, close corporations (other than Subchapter S corporations) are taxed as corporations, and must follow certain formalities to vary the normal centralized-management structure. Subchapter S corporations are more limited than LLCs in that they can have no more than 35 shareholders, can have only a single class of stock, and cannot have any foreign shareholders.

C.   DISREGARD OF CORPORATE ENTITY

1. **In General:** [§60]   Since a corporation is a legal entity distinct from its shareholders, the rights and obligations of a corporation are normally separate from those of the shareholders. Thus, a shareholder normally has no liability for corporate debts or other obligations. Instead, her liability—more accurately, her risk—is limited to the loss of her investment.

2. **Suits by Corporate Creditors Against Shareholders:** [§61]   Under certain circumstances, shareholders become liable to corporate creditors. In such cases, it is said, the courts "pierce the corporate veil." The tests for whether the corporate veil will be pierced are generally vague. Often, courts put the issue in terms of whether the corporation was the "alter ego" or "instrumentality" of its shareholders. Among the most important elements that may lead a court to pierce the corporate veil are the following:

a. **Commingling of assets:** [§62]   A commingling of the corporation's assets and the shareholders' personal assets occurs when the shareholders have dealt with the assets of the corporation as if those assets were their own, *e.g.,* by using corporate funds to pay private debts, or by using corporate assets for other private purposes.

b. **Lack of corporate formalities:** [§63]   Also relevant to piercing the corporate veil is whether basic corporate formalities were followed (*e.g.,* whether stock was issued, corporate records maintained, directors or officers elected, and regular meetings of directors and shareholders held).

(1) **Statutory close corporations:** [§64]   Many states today have special provisions for "statutory close corporations," which among other things permit less formal management of these corporations' affairs. *(See infra,* §§169-185.) Some of these statutes provide that the failure to hold formal meetings of the board of directors or shareholders, pursuant to shareholder agreement, is not to be considered a factor in determining whether the shareholders of a statutory close corporation should be held liable for the corporation's debts. [*See, e.g.,* Cal. Corp. Code §300(e)]

c. **Undercapitalization:** [§65]   An extremely important factor in deciding whether the corporate veil should be pierced is whether the corporation was organized with sufficient resources, by way of capital, liability insurance, or both, to meet the obligations that reasonably could be expected to arise in its business. [Minton v. Cavaney, 56 Cal. 2d 576 (1961)] The issue here is not whether the shareholders have respected and maintained the corporation as a separate entity; rather, the issue is whether the shareholders should reasonably have anticipated that the corporation would be unable to pay the debts it would be likely to incur. The rationale of piercing the veil on the basis of undercapitalization is that the legislature, in conferring limited liability, assumed that shareholders would in good faith put up encumbered capital (or insurance) reasonably adequate for its prospective liabilities.

d. **Domination and control by shareholder:** [§66]   Courts will often pierce the corporate veil of one corporation, C, when an individual or another corporation that owns most or all of C's stock so completely dominates C's policy and business practices that C can be said to have no separate mind, will, or existence of its own. The prime example occurs when a parent corporation directly determines the business policy of a subsidiary, rather than allowing that policy to be determined by the subsidiary's board. In contrast, the court is less likely to pierce a subsidiary's veil if the subsidiary's business policies are determined by its own board, even though the directors are elected by the parent, and even though they are also employees of the parent.

e. **"Alter ego"; "instrumentality"; "unity of interest":** [§67]   Courts that pierce the corporate veil often do so on the ground that no separate entity has been maintained and the corporation is only the "alter ego" or "instrumentality" of its shareholders, or there is a "unity of interest" between the corporation and its shareholders. Although the terms "alter ego," "instrumentality," and "unity of interest" are often treated as if they were grounds for piercing the corporate veil, more typically these terms are conclusory in nature, and applied only if other grounds (like those listed in a.-d., above) are present.

f. **Requirement of fraud, wrong, dishonesty, or injustice:** [§68]   It is sometimes said that the corporate veil will be pierced only if it was used to commit
fraud or wrong, perpetuate the violation of a statutory or other positive legal
duty, or commit a dishonest or unjust act in contravention of the creditor's legal right. [Zaist v. Olson, 227 A.2d 552 (Conn. 1967)] As a practical matter,
this means that certain elements that can lead to piercing, like the failure to
follow corporate formalities, may not lead to piercing unless the court also
concludes that an injustice of some sort would be done to the plaintiff if the
veil is not pierced.

g. **Application:** [§69]   Cases in which the courts pierce the corporate veil to
impose personal liability on shareholders are usually limited to corporations
with only a small number of shareholders (including corporations that are
wholly owned subsidiaries of other corporations).

3. **Piercing the Wall Between Affiliated Corporations:** [§70]   A related but somewhat different problem arises where a plaintiff with a claim against one corporation, C, seeks to satisfy the claim against the assets of an affiliated corporation, D,
under common ownership with C. Here, the plaintiff is not seeking to impose individual liability on C's *shareholders*, but to *aggregate* brother-sister corporations (C
and D) as if they were one corporation. [38 A.L.R. 3d 1102]

a. **Enterprise liability:** Some opinions suggest that this kind of aggregation
may be permitted where each affiliated corporate entity is not a free-standing
business enterprise, but only a fragment of an enterprise that is composed of
all the affiliated corporations. [Walkovszky v. Carlton, 18 N.Y.2d 414 (1966)]

b. **Rationale:** In permitting incorporation and limited liability, the legislature
contemplated the incorporation of business enterprises. Separate incorporation
of enterprise fragments was not within the legislative intent in granting limited
liability. [Berle, *The Theory of Enterprise Entity*, 47 Colum. L. Rev. 343 (1947);
Landers, *A Unified Approach to Parent, Subsidiary and Affiliate Questions in
Bankruptcy*, 42 U. Chi. L. Rev. 589 (1975)]

c. **Example:** Where a parent corporation operated through three wholly owned
subsidiaries, each of which actively implemented the activities of the other as
part of a single business enterprise, tort liabilities incurred by any one of the
subsidiaries could be imposed upon any of the other subsidiaries. [Sisco-
Hamilton Co. v. Lennon, 240 F.2d 68 (7th Cir. 1957)]

4. **Use of Corporate Form to Evade Statutory or Contract Obligations:** [§71]
The courts may ignore the corporate form when it is used to evade a statutory or
contractual obligation. Typically, the question in these cases is not whether the
shareholders are personally liable for the debts of the corporation. Rather, the question is one of statutory or contract interpretation: was a statute or contract that
nominally applies only to the corporation intended to also apply to the
corporation's shareholders?

a. **Example:** A statute prohibited railroads from giving rebates to shippers. The
statute was held to apply to rebates given to a corporation that was not itself a
shipper, but had been formed by a shipper's officers and principal shareholders for the purpose of obtaining what were in substance, although not in form,

rebates to a shipper. [United States v. Milwaukee Refrigerated Transit Co., 142 F. 247 (E.D. Wis. 1905)]

b. **Example:** A consent decree was entered against S Corporation, a subsidiary of P Corporation. P was controlled by a single family. The decree prohibited S from violating the Fair Labor Standards Act. Later, S was merged into T, another subsidiary of P. T had the same officers as S, and few assets. The court held that the consent decree was binding on T, and moreover that it applied not only to the employees at S's old operation, but also to a new operation T began after the merger. [Wirtz v. Ocala Gas Co., 336 F.2d 236 (5th Cir. 1964)]

5. **Disregard of Corporate Entity in Favor of Corporation or Its Shareholders:** [§72]   Only *third parties*, and not the corporation or its shareholders, are generally allowed to disregard the corporate entity. So, for example, in an action by P against Corporation C, C normally could not assert, as a set-off to P's claim against C, an obligation running from P to C's shareholders.

D. SUBORDINATION OF SHAREHOLDER DEBTS—"DEEP ROCK" DOCTRINE [§73]

If a corporation goes into bankruptcy, any debts owed by the corporation to *controlling* shareholders *may*, under certain circumstances, be subordinated to the claims of other creditors under the doctrine of equitable subordination. This means that the shareholders' debt claims against the corporation would not be paid unless and until all other corporate creditors are paid—even if the controlling shareholders' claims are secured, and all other creditor claims are unsecured. [Taylor v. Standard Gas & Electric Co., 306 U.S. 307 (1939)]

1. **Effect of Subordination:** [§74]   When shareholders' claims are subordinated in bankruptcy, "loans" from the shareholders to the corporation are treated as if they were not loans but *invested capital* (stock), at least vis-a-vis the claims of creditors who are not shareholders. In practice, this usually means that the shareholders' "loans" to the corporation will not be repaid, because if the corporation has gone into bankruptcy, typically there will not even be enough money to pay off the outside creditors' claims.

   a. **Compare to piercing:** [§75]   Subordination differs in a crucial way from piercing the corporate veil. When the corporate veil is pierced, the shareholder is ordered to *pay* the corporation's debts. In subordination, the shareholder's claims merely get placed behind the claims of nonshareholder debtors. The shareholder may lose his "loans" but she is not liable for corporate debts.

2. **Grounds:** [§76]   The doctrine of equitable subordination is often referred to as the "Deep Rock" doctrine, named after one of the corporations involved in the seminal case of *Taylor v. Standard Gas & Electric Co., supra,* §73. Under the Deep Rock doctrine, when a corporation is in bankruptcy, the claim of a controlling shareholder (which can be either an individual or a parent of a bankrupt subsidiary) may be subordinated to other claims, including the claims of preferred shareholders, on equitable grounds. [Costello v. Fazio, 256 F.2d 903 (9th Cir. 1958)] Among the factors that a court may regard as inequitable conduct that will justify subordination are:

   (i) *Fraud* or other wrongdoing;

(ii) **_Mismanagement_** in excess of simple negligence;

(iii) **_Undercapitalization_**;

(iv) **_Commingling of funds and properties_**;

(v) **_Failure to develop the corporation_** into an independently profitable business, overdependence of the corporation's business upon that of the shareholder, or both;

(vi) **_Excessive control_**, indicated by a failure to observe the formalities of separate corporations; and

(vii) Whether or not the transaction that gave rise to the shareholder's debt claim carries the earmarks of an **_arm's length bargain_**.

[Arnold v. Phillips, 117 F.2d 497 (5th Cir. 1941)]

II. ORGANIZING THE CORPORATION

chapter approach

This chapter details the formation (or "organization") of a corporation. If you see a question concerning the incorporation of a business, keep in mind that various formalities are required to perfect incorporation—that is, to perfect the formation of a corporation. Most exam questions in this area will probably concern defects in the formation process, which may subject would-be shareholders of a would-be corporation to personal liability. In analyzing such a question, ask yourself the following:

1. Was there **substantial compliance** with statutory requirements? If so, the would-be corporation may be a de jure corporation, which cannot be attacked by anyone.

2. Was there a **good faith and colorable attempt** to incorporate and **good faith actual use** of the corporate existence? If so, then even if the statutory compliance was insufficient to constitute a de jure corporation, it may be sufficient to create a de facto corporation. A de facto corporation has corporate status with respect to dealings with third parties, but not with respect to the state. However, statutes in many jurisdictions have abrogated or modified the de facto doctrine.

3. Even if there is no de jure or de facto corporation, do the circumstances suggest a **corporation by estoppel**? Persons who have claimed corporate status will generally be estopped to deny that status if suit is brought against the corporation. Likewise, a party who has dealt with a business as a corporation may be estopped from claiming that the business lacks corporate status.

4. If there is neither a de jure nor de facto corporation, nor a corporation by estoppel, who may be held liable? Under the traditional view, all the would-be shareholders are subject to liability for the would-be corporation's debts and other obligations. However, the modern trend is to impose liability only upon those owners who **participated** in management.

A. GENERAL CORPORATION LAWS [§77]

Under early English and American law, corporations were created by a "special charter" granted by the King or the legislature. Today, with only a few exceptions, corporations are created by compliance with a "general corporation law" or "business corporation law" of the state in which formation is sought.

B. FORMALITIES IN ORGANIZING CORPORATION

1. **Certificate or Articles of Incorporation:** [§78] Typically, a corporation is organized by the execution and filing of a "certificate" or "articles" of incorporation. (The nomenclature varies from state to state.) The articles of incorporation are executed by one or more "incorporators." What must and what may go into the articles of incorporation depends on state law. The Revised Model Business Corporation Act ("Model Act") is fairly typical.

a. **Required provisions:** [§79]   Under the Model Act, the articles of incorporation *must* set forth the corporate name, the number of shares the corporation is authorized to issue, the street address of the corporation's initial registered office and the name of its initial registered agent at that office, and the name and address of each incorporator. [Revised Model Business Corporation Act ("RMBCA") §2.02(a)]

b. **Optional provisions:** [§80]   In addition, the articles of incorporation *may* set forth the names and addresses of the individuals who are to serve as the initial directors, and provisions, not inconsistent with law, regarding:

   (i)   *The purpose* or purposes for which the corporation is organized;

   (ii) *Managing the business and regulating the powers* of the corporation, its board of directors, and shareholders;

   (iii) *The definition, limitation, and regulation* of the powers of the corporation, its board of directors, and shareholders;

   (iv) *A par value*, if any, for authorized shares or classes of shares;

   (v)   *The imposition of personal liability* on shareholders for the debts of the corporation to a specified extent and upon specified conditions;

   (vi) *Eliminating or limiting the liability* of a director to the corporation or its shareholders for money damages for any action taken, or any failure to take any action, as a director (except liability for the amount of a financial benefit received by a director to which he is not entitled, for an intentional infliction of harm on the corporation or the shareholders, for a violation of the rules governing the payment of dividends, or for an intentional violation of criminal law); and

   (vii) *Any provision that is required or permitted* to be set forth in the *bylaws*.

   [RMBCA §2.02(b)]

c. **Purpose clause:** [§81]   Before the adoption of modern statutes, the clauses in the articles of incorporation that stated the purpose for which the corporation was formed tended to be extremely elaborate, to avoid the problem of ultra vires (*see infra*, §140). Under modern statutes, elaborate purpose clauses are no longer necessary. For example, under the Model Act, every corporation has "the purpose of engaging in any lawful business unless a more limited purpose is set forth in the articles of incorporation." [RMBCA §3.01(a)] Similarly, under the Delaware statute it is sufficient to state, either alone or with other business purposes, that the purpose of the corporation is to engage in any lawful activity for which corporations may be organized. All lawful acts and activities are thus within the purposes of the corporation, except for express limitations, if any. [Del. Gen. Corp. Law §102(e)]

2. **Organizational Meeting:** [§82]   Filing the certificate of incorporation in proper form creates the corporation. However, several steps are required to complete the corporation's structure. These steps are taken at organizational meetings of either (i) the incorporators or (ii) the initial board of directors named in the articles, if the

statute provides for naming the initial board this way. [*See, e.g.*, Del. Gen. Corp. Law §§107, 108]

a. **Matters determined at organizational meeting of incorporators:** [§83] If initial directors are *not named* in the articles of incorporation, the incorporators, at their organizational meeting, will typically adopt bylaws, fix the number of directors (if the certificate of incorporation or bylaws do not fix that number), and elect directors to serve until the first shareholders' meeting. The directors so elected will then typically adopt a corporate seal and form of stock certificate, authorize the issuance of stock to designated persons at designated prices, elect officers, and designate the corporation's bank.

b. **Matters determined at organizational meeting of initial directors:** [§84] If initial directors are *named* in the certificate of incorporation, at their organizational meeting they will typically adopt bylaws, elect officers, adopt a form of corporate seal and a form of stock certificate, authorize the issuance of shares to designated persons at designated prices, elect officers, and designate the corporation's bank.

C. DEFECTS IN FORMATION PROCESS—"DE JURE" AND "DE FACTO" CORPORATIONS

1. **In General:** [§85] Sometimes there is a defect or irregularity in the process of forming a corporation. For example, fewer than the required number of incorporators may have signed the certificate of incorporation, the certificate may fail to include a required provision in proper form, or the certificate may not have been properly filed. The issue is then the effect of such a defect on corporate status. This issue is usually put in terms of whether the corporation exists "de jure," "de facto," "by estoppel," or not at all.

   a. **Liability actions:** [§86] This issue arises most commonly (but not exclusively) in cases in which a third party seeks to impose personal liability on would-be shareholders on the ground that corporate status was not attained and, therefore, neither was limited liability.

   b. **Quo warranto actions:** [§87] The issue of corporate status may also arise in a quo warranto proceeding brought by the state. Most states provide by statute for such proceedings, often without using the term "quo warranto." [*See, e.g.*, N.Y. Bus. Corp. Law §109; Cal. Corp. Code §180(a)]

2. **De Jure Corporation:** [§88] A de jure corporation is a corporation organized in compliance with the requirements of the state of incorporation. Its status as a corporation cannot be attacked by anyone, not even by the state in a quo warranto proceeding. [People v. Ford, 128 N.E. 479 (Ill. 1920)]

   a. **"Substantial compliance" sufficient:** [§89] Most courts hold that perfect compliance with statutory requirements is not required for de jure status. Instead, "substantial compliance" will suffice. Therefore, an enterprise that fails to meet all the requirements for incorporation may nevertheless be a de jure corporation if the noncompliance is insubstantial. What constitutes substantial compliance is determined on a case-by-case basis, according to the nature of the unsatisfied requirement and the extent to which compliance has been attempted. [People v. Montecito Water Co., 97 Cal. 276 (1893)]

(1) **Example:** If the articles were properly filed except that the address for the corporation's principal place of business inadvertently states the wrong street number, there would undoubtedly be substantial compliance.

b. **Distinction between mandatory and directory requirements:** [§90] Some courts hold that for a corporation to attain de jure status, there must be exact compliance with all mandatory statutory requirements, but that failure to comply with requirements that are only directory will not preclude de jure status. [J.W. Butler Paper Co. v. Cleveland, 77 N.E. 99 (Ill. 1906)] Whether a particular requirement is mandatory or directory is a matter of statutory interpretation. Factors to be considered include the wording of the statute (*e.g.,* "must," "shall," or "may") and the relative importance of the provision.

(1) **Example:** The attorney general filed a proceeding in the nature of a quo warranto against three incorporators who had failed to comply with a statutory requirement that the certificate of incorporation be sealed. The incorporators had used the secretary of state's forms, which neither contained nor mentioned a seal. The court concluded that a de jure status had been attained. The provision for a seal was only directory, it said, because the purpose of the statute was to make a public record, and a seal did not further that purpose. [People v. Ford, *supra*, §88]

3. **De Facto Corporation:** [§91] A de facto corporation is said to exist when there is insufficient compliance to constitute a de jure corporation vis-a-vis the *state*, but the steps taken toward formation are sufficient to treat the enterprise as a corporation with respect to its *dealings with third parties*. In such cases, the corporate status can be invalidated by the state through quo warranto proceedings, but not by creditors or other persons who have had dealings with the enterprise.

a. **Requirements:** [§92] A de facto corporation requires a colorable attempt to incorporate and some actual use or exercise of corporate privileges.

(1) **Example:** On November 21, the corporate name of Sunshine Greenery, Inc. was reserved for B by the secretary of state. On December 3, B and C executed a certificate of incorporation for that corporation. The certificate was sent by mail to the secretary of state on that same date, with a check for the filing fee, but for some unexplained reason the certificate was not officially filed until December 18, two days after the execution of a lease by Sunshine Greenery. *Held:* Sunshine Greenery was a de facto corporation prior to December 18, and therefore, B and C were not personally liable to the lessor. [Cantor v. Sunshine Greenery, Inc., 398 A.2d 571 (N.J. 1979)]

b. **Quo warranto:** [§93] A quo warranto proceeding can be maintained even against a de facto corporation, because the de facto theory is a defense only against a collateral attack on corporate status—in effect, only against a challenge raised by private parties—not against a challenge by the state itself.

4. **Corporation by Estoppel:** [§94] In appropriate cases, a party may be estopped from challenging the corporate status of an enterprise, even though the enterprise has not achieved de jure or de facto status, on the ground of "estoppel." The estoppel principle is not a single theory, but a cluster of different rules.

a. **Shareholders estopped to deny corporate status:** [§95]   The shareholders of a nominal corporation, having claimed corporate status in an earlier transaction with a third party, are estopped to deny that status in a suit brought by the third party against the corporation.

b. **Technical defenses:** [§96]   Sometimes the question of corporate status is raised in a technical procedural context. For example, in a suit brought against a third party by a nominal or "would-be" corporation, the third party may seek to raise the defense that the would-be corporation is not really a corporation and, therefore, cannot sue in a corporate name. The courts tend to regard such a defense as nonmeritorious, and hold that the third party is estopped from raising the defense, on the ground that the defense is technical and would defeat the interests of justice.

c. **Personal liability of would-be shareholders:** [§97]   A third party who has dealt with an enterprise as a corporation may seek to impose personal liability on would-be shareholders, who in turn raise estoppel as a defense. Here, the issue is whether, as a matter of equity, the third party, having dealt with the enterprise as if it were a corporation, should be prevented (*i.e.,* estopped) from treating it as anything else. Less must be shown to establish a corporation by estoppel than to establish a de facto corporation.

   (1) **Example:** Without the knowledge of the would-be shareholders, their attorney negligently failed to file the certificate of incorporation before the business entered into a transaction with a third party. A third party who dealt with the business as if it were a corporation was held to be estopped from suing the would-be shareholders. [Cranson v. IBM Corp., 200 A.2d 33 (Md. 1964)]

   (2) **Tort claims:** [§98]   The basis of estoppel theory in cases in which a third party seeks to impose liability on would-be shareholders is that the third party has dealt with the business as if it were a corporation. Therefore, the theory does not apply to bar suit against would-be shareholders by tort claimants or other involuntary creditors.

5. **Who May Be Held Liable:** [§99]   If a would-be corporation is neither a de jure nor de facto corporation, nor a corporation by estoppel, the courts have split on whether *all* of the would-be shareholders may be held personally liable for debts incurred in the corporation's name.

   a. **Traditional view:** [§100]   Older decisions imposed personal liability against all of the would-be shareholders, on the theory that if the enterprise is not a corporation, it is a partnership, and therefore, the would-be shareholders are general partners. [Hamill v. Davis, 168 F. 187 (8th Cir. 1909)]

   b. **Modern trend:** [§101]   The modern trend, however, imposes personal liability against only those owners who actively participated in the management of the business. Owners who actively participated are held personally liable as if they were partners, but passive investors are not. [Baker v. Bates-Street Shirt Co., 6 F.2d 854 (1st Cir. 1925)]

6. **Effect of Statutes:** [§102]   A number of statutes directly or indirectly address the de facto and estoppel doctrines.

a. **Effect of statutes on de facto doctrine:** [§103] Under the prior version of the Model Act, persons who act as a corporation without the authority of a properly issued certificate of incorporation are jointly and severally liable for all debts and liabilities incurred as a result of that action. [Model Business Corporations Act ("MBCA") §146 (1979)] This section was designed "to prohibit the application of any theory of de facto incorporation." [MBCA §146, comment] Accordingly, in those states with statutes based on this provision, the de facto doctrine was abolished. [Timberline Equipment Co. v. Davenport, 514 P.2d 1109 (Or. 1973); Robertson v. Levy, 197 A.2d 443 (D.C. 1964); *but see* Vincent Drug Co. v. Utah State Tax Commission, 407 P.2d 683 (Utah 1965)]

(1) **Revised Model Business Corporation Act:** [§104] The Revised Model Business Corporation Act makes a significant change in the prior Model Act language. Under the Revised Model Act, only persons acting as or on behalf of a corporation who **know** there was no incorporation are jointly and severally liable for all liabilities created while so acting. [RMBCA §2.04] The requirement that a defendant **knew** there was no incorporation protects would-be shareholders of defectively formed corporations against liability under a variety of circumstances. For example, this requirement affords protection in cases where the would-be shareholders honestly and reasonably, but erroneously, believe that a certificate of incorporation has been filed [Cranson v. IBM Corp., *supra*, §97], or in cases where an incorporator mails a certificate of incorporation to be filed, but either the letter is delayed in the mails or the secretary of state's office does not file the certificate immediately after receiving it [Cantor v. Sunshine Greenery, Inc., *supra*, §92].

b. **Effect of statutes on estoppel doctrine:** [§105] The effect of section 146 of the prior Model Act and section 2.04 of the Revised Model Act on estoppel doctrine is an unsettled point. [*See* Robertson v. Levy, *supra*, §103—section 146 abrogates the estoppel doctrine; Thompson & Green Machinery Co. v. Music City Lumber Co., 683 S.W.2d 340 (Tenn. 1984)—same; *but see* Namerdy v. Generalcar, 217 A.2d 109 (D.C. 1966)—contra; Timberline Equipment Co. v. Davenport, *supra*, §103—raises but does not resolve the issue]

c. **Effect of statutes on the issue of liability of passive investors:** [§106] Section 146 of the prior version of the Model Act, which imposes liability on all persons who act as a corporation without a properly issued certificate of incorporation, has been held not to include persons whose only connection with the enterprise is as an investor. Instead, the provision is interpreted to reach only those persons who not only have an investment in the enterprise, but also exercise control or actively participate in policy and operational decisions. [Timberline Equipment Co. v. Davenport, *supra*; Flanagan v. Jackson Wholesale Building Supply Co., 461 So. 2d 761 (Miss. 1984)] Presumably, section 2.04 of the Revised Model Act will be interpreted in much the same way.

III. LIABILITIES FOR TRANSACTIONS BEFORE INCORPORATION

chapter approach

Promoters participate in the formation of the corporation. Most exam questions about promoters concern the rights and liabilities of the promoter and the corporation with respect to contracts entered into by the promoter on the corporation's behalf prior to formation of the corporation. Your approach to this type of question should be as follows:

1. The first issue to consider is whether the corporation is liable. Under the American rule, the corporation is liable if it _ratifies or adopts_ the contract.

2. The second issue to consider is the _rights and liabilities of the promoter_. Recall that a promoter is not personally liable on these contracts if he has made it explicit that he is contracting solely on behalf of the proposed corporation. But if this is not explicit, the promoter is liable. If the corporation is never formed, the promoter may be permitted to enforce the contract himself; but if a corporation is formed and it adopts or ratifies the contract, only the corporation may enforce it.

A. PROMOTERS

1. **Definition:** [§107]   A promoter is one who participates in the formation of a corporation. The promoter usually arranges compliance with the legal requirements to form a corporation, secures initial capitalization, and enters into necessary contracts on behalf of the corporation before it is formed. Often the promoter remains active in the corporation after it comes into existence.

2. **Fiduciary Duties to Each Other:** [§108]   Prior to formation of the corporation, the promoters are regarded as joint venturers (similar to partners) and for that reason owe to each other a duty of _full disclosure_ and _fair dealing_ as to all matters pertaining to the corporation.

B. CONTRACTS MADE BY PROMOTERS ON CORPORATION'S BEHALF [§109]

Litigation frequently arises from contracts entered into by promoters on the corporation's behalf prior to formation of the corporation. For example, the promoter negotiates a lease in the name of the proposed corporation on property to be used as its principal office. What are the rights and liabilities of the corporation and the promoters on this lease?

1. **Rights and Liabilities of Corporation**

    a. **English rule:** [§110]   Under the English rule, the corporation cannot be held liable on contracts made on its behalf prior to incorporation—even where the corporation has adopted or ratified the contract. The corporation may become a party only by entering into a new contract or by formal novation.

        (1) **Rationale:** Under agency law, the promoter cannot be said to be acting as agent of the corporation, because the corporation was not yet in existence

and therefore could not have authorized the acts. Nor can a subsequent ratification by the corporation make it a party to the contract, since ratification relates back to the time the contract was made and the corporation was not then in existence. [Kelner v. Baxter, 2 L.R.-C.P. 174 (1866)]

(2) **Quasi-contractual liability:** [§111]   However, courts following this view recognize recovery in quasi-contract against the corporation for the value of any goods or services that it chose to accept after it came into being. If the corporation had a choice to accept or reject the services offered under a contract negotiated by the promoters, and chose to accept them, it would constitute unjust enrichment if the corporation were not required to pay the reasonable value thereof.

(3) **Massachusetts rule:** [§112]   Massachusetts has been thought to follow the English rule [Abbott v. Hapgood, 22 N.E. 907 (Mass. 1899)], but a more recent decision suggests that the corporation can be held liable on a promoter's contract if the other party performs and the corporation knowingly accepts the benefits of the contract [Framingham Savings Bank v. Szabo, 617 F.2d 897 (lst Cir. 1980)].

b. **American rule:** [§113]   Under the American rule, a corporation can be held liable on contracts negotiated on its behalf by its promoters prior to incorporation, but only if the corporation *ratifies or adopts* the contract. The ratification may be express or may be implied.

(1) **Rationale:** Some courts treat the promoter's contract as a continuing offer to the corporation, which it is free to accept or reject. Basically, however, the courts have developed a rule in response to commercial needs surrounding the formation of corporations.

(2) **What constitutes ratification or adoption by corporation:**   [§114] Corporations may *expressly* ratify or adopt promoters' contracts by a resolution by the board of directors. The more difficult problem is to determine the sufficiency of the acts constituting implied ratification or adoption of promoters' contracts. Usually, some affirmative act by the corporation is required, *e.g.*, accepting benefits or making use of services or materials obtained under the contract with knowledge of the contract. [D.A. McArthur v. Times Printing Co., 51 N.W. 216 (Minn. 1892)]

(a) **Example:** The corporation is clearly charged with knowledge of the promoters' contracts if the board of directors is wholly composed of promoters with such knowledge. And it *may* be deemed to have knowledge if the promoter who made the contract has become a director of the corporation or is a controlling shareholder. [Chartrand v. Barney's Club, Inc., 380 F.2d 97 (9th Cir. 1967)]

(b) **Note:** There is a split of authority on whether mere use of the corporate charter is sufficient "acceptance" of benefits to hold the corporation liable on pre-incorporation contracts for the services essential to its formation (attorneys' fees to incorporate, etc.). [Kridelbaugh v. Aldrehn Theatres Co., 191 N.W. 503 (Iowa 1923)]

(3) **Quasi-contractual liability:** [§115]   Even where the corporation expressly disavows its promoters' contracts, it cannot with impunity keep the benefits obtained thereby. Quasi-contractual liability can be imposed to the extent of the fair value of the services or materials obtained, although some courts do not impose quasi-contractual liability for preincorporation services that it had no real option to reject (*e.g.*, attorneys' fees, filing costs, etc.). [David v. Southern Import Wine Co., 171 So. 180 (La. 1936)]

c. **Corporation's right to enforce contract:** [§116]   Under both the English and American rules, the corporation may enforce the contract against the party with whom the promoter contracted, if it chooses to do so.

   (1) *Under the English rule* (no contract with corporation), the corporation must sue as *assignee* of the promoters.

   (2) *Under the American rule*, the corporation's adoption of the contract makes it a party thereto so that it can maintain the action directly. [Builders' Duntile Co. v. W.E. Dunn Manufacturing, 17 S.W.2d 715 (Ky. 1929)]

2. **Rights and Liabilities of Promoters**

   a. **Liability on pre-incorporation contract:** [§117]   Where the corporation never comes into existence, rejects the pre-formation contracts negotiated for it by its promoters, or ratifies the contract but never performs or pays as agreed, the other party to the contract frequently attempts to hold the promoters personally liable.

      (1) **No liability:** [§118]   If the contracting party *clearly intended* to contract with the proposed corporation and *not* with the promoters individually, it must rely solely on the credit of the proposed corporation and has no claim against the promoters individually. [Quaker Hill, Inc. v. Parr, 364 P.2d 1056 (Colo. 1961)]

         (a) **Rationale:** Where this is so, there really is *no contract* at all prior to the corporation's becoming a party thereto—only a continuing offer to be communicated to the corporation after its formation, which it can then accept (expressly or impliedly) or reject.

      (2) **Liability:** [§119]   However, where the promoters have *not* made it explicit that they are contracting solely on behalf of the proposed corporation, courts tend to hold the promoters *personally liable* on pre-formation contracts. This is particularly true where such contracts require the other party to render *performance prior* to formation of the corporation. [Stanley J. How & Associates v. Boss, 222 F. Supp. 936 (S.D. Iowa 1963)]

         (a) **Rationale:** Various theories for holding promoters liable have been advanced. Some courts talk about the promoters having impliedly warranted their authority, or having impliedly warranted that the corporation would be formed and, once formed, would adopt the pre-formation contract. Other courts talk about the promoter remaining personally liable as surety or guarantor of the corporation's performance.

(b) **Note:** Where the promoters have been held personally liable on pre-formation contracts, they have a right to be **reimbursed** or indemnified by the corporation for their expenses or losses, at least to the extent of any **benefits** received by the corporation under the contracts.

b. **Right to enforce against other party:** [§120] Only a few cases have dealt with an attempt by a promoter to enforce a contract made by him for a corporation to be formed. At least where the corporation was **never formed,** the promoter may be permitted to enforce the contract on the theory that since the promoter could have been held liable in event of breach (*see* above), there was sufficient "mutuality" to allow him to enforce it against the other party. Unless the contract was expressly limited to the proposed corporation, the failure to incorporate is not deemed an essential condition to the other party's duty to perform. [Erskine v. Chevrolet Motors Co., 117 S.E. 706 (N.C. 1923)]

(1) **Compare:** On the other hand, if the corporation is formed and adopts or ratifies the contract, it alone has the right to enforce the contract; thus, the promoter cannot sue. [Speedway Realty Co. v. Grasshoff Realty Corp., 216 N.E.2d 845 (Ind. 1966)]

C. OBLIGATIONS OF PREDECESSOR BUSINESS

1. **Introduction:** [§121] Although corporations may be created to undertake an entirely new venture, they are often formed to take over an existing business that is already being conducted by a sole proprietorship, a partnership, or a different corporation. The newly formed corporation frequently acquires all the assets of the predecessor business. The owners of the predecessor business (*i.e.*, the sole proprietor, the partners, or the earlier corporation) continue to be liable for its debts. But the newly formed corporation that takes over the predecessor business may also be liable to its creditors under certain circumstances.

2. **General Rule:** [§122] A corporation that acquires all the assets of a predecessor business does not ordinarily succeed to the predecessor's liabilities. There are, however, a series of exceptions to this general rule. [Tift v. Forage King Industries, Inc., 322 N.W.2d 14 (Wis. 1982)]

a. **Third-party beneficiary:** [§123] If the newly formed corporation expressly or impliedly assumes the obligations of its predecessor, then the creditors of the old business may hold the new corporation liable as third-party beneficiaries.

b. **Fraud:** [§124] The successor corporation will be held liable for the debts of the predecessor business if the sale of its assets was an attempt to defraud the predecessor's creditors.

(1) **Inadequate consideration:** [§125] This may arise if the successor corporation gives inadequate consideration for the assets received, thus rendering the predecessor business unable to pay its existing debts. [Ortiz v. South Bend Lathe, 120 Cal. Rptr. 556 (1975)]

c. **Merger:** [§126] The successor corporation will be held liable for the debts of the predecessor business if it is merged into, or absorbed by, the successor.

This reorganization ends the predecessor's existence and transforms it into a different enterprise. [McCarthy v. Litton Industries, Inc., 570 N.E.2d 1008 (Mass. 1991)]

d. **Continuation:** [§127] The successor corporation *may* be held liable for the debts of the predecessor business on the theory that the successor is merely a continuation of the predecessor. Some decisions (involving strict liability product defect claims) have found such a continuation simply because the successor corporation conducts the same business as the predecessor, using the same name and management. [Tift v. Forage King Industries, Inc., *supra*, §122] But most courts require a more formal "reorganization" of the predecessor business (as described *supra*). [J.F. Anderson Lumber Co. v. Myers, 206 N.W.2d 365 (Minn. 1973)—successor not liable even though predecessor corporation was insolvent; Pendergrass v. Care Care, Inc., 424 S.E.2d 391 (N.C. 1993)—successor corporation not liable, partners of predecessor partnership remain liable]

IV. POWERS OF THE CORPORATION

chapter approach

Generally, corporations have those powers expressly set forth in their certificate of incorporation and conferred by statute, and those implied powers necessary to carry out the express powers. Transactions beyond the purposes and powers of the corporation are ultra vires.

Although exam questions often raise the issue of ultra vires transactions, under modern statutes ultra vires is not usually a viable defense. It is no defense to tort or criminal actions. Even in contract actions, there are very few situations where ultra vires may be allowed:

(1) At common law, if a contract is *purely executory*, either party can raise ultra vires as a defense. However, most states now have *statutes* that prohibit the use of ultra vires as a defense in an action between the contracting parties.

(2) Most statutes do allow the corporation to *sue directors or officers* for damages for their ultra vires acts.

(3) Most statutes also allow shareholders to *enjoin performance* of an ultra vires contract.

A. CORPORATE POWERS

1. **Express and Implied Powers:** [§128]   At one time, a corporation's purposes and powers were generally limited to those purposes and powers set forth in the corporation's certificate of incorporation ("express powers") and those powers reasonably necessary to accomplish the purposes set forth in its certificate of incorporation ("implied powers"). This approach gave rise to various ultra vires problems and verbose certificates of incorporation intended to minimize such problems.

2. **Modern Statutes:** [§129]   Modern statutes minimize these problems in two ways. First, modern statutes dispense with the need for setting out a long list of corporate purposes, by simply providing that a corporation can engage in any lawful business. Second, modern statutes set out a long list of powers conferred on every corporation, whether or not those powers are stated in the certificate of incorporation. Under the Delaware statute, which is typical, a corporation is granted the following express powers, among others:

    (i)   To have *perpetual succession* (*i.e*, perpetual existence);

    (ii)   To *sue and be sued;*

    (iii) To have a *corporate seal;*

    (iv)   To *acquire, hold, and dispose of personal and real property;*

    (v)   To *appoint officers;*

    (vi)   To *adopt and amend bylaws;*

    (vii) To *conduct business* inside and outside the state;

(viii) To establish *pension and other incentive and compensation plans;*

(ix) To *acquire, hold, vote, and dispose of securities* in other corporations;

(x) To make *contracts of guaranty and suretyship;*

(xi) To *participate with others in any corporation, partnership, or other association* of any kind that it would have power to conduct by itself, whether or not such participation involves sharing or delegating control with others; and

(xii) To *make donations* for the public welfare or for charitable, scientific, or educational purposes, and in time of war or other national emergency, in aid thereof.

[Del. Gen. Corp. Law §122] The Delaware statute also provides that a certificate of incorporation can simply state that the purpose of the corporation is to engage in any lawful act or activity for which corporations may be organized under Delaware law. [Del. Gen. Corp. Law §102(a)(3)] As more and more corporations use this kind of sweeping purpose clause, the problem of corporate powers becomes less and less significant, since a corporation has implied powers to accomplish the purposes set forth in its certificate of incorporation.

3. **Traditional Problem Areas:** [§130]   The last three of the above listed powers are the most significant, in the sense that the existence of these powers was deemed questionable under the older statutes, which did not specifically confer them.

   a. **Guaranties:** [§131]   The older statutes typically did not explicitly confer upon corporations the power to guarantee the debts of others. Cases under these statutes held that the exercise of such a power was normally ultra vires. Modern statutes explicitly permit a corporation to make contracts of guaranty and suretyship. Like other corporate powers, however, this power can be exercised only in furtherance of the corporate business (*e.g.*, by guaranteeing a loan to a customer to enable the customer to buy the corporation's product).

   b. **Participation in a partnership:** [§132]   The older statutes did not explicitly confer upon corporations the power to be a partner. Cases under these statutes held that a corporation had no implied power to enter into a partnership (although a corporation could enter into a joint venture, which is usually temporary in nature and for a limited purpose). The rationale was that in a partnership the corporation would be bound by the acts of its partners, who are not its duly appointed agents and officers, and that such responsibility cannot be delegated by the board. [60 A.L.R.2d 920] Modern statutes make these cases moot by explicitly conferring upon corporations the power to be a partner.

   c. **Donations:** [§133]   The law concerning donations and other uses of the corporation's resources for public welfare, charitable, educational, or like purposes, in the absence of an explicit statutory power, has never been completely well-defined, partly because it is in a process of continual growth.

      (1) **General rule:** [§134]   The general rule is that the objective of the business corporation is to conduct business activity with a view to corporate profit and shareholder gain. [Dodge v. Ford Motor Co., 170 N.W. 668 (Mich. 1919)]

(2) **Traditional view:** [§135] Some cases, mostly arising at or before the turn of the century, built either on that rule or on a strict notion of ultra vires (or on both) to preclude use of corporate resources, by donation or otherwise, for humanitarian, educational, philanthropic, or other public activities. [*See, e.g.,* Brinson Railway v. Exchange Bank, 85 S.E. 634 (Ga. 1915); McCrory v. Chambers, 48 Ill. App. 445 (1892)] Normally, however, use of corporate resources for public welfare, humanitarian, philanthropic, or educational purposes can be justified on traditional profit grounds (*e.g.,* on the ground that it increases good will). Accordingly, this strict position was modified by cases holding that a corporation *could* use its resources for such purposes if the use was likely to produce a ***direct benefit*** to the corporation. [Whetstone v. Ottawa University, 10 Kan. 240 (1874); Corning Glass Works v. Lucase, 37 F.2d 798 (D.C. Cir. 1929), *cert. denied,* 281 U.S. 742 (1930)]

(3) **Modern view:** [§136] Modern cases have in effect dropped this direct-benefit test and permit the use of corporate resources for public welfare, humanitarian, educational, or philanthropic purposes without requiring a showing that a direct benefit is likely. Some cases reach this result by treating such uses as ***profit-maximizing*** and within the board's business judgment even where the evidence indicates that the motive behind the conduct was not a profit motive. [Shlensky v. Wrigley, 237 N.E.2d 776 (Ill. 1968); Union Pacific Railroad v. Trustees, Inc., 329 P.2d 398 (Utah 1958); Kelly v. Bell, 266 A.2d 878 (Del. 1970)] Other cases take the more direct approach that the use of corporate resources for such purposes is a ***legitimate end*** in itself, on the ground that (i) activity that maintains a healthy social system necessarily serves a long-run corporate purpose; or (ii) there is an independent social policy to maintain diversified centers of charitable, educational, etc., activity, and full effectuation of that policy depends upon, and therefore justifies, corporate support. [*See, e.g.,* A.P. Smith Manufacturing Co. v. Barlow, 98 A.2d 581 (N.J. 1953); Union Pacific Railroad v. Trustees, Inc., *supra*]

(a) **Limitation—reasonableness test:** [§137] The corporation's ability to make donations is not unlimited. The modern cases have invoked a limit of ***reasonableness*** on the use of corporate resources for public welfare, humanitarian, educational, or philanthropic purposes.

(4) **Statutes:** [§138] Many statutes, like Delaware's, explicitly confer upon corporations the power to make donations for charitable and like purposes. This power is also subject to an implied limit of reasonableness. Thus, even under such a statute, it would still be improper to give away most of the corporation's assets.

(5) **Restatement view:** [§139] According to the American Law Institute's Principles of Corporate Governance, the "objective of the business corporation is to conduct business activities with a view to corporate profit and shareholder gain, except that, even if corporate profit and shareholder gain are not thereby enhanced, the corporation, in the conduct of its business . . . may devote resources, within reasonable limits, to public welfare, humanitarian, educational, and philanthropic purposes." [A.L.I. Prin. Corp. Gov. §2.01]

B. ULTRA VIRES TRANSACTIONS

1. **In General:** [§140]   An "ultra vires" transaction is one that is *beyond the purposes and powers* of the corporation.

   a. **Implied powers:** [§141]   It was established even in early cases that corporate powers could be implied as well as explicit. [*See* Sutton's Hospital Case, 10 Coke 23a (1613)] The courts eventually became very liberal in finding implied powers, including implied powers to enter into business activities not specified in the articles. Thus, in *Jacksonville, Mayport, Pablo Railway & Navigation Co. v. Hooper,* 160 U.S. 514 (1896), the Supreme Court held that a Florida company whose purpose was to operate a railroad could also engage in leasing and running a resort hotel, on the ground that the latter activity was auxiliary or incidental to the former.

   b. **Effect of shareholder ratification:** [§142]   Even where an ultra vires defense would otherwise be allowed, under American common law a corporation was not permitted to assert the defense if all shareholders had given their consent to or acquiesced in the contract.

2. **Tort Actions:** [§143]   Under modern law, ultra vires is *no defense to tort liability*. A corporation cannot escape civil damages by claiming that it had no legal power to commit the wrongful act. [Nims v. Mt. Herman Boys' School, 35 N.E. 776 (Mass. 1893)]

   a. **Rationale:** The fact that a wrongful act exceeded the powers conferred upon the corporation by statute or its articles should not result in the loss falling on the innocent injured party, assuming the act was one for which the corporation would otherwise be civilly liable.

3. **Criminal Actions:** [§144]   Similarly, it is *no defense to criminal liability* that a corporate act was beyond the corporation's authorized powers.

4. **Contract Actions—Common Law:** [§145]   The most substantial questions at common law arose when a corporation entered into a contract that was not explicitly or impliedly authorized under its articles of incorporation or the relevant statute. The extent to which a plea of ultra vires was allowed in contract actions depended largely on the extent to which the contract had been performed.

   a. **Contract purely executory:** [§146]   Where there had been no performance on either side, the defense of ultra vires could be raised by either the corporation or the party with whom it had contracted. The rationale was that since the contract was beyond the corporation's powers, it was unenforceable *against* the corporation; and under the doctrine of mutuality of obligation, the contract was therefore unenforceable *by* the corporation. [Ashbury Railway Carriage & Iron Co. v. Riche, 7 L.R.-E. & I. App. 653 (1875)]

   b. **Contract fully performed on both sides:** [§147]   If the contract was fully performed by both parties, neither party could rescind on the ground that the contract had been ultra vires. The courts left the parties where they were. [Long v. Georgia Pacific Railway, 8 So. 706 (Ala. 1891)]

   c. **Contract partly performed:** [§148]   The difficult case occurred where the contract had been fully or partly performed on one side, and the nonperforming party then sought to assert ultra vires as a defense to enforcement of its side of the contract.

    (1) **Majority view—no defense:** [§149]   Under the majority view, the non-performing party, having received a benefit, was estopped to assert a defense of ultra vires. [Joseph Schlitz Brewing Co. v. Missouri Poultry & Game Co., 229 S.W. 813 (Mo. 1921)]

    (2) **Minority view (federal rule):** [§150]   Some cases held that the non-performing party could assert the defense of ultra vires on the ground that the contract was void ab initio (from the outset) and could not be enforced. However, even cases that adopted this minority rule recognized that a party who had received a benefit from the part performance would be liable in *quasi-contract* for the *value* of the benefit. [Central Transportation Co. v. Pullman's Palace Car Co., 139 U.S. 24 (1891)]

5.   **Statutes:** [§151]   Most states now have statutes that severely curtail the doctrine of ultra vires. The most common type of statute prohibits the use of ultra vires as a defense in a suit between the contracting parties, but permits ultra vires to be raised in certain other contexts. [RMBCA §304; Del. Gen. Corp. Law §124]

    a.   **Corporation and third party:** [§152]   Under this type of statute, neither the corporation nor the third party with whom it contracts can assert ultra vires as a *defense* to the other's suit to enforce the contract; and this is true regardless of whether the contract is still executory or has been performed in whole or in part.

    b.   **Suit against officers or directors:** [§153]   However, if the contract has been performed and has resulted in a loss to the corporation, the corporation can sue the officers or directors for damages for exceeding their authority. And, if the corporation refuses to sue, a shareholder may bring a derivative suit *(see infra, §675)*.

    c.   **Suit by the state:** [§154]   These statutes do not prohibit the state from suing to enjoin the corporation from transacting unauthorized business.

    d.   **Suit by shareholders:** [§155]   These statutes also permit a shareholder of the corporation to sue to *enjoin performance* of an ultra vires contract, provided all parties to the contract are made parties to the action and the court finds that injunctive relief would be equitable.

    (1) **Damages:** [§156]   If an injunction is granted, the court may allow compensation to the injured party for any damages resulting from noncompletion of the contract, *exclusive of lost profits*.

    (2) **Interpretation:** [§157]   These statutes do not provide that the court *must* enjoin an ultra vires contract upon the suit of a shareholder, but only that the court may do so if an injunction would be equitable. A shareholder who actively participated in authorizing an ultra vires contract, or who purchased a corporation knowing it had made such a contract, would probably be unable to enjoin performance of the contract,

because an injunction in favor of such a shareholder would normally be inequitable. [Goodman v. Ladd Estate Co., 427 P.2d 102 (Or. 1967)]

e. **Broad certificate provisions:** [§158]   Finally, if a corporation is incorporated under a statute like the Delaware statute, which provides that a certificate of incorporation can state that the purpose of the corporation is to engage in any lawful act or activity for which corporations may be organized [Del. Gen. Corp. Law §102(a)(3)], and the corporation's certificate of incorporation contains such a statement, ultra vires issues are very unlikely to arise.

V. MANAGEMENT AND CONTROL

chapter approach

This chapter covers a great deal of material, so to help you study, the most likely topics for exam questions are discussed below.

1. **Allocation of Powers Between Directors and Shareholders:** Remember that generally the power to manage the business of the corporation belongs to the board of directors, not the shareholders. However, in exam questions, look for indications of a **close corporation** (*e.g.,* small number of shareholders, no general market for stock, limitations on admission of shareholders, etc.), which may mean that shareholder participation in management is acceptable.

2. **Directors:** A likely topic for an exam question concerning directors is whether the directors have acted properly and effectively. Ask yourself the following questions: Was there proper **notice** of the meeting? Was a **quorum** present? Was the action **approved by the necessary majority**? If there was an **agreement** affecting board decisions, was it valid?

   A question concerning directors may also test your knowledge of the rights, duties, and liabilities of directors. Keep in mind that although directors owe the corporation the duty to exercise the care of **ordinarily prudent and diligent persons** in like positions under similar circumstances, they are **not** liable for mere bad business judgment. If a director fails to exercise the proper measure of care, he is personally liable for the losses resulting from the breach. A director is not liable for the wrongful acts of other directors or officers, unless he participated in the act, was negligent in discovering the misconduct, or was negligent in appointing the wrongdoer.

3. **Officers:** Any question concerning officers (other than one dealing with a conflict or "insider" status, *see* below) will probably center on the officer's authority to act on behalf of the corporation. Note that an officer may have **actual or apparent authority**. Even an unauthorized act may bind the corporation, if the act is **ratified** by the board. Remember that officers owe a duty of care and loyalty to the corporation similar to that owed by directors.

4. **Conflicts of Interest in Corporate Transactions:** This is a popular exam topic. Consider the five basic conflicts of interest situations:

   a. **Business dealings with corporations:** Whenever you see a question where a corporation contracts either directly with a director or officer, or with a company in which the director or officer is financially interested, you should analyze it as follows:

      (1) May the director **participate** in the meeting authorizing the transaction? Most statutes permit an interested director to be counted in a quorum and vote.

      (2) Was there **full disclosure** to an **independent** board, **and** is the transaction **fair**? Most courts hold that an interested director transaction is voidable by the corporation only if it is unfair. For the transaction to be fair, the director must

make a full disclosure to an independent board, and the transaction must be fair in price, terms, or other conditions. The burden of proof is on the interested director.

(3) Was there *shareholder ratification*, and if so, by how many? Unanimous shareholder ratification after full disclosure estops the corporation from challenging the transaction. Ratification by a majority of shareholders carries less weight, particularly when the interested director owns most of the shares.

(4) What is the appropriate *remedy*? If the interested director did not act in bad faith or profit personally, rescission may be the corporation's only remedy. Otherwise, the corporation may seek damages from the director.

b. **Interlocking directorates:** If the question concerns a contract between corporations having common directors, remember that most jurisdictions permit these transactions, subject to the same general requirements as *interested director transactions*.

c. **Corporate opportunity doctrine:** A director's fiduciary duty of loyalty bars her from personally taking any business opportunity that properly belongs to the corporation. To determine whether an opportunity properly belongs to the corporation, ask: Does the corporation have a *specific need* for it? Has the corporation *actively considered* acquiring it? Did the director discover the opportunity *while acting as a director*, and were any *corporate funds involved* in the discovery? Remember, if the director fully informs the board, and an independent board declines the opportunity, the director may usually pursue it. Similarly, if the corporation is financially unable to take advantage of the opportunity, or if doing so would be an ultra vires act, some courts allow the director to take advantage of it. However, if a director usurps a corporate opportunity, the corporation may seek a constructive trust of the property and profits, or if the property has been resold, damages in the amount of the director's profit.

d. **Competing with corporation:** Recall too that if a director or officer obtains an interest in a *business that competes* with the corporation, it is a conflict of interest and a possible breach of her fiduciary duty.

e. **Compensation for services to corporation:** Excessive compensation for services as a director, officer, or employee may be challenged as waste of corporate assets and thus a breach of the directors' duty of care. If this issue arises, discuss the following major issues: Was the compensation *duly authorized* by the board? Does the compensation bear a *reasonable relationship* to the value of services rendered?

A. ALLOCATION OF POWERS BETWEEN DIRECTORS AND SHAREHOLDERS

1. **Management of Corporation's Business:** [§159] Virtually all the corporate statutes provide that the business of a corporation shall be managed by or under the direction of a board of directors. Accordingly, except as provided by a valid agreement in a close corporation, the power to manage the business of the corporation is vested in its *board of directors*, not in the shareholders. At least in publicly held

corporations, therefore, the shareholders have no power over the management of corporate affairs and cannot order the board of directors to take a particular course of action in managing the corporation's business. [Charlestown Boot & Shoe Co. v. Dunsmore, 60 N.H. 85 (1880)]

a. **Limits on power—proper purpose:** [§160] The board may validly exercise its powers only for a proper purpose. For example, the board may not exercise its powers for the primary purpose of perpetuating itself in office by interfering in a shareholder vote. [*See, e.g.,* Schnell v. Chris-Craft Industries, Inc., 285 A.2d 437 (Del. 1971)—managers could not exercise a power to change the date of the annual shareholders' meeting for the purpose of obtaining an advantage in a proxy contest]

2. **Shareholder Approval of Fundamental Changes:** [§161] Shareholder approval is required for certain fundamental changes in the corporation—in particular, amendment of the articles of incorporation, merger, sale of substantially all assets, and dissolution. (*See infra,* §§998 *et seq.*)

3. **Power to Elect Directors:** [§162] Shareholders have the power to elect directors, although if the board is staggered (*i.e.,* if directors serve overlapping, multi-year terms) it can take two or more years before a new majority of directors can be elected.

4. **Power to Remove Directors**

a. **Shareholders:** [§163] Shareholders also have power to remove directors *for cause.* Under the common law, the shareholders can remove a director for cause, but cannot remove a director without cause absent specific authority in the certificate of incorporation or bylaws. However, a certificate or bylaw provision can permit the removal without cause of directors elected after the provision has been adopted. Furthermore, some statutes permit the shareholders to remove a director without cause. [*See, e.g.,* Cal. Corp. Code §303(a); RMBCA §8.08]

b. **Board of directors:** [§164] Under the common law, the board cannot remove a director, with or without cause. Some statutes permit the board to remove a director for cause or for specified reasons, such as conviction of a felony. A few statutes permit the board to remove a director for cause or for specified reasons if the certificate of incorporation so provides.

c. **Courts:** [§165] The cases are split on whether a court can remove directors for cause in the absence of statutory authority to do so. Some statutes permit the courts to remove a director for specified reasons, such as fraudulent or dishonest acts. These actions may be brought only by a designated percentage of the shareholders (most commonly 10%), by the attorney general, or in some cases, by either. [*See, e.g.,* Cal. Corp. Code §304; N.Y. Bus. Corp. Law §706(d); RMBCA §8.09]

5. **Power to Ratify:** [§166] Shareholders have power to ratify certain kinds of management transactions, and thereby either (i) insulate the transactions against a claim that the managers lacked authority, or (ii) shift the burden of proof or change the standard of proof that governs litigation concerning the transaction.

6. **Power to Adopt Precatory Resolutions:** [§167]   Shareholders have power to adopt precatory (advisory but nonbinding) resolutions on proper subjects of shareholder concern.

   a. **Example:** In *Auer v. Dressel*, 306 N.Y. 427 (1954), the court held that the shareholders were entitled to vote on a resolution endorsing the administration of the former president of the corporation, who had been ousted from office, and demanding his reinstatement: "The stockholders, by expressing their approval of Mr. Auer's conduct as president and their demand that he be put back in that office, will not be able, directly, to effect that change in officers, but there is nothing invalid in their so expressing themselves and thus putting on notice the directors who will stand for election at the annual meeting."

7. **Bylaws:** [§168]   Shareholders normally have the power to adopt and amend bylaws. Under some statutes, however, the board may have concurrent power to adopt and amend bylaws.

8. **Close Corporations:** [§169]   Special problems are raised when shareholders of a close corporation attempt to vary the normal rule that the power to manage the corporation's business is vested exclusively in the directors.

   a. **Definition:** [§170]   A "close corporation" is generally regarded as having these attributes:

      (1) *Ownership by a small number of shareholders*, most or all of whom are active in management of the corporation;

      (2) *No general market* for the corporation's stock; and, often,

      (3) *Some limitation upon the transferability* of stock.

   b. **Traditional view—shareholder agreements to control board discretion invalid:** [§171]   In the past, close corporations often were treated the same as any other corporation. Thus, courts tended to invalidate agreements among the shareholders of a close corporation that curtailed the powers of the board. [Long Park, Inc. v. Trenton-New Brunswick Theatres Co., 297 N.Y. 174 (1948); McQuade v. Stoneham & McGraw, 263 N.Y. 323 (1934)] However, agreements among *all* the shareholders of a close corporation that involved only a *slight* impingement on the statutory norms were generally upheld. [Clark v. Dodge, 269 N.Y. 410 (1936)]

   c. **Modern trend—special governance rules allowed:** [§172]   More recently, the courts have increasingly accommodated the needs and structure of the close corporation. In most respects, a close corporation is similar to a partnership, and it is therefore appropriate to permit the shareholders to adopt special governance rules. [Galler v. Galler, 203 N.E.2d 577 (Ill. 1964)] Also, many states now have statutory provisions that allow direct shareholder control of management in close corporations. Under the New York statute, for example, if a corporation's stock is not publicly traded, a certificate provision otherwise prohibited by law as improperly restrictive of the board's discretion is valid if authorized by all shareholders. [N.Y. Bus. Corp. Law §620] Other statutes go further and create a class of "statutory" close corporations.

9. **Statutory Close Corporation Status**

a. **Definition:** [§173]   To qualify as a "statutory close corporation" under the typical statute, the corporation must: (i) identify itself as such in its articles of incorporation (and also, under some statutes, in its share certificates); (ii) include certain limitations in its articles of incorporation as to number of shareholders, transferability of shares; or (iii) both. However, the precise requirements vary considerably in different jurisdictions.

(1) **Delaware statute:** [§174]   The Delaware statute defines a statutory close corporation as one whose articles of incorporation contain:

(i)   A provision that all of the stock shall be held by *not more than 30 persons*;

(ii) A provision making all of the stock *subject to a restriction on transferability*;

(iii) A provision that the corporation shall make *no public offering* of its stock; and

(iv) A *statement* that the corporation is a close corporation.

[Del. Gen. Corp. Law §§342, 343] There must also be "conspicuous notice," on the share certificate, of any qualifications that must be met by persons in order to be entitled to be holders of the corporation's shares and any provision in the articles of incorporation that confers management powers on the shareholders, rather than the directors (*see* below). [Del. Gen. Corp. Law §351]

(2) **California statute:** [§175]   The California statute defines a statutory close corporation as one whose articles provide that its stock shall not be held by more than 35 record shareholders and contain an express statement that "this corporation is a close corporation." [Cal. Corp. Code §158(a)] Share certificates for the corporation must also contain a conspicuous legend to the following effect: "This corporation is a close corporation. The number of holders of record cannot exceed _____ [a number not in excess of 35]. Any attempted voluntary inter vivos transfer that would violate this requirement is void. Refer to the articles, bylaws, and shareholder agreements on file with the secretary of the corporation for further restrictions." [Cal. Corp. Code §418(c)] If such a statement is *not* placed on the share certificate and there is a transfer resulting in the corporation having more than the maximum number of shareholders specified in its articles of incorporation, the corporation's status as a close corporation automatically terminates. [Cal. Corp. Code §158(e)]

b. **Functioning as a statutory close corporation:** [§176]   A corporation that qualifies as a statutory close corporation has great flexibility concerning management.

(1) **Shareholder agreements concerning management:** [§177]   Typically, the close corporation statutes provide that an agreement among the shareholders of a statutory close corporation relating to any phase of the

corporation's affairs (*e.g.*, election of officers, payment of salaries, or distribution of dividends) is not subject to attack on the grounds that it interferes with the discretion of the directors or treats the corporation as if it were a partnership. [Del. Gen. Corp. Law §§350, 354; Cal. Corp. Code §§186, 300(b)] Some statutes provide that such agreements are valid only if entered into by *all* shareholders. [Cal. Corp. Code §§186, 300(b)] Others appear to permit a majority of the shareholders to enter into such agreements. [Del. Gen. Corp. Law §350]

(2) **Management by shareholders:** [§178]   Under some statutes, the business of a statutory close corporation may be managed directly by the shareholders, rather than by directors. [Del. Gen. Corp. Law §351]

   (a) **Liabilities for management:** [§179]   To the extent that the shareholders of a statutory close corporation are authorized to and do manage the affairs of the corporation, they become personally liable for managerial acts or omissions for which directors would be liable. [Del. Gen. Corp. Law §350; Cal. Corp. Code §300(d)]

(3) **Rights and liabilities of transferees:** [§180]   Close corporation statutes frequently provide that the share certificates of a statutory close corporation must contain a conspicuous notation of the corporation's status and the existence of shareholder agreements that impose special rules for the management of the corporation or other matters. The statutes address the problem of transfers to ineligible or unknowing transferees in a variety of ways:

   (a) **Delaware statute:** [§181]   Under the Delaware statute, whenever any transferee has actual notice, or is conclusively presumed to have notice, that either (i) she is ineligible to be a shareholder of the corporation, (ii) the transfer would cause the corporation's stock to be held by more than the number of persons permitted by its articles of incorporation, or (iii) the transfer is in violation of a valid restriction on transfer, the corporation may refuse to register the transfer. [Del. Gen. Corp. Law §347]

      1) **Transfer to a person who is not entitled to be a holder:** [§182]   If stock of a Delaware statutory close corporation is issued or transferred to any person who is not entitled, under a valid provision of the articles of incorporation, to be a holder of the corporation's stock, and if the stock certificate conspicuously notes the qualifications of the persons entitled to be holders of the corporation's stock, the transferee is conclusively presumed to have notice of her ineligibility to be a stockholder.

      2) **Transfer that will cause the number of holders to exceed permitted number:** [§183]   If the articles of incorporation of a Delaware statutory close corporation state the number of persons (not in excess of 30) who are entitled to be holders of record of its stock, the stock certificate conspicuously states that number, and the issuance or transfer of stock to any person would cause the corporation's stock to be held by more than that number of persons, the transferee is conclusively presumed to have notice of this fact.

3) **Transfer that violates a valid restriction on transfer:** [§184] If the stock certificate of a Delaware statutory close corporation conspicuously notes a valid restriction on the transfer of stock of the corporation, a transferee who acquires stock in violation of the restriction is conclusively presumed to have notice of that fact as well.

(b) **Model Statutory Close Corporation Supplement:** [§185] Under the Model Statutory Close Corporation Supplement ("MSCCS"), the following statement must appear conspicuously on each share certificate issued by a statutory close corporation: "The rights of shareholders in a statutory close corporation may differ materially from the rights of shareholders in other corporations. Copies of the articles of incorporation and bylaws, shareholders' agreements, and other documents, any of which may restrict transfers and affect voting and other rights, may be obtained by a shareholder on written request to the corporation." [MSCCS §10] If a statutory close corporation has complied with the notice requirement, a transferee is bound by the documents referred to in the notice. If a statutory close corporation has not complied with the notice requirement, a transferee is bound by any documents of which he has knowledge or notice.

B. DIRECTORS

1. **Appointment of Directors:** [§186] The initial directors of the corporation are either designated in the articles of incorporation or elected at a meeting of the incorporators. Thereafter, the board is elected by the shareholders at their annual meetings, except that the board members themselves may fill vacancies on the board that occur between shareholders' meetings.

   a. **Number:** [§187] The number of directors is usually prescribed in the articles or the bylaws. At one time, the statutes required a minimum of three directors, but that is now much less common. For example, both Delaware and the Model Act require only that the board consist of one or more members. [Del. Gen. Corp. Law §141; RMBCA §8.03(a)]

   b. **Qualifications:** [§188] Unless otherwise provided in the articles of incorporation or bylaws, persons may be elected or appointed as directors even though they are not shareholders of the corporation or residents of the state of incorporation. [RMBCA §8.02]

   c. **Vacancies:** [§189] Statutes vary somewhat in their treatment of vacancies. Under the Model Act, unless the articles of incorporation provide otherwise, if a vacancy occurs on a board of directors, including a vacancy resulting from an increase in the number of directors: (i) the shareholders may fill the vacancy; (ii) the board of directors may fill the vacancy; or (iii) if the directors remaining in office constitute fewer than a quorum of the board, they may fill the vacancy by the affirmative vote of a majority of all the directors remaining in office. [RMBCA §8.10]

      (1) **Compare—removal of directors:** [§190] Under some statutes, vacancies on the board caused by *removal* of a director (*see* below) must be

filled by the *shareholders*, unless the articles or bylaws give the directors that authority. [Cal. Corp. Code §305(a)]

2. Tenure of Office

a. **Term of appointment:** [§191]   Statutes generally provide that directors of a corporation hold office until the next annual meeting, unless the board is "classified." [RMBCA §8.03(d)]

   (1) **"Classified" boards:** [§192]   A number of statutes permit the board to be divided into some maximum number of classes, usually three to five. [*See, e.g.,* Del. Gen. Corp. Law §141 and RMBCA §8.06—up to three classes] The directors in each class are then elected for a multiyear term whose length corresponds to the number of classes into which the board is divided. For example, in a board consisting of nine directors divided into three classes, three new directors will be elected each year for three-year terms.

b. **Power to bind corporation beyond term:** [§193]   Unless limited by the articles of incorporation, the board has power to make contracts that bind the corporation beyond the directors' terms of office.

c. **Removal of director during term**

   (1) **Removal by shareholders:** [§194]   Under the common law, the shareholders can remove a director during his term of office only for *cause* (*e.g.,* fraud, incompetence, dishonesty); the shareholders cannot remove a director without cause unless there is specific authority in the articles of incorporation or bylaws. [Frank v. Anthony, 107 So. 2d 136 (Fla. 1958)] However, an article or bylaw provision can permit the removal, without cause, of directors elected after the provision has been adopted. [Everett v. Transnational Development Corp., 267 A.2d 627 (Del. 1970)]

      (a) **Hearing:** [§195]   When a director is to be removed for cause, he is entitled to a hearing by the shareholders before a vote to remove. [Auer v. Dressel, *supra,* §167; Campbell v. Loew's, Inc., 134 A.2d 852 (Del. 1957)]

      (b) **Compare—statutes:** [§196]   In contrast to the common law, a number of statutes permit the shareholders to remove a director without cause, unless otherwise provided in the articles of incorporation. [Del. Gen. Corp. Law §141(k); RMBCA §8.08]

   (2) **Removal by board:** [§197]   Under common law, the board cannot remove a director, with or without cause. [Bruch v. National Guarantee Credit Corp., 116 A. 738 (Del. 1922)] However, some statutes permit the board to remove a director for cause [Mass. Gen. L. ch. 156B, §51(c)] or for specified reasons, such as conviction of a felony [Cal. Corp. Code §302].

   (3) **Removal by court:** [§198]   The cases are split on whether a court can remove directors for cause. [Webber v. Webber Oil Co., 495 A.2d 1215

(Me. 1985)—courts do not have power to remove directors; Brown v. North Ventura Road Development Co., 216 Cal. App. 227 (1963)—courts have power to remove directors, at least for fraud or the like]

(a) **Statutes:** [§199]   Some statutes permit the courts to remove a director for specified reasons, such as fraudulent or dishonest acts. These statutes usually provide that a petition for such removal can be brought only by a designated percentage of the shareholders (most commonly 10%), by the attorney general, or in some cases, by either. [Cal. Corp. Code §304; N.Y. Bus. Corp. Law §706(d); RMBCA §8.09]

3. **Functioning of Board**

a. **Meetings:** [§200]   Absent a statute, directors can act only at a duly convened meeting at which a quorum is present. However, most statutes provide that a meeting of the board can be conducted by conference telephone or any other means of communication through which all participating directors can simultaneously hear each other. [RMBCA §8.20] Most statutes also permit the board to act by unanimous written consent, without a meeting of any kind. [RMBCA §8.21]

(1) **Notice:** [§201]   Formal notice is not required for a regular board meeting. In the case of a special meeting, however, notice of date, time, and place must be given to every director. The notice need not state the purpose of a meeting unless the articles of incorporation or the bylaws otherwise provide. Most statutes provide that notice can be waived in writing before or after a meeting, and that attendance at a meeting constitutes a waiver unless the director attends only to protest the holding of the meeting.

(2) **Quorum:** [§202]   A quorum consists of a majority of the *authorized number of directors*—not a majority of the directors then in office. Many statutes permit the articles of incorporation or bylaws to require a greater number for a quorum than a majority of the full board. A substantial minority of the statutes, including the Delaware statute and the Model Act, permit the articles or bylaws to set a lower number, but usually no less than one-third of the full board.

(3) **Voting:** [§203]   Assuming that a quorum is present when a vote is taken, the affirmative vote of a *majority of those present* (not simply a majority of those voting) is required. Most statutes provide that the articles or bylaws can require a greater-than-majority vote for board action.

b. **Effect of noncompliance with formalities**

(1) **Unanimous but informal approval:** [§204]   Some older cases hold that informal approval by directors is ineffective even if the approval is explicit and unanimous. [Baldwin v. Canfield, 1 N.W. 261 (Minn. 1879)] However, most modern courts would hold that informal but *explicit approval* by *all* the directors is effective, particularly where all the shareholders are directors or have acquiesced in the transaction or in a past practice of informal board action. [Gerard v. Empire Square Realty Co.,

195 A.D. 244 (1921); Anderson v. K.G. Moore, Inc., 376 N.E.2d 1238 (Mass. 1978), *cert. denied*, 439 U.S. 1116 (1979)]

(2) **Unanimous acquiescence:** [§205]   Most modern courts will also treat as effective the *explicit approval by a majority* of the directors without a meeting together with *acquiescence by the remaining directors*. [Winchell v. Plywood Corp., 85 N.E.2d 313 (Mass. 1949)]

(3) **Majority acquiescence:** [§206]   Where a majority of the directors approve a transaction explicitly or by acquiescence, without a meeting, but the remaining directors lack knowledge of the transaction, some courts hold the corporation is not liable [Hurley v. Ornsteen, 42 N.E.2d 273 (Mass. 1942)], while other courts hold it is liable, at least if the *shareholders* acquiesced in the transaction, or the shareholders or the remaining directors acquiesced in a practice of informal action by the directors [Holy Cross Gold Mining & Milling Co. v. Goodwin, 223 P. 58 (Colo. 1994)].

c. **Delegation of authority:** [§207]   It is within the power of the board, and is in fact a common practice, to appoint committees of its own members to act for the board either in particular kinds of matters (*e.g.,* a nominating committee, an audit committee, a compensation committee) or to handle day-to-day management in the intervals between board meetings.

(1) **Executive committees:** [§208]   Statutes in many states authorize the board to appoint a committee of its members (frequently called "executive committees") to exercise the authority of the board within certain limits. [Del. Gen. Corp. Law §141]

(a) **Limitations:** [§209]   Typically, the statutes carve out certain powers that *cannot* be delegated to a board committee. For example, the Delaware statute prohibits delegating to a committee the power or authority to:

(i) *Amend the articles of incorporation;*

(ii) *Adopt an agreement of merger or consolidation;*

(iii) *Recommend* to the shareholders the *sale, lease, or exchange* of all or substantially all of the corporation's property and assets;

(iv) *Recommend* to the shareholders a *dissolution* of the corporation;

(v) *Recommend* to the shareholders an *amendment of the bylaws*; or

(vi) *Declare a dividend or authorize the issuance of stock,* unless a board resolution, the bylaws, or the articles of incorporation expressly so provide.

[Del. Gen. Corp. Law §141; *and see* RMBCA §8.25(e)]

(2) **General qualification:** [§210]   Although the board may delegate general operation of the corporation's business to an officer or to a management company, this authority must be exercised under the ultimate control of the board. [Cal. Corp. Code §300(a)] While what constitutes "undue delegation" has not been precisely defined, it is clear that the board may not assign to others its complete function to govern. [Kennerson v. Burbank Amusement Co., 120 Cal. App. 2d 157 (1953)]

d. **Provisional directors:** [§211]   A growing number of statutes provide that where the board is deadlocked and the business of the corporation is endangered, a court may appoint an impartial person as a "custodian" or "provisional director," to prevent impairment of business resulting from the deadlock. Such a provisional director serves with all the rights and powers of a director until the deadlock is broken, or until she is removed from office by court order or by vote or written consent of a majority of the shareholders. [Cal. Corp. Code §308]

(1) **Close corporations:** [§212]   Some of these statutes apply only to close corporations, as statutorily defined. [Del. Gen. Corp. Law §353]

(2) **Criteria for appointment:** [§213]   Pursuant to these statutes, a provisional director (or custodian) may be appointed when the board is deadlocked even though there may be no showing of special or irreparable injury to the corporation. [Giuricich v. Emtrol Corp., 449 A.2d 232 (Del. 1982)]

e. **Voting agreements among directors:** [§214]   Although the laws allow shareholders to make binding agreements as to how they will vote their shares (*see infra,* §§563-573), traditionally, an agreement in advance among shareholder-directors as to how they will vote *as directors* was void as contrary to public policy. [McQuade v. Stoneham & McGraw, *supra,* §171] *Rationale:* Directors are fiduciaries of the corporation and must have unfettered discretion in voting on corporate affairs. However, courts have become more liberal in permitting special rules of governance in close corporations, and thus, modern courts will usually permit such an agreement, at least when all of the shareholders agree, and particularly if the agreement covers only certain matters. [Galler v. Galler, *supra,* §172] Some statutes specifically validate such agreements in the case of statutory close corporations. For example, the Delaware statute provides that a written agreement among a majority of stockholders of a statutory close corporation is not invalid on the ground that it restricts or interferes with the discretion or powers of the board of directors. [Del. Gen. Corp. Law §350; *and see* N.Y. Bus. Corp. Law §620]

4. **Compensation**

a. **Compensation for services as director:** [§215]   The traditional rule is that a director is *not* entitled to compensation for services *as director,* unless the services are extraordinary (*see* below) or compensation is provided for in the articles or by a resolution of the board passed *before* the services are rendered.

(1) **Extraordinary services:** [§216]   Where the services rendered are *beyond the scope* of normal duties of a director, and where properly authorized corporate officials either request the services or accept the

benefits for the corporation, recovery in quasi-contract may be allowed for their reasonable value even without a specific agreement (*e.g.,* a member of the board travels cross-country to investigate possible corporate business opportunity).

b. **Compensation for services as officer or employee:** [§217]   A director who also serves as an officer or employee of the corporation is entitled to compensation for such services—even where the rate of compensation is *not* set in advance.

  (1) **Limitation—conflict of interest problem:** [§218]   A director-officer has a conflict of interest in connection with any action by the board adopting or approving a contract fixing compensation for his services as an officer or employee of the corporation. (As to the effect of such conflict of interest on his right to participate in the board action, *see* discussion *infra,* §§310-332.)

  (2) **Limitation—waste:** [§219]   Executive compensation is also subject to the test of waste. Even where approved by a disinterested board, an agreement to pay executive compensation that is unreasonable or excessive may be held unenforceable against the corporation (*see infra,* §§321-332).

5. **Directors' Rights, Duties, and Liabilities**

a. **Right to inspect corporate records:** [§220]   A director is ordinarily entitled to inspect corporate records or properties firsthand to enable him to discharge his fiduciary duties.

  (1) **Limitation:** [§221]   This right of inspection is often said to be "absolute." [Cohen v. Cocoline Products, Inc., 309 N.Y. 119 (1955)] However, some cases have held that the inspection must be in *good faith* and for some purpose germane to the director's position. Thus, a court *might* not order the corporation to permit inspection if it appeared that the director was attempting to obtain information for a purpose that would deliberately hurt the corporation (*e.g.,* to obtain lists of its customers to hand over to a competitor). [Henshaw v. American Cement Corp., 252 A.2d 125 (Del. 1969)]

  (2) **Basis of right:** [§222]   The director's right to inspect corporate records is usually governed by common law principles. However, a few states have *statutes* recognizing such right. Where the statute provides that the director's right is "absolute" [*see, e.g.,* Cal. Corp. Code §1602; Del. Gen. Corp. Law §220(d)], courts may be less inclined to read in any exceptions.

b. **Duty of care:** [§223]   Directors occupy a fiduciary relationship to the corporation and must exercise the care of *ordinarily prudent and diligent persons* in like positions under similar circumstances. [Francis v. United Jersey Bank, 432 A.2d 814 (N.J. 1981)] In many states this duty is codified by statute. For example, California requires that a director perform his duties "in good faith, in a manner such director believes to be in the best interests of the corporation, and with such care, including reasonable inquiry, as an ordinarily prudent person in a like position would use under similar circumstances." [Cal. Corp.

Code §309(a)] Most other state statutes are basically similar. [RMBCA §8.30(a); N.Y. Bus. Corp. Law §717; A.L.I. Principles of Corporate Governance ("Prin. Corp. Gov.") §4.01(a)]

(1) **Amount of care required:** [§224] The standard of "reasonable care and prudence" is often difficult to apply to the judgmental decisions on "business risks," which directors are often called upon to make. Courts recognize that (i) since potential profit often corresponds to the potential risk, shareholders often assume the risk of bad business judgment; (ii) after-the-fact judgment is a most imperfect device to evaluate business decisions; and (iii) if liability were imposed too readily, it might deter many persons from serving as directors. [Joy v. North, 692 F.2d 880 (2d Cir. 1982)]

(a) **"Business judgment rule":** [§225] For these reasons, some courts have adopted the rule that where the act or omission involves no fraud, illegality, or conflict of interest but is a question of policy or business judgment, a director who acts in good faith is not personally liable for mere errors of judgment or want of prudence, short of *clear and gross negligence*. [Shlensky v. Wrigley, *supra*, §136]

1) **Majority view:** [§226] Most courts conclude that a director cannot invoke the business judgment rule if he has not been *"reasonably diligent*," as where he knew or should have known that he did not have sufficient facts to make a judgment, yet failed to make reasonable efforts to inform himself. [Francis v. United Jersey Bank, *supra*] Some courts have stated that "*gross* negligence is the standard for determining whether a business judgment reached by the board of directors was an informed one." [Smith v. Van Gorkom, 488 A.2d 858 (Del. 1985)] And there are some decisions that have adopted a standard of "ordinary negligence." [Brane v. Roth, 590 N.E.2d 587 (Ind. 1992)]

2) **Illegality:** [§227] A director cannot invoke the business judgment rule if he causes the corporation to engage in acts that are illegal or contrary to public policy. A director is liable for any loss sustained by the corporation because of such acts, even if undertaken for the benefit of the corporation. [Miller v. American Telephone & Telegraph Co., 507 F.2d 759 (3d Cir. 1974)]

3) **Profit maximization and "other constituencies":** [§228] A director may invoke the business judgment rule even though he causes the corporation to undertake action that is not profit-maximizing, but instead considers the interests of employees, creditors, local communities, or other constituencies. [N.Y. Bus. Corp. Law §717(b)] It would seem that a limit of *reasonableness* would apply here, as it does in respect to other uses of corporate resources for public welfare, humanitarian, educational, or philanthropic purposes. *(See supra, §136.)*

(b) **Directors of banks and other financial institutions:** [§229] Many early cases impose a higher duty of care on directors of banks and other financial institutions, particularly in overseeing the activities of officers and management. Such directors may be found negligent for deviation from generally accepted banking principles. *Rationale:* Public interest in the safety of banks requires a higher fiduciary duty of care by bank directors. [Bates v. Dresser, 251 U.S. 524 (1920)]

(2) **Extent of liability**

(a) **Injury and causation:** [§230] Even where a director has not exercised the proper measure of care, he will be held personally liable only for corporate losses suffered as the *direct and proximate result* of his breach of duty—*i.e.,* injury to the corporation and causation must still be shown. [Barnes v. Andrews, 298 F. 614 (S.D.N.Y. 1924)]

  1) **Note:** A recent decision of the Delaware Supreme Court has rejected the tort principle of proximate cause. Under that ruling, when there has been a breach of the duty of care, the burden of proof shifts to the directors to demonstrate that the transaction was entirely fair. [Cede & Co. v. Technicolor, Inc., 634 A.2d 345 (Del. 1993); *and see infra,* §266]

(b) **Acts of others:** [§231] A director is liable for the wrongful acts of other officers and directors only if he *participated* therein, was *negligent in failing to discover* the misconduct (he has the duty to inquire under the general standard of care above), *or* was *negligent in appointing* the wrongdoer. [Graham v. Allis-Chalmers Manufacturing Co., 188 A.2d 125 (Del. 1963)]

  1) **Note:** A director may seek to avoid being held liable for acts of the board by recording his *dissent*. However, in some circumstances, he may have to pursue other means such as threatening suit. [Francis v. United Jersey Bank, *supra,* §223]

(c) **Abolishing liability:** [§232] Many state statutes permit the articles of incorporation to *limit or eliminate* the directors' liability for breach of the duty of care—apart from action in bad faith, intentional misconduct, or knowing violation of law. [*See, e.g.,* Del. Gen. Corp. Law §102(b)(7)] A few statutes either impose a maximum amount of liability [Va. Stock Corp. Act §692.1—greater of $100,000 or cash compensation during preceding 12 months], or authorize the shareholders to do so [A.L.I. Prin. Corp. Gov. §7.19]. Others have directly modified the standard of liability. [*See, e.g.,* Va. Stock Corp. Act §690A—"good faith business judgment of the best interests of the corporation"]

(3) **Defenses to liability**

(a) **Nominal directors:** [§233] It is usually no defense that the director was serving gratuitously or merely as a figurehead. [Francis v.

United Jersey Bank, *supra,* §231; *but see* Harman v. Willbern, 520 F.2d 1333 (10th Cir. 1975)—contra]

(b) **Disabilities:** [§234]   Ill health, old age, and lack of experience have been held not to constitute defenses, on the theory that a person subject to one of these disabilities should not have accepted (or should have resigned from) the directorship. [McDonell v. American Leduc Petroleums, Ltd., 491 F.2d 380 (2d Cir. 1974)]

(c) **Reliance on reports of management:** [§235]   Directors are not required to make firsthand investigations of every detail of corporate business, at least in the absence of suspicious circumstances. As long as the director acts in good faith, he is entitled to rely on statements and reports made to him by corporate officers or employees and on reports by any committee of the board of which he is not a member, as to matters within their authority that appear to merit confidence. [RMBCA §8.30(b); A.L.I. Prin. Corp. Gov. §4.02]

   1) **Compare:** This may not be a defense to a federal securities act violation (*see infra,* §§915-917).

(d) **Reliance on expert opinion:** [§236]   A director is also entitled to rely on the advice given by attorneys, accountants, engineers, or other persons as to matters the director reasonably believes to be within that person's expertise. As long as the director's reliance was reasonable and in good faith, it is a defense to liability even if the opinion proves to be erroneous. [RMBCA §8.30(b); A.L.I. Prin. Corp. Gov. §4.02(b)]

(e) **Shareholder ratification of directors' failure to exercise due care:** [§237]   This issue is discussed *infra,* §§702-710.

c. **Duty of loyalty:** [§238]   Directors have a duty of loyalty in all dealings with the corporation. (*See infra,* §§256 *et seq.*)

d. **Statutory duties and liabilities regarding management:** [§239]   In addition to the general duty of care (above), various duties and liabilities are imposed on directors by federal and state statutes. These provisions seek to protect a bread range of public interests in addition to those of corporate shareholders and creditors.

(1) **Securities Act of 1933:** [§240]   This statute makes directors liable for misstatements or omissions of material fact in a registration statement, unless they exercise **due diligence**. (*See infra,* §§904-922.)

(2) **Rule 10b-5:** [§241]   Directors are liable for fraudulent misstatements or omissions of material fact by the corporation if they **participated** in or had **knowledge** of the fraud, or if their lack of knowledge resulted from **willful or reckless disregard of the truth**. (*See infra,* §§339 *et seq.*)

(3) **Illegal dividends:** [§242]   Directors who participate in declaring a dividend from an unlawful source, or under other circumstances making a dividend illegal, are jointly and severally liable to the extent of the injury to creditors and preferred shareholders. (*See infra,* §§971-975.)

(4) **Criminal liability:** [§243]   A wide variety of state and federal statutes impose criminal liability on corporate managers for unlawful corporate action. This liability may arise if the managers personally engage in or cause the unlawful act [*see, e.g.,* N.Y. Penal Law §20.25], or if they have control over the corporate employees who commit the unlawful act [United States v. Park, 421 U.S. 658 (1975)—president of national retail food chain criminally liable for violation of Federal Food, Drug, and Cosmetic Act because of unsanitary conditions in a corporate warehouse].

C.   OFFICERS

1. **Election:** [§244]   Under most statutes, the major officers of a corporation are elected by the board, although some statutes permit election of officers by shareholders. Officers hold their office at the pleasure of the board. Even if they have contracts, they can be discharged, subject to their right to damages for breach of contract. Minor officers (assistant treasurer, assistant secretary, etc.) may be appointed by the board, by the chief executive officer, or by other officers.

2. **Authority of Corporate Officers—Liability of Corporation to Outsiders**

   a. **Types of authority:** [§245]   A corporate officer may have any of the following types of authority:

      (1) **Actual authority:** [§246]   Actual authority is the authority that a reasonable person in the officer's position would believe had been conferred upon him by the corporation. Actual authority may be *expressly* conferred on the officer by the bylaws, resolutions of the board of directors, a valid delegation from a superior, or acquiescence by the board or superior officers in a past pattern of conduct. An officer also has *implied* actual authority to do what can reasonably be implied from a grant of express authority.

      (2) **Apparent authority:** [§247]   Apparent authority is authority that the corporation allows third parties to reasonably believe an officer possesses. Apparent authority can arise from intentional or negligent representations by the corporation to the third party, or through permitting an officer or employee to assume certain powers and functions on a continuing basis with the third party's knowledge.

      (3) **Power of position:** [§248]   This is a special type of apparent authority, which arises by reason of the officer holding a particular position in the corporation that normally carries certain authority. For example, a vice president for sales would probably have power of position to hire a salesperson.

      (4) **Ratification:** [§249]   Even an unauthorized act by a corporate officer may bind the corporation, if the officer purports to act on the corporation's behalf and the act is later ratified by the board.

   b. **Authority of president:** [§250]   A common authority issue is the scope of authority possessed by the president by virtue of that title. There are three competing views:

(1) **Only the power of a director:** [§251] Under one view, the president has only those powers possessed by any other director, except for the power of presiding at corporate meetings. This is obviously unrealistic and probably not good law today.

(2) **Broad power to act:** [§252] A second view, known as the "New York rule" (although it is not clear whether New York courts or any other courts still subscribe to it), holds that the president has presumptive or prima facie power to do any act that the board could authorize or ratify. [Schwartz v. United Merchants & Manufacturers, Inc., 72 F.2d 256 (2d Cir. 1934)]

(3) **Power to bind corporation in regular course of business:** [§253] A third view, which is the law in virtually all jurisdictions today, is that the president has the power to bind the corporation in transactions arising in the "usual and regular course of business," but not in "extraordinary" transactions. [Joseph Greenspon's Sons Iron & Steel Co. v. Pecos Valley Gas Co., 156 A. 350 (Del. 1931)]

    (a) **Compare:** A variant of this rule is that the president has such power if—but only if—he is the "general manager" of the corporation by title or in fact. [Memorial Hospital Association v. Pacific Grape Products Co., 45 Cal. 2d 634 (1955)]

    (b) **"Ordinary and regular course of business":** [§254] Modern courts following this approach often take an expansive view of what constitutes the ordinary and regular course of business. [Lee v. Jenkins Bros., 268 F.2d 357 (2d Cir. 1959)] However, even under an expansive view, presidential authority would not extend to all corporate actions. It would not, for example, cover the sale of a major part of the corporate assets without the consent of the board. Such a transaction is clearly outside the usual and regular course of business of the corporation.

3. **Duties of Corporate Officers:** [§255] Officers owe a duty of care to the corporation similar to that owed by directors (*supra*, §223). Indeed, since the officers may have more intimate knowledge of the corporate affairs than nonofficer directors, they may be held to a higher standard of care. Officers, like directors, also owe a duty of loyalty in their dealings with the corporation (*see* below).

D. CONFLICTS OF INTEREST IN CORPORATE TRANSACTIONS

1. **Duty of Loyalty:** [§256] As a further consequence of their fiduciary relationship with the corporation, officers and directors are held to a duty of *loyalty* in all dealings with the corporation—*i.e.*, the duty to promote the interests of the corporation without regard for personal gain.

2. **Business Dealings with Corporations:** [§257] Conflict of interest issues arise whenever a corporation contracts directly with one of its officers or directors, or with a company in which the officer or director is financially interested. For example, if Corporation contracts to purchase property in which Director has a financial interest, or to sell corporate assets to an entity in which Director has a financial

interest, does Director's adverse interest disqualify her from voting on the contract? Does it render the contract voidable by the corporation, even where her adverse interest was disclosed at the meeting?

a. **Effect of director's self-interest on right to participate in meeting authorizing transaction**

(1) **Common law:** [§258]   At common law, directors who had interests adverse to the corporation could not be counted for purposes of making up a quorum, or for purposes of making up a majority vote at the meeting in which the transaction was approved. [Weiss Medical Complex, Ltd. v. Kim, 408 N.E.2d 959 (Ill. 1980)]

(2) **Statutes:** [§259]   Today, most statutes permit an "interested" director to be counted in determining the presence of a quorum, and further provide that interested director transactions are *not automatically voidable* by the corporation simply because the interested director's vote was necessary for approval. [Cal. Corp. Code §310(a); N.Y. Bus. Corp. Law §713; Del. Gen. Corp. Law §144] Under these statutes, such transactions may still be valid if other conditions are met. (*See infra*, §277.)

b. **Effect of director's self-interest in rendering transaction voidable by corporation**

(1) **Strict view:** [§260]   The historic common law rule was that any contract in which a director is financially interested is *voidable* at the option of the corporation—without regard to fairness or whether the director's adverse interest was disclosed in advance to the directors who then approved the transaction.

(2) **Modern view:** [§261]   Most courts today adopt the more liberal position that contracts and dealings in which a director has a financial interest are voidable by the corporation only where the contract is found to be *unfair* to the corporation considering all the relevant circumstances.

(a) **Disclosure requirement:** [§262]   Following this view, it has been held that failure of an interested director to make *full disclosure* to an *independent* board respecting the transaction is in itself "unfair" to the corporation. [State *ex rel.* Hayes Oyster Co. v. Keypoint Oyster Co., 391 P.2d 979 (Wash. 1964)] The Principles of Corporate Governance adopt this rule. [A.L.I. Prin. Corp. Gov. §5.02]

1) **"Full disclosure":** [§263]   "Full disclosure" requires that the director inform the board as to all matters affecting the *value* of the property involved and perhaps also the *amount of the director's profit*.

2) **"Independent board":** [§264]   An "independent board" is one where majority of the directors are not under the control of the interested director (directly or indirectly).

(b) **Fairness requirement:** [§265]   Even if there has been a full disclosure to an independent board, courts following the modern view generally hold that the transaction is still voidable by the corporation (*e.g.,* where the board later changes its mind, new directors take office and reevaluate the transaction, a trustee in bankruptcy takes over, or a shareholder brings a derivative suit challenging the transaction) if it is unfair to the corporation in price, terms, or other conditions. [Globe Woolen Co. v. Utica Gas & Electric Co., 224 N.Y. 483 (1918)—sale of valuable corporate asset to director who is otherwise insolvent, for a token down payment, with balance of purchase payable over many years and without adequate security, is voidable by corporation]

1) **Burden of proof:** [§266]   The burden of establishing the fairness of the transaction is usually placed on the interested director. In effect, there is a *presumption of unfairness* that must be rebutted. [Cookies Food Products, Inc. v. Lakes Warehouse Distributing, Inc., 430 N.W.2d 447 (Iowa 1988); *but see* Durfee v. Durfee & Canning, Inc., 80 N.E.2d 522 (Mass. 1948)—"Massachusetts rule"]

2) **Fairness where no ability to disclose:** [§267]   Where disclosure to an independent board is not possible (as where the interested director controls a majority of the board), dealings between the corporation and an interested director will be upheld as long as the interested director proves that the transaction was fair and reasonable to the corporation. [Shlensky v. South Parkway Building Corp., 159 N.E.2d 31 (Ill. 1959)]

(c) **Effect of shareholder ratification**

1) **Unanimous ratification:** [§268]   If after *full disclosure* the shareholder *unanimously* ratify the corporation's dealings with the interested director, the corporation will be estopped from later challenging the transaction (and so will any shareholder bringing a derivative suit).

   a) **But note:** No such estoppel is invoked unless there was *full* disclosure. [Rivoli Theatre Co. v. Allison, 152 A.2d 449 (Pa. 1959)]

   b) **Compare:** And although unanimous shareholder ratification will bar suits by or on behalf of the corporation, it may not preclude *creditors' suits* if the effect of the transaction was to deplete corporate assets and thereby render the corporation *insolvent* and unable to pay its debts—at least where the ratifying shareholders are also interested in the transaction.

2) **Less-than-unanimous ratification:** [§269]   The effect of a *majority* (but less than all) of the shareholders voting to ratify dealings with an interested director usually turns on whether the majority shares were also *owned or controlled* by the interested director.

a) **Ratification by "disinterested" majority:** [§270] If the majority shareholders approving the transaction have full disclosure and have no financial interest in the transaction, some courts hold that the transaction cannot be attacked by the corporation (or by a shareholder bringing a derivative suit). Other courts hold that such ratification *shifts the burden of proving "unfairness"* to the corporation (or derivative suit plaintiff) challenging the transaction. [Eliasberg v. Standard Oil Co., 92 A.2d 862 (N.J. 1952)]

    1/ **Waste:** [§271] Even if a disinterested majority of the shareholders ratifies the transaction, if the interested director is charged with "waste," it has been held that the court itself must examine the facts to determine whether they fall within the realm of business judgment. [Cohen v. Ayers, 596 F.2d 733 (7th Cir. 1979)]

b) **Ratification by "interested" majority:** [§272] Less weight is generally given to shareholder ratification where the majority shares are owned or controlled (directly or indirectly) by the interested director.

    1/ **Corporation can later rescind:** [§273] Some courts hold an interested majority's ratification makes no difference even when most of the *disinterested* shareholders also approved the transaction. If even a single shareholder disapproved, the corporation (or derivative suit plaintiff) can later sue to rescind for unfairness, and the burden of proving fairness remains on the interested director. [Pappas v. Moss, 393 F.2d 865 (3d Cir. 1968)]

    2/ **Subsequent attack precluded or burden shifted:** [§274] Other courts, however, are more lenient in holding that ratification by a majority of the disinterested shareholders (even though they are a minority in the corporation) precludes subsequent attack by the corporation, or at least shifts the burden of proving "unfairness" to the corporation (or derivative suit plaintiff).

    3/ **Older cases—corporation estopped even without disinterested majority:** [§275] Some older cases go further and estop the corporation even where the shares of the interested director(s) were necessary to make up the majority shareholder vote ratifying the transaction. [Kirwan v. Parkway Distillery, Inc., 148 S.W.2d 720 (Ky. 1941)]

c) **Estoppel against shareholder:** [§276]   In any event, a shareholder who received full disclosure and voted to approve the corporation's dealings with the interested director(s) would probably be estopped from later bringing a derivative suit charging "unfairness."

(3) **Statutes:** [§277]   Most states have adopted statutes regulating interested director transactions. The Delaware law is illustrative. It provides that such transactions are not voidable by the corporation for conflict of interest if (i) the material facts as to the director's interest and the transaction were disclosed or known to the board and the transaction was nonetheless approved in good faith by a disinterested majority of the board; or (ii) the same information was disclosed or known to the shareholders, and a *majority of the shareholders* approves; or (iii) the transaction is fair to the corporation. [Del. Gen. Corp. Law §144]

(a) **Fairness required notwithstanding disclosure:** [§278]   Although "fairness" and "approval after disclosure" seem to be alternatives under these statutes, courts have interpreted the statutes as requiring fairness in any event. Thus, an interested director transaction may be set aside if unfair to the corporation, notwithstanding that there was full disclosure to and approval by the majority of the directors or shareholders. [Remillard Brick Co. v. Remillard-Dandini Co., 109 Cal. App. 2d 405 (1952); Flieger v. Lawrence, 361 A.2d 218 (Del. 1976); *but see* Marciano v. Nakash, 535 A.2d 400 (Del. 1987)—contra (dictum*)*] Indeed, this is now expressly required under the California statute. Transactions between a corporation and one of its directors must be "just and reasonable as to the corporation" notwithstanding full disclosure and approval by the directors. [Cal. Corp. Code §310(a)(2)] This provision is *not applicable*, however, where there has been disclosure to and approval by *shareholders*. [Cal. Corp. Code §310(a)(1)]

1) **Model statutes:** [§279]   The Principles of Corporate Governance and Model Business Corporation Act take differing approaches. The Principles of Corporate Governance require that, notwithstanding full disclosure and approval, disinterested directors "could reasonably have concluded that the transaction was fair to the corporation." [A.L.I. Prin. Corp. Gov. §5.02(a)(2)(B)] On the other hand, the Model Act appears to eliminate the fairness requirement if there has been compliance with the other statutory procedures. [RMBCA §§8.61, 8.62]

(b) **Shareholder approval:** [§280]   Some statutes provide that the requisite shareholder approval must occur *without* counting the shares owned by interested directors. [Cal. Corp. Code §310(a)(1)] Others are less clear on whether such shares may be counted. [*See* Del. Gen. Corp. Law §144; N.Y. Bus. Corp. Law §713]

(c) **Burden of proof:** [§281]   Some statutes are silent on whether the interested director has the burden of proving compliance with the statute. [Del. Gen. Corp. Law §144] Other statutes provide that if an interested director transaction is defended on grounds of "fairness," the interested director has the burden of proof. [N.Y. Bus. Corp. Law §713(b); Cal. Corp. Code §310(a)(3)]

(d) **"Interested":** [§282]   Although only a few state statutes define what is meant by an "interested" director, the model statutes provide greater detail: "A director or officer is 'interested' in a transaction . . . [if the] director or officer has a business, financial, or familial relationship with a party to the transaction or conduct, and that relationship would reasonably be expected to affect the director's or officer's judgment with respect to the transaction or conduct in a manner adverse to the corporation . . . ." [A.L.I. Prin. Corp. Gov. §1.23(a); *and see* RMBCA §8.60]

c. **Remedy:** [§283]   If the transaction is voidable under any of the views above, the corporation is entitled to *rescind* (unwind the transaction). Alternatively, it may affirm the contract and hold the interested director liable for damages.

(1) **Measure of damages:** [§284]   Where damages are granted, the usual measure is the amount of the *unfair profit* made on the transaction, *i.e.,* the difference between fair value and the price at which the transaction was consummated. Thus, where the interested director sold personal assets to the corporation at an inflated value, the corporation can recover the excess over the fair value. Or where the interested director purchased corporate assets at an inadequate price, the corporation can recover the *additional amounts* it should have received. [Shlensky v. South Parkway Building Corp., *supra,* §267]

(a) **Loss of salary:** [§285]   In addition to damages, some courts have held that the interested director must repay any salary earned during the period of fiduciary breach. [American Timber & Trading Co. v. Niedermeyer, 558 P.2d 1211 (Or. 1976)]

(b) **Punitive damages:** [§286]   Some courts have awarded punitive damages against directors who have breached their fiduciary duty. [Rowen v. LeMars Mutual Insurance Co. of Iowa, 282 N.W.2d 639 (Iowa 1979)]

(2) **Alternate measure of damages:** [§287]   Alternatively (particularly in cases of *trickery* or *fraud,* or where the director acquired assets for the purpose of reselling to the corporation at an excessive price), some courts penalize the director by awarding damages based on the difference between the price paid by the corporation and the interested director's acquisition cost. This effectively *deprives the director of the profit* she could have made on a sale of such assets to any third party.

(a) **Example:** Director buys assets for $5,000 for the purpose of resale to Corporation at $20,000, although fair value is only $12,000. Under the normal measure, Corporation could recover $8,000. Under this "penal" measure it can recover $15,000. Director is thus deprived of the $7,000 she could have made had she sold to a third party.

(3) **Rescission as sole remedy:** [§288]   If the interested director did not act in *bad faith* or *profit personally* from the transaction (as where her corporation sells property to another corporation in which she is a director but owns no shares, *see* below), courts may decide not to hold her personally liable for damages. In such cases, the corporation's *only remedy is to rescind*. [Chelrob, Inc. v. Barrett, 293 N.Y. 442 (1944)]

   (a) **Note:** Some older decisions have held that damages should not be awarded against an interested director in *any* transaction unless rescission is practicable. [New York Trust Co. v. American Realty Co., 244 N.Y. 209 (1926)]

3. **Interlocking Directorates:** [§289]   Conflicts of interest may also arise when the same individual sits as a director of two corporations that contract with each other. The conflict stems from the fact that the director owes each corporation the duty to make the best possible deal for it. The problem is even more acute when the boards of both corporations are composed entirely of the same individuals (which is frequently the case with parent and subsidiary corporations).

   a. **Strict view:** [§290]   The historic common law rule held that contracts between corporations having common directors may be avoided by either corporation because of the conflict of interest—regardless of the fairness of the transaction.

   b. **Modern view:** [§291]   However, the clear weight of authority today permits such intercorporate transactions subject to the same general requirements as for interested director transactions (*i.e.,* full disclosure and fairness).

      (1) **Statutes:** [§292]   Some statutes suggest that intercorporate dealings are not voidable for conflict of interest if the director who sits on both boards of the contracting corporations owns stock in neither. For example, the California statute provides that "a mere common directorship does not constitute a material financial interest" that should be disclosed. [Cal. Corp. Code §310(a)(3)]

      (2) **Parent-subsidiary transactions:** [§293]   There is no conflict of interest where one corporation is a wholly owned subsidiary of another. But conflicts frequently arise where the parent owns only a majority of the subsidiary's shares, and there are other (minority) shareholders who may be affected by parent-subsidiary dealings. The basic question in each case is whether the transaction was *fair* to the subsidiary.

         (a) **Burden of proof on parent:** [§294]   As in interested director cases generally, the burden of proof is usually on the parent corporation to demonstrate that it has taken no unfair advantage of the subsidiary through control of its board. [Sterling v. Mayflower Hotel Corp., 93 A.2d 107 (Del. 1952)] The Principles of Corporate Governance adopt this position—except for transactions in the ordinary course of business, in which case the burden of coming forward with evidence of unfairness is on the person challenging. [A.L.I. Prin. Corp. Gov. §5.10]

         (b) **Limitation:** [§295]   However, some courts place this burden on the parent only where, by virtue of its domination, it has received something from the subsidiary to the *exclusion* of the minority shareholders of the subsidiary. For example, it has been held that minority shareholders of a subsidiary corporation cannot complain that the majority shareholder (parent) caused the subsidiary to pay "excessive" dividends (draining too much capital out of the subsidiary and injuring its operations) because the minority shareholders had received their proportionate share of the dividends. [Sinclair Oil Corp. v. Levien, 280 A.2d 717 (Del. 1971)]

4. **Corporate Opportunity Doctrine:** [§296]   The fiduciary duty of loyalty, discussed above, bars a director from taking for herself any advantage or business opportunity that properly belongs to the corporation. As to any such opportunity, a director must first offer it to the corporation. [A.L.I. Prin. Corp. Gov. §5.05(a)] The director owes the corporation at least a *right of first refusal, i.e.,* the right to acquire it on the same terms offered to her.

   a. **What constitutes a corporate opportunity:** [§297]   There is no clear-cut definition of what constitutes a corporate opportunity. Rather, it depends upon whether, under all the circumstances, it would be *unfair* for the director to exploit the opportunity. [Johnston v. Greene, 121 A.2d 919 (Del. 1956)] The following factors are those most frequently relied upon by courts in holding that an opportunity is "corporate" and hence may not legitimately be taken advantage of by the directors personally:

      (1) **Corporate plans and expectations:** [§298]   If the corporation has a present interest or "tangible expectancy" in the opportunity in the sense that it has a specific need for it, has resolved to acquire it, or has *actively considered* its acquisition, it may not be taken advantage of by a director.

         (a) **Note—"useful" not enough:** [§299]   The mere fact that the property or opportunity would be "useful" to the corporation is ordinarily not in itself enough to render it a corporate opportunity. [Burg v. Horn, 380 F.2d 897 (2d Cir. 1967)]

      (2) **Director's capacity in dealing:** [§300]   If the opportunity was discovered by the director in her *capacity as director* of the corporation (*e.g.,* offer delivered to the director intended for the corporation), it is a corporate opportunity. [*See* Johnston v. Greene, *supra*]

         (a) **Note:** The fact that an opportunity relates to the corporation's "line of business" does *not* necessarily mean that the director must deal with it on behalf of the corporation—particularly where it also falls within the director's personal business interests that are outside the capacity of director of the corporation. [Burg v. Horn, *supra*]

      (3) **Funds used:** [§301]   If the corporation's property, information, or funds were involved in the director's discovering or acquiring the opportunity, or if the corporation's *facilities or employees* were used in developing it, the opportunity may not be personally taken advantage of by a director. [Guth v. Loft, Inc., 5 A.2d 503 (Del. 1939)]

b. **Where corporation unable to take advantage:** [§302]   Although much depends on the particular facts of the case, it is frequently stated that directors *may* take advantage of corporate business opportunities of which the corporation is unable to take advantage. Thus, if the corporation is *insolvent or financially unable* to make the investment required, it has been held that the director is free to do so. [Miller v. Miller, 222 N.W.2d 71 (Minn. 1974)]

   (1) **Disclosure:** [§303]   Some courts have held that the director must promptly disclose all known material facts to the disinterested directors (or, if there are none, to the disinterested shareholders). The rationale is that if the investment is sufficiently attractive, the corporation might itself be able to raise the necessary funds. After full disclosure, the director may take advantage of the business opportunity if it is rejected by the corporation, or if the director proves that the corporation unreasonably failed to reject it and it would be otherwise fair for the director to personally take the opportunity. [Klinicki v. Lundgren, 695 P.2d 906 (Or. 1985)]

       (a) **Compare:** Other courts have held that the director's fiduciary duty *precludes* her taking advantage of such opportunities, reasoning that to permit her to do so might discourage her making her best efforts *to obtain* the needed money for the corporation. [Irving Trust Co. v. Deutsch, 73 F.2d 121 (2d Cir. 1934)]

   (2) **Ultra vires transaction:** [§304]   If the acquisition would be ultra vires by the corporation (*e.g.,* the corporation was not authorized to enter the particular business), a number of cases hold that the director may make use of the opportunity. [Alexander & Alexander of New York, Inc. v. Fritzen, 147 A.D.2d 241 (1989)] *But note*: There is a strong contrary argument on the rationale that the corporation should at least have the right to consider the investment. It might be so advantageous that it would justify amending the articles or taking other action to enable it to engage in the business.

c. **Where corporation unwilling to take advantage:** [§305]   If the director *fully* informs the board of the opportunity, and an independent board declines to take it, the director generally may pursue it for herself. [*See* Kerrigan v. Unity Savings Association, 317 N.E.2d 39 (Ill. 1974)]

d. **Remedies:** [§306]   If a director usurps a corporate opportunity, the corporation may invoke any of the following remedies:

   (1) **Constructive trust:** [§307]   Courts may declare that the director holds the opportunity as constructive trustee for the corporation, forcing a *conveyance* of the property to the corporation at the cost to the director and an accounting to the corporation for any *rents, income, or profits derived* through ownership thereof. [Irving Trust Co. v. Deutsch, *supra*]

   (2) **Damages:** [§308]   If the director has already *resold* the property, a suit will lie for damages for breach of fiduciary duty—forcing the director to disgorge all profits made on the transaction.

5. **Competing with Corporation:** [§309]   A director (or officer) who obtains a financial interest in a business that competes with that of the corporation puts herself

in a conflict of interest situation—even where the competing business is *not* a corporate opportunity. Depending on all the circumstances, competition by a director or officer may be held a breach of fiduciary duty, in which event she may be barred from such competition or held liable for damages. [Lincoln Stores, Inc. v. Grant, 34 N.E.2d 704 (Mass. 1941)]

a. **Example:** A breach of fiduciary duty will most likely be found where the director has used corporate funds, facilities, or employees (or corporate secrets) in starting up or acquiring the competing business. [Guth v. Loft, Inc., *supra,* §301]

b. **Compare:** However, the mere fact that an officer or director makes *preparations* to compete with the corporation before resigning from office does not in itself establish a breach of fiduciary duty; nor does the failure to disclose to the board any plans to compete. [Maryland Metals, Inc. v. Metzner, 382 A.2d 564 (Md. 1978)] But if there are added circumstances (*e.g.,* concealment of material facts, use of corporate facilities or assets, or "raids" on key corporate personnel), this clearly constitutes a breach of fiduciary duty. [Veco Corp. v. Babcock, 611 N.E.2d 1054 (Ill. 1993)]

6. **Compensation for Services to Corporation:** [§310]   Finally, a conflict of interest issue arises in dealings between the corporation and one of its directors relative to compensation for services as director, officer, or employee of the corporation. Such compensation may take various forms—*e.g.,* salary, bonuses, profit-sharing and pension plans, stock options, expense accounts, etc. Usually, the conflict of interest issue is raised by a dissident minority shareholder in a derivative suit charging excessive compensation to the director and resultant unfairness to the corporation.

a. **Authorization:** [§311]   The first question is whether the compensation arrangement has been *duly authorized* by the board. This often turns on whether the interested director is entitled to participate in the meeting and to vote on her own compensation.

(1) **Issues:** [§312]   Since this is simply another form of interested director transaction, the various common law and statutory rules (*supra,* §§257-288) govern (i) whether the director may be counted in determining the presence of a quorum at the meeting, (ii) whether her vote may be counted on her own compensation, and (iii) the effect of shareholder ratification and the like.

(2) **Statutory resolution:** [§313]   Statutes in some states resolve the problem by expressly authorizing members of the board to establish reasonable compensation for directors notwithstanding their personal interest in such matters (provided there are no contrary provisions in the articles or bylaws). [*See* Ill. Bus. Corp. Act §8.05]

b. **"Reasonableness":** [§314]   Assuming the compensation plan is duly authorized and adopted by the board, the next question is whether the terms of the plan are *reasonable*. If not, it may be challenged as a waste of corporate assets by the directors, and hence a violation of their duty of care to the corporation.

(1) **Disinterested directors protected by business judgment rule:** [§315] Good faith and the business judgment rule (*supra,* §225) will ***ordinarily*** protect disinterested directors from liability to the corporation for approving executive compensation plans to other directors, officers, or employees of the corporation. Courts are reluctant to second guess the directors' business decisions on the value of an employee's services.

    (a) **Publicly held corporations:** [§316] Despite recent criticism of the large amounts of compensation paid to executives of America's biggest companies, the business judgment rule has resulted in virtually no modern judicial decisions finding excessive pay in this context.

        1) **Federal action:** [§317] Nonetheless, the SEC has greatly increased the type and amount of information about executive compensation that must be disclosed by large corporations (*see infra,* §§531, 876), and has authorized shareholders to make proposals about executive pay in management's proxy materials. (*See infra,* §§533 *et seq.*) And the Internal Revenue Code now limits expense deductions from the federal income tax for executive pay over $1 million unless tied to the corporation's performance [I.R.C. §162(m)], and also imposes a special surtax on incomes above $250,000.

        2) **Compare—close corporations:** [§318] In contrast, courts often hold executive compensation to be unreasonable in the context of closely held corporations when the compensation is not approved by either disinterested directors or disinterested shareholders. [Crowley v. Communications for Hospitals, Inc., 573 N.E.2d 996 (Mass. 1991)]

    (b) **Recipients also protected:** [§319] And where the compensation was authorized by disinterested directors, recipients of the compensation will usually be protected against a suit by the corporation (or a shareholder's derivative suit) for rescission or return of allegedly excessive compensation.

    (c) **Caution—"mutual back scratching":** [§320] Directors who vote for each other's compensation plans or for trade-offs in some other capacity (*e.g.,* retainer fee as attorney for the corporation) are ***not*** considered disinterested.

(2) **Limitation—doctrine of waste:** [§321] Even disinterested directors have no power to "give away" or "waste" corporate assets, absent unanimous shareholder approval. Nor may a mere majority of the shareholders condone a waste or gift of the corporate assets to the prejudice of the minority. Consequently, courts have placed limitations on executive compensation plans ***notwithstanding approval*** by disinterested directors and/ or a majority of the disinterested shareholders.

(a) **Legally sufficient consideration to corporation:** [§322]   Courts have held that it must appear that the compensation is paid for services that constituted legally sufficient consideration to the corporation for such payment.

1) **Expressly or impliedly authorized:** [§323]   It must appear that the services rendered by the officer or director were expressly or impliedly authorized by the corporation. Normally, the fact that the services are reasonably related to the corporation's business is sufficient.

2) **Compensation for past services:** [§324]   Courts have generally *invalidated* agreements by the corporation to pay an officer or director (or the surviving spouse of an officer or director) for past services (or to increase compensation retroactively), on the rationale that there is no legal consideration for the agreement. [Adams v. Smith, 153 So. 2d 221 (Ala. 1963)]

   a) **Future consulting fees:** [§325]   One way to avoid this rule is for the corporation to grant compensation to a departing employee in exchange for a promise to be available to "advise" or "consult" with the corporation in the *future* or for a promise not to compete with the corporation. [Osborne v. Locke Steel Chain Co., 218 A.2d 526 (Conn. 1966)]

   b) **Bonuses:** [§326]   Some courts hold that reasonable bonuses (or the like) may be paid to officers and employees for recent past services, if approved by a majority of the shareholders. [Chambers v. Beaver-Advance Corp., 14 A.2d 808 (Pa. 1958)]

   c) **Retirement benefits:** [§327]   And some statutes now specifically authorize the board to provide pensions and retirement benefits in recognition of past services. [*See* Pa. Bus. Corp. Law §316]

3) **Compensation for future services:** [§328]   Compensation for services to be rendered in the future may be held improper if there is no reasonable assurance that the corporation will ultimately receive the benefit of the services for which it is paying.

   a) **Stock options:** [§329]   Some courts have invalidated the grant of stock options exercisable by officers and employees in future years when the options were *not conditioned* on the recipient's remaining in the corporation's employ for any designated period of time and when the option would be exercised even after the recipient left the corporation's employ. [Kerbs v. California Eastern Airways, 90 A.2d 652 (Del. 1952)] Other courts have upheld such plans (when adopted by a disinterested board) as an exercise of "reasonable business judgment." [Beard v. Elster, 160 A.2d 731 (Del. 1960)]

(b) **Value of services rendered:** [§330]   There must be some *reasonable relationship* between the amount paid by the corporation and the value of the services rendered. [Rogers v. Hill, 289 U.S. 582 (1933)]

    1) **"Reasonable":** [§331]   What constitutes "reasonable" (as opposed to "excessive" or "wasteful") compensation is determined by all the facts and circumstances, such as: the recipient's qualifications; time spent and responsibilities assumed; the size and complexity of the corporation's business; the amount of its income; and amounts paid to comparable persons performing similar services for other corporations. [Ruetz v. Topping, 453 S.W.2d 624 (Mo. 1970)]

    2) **Percentage of profits:** [§332]   The mere fact that the officer or employee is to receive a percentage of corporate profits is *not* ordinarily enough by itself to show the compensation "excessive," even though another individual could be found to do the same work on a straight salary basis. [*Compare* Rogers v. Hill, *supra*—bonus percentage, valid when established 18 years earlier, might amount to waste due to enormous increase in corporate profits]

VI. INSIDER TRADING

chapter approach

This chapter considers securities trading by corporate insiders, such as officers, directors, and controlling shareholders. Most exam questions in this area concern the *federal* securities laws that regulate insider trading; thus, that is the primary focus of this chapter. Whenever you have a question involving trading by insiders, or by persons to whom they have given inside information (tippees), consider applying rule 10b-5 and section 16(b).

1. **Rule 10b-5:** Analyze rule 10b-5 issues as follows:

   a. Look for a *material misrepresentation,* or an *omission* of material nonpublic information in connection with the sale or purchase of *any* security.

   b. In the case of an omission (as opposed to a misrepresentation), consider whether the person who trades is an *insider*.

   c. If, in an omission case, the person who trades is *not* an insider, consider whether she is a *tippee*. If so, analyze her liability by determining whether: (i) the insider-tipper breached her *fiduciary duty*, (ii) the insider-tipper communicated the information *for her own advantage*, and (iii) the *tippee knew of the breach*.

   d. If the facts of your question do not involve a traditional insider or tippee, consider whether the person trading on the material, nonpublic information obtained the information by *misappropriation*. For example, did she obtain the information through a breach of duty to her employer?

   e. Remember that a suit can be brought under rule 10b-5 either by a private plaintiff who is a *purchaser or seller* or by the *Securities Exchange Commission*. Keep in mind that even nontrading parties (*e.g.*, a corporation that makes a material misrepresentation) may be liable under rule 10b-5.

   f. Consider the *defenses* to a 10b-5 action—such as *lack of scienter, lack of reliance, lack of causation, lack of due diligence,* or *in pari delicto*—and determine whether one of the defenses applies to the facts in question.

   g. Finally, discuss the *remedies*. Potential *remedies* for private plaintiffs are damages and restitutionary forms of relief. Remedies available to the government include injunctive relief, criminal sanctions, and civil penalties.

2. **Section 16(b):** Whenever you encounter a question concerning an acquisition or disposition of securities by a corporation with a class of securities that must be *registered* under section 12 of the 1934 Act, consider the application of section 16(b). Under this section, a corporation can recover any profit made by an insider from any *purchase and sale* (or sale and purchase) of its securities made *within a six-month period*. Remember that, for this purpose, *officers, directors, and beneficial owners of more than 10% of the shares* are considered insiders, and that any transaction in which an acquisition or disposition of securities occurs (such as a merger) may involve a "purchase" or "sale" for purposes of section 16(b).

a. When analyzing a question under section 16(b), first determine whether the person is a statutory insider and, if so, *at what time* she became an insider. Then, try to *pair up* an acquisition and a disposition within a six-month period and calculate the short-swing profits.

3. **Common Law:** Remember that some courts now impose liability on insiders in favor of the corporation as a matter of common law.

A. INTRODUCTION [§333]

The purchase and sale of a corporation's stock by a director, officer, or other insider raises important and complex issues of fiduciary responsibility. The basic problem is the possibility that an insider has an unfair advantage because he knows facts about the corporation that are not known to those with whom he deals, and he knows those facts only because of his fiduciary position, not because he has exercised skill or diligence.

B. COMMON LAW

1. **Duty to Shareholders:** [§334]   It was clear at common law that a director or officer was liable if he made misrepresentations, or stated half-truths, in connection with the purchase or sale of the corporation's stock. However, the courts were divided concerning the liability of officers and directors who purchased or sold stock without making misrepresentations or stating half-truths, but failed to disclose material facts of which they had inside knowledge.

   a. **Majority rule:** [§335]   The majority rule at common law was that an officer or director had no duty of disclosure, when buying or selling the corporation's securities, regarding any inside information that might affect the value of the securities, because officers and directors owed fiduciary duties only to the corporation. [Goodwin v. Aggasiz, 186 N.E. 659 (Mass. 1933)]

      (1) **"Special facts" exception:** [§336]   A number of jurisdictions that followed the majority rule nevertheless adopted an exception under which an insider did have a duty of disclosure if there were "special facts" that made nondisclosure unfair to the person with whom the insider dealt. [Strong v. Repide, 213 U.S. 419 (1909)] This exception was most typically applied where the parties dealt face-to-face, rather than over a stock exchange. However, "special facts" were found in so many cases that the exception sometimes overshadowed the rule. [Taylor v. Wright, 69 Cal. App. 2d 371 (1945)]

   b. **Minority rule:** [§337]   Under a minority rule, an insider was considered a fiduciary for the shareholders, as well as the corporation, and was required to disclose any material information she had obtained as an insider that might affect the value of the shares, even in the absence of special facts. [King Manufacturing Co. v. Clay, 118 S.E.2d 581 (Ga. 1961)]

C. SECURITIES EXCHANGE ACT OF 1934—IN GENERAL [§338]

The common law rules governing insider trading have been largely superseded by the Securities Exchange Act of 1934. [15 U.S.C. §§78a *et seq.*] The principal focus of the 1934 Act is the regulation of trading in securities after their initial issuance. Most, but not all, of the Act's provisions are keyed to whether securities are required to be registered with the Securities Exchange Commission ("SEC") under section 12 of the Act. Generally speaking, section 12 and the rules thereunder require registration of (i) any security that is **traded on a national securities exchange**, and (ii) any equity security that is issued by a corporation that has **total assets** (not net worth) **exceeding $5 million** and is held by **500 or more persons**. [15 U.S.C. §781] However, **section 10(b)** of the Act is **not** keyed to whether securities are required to be registered; it applies to all securities, even shares in close corporations.

D. SECTION 10(b) AND RULE 10b-5 [§339]

Section 10(b) of the 1934 Act makes it unlawful "to use or employ . . . any manipulative or deceptive device" in contravention of SEC rules, in connection with the purchase or sale of any security. [16 U.S.C. §78j] To implement section 10(b), the SEC promulgated Securities Exchange Act ("Exchange Act") Rule 10b-5. Under rule 10b-5, it is unlawful, in connection with the purchase or sale of any security, by use of the mails or any means of interstate commerce to:

(i) Employ any **device, scheme, or artifice to defraud**;

(ii) Make any **untrue statement of a material fact** or **omit a material fact** necessary to make the statements made not misleading; or

(iii) Engage in any **act, practice, or course of business that operates as fraud or deceit** upon any person

in connection with a purchase or sale of securities.

1. **Covered Conduct—Misrepresentation and Nondisclosure**: [§340]   Rule 10b-5 applies not only to misrepresentations, but also to nondisclosure by insiders and, in certain cases, by tippees. [*In re* Cady, Roberts & Co., 40 S.E.C. 907 (1961)]

2. **Covered Persons:** [§341]   Rule 10b-5 is often referred to as an insider-trading rule, because its major significance is to prohibit insider trading. In fact, however, rule 10b-5 extends well beyond insider trading. For example, **any person** who makes a misrepresentation in connection with the purchase or sale of stock may be liable under rule 10b-5, whether or not he is an insider.

3. **Covered Securities:** [§342]   Rule 10b-5 applies to the purchase or sale of **any security**, whether or not required to be registered under section 12. The rule applies whether the corporation is large or small, and whether its shares are widely or closely held. [Hooper v. Mountain States Securities Corp., 282 F.2d 195 (5th Cir. 1960); Kardon v. National Gypsum Co., 83 F. Supp. 613 (E.D. Pa. 1947)] The only limitation is jurisdictional: The violation must involve the use of some instrumentality of interstate commerce. However, this limitation is seldom a problem, because use of the telephone or mail (for example) satisfies the interstate-commerce requirement.

4. **Who Can Bring Suit Under Rule 10b-5**

   a. **Suit by SEC:** [§343]   A suit for violation of rule 10b-5 may be brought by the SEC. [SEC v. Texas Gulf Sulphur Co., 401 F.2d 833 (2d Cir. 1968)]

   b. **Suit by private plaintiff:** [§344]   Although neither section 10(b) nor rule 10b-5 expressly provides that a private person who is injured by a violation of the rule can bring suit, it is well established that section 10(b) and rule 10b-5 create an "implied" private right of action in favor of an injured private party. [Superintendent of Insurance v. Bankers Life & Casualty Co., 404 U.S. 6 (1971); Kardon v. National Gypsum Co., *supra*, §342]

5. **Materiality:** [§345]   Rule 10b-5 is applicable to misrepresentations and nondisclosures only if the misrepresented or omitted fact is ***material***. An "omitted fact is material if there is a substantial likelihood that a reasonable shareholder would consider it important in deciding" on her course of action. There "must be a substantial likelihood that the disclosure of the omitted fact would have been viewed by the reasonable investor as having significantly altered the 'total mix' of information made available." [Basic, Inc. v. Levinson, 485 U.S. 224 (1988)] Materiality depends "at any given time upon a balancing of both the indicated probability that the event will occur and the anticipated magnitude of the event in light of the totality of the company activity." [Basic, Inc. v. Levinson, *supra—quoting* SEC v. Texas Gulf Sulphur Co., *supra*, §343]

   a. **Example:** Where insiders knew that the corporation had done exploratory drilling that gave a promise of a gigantic mineral strike, the knowledge was deemed material even though it was possible that after thorough exploration it would turn out that the company did not have a minable body of ore. Knowledge of the possibility of a gigantic mine could affect the price of stock. If it turned out there was a minable body of ore, the market price would rise substantially when that news was disclosed. If it turned out there was no minable body of ore, the market price of the stock would not fall, assuming the information about the exploratory drilling was neither leaked nor acted upon by insiders. [SEC v. Texas Gulf Sulphur Co., *supra*]

6. **Fault Required—Scienter:** [§346]   A material misrepresentation or omission will not violate rule 10b-5 if the defendant was without fault or merely negligent. Liability can be imposed under rule 10b-5 only if the defendant had scienter. [Ernst & Ernst v. Hochfelder, 425 U.S. 185 (1976)]

   a. **Definition of scienter—recklessness:** [§347]   Under tort law, scienter is satisfied by an intent to deceive, to mislead, or to convey a false impression. Decisions since *Ernst & Ernst* have unanimously held that recklessness also satisfies the scienter requirement. [Rolf v. Blyth, Eastman Dillon & Co., 570 F.2d 38 (2d Cir. 1976), *cert. denied*, 439 U.S. 1039 (1978)] Many courts have adopted a definition under which "recklessness" is highly unreasonable conduct, "involving not merely simple or even inexcusable negligence, but an extreme departure from the standards of ordinary care, and which presents a danger of misleading buyers or sellers that is either known to the defendant or is so obvious that the actor must have been aware of it." [Sundstrand Corp. v. Sun Chemical Corp., 553 F.2d 1033 (7th Cir. 1977), *cert. denied*, 434 U.S. 875 (1977)]

   b. **Injunctive relief:** [§348]   Scienter is also a requirement in an injunctive action under rule 10b-5. [Aaron v. SEC, 446 U.S. 680 (1980)]

7. **Causation and Reliance:** [§349]   The plaintiff in a rule 10b-5 case must prove that the rule 10b-5 violation caused her loss. In theory, this means that the plaintiff

must prove that she relied on the defendant's wrongful statement or omission. In practice, however, the reliance requirement has been greatly attenuated.

a. **Omissions:** [§350]   In omissions cases, "positive proof of reliance is not a prerequisite to recovery. All that is necessary is that the facts withheld be material in the sense that a reasonable investor might have considered them important" in the making of her decision. [Affiliated Ute Citizens of Utah v. United States, 406 U.S. 128 (1972)]

(1) **Presumption of reliance:** Subsequent court of appeals cases have held that *Ute* "merely established a presumption that made it possible for the plaintiffs to meet their burden." [Shores v. Sklar, 647 F.2d 462 (5th Cir. 1981) (en banc), *cert. denied*, 459 U.S. 1102 (1983)] The defendant can rebut this presumption by showing that the plaintiff would have followed the same course of conduct even with full disclosure. For example, the defendant might show that the plaintiff learned the omitted fact from an independent source before making her investment, so that the investment could not have been caused by the defendant's nondisclosure.

b. **"Fraud on the market":** [§351]   Where securities are sold in a well-developed market (rather than in a face-to-face transaction), a plaintiff may be able to prove reliance on a misrepresentation by alleging that she relied on the integrity of the market. This is known as the "fraud on the market" theory. [Basic, Inc. v. Levinson, *supra*]

(1) **Rationale:** In an open and well-developed securities market, material misrepresentations (or the withholding of material information) generally affect the price of the stock. Since purchasers rely on the price of the stock as a reflection of its value, they may be defrauded even if they do not directly rely on the misrepresentations. [Basic, Inc. v. Levinson, *supra*]

(2) **Effect:** The effect of the fraud-on-the-market theory is to create a *presumption* of reliance. The defendant can rebut the presumption by showing, for example, that a misrepresentation in fact did not lead to a distortion of price, that an individual plaintiff traded or would have traded despite knowing the statement was false, or that before the plaintiff traded the correct information entered the market.

c. **Face-to-face misrepresentations:** [§352]   In an action based on a face-to-face misrepresentation, the plaintiff has the burden of showing actual reliance on the misrepresentation. [REA Express, Inc. v. Interway Corp., 538 F.2d 953 (2d Cir. 1976); Holdsworth v. Strong, 545 F.2d 687 (10th Cir. 1976)] However, the plaintiff can normally satisfy this burden by showing that the misrepresentation was material, testifying that she relied on it, and showing that she traded soon after the misrepresentation. [Robinson v. Cupples Container Co., 513 F.2d 1274 (9th Cir. 1975)] The burden will then shift to the defendant to show that the plaintiff did not rely on the misrepresentation. For example, the defendant might be able to show that the plaintiff knew from other sources that the misrepresentation was false.

8. **When Nondisclosure Constitutes a Violation:** [§353]   Assuming that materiality and scienter are established, rule 10b-5 is clearly violated when a person makes

a misrepresentation or states a half-truth in connection with the purchase or sale of stock. Most such cases would constitute common law fraud as well as a violation of rule 10b-5. The primary advantages of rule 10b-5 in such cases are the ability to bring suit in federal court, the liberal venue and service-of-process provisions of the 1934 Act, and a relatively expansive view of what constitutes a misrepresentation or half-truth. More difficult issues are presented, however, where the defendant is claimed to have violated rule 10b-5 not by a misrepresentation or half-truth, but by failure to make disclosure.

a. **Mere possession of material information:** [§354]   Broadly speaking, nondisclosure of material nonpublic information violates rule 10b-5 *only* when there is a duty, ***independent of rule 10b-5***, to disclose. A duty to disclose under rule 10b-5 does not arise from the mere possession of nonpublic information. [Chiarella v. United States, 445 U.S. 222 (1980); Dirks v. SEC, 463 U.S. 646 (1983)] So, for example, a person who acquires material nonpublic information solely by skill and diligence in searching out the information, without using an insider position or any wrongful methods, does not violate rule 10b-5 if he trades on the basis of that information. Similarly, a person who innocently overhears material nonpublic information can make use of the information in trading without violating rule 10b-5.

b. **Trading by insiders:** [§355]   At the other end of the spectrum, it is clear that insiders—directors, officers, controlling shareholders, and corporate employees—violate rule 10b-5 if they trade on the basis of material nonpublic information that they obtained through their positions ("inside information"). The duty of such persons to disclose such information before trading rests on the existence of a relationship giving them access to information intended to be available only for a corporate purpose, and the unfairness of allowing a corporate insider to take advantage of that information by trading without disclosure. [*In re* Cady, Roberts & Co., *supra*, §340; Chiarella v. United States, *supra*] Trading by insiders on the basis of inside information is commonly referred to as "insider trading."

c. **Misappropriation:** [§356]   Between the extremes of skillfully or innocently acquired nonpublic information on the one hand, and inside information on the other, is information that a noninsider wrongfully acquires, *i.e.,* "misappropriates." The misappropriation theory is most useful where the defendant had no independent fiduciary duty to the party with whom he traded. However, whether a person who trades on the basis of such information is liable under rule 10b-5, and if so, the extent of that liability, are questions that are not completely settled.

(1) ***Chiarella v. United States:*** [§357]   In *Chiarella v. United States, supra,* §355, Chiarella worked in the composing room of a financial printer and learned of prospective takeover bids before they were made public. In violation of his employer's rules, Chiarella acquired stock in the target before the tender offer was made, and sold the target's stock at a profit after the tender offer was made. Chiarella was indicted for violation of section 10(b) and rule 10b-5. The trial court instructed the jury that Chiarella should be found guilty if he used material nonpublic information at a time when he knew that other people trading in the securities market did not have access to the same information. The jury convicted Chiarella.

The United States Supreme Court reversed, holding that the trial court's instruction imposed too broad a duty, because under the instruction Chiarella would be guilty even if he had obtained material information rightfully. However, the Court reserved decision on whether Chiarella could have been convicted on the theory that he breached a duty to the acquiring corporation when he acted upon information that he obtained by virtue of his position as an employee of a printer employed by that corporation. Furthermore, at least four Justices explicitly embraced the theory that trading on the basis of improperly obtained nonpublic information violated rule 10b-5 (the "misappropriation theory").

(2) **Misappropriation theory applied—*SEC v. Materia*:** [§358]   In *SEC v. Materia*, 745 F.2d 197 (2d Cir. 1984), *cert. denied*, 471 U.S. 1053 (1985), Materia (like Chiarella) was employed by a financial printer and used confidential information obtained in that capacity to trade in the stock of target corporations. The Second Circuit held that Materia had criminally violated rule 10b-5 under the misappropriation theory. *Chiarella* was distinguished on the ground that the instruction to the jury in that case had been much broader than the misappropriation theory.

(3) **Violation of duty to employer—*United States v. Newman*:** [§359]   In *United States v. Newman*, 664 F.2d 12 (2d Cir. 1981), *cert. denied*, 464 U.S. 863 (1983), Courtois was employed in the mergers and acquisitions department of Morgan Stanley, an investment banking firm. Warner-Lambert Corporation retained Morgan Stanley to assess the desirability of making a tender offer for Deseret Pharmaceutical Corporation. Courtois learned of Warner's plan, and, acting with and through others, purchased Deseret stock at $28 per share. When Warner publicly announced the tender offer, the Deseret stock jumped to $38. The Second Circuit held that Courtois had criminally violated rule 10b-5, based on the misappropriation theory.

(4) **Private actions:** [§360]   In a private (rather than a criminal) action based on the same facts as *Newman, supra,* the Second Circuit held that although Newman and his associates had criminally violated rule 10b-5 by trading on the basis of information they used in violation of Newman's fiduciary duty to his employer, they were not liable in private actions by those persons with whom they actually traded. The court held that a noninsider's duty to "abstain or disclose" with respect to his ***employer*** does not stretch to encompass a duty to disclose to the ***general public***. [Moss v. Morgan Stanley, Inc., 719 F.2d 5 (2d Cir. 1983), *cert. denied*, 465 U.S. 1025 (1984)]

(a) **Insider Trading and Securities Fraud Enforcement Act:** [§361] The Insider Trading and Securities Fraud Enforcement Act of 1988 is intended in part to overrule the result in *Moss v. Morgan Stanley.* Under section 20A of that Act, any person who violates rule 10b-5 by purchasing or selling a security while in the possession of material nonpublic information is liable to ***any person*** who, contemporaneously with the purchase or sale, purchased or sold (as the case may be) securities of the same class. Liability under this provision is limited to the profit the defendant gained or the loss he avoided.

(5) **Misappropriation theory rejected—*United States v. Bryan*:** [§362] Although several circuits have adopted the misappropriation theory, the Fourth Circuit has rejected it in a criminal action. [United States v. Bryan, 58 F.3d 933 (4th Cir. 1995)] The *Bryan* court recognized that the language of section 10(b) and rule 10b-5 "sweeps broadly," and "could plausibly accommodate the misappropriation theory." However, the court in *Bryan* said, "the Supreme Court has repeatedly warned against expanding the concept of fraud in the securities context beyond what the words of the Act reasonably will bear," and "[m]anipulation and deception are the touchstones of section 10(b) liability." Based on those propositions, the court concluded that the misappropriation theory should not be adopted.

(6) **Mail fraud—*United States v. Carpenter*:** [§363] The federal mail fraud act [18 U.S.C. §§1341, 1343] makes it a criminal offense to employ false or fraudulent pretenses, representations, or promises in furtherance of a scheme or artifice to defraud, if any matter is transmitted by mail or wire to execute the scheme or artifice. In *United States v. Carpenter*, 791 F.2d 1024, *aff'd*, 484 U.S. 19 (1987), a *Wall Street Journal* reporter who wrote a widely read and influential column, participated, in violation of the *Journal's* rules, in a scheme in which he provided two stockbrokers with securities-related information that was scheduled to appear in his column. Based on this advance information, the two brokers would buy or sell the securities before the column appeared, and sell or buy immediately thereafter. The reporter was found guilty of criminally violating rule 10b-5, based on the misappropriation theory, and was also found guilty of mail and wire fraud. The mail fraud conviction was unanimously affirmed by the Supreme Court. The Court held that the interest of the *Journal's* owner in the confidentiality of the *Journal's* contents was a property right, and that by using the information for his own purposes the reporter had obtained "money or property" from the *Journal* by fraud. The rule 10b-5 violation was affirmed by an equally divided Supreme Court, without an opinion. Therefore, the Supreme Court's view of the misappropriation theory is still not clear.

(a) **Comment:** As a practical matter, the status of the misappropriation theory under rule 10b-5 has been rendered somewhat less important by the Court's adoption of a comparable theory in the interpretation of the mail and wire fraud statute. Most persons who misappropriate and then trade on information will now be guilty of the crime of mail and wire fraud, whether or not they are guilty of criminally violating rule 10b-5. However, unlike rule 10b-5, the mail and wire fraud statute may not give rise to private actions.

(7) **Special rule for tender offers:** [§364] Exchange Act Rule 14e-3 provides that if any person has taken substantial steps to begin, or has begun, a tender offer, it is a fraudulent, deceptive, or manipulative act or practice for any other person who is in possession of material information relating to the tender offer to purchase or sell any of the target's securities if the person knows (or has reason to know) that the information is nonpublic and has been acquired directly or indirectly from the bidder, the target, or a director, officer, or other person acting on the bidder's or the target's

behalf. In effect, rule 14e-3 reverses the rule in *Chiarella* where the relevant information concerns a tender offer. [*See* United States v. Chestman, 947 F.2d 551 (2d Cir. 1991), *cert. denied*, 503 U.S. 1004 (1992)—Second Circuit held rule 14e-3 valid, upholding the conviction of defendant who had traded on basis of material information relating to tender offer, even though, in the court's view, under *Chiarella* the defendant had not violated rule 10b-5; *accord*, SEC v. Peters, 978 F.2d 1162 (10th Cir. 1992)]

d. **"Disclose or abstain":** [§365]   Where a person has a duty to disclose material nonpublic information in his possession before he trades, the applicable rule is often expressed as "disclose or abstain." That is, nondisclosure *in itself* normally does not violate rule 10b-5. Nondisclosure by a person with a duty to disclose violates rule 10b-5 *only* if the person trades. Such a person has a choice: disclose and trade, or do not disclose and do not trade.

9. **Liability of Nontrading Persons for Misrepresentations:** [§366]   Normally, a rule 10b-5 action is brought against a person who traded in stock. However, even persons who do not trade may be liable under rule 10b-5 in certain types of cases. [Basic, Inc. v. Levinson, *supra*, §351] In particular, a corporation or other person who makes a misrepresentation that would cause reasonable investors to rely thereon in the purchase or sale of securities would be liable under rule 10b-5, even though the corporation or other person does not trade. So, for example, a nontrading corporation may be liable under rule 10b-5 if it issues a misleading press release that would be likely to affect investment decisions, provided scienter is present. [SEC v. Texas Gulf Sulphur Co., *supra*, §345]

a. **Scienter required:** [§367]   A nontrading corporation or other person, like any other defendant, will be liable under rule 10b-5 only if it had scienter. [Ernst & Ernst v. Hochfelder, *supra*, §346] A misrepresentation that is without fault, or that results only from negligence, will not result in rule 10b-5 liability.

b. **Liability of nontrading corporation for nondisclosure:** [§368]   In the case of nondisclosure (as opposed to misrepresentation), the basic principle of rule 10b-5 is "disclose or abstain." Accordingly, a nontrading corporation is unlikely to be liable under rule 10b-5 for nondisclosure of material facts even though persons who do trade would have deemed the information material and made different investment decisions if they had known the undisclosed information. The general rule is that the timing of disclosure of material facts by a corporation is "a matter for the business judgment of the corporate officers entrusted with the management of the corporation within the affirmative disclosure requirements promulgated by the exchanges and by the SEC." [SEC v. Texas Gulf Sulphur Co., *supra*; Financial Industrial Fund, Inc. v. McDonnell Douglas Corp., 474 F.2d 514 (10th Cir.), *cert. denied*, 414 U.S. 874 (1973); Electronic Specialty Co. v. International Controls Corp., 409 F.2d 937 (2d Cir. 1969)] There are, however, several exceptions to this rule.

(1) **Duty to correct statement:** [§369]   If the corporation makes a statement that is misleading (inaccurate) when made, even though not intentionally so, and the corporation later learns that the statement was misleading, it is under a duty to *correct* the statement if the statement is still "alive," rather than "stale"—*i.e.*, if the statement would still be likely

to be material to investors. [*See, e.g.*, Backman v. Polaroid Corp., 910 F.2d 10 (1st Cir. 1990)]

(2) **Duty to update statement:** [§370]   Several courts have held that if a corporation makes a public statement that is correct when made, but that has become materially misleading in light of subsequent events, the corporation may have a duty to **update** the statement. [*See* Backman v. Polaroid Corp., *supra*—qualified this position by taking view that duty to update applies only to forward-looking statements; Greenfield v. Heublein, Inc., 742 F.2d 751 (3d Cir. 1984), *cert. denied*, 469 U.S. 1215 (1985)]

(3) **Assumption of duty to correct others' statements:** [§371]   A corporation may so involve itself in the preparation of statements about the corporation by outsiders—such as analysts' reports or earnings projections—that it assumes a duty to correct material errors in those statements. Such a duty "may occur when officials of the company have, by their activity, made an implied representation that the information they have reviewed is true or at least in accordance with the company's views." [Elkind v. Liggett & Myers, Inc., 635 F.2d 156 (2d Cir. 1980)]

(4) **Duty to correct rumors:** [§372]   A corporation may be under a duty to correct erroneous rumors resulting from leaks by the corporation or its agents. [*See* State Teachers Retirement Board v. Fluor Corp., 654 F.2d 843 (2d Cir. 1981)]

10. **Tippee and Tipper Liability—*Dirks v. SEC*:** [§373]   A *tippee* is a person who is not an insider, but who trades on information she has received from an insider. The basic principles of tippee liability were laid down by the Supreme Court in *Dirks v. SEC* (*supra*, §354).

   a. **Broad rule rejected:** [§374]   The Court in *Dirks* rejected the broad rule that a person would be liable, as a tippee, solely because she knowingly received material nonpublic information from an insider and traded on it. Such a broad rule would conflict with the conclusion in *Chiarella* (*supra*, §§354-357) that trading while in the possession of material nonpublic information is not in and of itself a violation of rule 10b-5. (That is, it matters how the information was obtained.) The Court was also concerned that a broad rule would inhibit the role of market analysts, who often, as part of their research into particular stocks, interview corporate executives and acquire information that may not have theretofore been public. However, the Court identified certain situations in which tippees would be liable.

   b. **Tippee liability based on fiduciary obligations of tipper:** [§375]   A person who receives information from an insider and trades on it is liable if (i) the insider breached a fiduciary duty in communicating the information and (ii) the tippee knew or should have known of the breach, and therefore, knew that she (the tippee) had received the information improperly. The primary test for determining whether the communication of information by an insider constitutes a breach of fiduciary duty is whether the insider communicated the information to realize a gain or advantage. [Dirks v. SEC, *supra*]

(1) **Breach of insider's fiduciary duty:** [§376]   Not only are insiders forbidden by their fiduciary relationship from personally using undisclosed corporate information for the purpose of reaping personal gain or advantage, but they may not give such information to others for that purpose. An insider who tips for that purpose breaches his fiduciary duty to the corporation. Correspondingly, a tippee who knows or should know that the tipper, in disclosing inside information to the tippee, has breached his fiduciary duty to the corporation by using corporate information for his own gain or advantage, will be liable as a knowing participant in a breach of fiduciary duty. On the surface, this test seems narrow. However, the Court defined gain or advantage, in this connection, so broadly as to include most tipping activity.

(a) **Tips to friends or relatives:** There is, for example, a gain or advantage to the insider when he makes a gift of confidential information to a trading relative or friend. The tip to the relative or friend, followed by a trade by the tippee, is like a trade by the insider followed by a gift of his profits from the trade. [Dirks v. SEC, *supra*]

(2) **Quid pro quo for past or future benefits:** [§377]   Even if the tippee is not a friend or a relative, the insider breaches his fiduciary duty, and the tippee is therefore liable, if there is a relationship between the insider and the tippee that suggests that the tip is a quid pro quo for a past or future benefit from the tippee. [Dirks v. SEC, *supra*]

(3) **Tippers:** [§378]   Under *Dirks*, if a tippee will be liable, so will the tipper.

(4) **Outsiders in special confidential relationships:** [§379]   Outsiders who receive information from the corporation as a result of a *special confidential relationship* could be liable under a separate principle (*see* below). [Dirks v. SEC, *supra*]

11. **"Temporary Insiders":** [§380]   Where corporate information is legitimately revealed to an underwriter, accountant, lawyer, or other professional or consultant working for the corporation, that person may become a fiduciary of the corporation's shareholders regarding that information. [Dirks v. SEC, *supra*] The theory is that the person has entered into a special confidential relationship with the corporation and is given access to the information solely for corporate purposes. If such a person trades on the information, he will be just as liable as an ordinary insider (and he will be liable as a tipper if he improperly tips the information). Persons who acquire information in this way are sometimes referred to as "temporary insiders."

12. **Aiders and Abettors:** [§381]   An aider and abettor is a person who aids or abets someone who improperly trades. For example, an accountant or lawyer may aid or abet a client's wrongful trading, or a banker may finance such trading. In *Central Bank of Denver v. First Interstate Bank of Denver*, 114 S. Ct. 1439 (1994), the Supreme Court held that *liability cannot be imposed* on a person under rule 10b-5 solely because that person aided and abetted a violation of the rule.

a. **Note:** Prior to *Central Bank*, issues concerning aiding-and-abetting liability under rule 10b-5 usually arose in the context of a suit against a primary violator in which the plaintiff joined as defendants such secondary actors as lawyers, accountants, or banks who had somehow furthered the primary violator's course of conduct. The *Central Bank* opinion held that such secondary actors could not be sued on an aiding-and-abetting theory, but left open the possibility of suing such actors as primary violators in appropriate cases.

13. **Application of Rule 10b-5 to Breach of Fiduciary Duties by Directors, Officers, or Controlling Shareholders**

   a. **"Ordinary mismanagement" without misrepresentation, nondisclosure, or manipulation—the *Santa Fe* rule:** [§382]   A breach of fiduciary duty by a corporate manager that does not involve a misrepresentation, nondisclosure, or manipulation does not violate rule 10b-5 even if it involves the purchase or sale of stock. [Santa Fe Industries, Inc. v. Green, 430 U.S. 462 (1977)] This kind of rule 10b-5 case is often referred to as an "ordinary mismanagement" case.

      (1) **Example:** A Corp. and B Corp. are both incorporated in State X. A owns 90% of B. Under the law of State X, a short-form merger can be used to cash out minority shareholders if the parent owns at least 90% of the subsidiary. A minority shareholder who is dissatisfied with the price offered for his shares may demand appraisal, but this is his only state law remedy. A Corp. proposes to merge B Corp. into itself by a short-form merger for a cash price that is wholly inadequate, but A Corp. discloses all the relevant facts concerning the value of B Corp., from which the inadequacy of the price could be determined. B Corp.'s minority shareholders have no cause of action against A Corp. under rule 10b-5, even if the inadequacy of the price violates A Corp.'s fiduciary duties. [Santa Fe Industries, Inc. v. Green, *supra*]

   b. **Purchase or sale of stock by fiduciary on the basis of misrepresentation or nondisclosure:** [§383]   Notwithstanding the general rule established in *Santa Fe*, if a director or officer purchases stock from or sells stock to the corporation on the basis of a misrepresentation or nondisclosure, the corporation can sue the fiduciary under rule 10b-5, even though it can *also* sue her for breach of fiduciary duty.

      (1) **Derivative suits:** [§384]   If the corporation does not sue in such a case, a minority shareholder can maintain a derivative suit on the corporation's behalf (*see infra*, §675). The *Blue Chip* rule (*infra*, § 390), which prohibits a private action by a person other than a purchaser or seller of the securities, would not be a barrier to such an action because the corporation is a purchaser or seller, and the action is maintained on its behalf.

   c. **Purchase or sale of stock by controlling shareholder with approval of majority of directors:** [§385]   Suppose that a controlling shareholder causes a corporation to issue stock to him, or buy stock from him, at an unfair price, and the material facts are not disclosed to the minority shareholders. A derivative action can be brought against the controlling shareholder under rule 10b-5 in such a case if the nondisclosure caused a loss to the minority shareholders. [Goldberg v. Meridor, 567 F.2d 209 (2d Cir. 1977), *cert. denied*, 434 U.S. 1069 (1978)]

      (1) **Causation:** [§386]   To show that the nondisclosure caused a loss to the minority shareholders in such a case, the plaintiff must establish that *an*

effective state remedy was forgone as a result of the nondisclosure to the minority shareholders. The plaintiff usually attempts to satisfy this requirement by arguing that if disclosure had been made to the minority shareholders, they could have sued for injunctive relief against the proposed transaction under state law. The courts are divided on the issue of what the plaintiff must show concerning the likelihood that the suit would have been successful.

(a) **Actual success:** [§387]   Some courts hold that the plaintiff must show that the shareholders would actually have succeeded if they had brought the forgone suit. [Kidwell *ex rel.* Penfield v. Meikle, 597 F.2d 1273 (9th Cir. 1979)]

(b) **Reasonable probability of success:** [§388]   Other courts hold that the plaintiff must show "there was a reasonable probability of ultimate success." [Healey v. Catalyst Recovery, 616 F.2d 641 (3d Cir. 1980)]

(c) **Prima facie case for relief:** [§389]   Still other courts have adopted a requirement "that the facts shown make out a prima facie case for relief." [Alabama Farm Bureau Mutual Casualty Co. v. American Fidelity Life Insurance Co., 606 F.2d 602 (5th Cir. 1979), *cert. denied*, 449 U.S. 820 (1980)]

14. *Blue Chip* **Rule—Private Plaintiff Must Be Purchaser or Seller:** [§390]   A private cause of action can be maintained only by a person who actually purchased or sold the securities to which the violation of rule 10b-5 relates. It is not enough that the violation caused the plaintiff *not* to buy or *not* to sell. [Blue Chip Stamps v. Manor Drug Stores, 421 U.S. 723 (1975)]

a. **Rationale:** The *Blue Chip* rule is based largely on considerations of administrability. The Supreme Court was concerned that it would be too easy for a person to bring a contrived suit under rule 10b-5, based on the allegation, which could be supported only by the plaintiff's oral testimony and therefore would be difficult to disprove, that the plaintiff failed to buy or sell because of defendant's misrepresentation or omission. In contrast, when a plaintiff has actually bought or sold, there is an objective and documented action, not merely a claim of subjective response.

b. **Meaning of "sale":** [§391]   Although *Blue Chip* allows private actions to be brought only by persons who have actually purchased or sold, the term "sale" has an expansive meaning under the securities acts.

(1) **Stock for assets:** [§392]   An exchange of stock for assets, property, or other stock is a "sale" within the meaning of rule 10b-5.

(2) **Mergers and liquidations:** [§393]   A merger can be a sale under rule 10b-5. [Vine v. Beneficial Finance Co., 374 F.2d 627 (2d Cir. 1967)]

(3) **Contracts to sell stock:** [§394]   An executory contract to sell stock is a sale under rule 10b-5. [A.T. Brod & Co. v. Perlow, 375 F.2d 393 (2d Cir. 1967)]

(4) **Pledges:** [§395]   A pledge can be a sale under rule 10b-5. [Rubin v. United States, 449 U.S. 424 (1981); Chemical Bank v. Arthur Andersen & Co., 726 F.2d 930 (2d Cir. 1984)]

c.   **Standing of SEC:** [§396]   The *Blue Chip* rule bars only actions under rule 10b-5 by private persons who have neither purchased nor sold the securities. The *SEC* can bring an action against a violator of rule 10b-5 even though the SEC neither purchased nor sold the securities. By its nature, the SEC is never a purchaser or a seller. Furthermore, the SEC is unlikely to bring contrived suits.

15. **Defenses:** [§397]   Two important defenses to a rule 10b-5 claim are the "due diligence" and "in pari delicto" defenses.

a.   **Due diligence:** [§398]   If the plaintiff was *at fault* in relying on the defendant's misrepresentation, or in failing to learn an omitted fact, in the sense that had the plaintiff used due diligence he would not have been misled, that fault may bar recovery. Mere negligence by the plaintiff will not constitute a lack of due diligence for rule 10b-5 purposes. Since a *defendant* is not liable for negligence under rule 10b-5 (*see supra*, §367), it would be anomalous to hold the *plaintiff* to a higher standard. [Dupuy v. Dupuy, 551 F.2d 1005 (5th Cir.), *cert. denied*, 434 U.S. 911 (1977); Holdsworth v. Strong, *supra*, §352] However, the plaintiff will be barred from recovery by his own intentional misconduct, and may also be barred, under the due-diligence defense, by his own recklessness if the defendant's conduct was merely reckless rather than intentional. It is not yet clear whether the plaintiff will be barred by his own recklessness if the defendant was guilty of intentional misconduct.

(1) **Example:** Seller recklessly makes incorrect oral statements to Buyer, a sophisticated businessperson, about C stock. Subsequently, however, and before Buyer agrees to purchase C stock, Seller furnishes Buyer with documents that correctly state the facts about C. Buyer does not read the documents. In a suit by Buyer against Seller under rule 10b-5, Seller may prevail under the due diligence defense. [Zobrist v. Coal-X, Inc.,708 F.2d 1511 (10th Cir. 1983)]

b.   **In pari delicto—*Bateman Eichler, Hill Richards, Inc. v. Berner*:** [§399] "In pari delicto" is a shorthand phrase for the doctrine that in a case of equal fault, the position of the defendant is better. In a rule 10b-5 context, the doctrine refers to the fault of a plaintiff who sues for a violation of rule 10b-5, but who has *himself* violated rule 10b-5. (The doctrine is most commonly raised in suits by a tippee against a tipper for misrepresentation of alleged inside information. The tipper replies that the tippee was in pari delicto because he violated rule 10b-5 by trading on the tipped information.) In *Bateman Eichler, Hill Richards, Inc. v. Berner*, 472 U.S. 299 (1985), the Supreme Court held that a private action for damages under the securities laws may be barred under the principle of in pari delicto on the grounds of the plaintiff's culpability, but only where (i) as a direct result of his own actions the plaintiff bears at least *substantially equal responsibility* with the defendant for the violation that the plaintiff seeks to redress, and (ii) preclusion of the plaintiff's suit would not *significantly interfere* with the effective enforcement of the securities laws and the protection of the investing public. Note that an investor who engages in insider trading as a tippee is not necessarily as blameworthy as a corporate insider who discloses the information for personal gain.

(1) **Effect:** Although *Bateman Eichler* severely limited the in pari delicto defense in rule 10b-5 cases, it did not foreclose that defense in situations "in which the relative culpabilities of the tippee and his insider source merit a different mix of deterrent incentives." [Rothberg v. Rosenbloom, 808 F.2d 252 (3d Cir. 1986)]

(2) **Note:** In *Pinter v. Dahl*, 486 U.S. 622 (1988), the Supreme Court elaborated on the first prong of the *Bateman Eichler* test, concerning when the plaintiff, as a direct result of his own actions, bears at least substantially equal responsibility for the underlying illegality. The Court held that the plaintiff must be an "active, voluntary participant in the unlawful activity that is the subject of the suit," *i.e.*, the plaintiff must himself have violated the law in cooperation with the defendant, in order to be in pari delicto. Thus, unless the degrees of fault are essentially indistinguishable or the plaintiff's responsibility is clearly greater, the in pari delicto defense should not be allowed, and the plaintiff should be compensated.

16. **Remedies:** [§400]   A great variety of remedies are available for violations of rule 10b-5.

   a. **Potential remedies:** [§401]   Before examining exactly which remedies are available in which kinds of cases, it is helpful to understand the meaning of various remedies.

      (1) **Out-of-pocket damages:** [§402]   Out-of-pocket damages are the difference between the price paid for stock and its actual value. This measure is designed to put the injured person back in the same financial position he was in before the transaction occurred, but not to give him the benefit of the bargain.

         (a) **Compare—benefit-of-the-bargain damages:** [§403]   Benefit-of-the-bargain damages are measured by the difference between the value of stock as it really is and the value the stock would have had if a misrepresentation had been true. The difference between out-of-pocket and benefit-of-the-bargain damages can be illustrated as follows: Buyer paid $20,000 for O Oil Company stock based on Seller's representation that O had just struck a new well. O stock would have been worth $22,000 if the representation had been true. In fact, O had not just struck a new well, and the stock was worth only $19,000. Benefit-of-the-bargain damages would be $3,000—the difference between the actual value of the O stock ($19,000) and the value it would have had if it had struck a new well ($22,000). Out-of-pocket damages, however, are only $1,000—the difference between the amount Buyer paid ($20,000) and the value of the stock ($19,000).

(b) **Standard measure of conventional damages in rule 10b-5 cases:** [§404] In private actions under rule 10b-5 in which the plaintiff seeks conventional damages, *out-of-pocket damages* is the standard measure; benefit-of-the-bargain damages are generally not granted. [Estate Counseling Service, Inc. v. Merrill Lynch, Pierce, Fenner & Smith, Inc., 303 F.2d 527 (10th Cir. 1962); Green v. Occidental Petroleum Co., 541 F.2d 1335 (9th Cir. 1976)]

(2) **Restitutionary relief:** [§405] A plaintiff may seek restitutionary relief rather than conventional damages.

(a) **Rescission:** [§406] The most common form of restitutionary relief is rescission. If a seller sues for rescission and succeeds, she returns the purchase price and gets back the stock she sold. If a buyer sues for rescission and succeeds, he returns the stock he bought and gets back his purchase price.

(b) **Rescissionary or restitutionary damages:** [§407] Another form of restitutionary relief is rescissionary or restitutionary damages. Such damages are the money equivalent of rescission. They are measured by the difference between the value of what plaintiff gave up and the value of what the defendant received.

(c) **Difference between conventional damages and restitutionary relief:** [§408] The major difference between conventional damages and restitutionary relief (whether rescission or rescissionary damages) is that out-of-pocket damages are based on the *plaintiff's loss*, while restitutionary relief is based on the *defendant's wrongful gain*.

1) **Comment:** Rescission or rescissionary damages may be especially attractive remedies to a plaintiff when the value of the stock in question changed radically after the transaction. For example, suppose the facts of the oil company hypothetical (*supra*, §403) are reversed: O Oil Company *has* struck a new well, but Buyer tells Seller that it has not. As a result, Seller sells Buyer O stock for $20,000, when it was really worth $22,000. By the time of the trial, however, the O stock is worth $40,000. Under the conventional out-of-pocket damages measure, Seller would be entitled to $2,000, the difference between the value of what she gave up (stock worth $22,000) and the value of what she got ($20,000 in cash). Seller is much better off if she can either get back the stock itself (which will give her $40,000 worth of O stock in return for repaying only $20,000 in cash) or rescissionary damages (which will be $20,000—the value of the stock minus the value of what she received for it).

b. **Application of remedy provisions:** [§409] The next several sections show how these potential remedies are actually used to remedy violations of rule 10b-5. Which remedies are available in which cases depends to a considerable extent on whether the stock is closely or publicly held.

(1) **Remedies for 10b-5 violations in connection with stock of closely held corporations:** [§410]   Suppose that Seller owns stock in C, a closely held corporation. Buyer makes a material representation to Seller concerning C. If the representation were true, it would have a negative impact on the value of C stock. In fact, it is false. In reliance on the misrepresentation, Seller sells his C stock to Buyer. Later, Seller learns that he was deceived.

    (a) **Out-of-pocket damages:** [§411]   Seller can sue for conventional damages under rule 10b-5. In that case, his recovery will normally be based on the out-of-pocket measure; thus, he will be awarded the difference between the price he received for his stock and its actual higher value. (Similarly, a buyer can sue for out-of-pocket damages based on a misrepresentation by a seller. And either a seller or a buyer can sue for out-of-pocket damages based on failure to disclose a material fact where disclosure is required.)

    (b) **Restitutionary relief:** [§412]   Alternatively, a seller or buyer of stock in a close corporation who sold or bought on the basis of a misrepresentation or a wrongful nondisclosure can sue for restitutionary relief.

        1) **When plaintiff is a seller:** [§413]   If the plaintiff is a seller, and sues for rescission, he would return the purchase price to the buyer and recover the stock. Suppose that, in the above example (§410), Buyer has already resold the stock. In that case, Seller may be able to recover Buyer's *profit on resale*, i.e., the difference between the price at which Seller sold the stock to Buyer, and the price at which Buyer resold the stock. The theory of such a recovery is that Buyer holds the profit in constructive trust for Seller. In effect, the money Buyer received when he resold the stock replaced the stock to which Seller was entitled. Seller should get the equivalent of rescission, by recovering the difference between the price at which he sold to Buyer and the proceeds of Buyer's resale. [Janigan v. Taylor, 344 F.2d 781 (1st Cir.), *cert. denied*, 382 U.S. 879 (1965); Affiliated Ute Citizens of Utah v. United States, *supra*, §350; Harris v. American Investment Co., 523 F.2d 220 (8th Cir. 1975), *cert. denied*, 423 U.S. 1054 (1976)] This is a form of rescissionary damages.

        2) **When plaintiff is a buyer:** [§414]   Similarly, if the injured party is a buyer, she may return the stock and recover the purchase price. If she resold the stock at a lower price before she discovered the violation of rule 10b-5, she should be able to recover the difference between the price she paid and the resale price. [Chasins v. Smith, Barney & Co., 438 F.2d 1167 (2d Cir. 1970), *aff'g* 306 F. Supp. 177 (S.D.N.Y. 1969); Randall v. Loftsgaarden, 478 U.S. 647 (1986)]

(2) **Remedies for 10b-5 violations in connection with stock in publicly held corporations:** [§415]   When a rule 10b-5 case involves stock in a

publicly held corporation, the situation is much different. To keep the discussion as simple as possible, the focus will be on cases where the injured party is a seller. The same principles generally apply where the injured party is a buyer.

(a) **Plaintiff deals directly with defendant:** [§416] Suppose that Seller owns stock in P, a publicly held corporation. Buyer publicly makes a material misrepresentation concerning P, which has a negative impact on the value of P stock. In reliance on the misrepresentation, Seller sells his stock to Buyer.

1) **Damages:** [§417] Assume first that Seller sues Buyer for conventional damages. Under the out-of-pocket measure, Seller would recover the difference between the price at which he sold stock in P and the actual value of the stock. There is a good reason, however, for measuring the actual value of the stock, not by its price *at the time of the wrong*, but by its price *at the time of disclosure of the correct information*. The market price of P stock at the time of the wrong is *not* a good indicator of the actual value of the stock at that time, because the market will have been affected by Buyer's misrepresentation. In contrast, the market price of P stock after the misrepresentation is corrected normally is a good indicator of the actual value of the stock at the time of the wrong, because that price will reflect the market's valuation of P stock in light of the new, correct information. [Harris v. American Investment Co., *supra*, §413] The use of market price at the time of disclosure to determine the actual value of the stock at the time of the wrong is sometimes referred to as the "modified" out-of-pocket measure.

a) **Conversion measure:** [§418] Some cases put a slight twist on this rule, and allow the seller to measure damages by the highest price within a reasonable time after disclosure. The theory is that if Buyer had not caused Seller to sell his P stock at an unfairly low price, Seller might have sold the stock at the highest price available in the market during a reasonable time after he learned the true facts. Of course, we cannot know exactly what price Seller would have obtained—he might have sold at less than the highest price—but the wrongdoer should bear the burden of this uncertainty, since she created it. [Mitchell v. Texas Gulf Sulphur Co., 446 F.2d 90 (10th Cir.), *cert. denied*, 404 U.S. 1004 (1971)] This is sometimes known as the "conversion" measure.

2) **Restitutionary relief:** [§419] Restitutionary relief (rescission and rescissional damages) is usually *unavailable* in the case of publicly held stock, because such relief is unnecessary to compensate the seller or prevent unjust enrichment of the buyer. Where publicly held stock is involved, once the misrepresentation is corrected, the seller can replace himself by purchasing the stock on the market.

a) **Example:** On January 10, Seller sells P stock to Buyer, who had made a material misrepresentation that P is badly off, when in fact it is not. The price is $30. On February 20, public disclosure is made of the true facts, and P stock goes up to $35, where it hovers until March 20. A year later, at the time of trial, P stock is at $60. Seller's failure to realize a gain from the further increase in the value of P stock from $35 to $60 after February 20 does not derive from Buyer's misrepresentation, but from Seller's fully informed decision not to buy P stock at $35. Similarly, Buyer's gain after February 20 reflects not her fraud, but her decision to retain the P stock, which she could have purchased at $35 on February 20 even without having made the misrepresentation. [SEC v. MacDonald, 699 F.2d 47 (1st Cir. 1983)]

b) **Compare—close corporations:** [§420] The rule that restitutionary relief is generally not available under rule 10b-5 in the case of stock in publicly held corporations is not inconsistent with the rule that restitutionary relief generally *is* available under rule 10b-5 in the case of close corporation stock. Where a close corporation is involved, disclosure normally does not put the plaintiff and defendant on an equal footing: Since stock in a close corporation cannot be purchased and sold on the market, the injured seller cannot replace himself by buying shares of the stock on the market after disclosure is made.

(b) **Plaintiff does not deal directly with defendant:** [§421] Suppose that, although Buyer violates rule 10b-5 by a misrepresentation or wrongful omission, she does not deal directly with Seller. In other words, Seller did sell, and would not have sold but for the misrepresentation or omission, but Buyer did not buy from Seller.

1) **Misrepresentation:** [§422] If the defendant made a public misrepresentation that had the foreseeable effect of causing members of the public to buy or sell the stock, she will probably be liable for all the resulting damages. [Mitchell v. Texas Gulf Sulphur Co., *supra*, §418; Blackie v. Barrack, 524 F.2d 891 (9th Cir. 1975), *cert. denied*, 429 U.S. 816 (1976)]

2) **Omission:** [§423] Suppose the defendant did not make a public misrepresentation, but traded on the basis of inside information without having made disclosure.

a) **Case law:** [§424] Two leading cases in the Second Circuit, *Shapiro v. Merrill Lynch, Pierce, Fenner & Smith, Inc.*, 495 F.2d 228 (2d Cir. 1974) and *Elkind v. Liggett & Myers, Inc.*, 635 F.2d 156 (2d Cir. 1980), imposed liability in such cases. However, *Elkind* limited damages to a "disgorgement" measure, in which the defendant is obliged only to surrender profits, not to compensate everyone who traded at the same time for the difference between the price they realized and the value of the stock. A Sixth Circuit case, *Fridrich v. Bradford*, 542 F.2d 307 (6th Cir. 1976) (decided after *Shapiro* but before *Elkind*), refused to impose liability, partly out of concern that to do so would "unduly" extend liability under rule 10b-5—a problem that is cured by using the disgorgement measure to limit damages.

b) **Insider Trading Act of 1988:** [§425]   Under the Insider Trading and Securities Fraud Enforcement Act of 1988, any person who violates rule 10b-5 by purchasing or selling a security while in the possession of material nonpublic information is expressly made liable to any other person who, contemporaneously with the purchase or sale, sold or purchased securities of the same class. Liability under this provision is limited to the profit the defendant gained, or the loss avoided. The Act therefore seems to adopt the approach taken in *Elkind*.

(3) **Remedies available to the government:** [§426]   The SEC, as a government agency, rather than a buyer or a seller, cannot sue for damages in the normal sense. However, the SEC can seek several different remedies for violation of rule 10b-5, including special monetary remedies.

(a) **Injunctive relief:** [§427]   The SEC can, and commonly does, seek injunctive relief. In seeking injunctive relief, the SEC often requests ancillary monetary relief in the form of disgorgement of profits, or other payments, that can be used as a fund for private parties injured by the defendant's violation. [SEC v. Texas Gulf Sulphur, *supra*, §368—insiders ordered to pay their profits from insider trading to corporation, corporation ordered to hold profits in escrow for five years for claimants, and at the end of the five-year period, balance to become property of corporation]

(b) **Criminal sanctions:** [§428]   Violation of rule 10b-5 is a criminal act. The Justice Department often seeks fines and sometimes jail sentences for such violations.

(c) **Civil penalties:** [§429]   Under the Insider Trading Sanctions Act, a person who purchases or sells securities while in the possession of material nonpublic information may be ordered, in an action by the SEC or the Attorney General, to pay a civil penalty to the Treasury of up to three times the profit gained or loss avoided as a result of the purchase or sale. [15 U.S.C. §§78c, 78o, 78t, 78u, 78ff]

17. Jurisdiction, Venue, and Service of Process

a. **Jurisdiction:** [§430]   Suits under rule 10b-5 are based on the 1934 Act. Under section 27 of that Act, the federal district courts have exclusive federal question jurisdiction of violations of the Act and of the rules promulgated thereunder.

(1) **Supplemental jurisdiction of state claims:** [§431]   Under the doctrine of "supplemental jurisdiction" (formerly known as "pendant jurisdiction"), the plaintiff may join, with a rule 10b-5 claim, any claim that he has under state law relating to the same transaction (*e.g.*, for fraud, breach of a common law duty of disclosure, or violation of a state securities statute).

b. **Venue and service of process:** [§432]   Actions under rule 10b-5 are governed by the liberal venue provisions of the 1934 Act. Under those provisions, an action under rule 10b-5 can be filed wherever *any* act or transaction constituting a violation occurred, or in the district where the defendant is found or transacts business. Service of process is also governed by a liberal provision: Process can be served in any district where the defendant can be found, or of which defendant is an inhabitant (whether or not it is the district in which the action was brought). [15 U.S.C. §78aa]

18. **Statute of Limitations:** [§433]   No statute of limitations is provided in the 1934 Act for *private* rule 10b-5 actions. However, in *Lampf, Pleva, Lipkind, Prupis & Petrogrow v. Gilbertson*, 501 U.S. 305 (1991), the Supreme Court held that under rule 10b-5 a private action cannot be brought more than *one year* after discovery of the facts constituting the cause of action or more than *three years* following accrual of the cause of action.

a. **Tolling inapplicable:** [§434]   The Court also held that the doctrine of tolling—a legal doctrine under which the statute of limitations stops running during the continuation of certain circumstances, such as efforts on the part of the defendant to conceal knowledge of his wrong from discovery—is inapplicable to private actions under rule 10b-5.

b. **Retroactivity:** [§435]   The Court held that the new limitation period applied retroactively, even to cases that were brought before *Lampf, Pleva* but were still pending. In response, Congress amended the Securities Exchange Act by adding section 27A, which made *Lampf, Pleva* nonretroactive as to pending actions and even as to actions that had already been dismissed on the authority of *Lampf, Pleva*.

(1) **Constitutionality of section 27A:** [§436]   The constitutionality of section 27A has been challenged in a number of cases. Various circuit courts have upheld the constitutionality of section 27A as applied to cases that were *pending* when section 27A was enacted. [*See, e.g.*, Gray v. First Winthrop Corp., 989 F.2d 1564 (9th Cir. 1993)] However, in *Plaut v. Spendthrift Farms*, 115 S. Ct. 1447 (1995), the Supreme Court held that section 27A was unconstitutional as applied to cases that had been *dismissed* under *Lampf, Pleva* prior to the enactment of that section.

c. **Exceptions to *Lampf* period:** [§437]   The one-and-three-year structure adopted in *Lampf, Pleva* does not apply to all private actions under rule 10b-5. For example, under section 20A of the Securities Exchange Act, there is a five-year statute of limitations for private rights of action based on suits by contemporaneous traders against persons who purchase or sell in violation of rules that prohibit trading while in possession of material, nonpublic information. In addition, the SEC is not subject to any statute of limitations in civil enforcement actions. [*See* SEC v. Maurice Rind, 991 F.2d 1486 (9th Cir. 1993), *cert. denied*, 114 S. Ct. 439 (1993)]

E. SECTION 16 OF THE 1934 ACT [§438]

A second major provision of the 1934 Act governing insider trading is section 16, which relates to purchases followed by sales, or sales followed by purchases, by certain types of insiders, within a six-month period. Such trading is known as "short-swing trading." [15 U.S.C. §78p]

1. **Securities Affected Under Section 16:** [§439]   Section 16 applies only to trading in equity securities of those corporations that have a class of equity securities that must be registered under section 12 of the 1934 Act. Basically, this means a class of equity securities (i) *traded on a national securities exchange*, or (ii) held by at least *500 shareholders* and issued by a corporation having *total assets exceeding $5 million*. (*See supra*, §338.)

   a. **Note:** It is enough to trigger section 16 that *any class* of the corporation's equity securities is registered under section 12. If so, trading in *all* of the corporation's equity securities is subject to section 16. For example, if a corporation has outstanding an issue of common stock registered under section 12, trading in the corporation's preferred stock is subject to section 16 even though that stock is not required to be registered (because, for example, it is not listed and is held by less than 500 persons).

2. **Disclosure Requirement—Section 16(a):** [§440]   Section 16(a) requires that every person who is directly or indirectly the *beneficial owner of more than 10%* of any class of equity securities registered under section 12, or who is a *director or officer* of a corporation that has issued such a class of securities, must file periodic reports showing the amount of the corporation's securities that he beneficially owns, and any changes in those holdings.

   a. **Place of filing:** [§441]   These reports must be filed with the SEC and with any national securities exchange on which the stock is traded.

   b. **Time of filing:** [§442]   The initial report must be filed within 10 days after the person has become a more-than-10% beneficial owner, officer, or director. Subsequent reports must be filed within 10 days after the end of any calendar month in which there have been any changes in beneficial ownership.

3. **Liability—Section 16(b):** [§443]   To prevent the unfair use of information that may have been obtained by a more-than-10% beneficial owner, director, or officer by reason of his relationship to the issuer, a corporation can recover any profit realized by such a person from a *purchase and sale* (or *sale and purchase*), within less than six months, of equity securities of a corporation that has a class of equity securities registered under section 12.

   a. **Coverage of section 16(b):** [§444]   Although section 16(b) is popularly referred to as an insider-trading provision, it does not actually use the term "insider," does not cover all insider trading, and is not limited to trades based on inside information. On the one hand, section 16(b) covers short-swing trading by directors, officers, and more-than-10% beneficial owners, even if the trading is not based on inside information. On the other hand, a person who is not a director, officer, or more-than-10% beneficial owner normally does not fall within section 16(b), even if he does trade on the basis of inside information.

b. **Calculation of short-swing profit:** [§445]   The profit recoverable under section 16(b) is calculated by subtracting, from the price of stock sold, the price of an equal amount of stock purchased within six months *before or after* the sale.

(1) **Example:** On January 2, D, a director of C Corp. (whose common stock is registered under section 12 of the 1934 Act), sells 500 shares of C common stock at $40 per share. Four months later, on May 1, D purchases 400 shares of C common stock at $30 per share. D has realized a $4,000 profit within the meaning of section 16(b), *i.e.*, the excess of the $40 sale price over the $30 purchase price, multiplied by 400 shares.

(2) **Multiple transactions:** [§446]   If there is more than one purchase or sale transaction within the six-month period, the court pairs off transactions by matching the highest sale price with the lowest purchase price, the next highest sale price with the next lowest purchase price, and so on. [Gratz v. Claughton, 187 F.2d 46 (2d Cir. 1951)]   Of course, once any two transactions have been paired off with each other, neither can be paired off with a third transaction.

(a) **Rationale:** The purpose of such matching is to squeeze all possible profits out of short-swing trading by insiders.

(b) **Example:** As a result of this formula, what looks to the untrained eye like a series of losses may be turned into a profit for purposes of section 16(b). For example, assume the following trading by Director D in C Corp.'s common stock:

Date	Purchases or Sells	Number of Shares	Price
6/1	Purchases	1,000	$60
7/1	Sells	1,000	$55
8/1	Purchases	1,000	$50
9/1	Sells	1,000	$45

D may believe that she has lost $10,000 on her trading ($60 - $55 x 1,000; and $50 - $45 x 1,000). However, for purposes of section 16(b), D has a $5,000 profit, since the purchase at $50 on August 1 can be matched with the sale at $55 on July 1.

(3) **Time computation:** [§447]   The court can look six months forward or backward from any sale to find a purchase, or from any purchase to find a sale. If there is *any pair* of transactions within a six-month period in which the sale price is higher than the purchase price, the officer, director, or more-than-10% beneficial owner must account for it even if there were other transactions during the period that involved losses.

c. **Who is entitled to recover:** [§448]   The profit derived by the officer, director, or more-than-10% beneficial owner belongs to the corporation (rather than the shareholders with whom the insider dealt), and the corporation alone is entitled to recover that profit.

(1) **Shareholder action on corporation's behalf:** [§449]   If the corporation fails to sue within 60 days after demand by a shareholder, the shareholder may bring an action on the corporation's behalf. However, this is not a typical derivative suit (*see infra*, §716). The cause of action is federal. Therefore, state security-for-expenses provisions (*see infra*, §§729-741) do not apply. Moreover, the "contemporaneous shareholder" requirement normally applicable to derivative suits (*see infra*, §714) does not apply; thus, the shareholder maintaining the action need not have been a holder at the time of the transactions in question. [Dottenheim v. Murchison, 227 F.2d 737 (5th Cir. 1955)]

(a) **"Security" requirement:** [§450]   Although plaintiffs seeking to sue under the statute must own a "security," section 16(b) places no significant restriction on the type of security adequate to confer standing. Any security suffices. The statutory definition is broad enough to include stock, notes, warrants, bonds, debentures, puts, calls, and a variety of other financial instruments. It expressly excludes only "currency or any note, draft, bill of exchange, or banker's acceptance which has a maturity at the time of issuance of not exceeding nine months. . . ." [Gollust v. Mendel, 501 U.S. 115 (1991)]

d. **"Insiders" under section 16(b):** [§451]   As mentioned, section 16(b) covers persons who are officers or directors at the time of either the purchase or the sale, and persons who are more-than-10% beneficial owners at the time of both the purchase and the sale. (*See infra*, §§455-465.)

(1) **"Officer":** [§452]   The term "officer" means an issuer's president; principal financial or accounting officer (or, if there is no such principal accounting officer, the controller); any vice-president of the issuer in charge of a principal business unit, division, or function (such as sales, administration or finance); any other officer who performs a significant policymaking function, or any other person who performs similar policymaking functions for the issuer. [Exchange Act Rule 16a-1(f)]

(a) **Note:** A person's functions, and not simply her title, determine the applicability of section 16. Therefore, "individuals with executive functions do not avoid liability under section 16 simply by forgoing a title, and conversely, persons with a title but no significant executive responsibilities are not subject to the automatic short-swing profit liability of section 16(b). Thus, for example, a vice-president of a bank who has no policymaking responsibility would not have to be concerned with possible liability under section 16(b), if because of an unexpected family emergency, he needed to sell securities." [Barron, *Control and Restricted Securities*, 19 Sec. Reg. L.J. 292, 294-95 (1991)]

(2) **"Director":** [§453]   The term "director" clearly covers persons actually named as directors. In addition, it covers anyone who has *deputized* another to act as director for him. The person making such a deputization will himself be deemed a director.

    (a) **Example:** C Corp. deputizes one of its officers, D, to sit as C's representative on the board of X Corp., in which C holds less than 10% of the stock. D is a director of X Corp. for purposes of section 16(b), and so is C Corp.

    (b) **What constitutes "deputization":** [§454]   Suppose that C Corp. holds stock in X Corp. and that D is both an officer of C Corp. and a director of X Corp. Deputization will be found if it was agreed that in serving as a director of X, D would represent C's interests. Deputization will also be found if D regularly passes on inside information to C Corp., even in the absence of any agreement to do so. Short of these two situations, however, what constitutes "deputization" is unsettled.

        1) **Example:** D was a partner in L Bros., a large investment-banking partnership. D was also a director of Oil Co. L Bros. traded in Oil Co. stock. Although D had succeeded another L Bros. partner on the Oil Co. board, L Bros. was found *not* to have deputized D to represent its interests in Oil Co. because (i) there was no express understanding that D was to represent L Bros.' interests; (ii) D had never discussed the operating details of Oil Co.'s affairs with any member of L Bros.; and (iii) L Bros.' purchase and sale of Oil Co. securities did not result from receipt of inside information from D. Thus, L Bros. was not a director of Oil Co. within the meaning of section 16(b). [Blau v. Lehman, 368 U.S. 403 (1962)]

        2) **Compare:** Martin Marietta owned Sperry Rand stock, and Martin Marietta's president, P, sat on Sperry Rand's board. Although there was no express understanding that P was to represent Martin Marietta's interests, and P had not passed any inside information to Martin Marietta, a number of facts showed deputization for section 16(b) purposes: P was ultimately responsible for the total operation of Martin Marietta, and personally approved all of its financial investments—in particular, its purchase of the Sperry stock. P's control over Martin Marietta, coupled with his membership on Sperry's board, placed him in a position in which he could acquire inside information concerning Sperry and could use such information for Martin. Furthermore, P admitted discussing Sperry's affairs with two officials at Martin Marietta and participating in sessions when Martin Marietta's investment in Sperry was reviewed. P's ultimate letter of resignation stated that "When I became a member of the [Sperry] board . . . it appeared to your associates that the Martin Marietta ownership of a substantial number of shares of Sperry Rand should have representation on your Board." On these facts, the court held that P, in his capacity as a director of Sperry Rand, served as a deputy of Martin

Marietta. Therefore, Martin Marietta was itself a director of Sperry Rand for purposes of section 16(b), and a purchase and sale by Martin Marietta of Sperry Rand stock within six months fell within that section. [Feder v. Martin Marietta Corp., 406 F.2d 260 (2d Cir. 1969), *cert. denied*, 396 U.S. 1036 (1970)]

(3) Time at which insider status of officers and directors determined

(a) **Office held at one end of swing:** [§455]   A director or officer who purchases or sells stock while in office, and then sells or purchases after leaving office but within six months of the first end of the swing, is liable under section 16(b). [Feder v. Martin Marietta Corp., *supra*] However, Exchange Act Rule 16a-2(a) exempts from the operation of section 16 a purchase or sale by a director or officer *before* she became a director or officer, even though the transaction could be matched with a sale or purchase that occurred after she became a director or officer and within six months of the transaction.

  1) **Example:** D, a director, purchases stock in her corporation, resigns her position, and makes a sale within six months of the purchase. D is liable under section 16(b). D would also be liable if she sells stock while a director, resigns, and then makes a purchase within six months of the sale. [Feder v. Martin Marietta Corp., *supra*]

(b) **Office not held at either end of swing:** [§456]   Section 16(b) does not apply unless at least one end of the short-swing transaction occurred while the defendant was an officer or director. [Lewis v. Varnes, 505 F.2d 785 (2d Cir. 1974); Lewis v. Mellon Bank, 513 F.2d 921 (3d Cir. 1975)]

  1) **Example:** D is a director and officer of C Corp. On January 2, D purchases 5,000 shares of C stock. On February 1, D retires. On March 1, D purchases an additional 5,000 shares. On July 6, D sells 5,000 shares. D is not liable under section 16(b). Although the July 6 sale occurred within six months of the March 1 purchase, both ends of that purchase and sale occurred while she was no longer an officer or director. The July 6 sale cannot be matched with the January 2 purchase, because more than six months separated these two transactions.

(4) **Beneficial ownership under section 16(b):** [§457]   If a person is the record owner of an equity security and also has a pecuniary interest in the security, he is undoubtedly a beneficial owner for all purposes under section 16. Problems of interpretation arise, however, if a person is a record owner of shares but has no pecuniary interest; or if a person has a pecuniary interest but is not the record owner; or if a person is neither the record owner nor has a pecuniary interest, but there is nevertheless an important relationship between the person and the security, like the right to control the security. These problems are addressed by the rules under section 16.

Those rules draw a distinction between (i) what constitutes beneficial ownership for purposes of determining *whether a person is a 10% owner* [Exchange Act Rule 16a-1(a)(1)], and (ii) what constitutes beneficial ownership for purposes of determining whether a person who *is* a 10% owner, or a director or officer, must *report* under section 16(a) and may *be liable* for short-swing profits under section 16(b) [Exchange Act Rule 16a-1(a)(2)].

(a) **Determining more-than-ten-percent ownership:** [§458]   For the purpose of determining whether a person *is* a beneficial owner of more than 10% of any class of equity securities, "beneficial owner" means "any person who, directly or indirectly, through any contract, arrangement, understanding, relationship, or otherwise" has or shares: (i) *voting power*, including the power to direct the voting of the security; and/or (ii) *investment power*, including the power to dispose of (or direct the disposition of) the security. [Exchange Act Rules 16a-1(a)(1), 13d-3] In short, in determining whether a person is a more-than-10% owner of stock, the emphasis under rule 16a-1 is on the person's *control* over the stock.

(b) **"Beneficial ownership" for reporting and liability purposes:** [§459]   In contrast, for the purposes of reporting requirements and liability, a "beneficial owner" is "any person who, directly or indirectly, through any contract, arrangement, understanding, relationship or otherwise, has or shares a direct or indirect pecuniary interest in the equity securities. . . ." "Pecuniary interest" in any class of equity securities means "the opportunity, directly or indirectly, to profit or share in any profit derived from a transaction in the subject securities." [Exchange Act Rule 16a-1(a)(2)] In short, unlike rule 16a-1(a)(1), which emphasizes *control* for purposes of determining who is a more-than-10% owner, rule 16a-1(a)(2) emphasizes *pecuniary interest* for purposes of determining what transactions in equity securities may give rise to *reporting obligations and liability*. After stating the pecuniary-interest test as a general principle to govern the determination of beneficial ownership for reporting and liability purposes, rule 16a-1(a)(2) then goes on to deal with certain recurring cases:

  1) **Family members:** [§460]   The term "indirect pecuniary interest" includes securities held by members of a person's immediate family sharing the same household, but this presumption of beneficial ownership may be rebutted. [Exchange Act Rule 16a-1(a)(2)(ii)(A)] "Immediate family" means "any child, stepchild, grandchild, parent, stepparent, grandparent, spouse, sibling, mother-in-law, father-in-law, son-in-law, daughter-in-law, brother-in-law, or sister-in-law, and . . . adoptive relationships." [Exchange Act Rule 16a-1(e)]

  2) **Partnerships:** [§461]   A general partner's proportionate interest in the portfolio securities held by a general or limited partnership is also an indirect pecuniary interest. [Exchange Act Rule 16a-1(a)(2)(ii)(B)]

3) **Corporations:** [§462]   A shareholder is not deemed to have a pecuniary interest in the portfolio securities held by a corporation or similar entity in which the person owns securities if the shareholder is not a controlling shareholder of the entity and does not have or share investment control over the entity's portfolio. [Exchange Act Rule 16a-1(a)(2)(iii)] Note that this rule does not specify a general principle for determining when a corporation's portfolio securities will be attributed to shareholders in the corporation, but only provides a safe harbor in the cases that the rule specifies.

4) **Note:** The rules under section 16 also contain elaborate provisions dealing with such matters as when a trustee is a beneficial owner for reporting and liability purposes, and when the ownership of a derivative security makes a person the beneficial owner of the derivative security.

(5) **Time at which insider status of more-than-ten-percent beneficial owner determined:** [§463]   Unlike the case of an officer or director, liability for short-swing profits is imposed on a more-than-10% beneficial owner only if the person owned more than 10% of the shares at the time of *both* the purchase and the sale.

(a) **Purchase by stages:** [§464]   Section 16(b) does not cover any transaction where a more-than-10% beneficial owner was not such "both at the time of the purchase and sale, or the sale and purchase, of the security involved." [15 U.S.C. §78p] In *Foremost-McKesson, Inc. v. Provident Securities Co.*, 423 U.S. 232 (1976), the Supreme Court held that in the case of a purchase-sale sequence, a more-than-10% beneficial owner is not liable under section 16(b) unless he was a more-than-10% beneficial owner *before* he made the purchase in question. To put this differently, the purchase that first lifts a beneficial owner above 10% cannot be matched with a subsequent sale under section 16(b).

1) **Example:** D purchases 6% of the outstanding shares of C Corp. on January 2, an additional 6% on February 1, and another 6% on March 1. D sells all of these shares at a substantial profit on April 1. The profit on the January 2 and February 1 purchases is not subject to section 16(b), because D was not a more-than-10% beneficial owner at the time he made either purchase. The profits on the March 1 purchase are subject to section 16(b), because D held a 12% interest at that time.

2) **Sale followed by purchase:** [§465]   The *Foremost* case involved a purchase followed by a sale. However, a sale by a more-than-10% beneficial owner that reduces his interest to less than 10%, followed by a purchase within six months, presents greater potential for abuse. In such a case, the defendant would presumptively have had access to inside information prior to the first leg of the swing, and such information might

well carry over to the second leg. Thus, the opinion in *Foremost* left open the question whether a sale-purchase sequence (as opposed to a purchase-sale sequence) by a person who was a more-than-10% beneficial owner at the time of the sale might result in liability under section 16(b).

e. **What constitutes a "purchase" or "sale" under section 16(b)**

(1) **Garden-variety transactions:** [§466] Any "garden-variety" purchase or sale of stock—in particular, an exchange of shares for cash—is a purchase or sale. This is true regardless of motive, *i.e.*, whether or not the purchase or sale was based on inside information.

(2) **Unorthodox transactions:** [§467] The terms "purchase" and "sale" in section 16(b) are not limited to garden-variety purchases and sales. Rather, these terms potentially encompass *any* acquisition or disposition of stock. Acquisitions or dispositions other than garden-variety purchases or sales are sometimes referred to as "unorthodox transactions."

   (a) **Example:** A merger in which stock in C Corp. is exchanged for stock in D Corp. may be treated as a purchase or sale under section 16(b). Likewise, a conversion or redemption of stock, or the exercise of a stock option, may be treated as a purchase or sale under section 16(b). The SEC has adopted elaborate and complex rules under section 16(b) that exempt certain transactions, like conversions and the exercise of options, if designated conditions are satisfied, from the operation of section 16(b). However, these rules do not cover all types of unorthodox transactions, so that the courts must frequently determine whether such a transaction falls within section 16(b).

   (b) **Application of section 16(b)—theories of interpretation:** [§468] Courts have relied on two conflicting theories in interpreting section 16(b) in cases involving unorthodox transactions.

      1) **"Objective" theory:** [§469] Some decisions follow the theory that section 16(b) should be applied broadly to every transaction it can be read to reach, regardless of whether the result is necessary to effectuate the stated purpose of section 16(b) (to prevent the unfair use of inside information). [*See* Smolowe v. Delendo Corp., 136 F.2d 231 (2d Cir.), *cert. denied*, 320 U.S. 751 (1943)] This is known as the "objective" theory.

      2) **"Subjective" or "pragmatic" theory:** [§470] Under an alternative approach, known as the "subjective" or "pragmatic" theory, section 16(b) is applied only to those unorthodox transactions that give rise to a potential for abuse. Under this theory, assuming that an unorthodox transaction *may* be deemed a purchase or sale, whether it *will* be deemed a purchase or sale depends in large part on whether the transaction is of *a type that has a potential for insider abuse*.

         a) **Example:** Occidental Petroleum acquired more than 10% of the stock of Kern County Land as the result of a tender offer. To avoid a takeover by Occidental, Kern County entered into a merger with a subsidiary of Tenneco Corporation. The merger was consummated less than six months after the tender offer, and liability was sought against Occidental under section 16(b), on the theory that the share exchange pursuant to the merger constituted a sale by Occidental of its Kern stock. The Supreme Court held for Occidental on the ground that while a merger *could* constitute a sale of stock for purposes of section 16(b), under the circumstances of this case—the merger was involuntarily thrust upon Occidental by an antagonistic corporation—there was no real potential for speculative abuse by Occidental of the kind section 16(b) was designed to prevent. [Kern County Land Co. v. Occidental Petroleum Corp., 411 U.S. 582 (1973)]

3) **Significance:** [§471] Although the tension between the approaches to the interpretation of section 16(b) is real and important, it is a tension only at the margins. Most of the transactions that have been considered "unorthodox" within the narrow exception announced in *Kern County* involve exchanges of stock pursuant to a merger. The great bulk of potential cases involve garden-variety transactions that cannot be regarded as unorthodox. In these cases, the pragmatic approach is not applicable, and the application of section 16(b) is relatively straightforward. Furthermore, the pragmatic approach normally will be applied only to *involuntary* transactions, *i.e.*, to transactions over which the insider had no control. So, for example, if a section 16(b) insider has control over her corporation's decision to enter into a merger, the merger will be treated as a sale for section 16(b) purposes. And even if the insider had no control over the transaction, she may be liable if she had access to inside information.

F. SECTION 16(b) COMPARED TO RULE 10b-5

1. **Covered Securities:** [§472] Section 16(b) applies only to securities of corporations that have a class of securities required to be registered under the 1934 Act. Rule 10b-5 applies to all securities.

2. **Inside Information:** [§473] Short-swing profits are recoverable under section 16(b) whether or not they are attributable to misrepresentations, inside information, or misappropriation. Recovery is available under rule 10b-5 only where the defendant has made a misrepresentation or has traded on the basis of inside or misappropriated information.

3. **Plaintiff:** [§474] Recovery under section 16(b) belongs to the corporation. Recovery under rule 10b-5 belongs to the injured purchaser or seller.

4. **Overlapping Liability:** [§475] It is conceivable that insiders who make short-swing profits by the use of inside information could end up subject to both a claim by the corporation suing under section 16(b) and a claim by the injured seller or buyer under rule 10b-5. However, section 16(b) provides for recovery of the "profits realized" by the defendant, and damages that a defendant must pay because of a

rule 10b-5 claim arising out of the same transaction would probably reduce the "profits realized" within the meaning of section 16(b).

G. COMMON LAW LIABILITY FOR INSIDER TRADING [§476]

As discussed at the very beginning of this topic, the majority rule at common law was that shareholders could not recover against directors or officers who traded with them without disclosing inside information, partly on the theory that directors and officers owed a fiduciary duty only to the corporation, not to shareholders (*see supra*, §335). Several modern cases have held that as a matter of common law, insider trading does constitute a breach of fiduciary duties owed to the *corporation*—specifically, a breach of the duty not to use corporate assets (inside information) for other than corporate purposes. Under this approach, the *corporation* can recover profits made by insider trading. [Diamond v. Oreamuno, 24 N.Y.2d 494 (1969); Brophy v. Cities Service Co., 70 A.2d 5 (Del. 1949); *but see* Schein v. Chasen, 313 So. 2d 73 (Fla. 1975); Freeman v. Decio, 584 F.2d 186 (7th Cir. 1978)—contra]

1. **Common Law Liability Compared to Liability Under Section 16(b): [§477]** Like liability under section 16(b), common law liability runs against insiders and in favor of the corporation. In other respects, however, common law liability differs from liability under section 16(b):

   a. **Scope: [§478]** The common law theory applies to all corporations. Section 16(b) applies only to corporations with a class of equity securities required to be registered under section 12 of the 1934 Act.

   b. **Defendants: [§479]** Under the common law theory, recovery can be had against any corporate insider. Recovery under section 16(b) is allowed only against officers, directors, or more-than-10% beneficial owners.

   c. **Short-swing requirement: [§480]** The common law theory is available even though the purchase and sale did not occur within a six-month period. Section 16(b) is applicable only to a purchase and sale that occurs within a six-month period.

   d. **Informational requirement: [§481]** The common law theory applies only if an insider uses inside information. Section 16(b) applies whether or not inside information is used.

2. **Common Law Liability Compared to Liability Under Rule 10b-5: [§482]** Liability under the common law also differs from rule 10b-5 liability, in that it runs to the corporation rather than to the injured purchaser or seller. In other respects, the two kinds of liability are highly comparable. However, they do differ in some ways.

   a. **No purchaser or seller requirement: [§483]** Under rule 10b-5, the plaintiff must be either a purchaser or a seller. The common law theory permits recovery by the corporation even when the corporation was neither a purchaser nor a seller.

   b. **Tippees, etc.: [§484]** Common law liability has so far been imposed only against corporate insiders. It is still unclear whether courts would allow recovery under the common law theory against noninsiders (such as tippees), which may be allowed under rule 10b-5 under certain conditions (*see supra*, §§373-379, 381).

VII. RIGHTS OF SHAREHOLDERS

chapter approach

This chapter details shareholders' rights with respect to voting, transferring shares, inspecting corporate records, and bringing direct and derivative actions. It also considers the fiduciary obligations of controlling shareholders. A great deal of important information is covered in this chapter. Some key things to remember for exam purposes are discussed below.

1. **Voting Rights:** Generally shareholders may vote (i) for the election and removal of directors, (ii) to amend the articles or bylaws, and (iii) on "fundamental" corporate changes. Besides that rule, the things you should know about voting rights are:

   a. **Straight voting:** Remember that except for the election of directors, or if the articles otherwise provide, shareholders are generally entitled to *one vote per share*.

   b. **Cumulative voting:** Most states permit cumulative voting for directors, which means that each share is given *one vote for each director to be elected*. The purpose is to give minority shareholders a voice on the board. You may have to memorize the formula for electing directors by cumulative voting so that you can calculate the ability of particular shareholders to elect directors. Keep in mind that the majority shareholders may wish to employ devices such as staggering directors' terms, removing directors elected by the minority, and reducing the size of the board, to avoid the effects of cumulative voting.

   c. **Voting by proxy:** A proxy is a power granted by a shareholder to exercise his voting rights. If you see a proxy question on your exam, make sure that the proxy is in writing and is being exercised during its statutory effective period. Remember too that, unless coupled with an interest, a proxy is *revocable* at any time.

      (1) **Proxy solicitation:** This is a likely source of exam questions. In publicly held corporations, nearly all shareholders vote by proxy. Management solicits proxies for reelection of directors and approval of corporate actions. Occasionally, insurgent groups try to take control of the corporation through a proxy solicitation. Most exam questions will want you to apply the *federal proxy rules* to these situations. These rules forbid misstatements or omissions of *material* facts in proxy materials. In addition, the rules contain detailed *disclosure requirements*, particularly with respect to director-nominees and committees. Generally, shareholder proposals must be included in corporate proxy materials. If this issue comes up on your exam, however, be aware of the lengthy list of exceptions.

         (a) **Remedies:** The SEC may institute a suit for a violation of section 14(a) or the proxy rules. The proxy rules also provide for a *private cause of action* for material misstatements or omissions with respect to proxy solicitations. For these private actions, the crucial elements are: materiality, causation (although this is satisfied by a showing of materiality), standing, and fault. Remember that fairness is no defense. Rescission and damages are the remedies available under this private action.

         (b) **Expenses:** An important possible exam issue is whether corporate funds may be used to reimburse the expenses of a proxy fight. Remember that *management's expenses* may be reimbursed for (i) soliciting proxies to obtain a quorum, and (ii) a proxy fight involving corporate policy, not personnel. *Insurgents* never have a *right* to reimbursement of their proxy expenses, but the corporation may voluntarily reimburse the expenses of insurgents who win a contest involving policy.

    d.   **Combining votes for control—close corporations:** If your exam question involves a *close corporation*, the shareholders may be able to control corporate policy through the following voting devices: shareholder voting agreements, agreements requiring greater-than-majority approval, shareholder agreements binding votes as directors, and voting trusts.

2.   **Restrictions on Transfer of Shares:** Transfer restrictions are often used by close corporations to limit the number of shareholders, prevent entry of unwanted shareholders, or avoid a shift of control. (These restrictions are also used on certain classes of shares by large corporations.) If this comes up in an exam question, remember that, to be valid, the restriction must be *reasonable* and *noted conspicuously* on the certificate. Also, recall that restrictions are not favored and will be strictly construed.

3.   **Shareholders' Right to Inspect Corporate Records:** Generally, a shareholder acting for a *proper purpose* has a right to inspect corporate books and records at reasonable times. At common law, the shareholder has the burden of proving a proper purpose. Most statutes, however, shift the burden to the corporation to prove improper purpose. To determine whether a purpose is proper, ask yourself whether the shareholder is seeking inspection *primarily to protect his interest as a shareholder*, rather than as a potential business rival or litigant.

4.   **Fiduciary Obligations of Controlling Shareholders:** A controlling shareholder owes a fiduciary duty to minority shareholders to act *with good faith and inherent fairness* toward them. The obligation is even greater in close corporations. Thus, when a question arises concerning a controlling shareholder's business dealings with the corporation, ask whether the transactions are fair. The burden of proof is on the controlling shareholder. Likewise, if a controlling shareholder causes a fundamental corporate change, ask whether it promotes his own self-interest at the expense of the minority. Be sure that when the controlling shareholder deals with the minority, he makes a *full disclosure*.

Although a controlling shareholder may sell his control stock at a *premium*, the following transactions are forbidden: A bare sale of directorships or corporate offices is invalid. Similarly, under the theory of corporate action, transactions where controlling shareholders are considered to have usurped a corporate opportunity are breaches of the fiduciary duty, as are sales where the controlling shareholder persuades the minority to sell on less favorable terms than he receives. It is also a breach for a controlling shareholder to sell control to a transferee whom he knows will deal unfairly with the corporation.

5.   **Shareholder Suits:** Direct suits by shareholders, which concern the breach of duties *owed to shareholders as individuals*, are rare exam topics. In contrast, derivative suits, which concern the breach of duties *owed to corporations*, are exam favorites. Whenever a breach of a duty owed to the corporation arises, consider whether a shareholder derivative suit is appropriate. Ask yourself: Have the *corporate remedies* been exhausted (*e.g.*, has a demand for suit been made on directors and, if required, shareholders)? Is the plaintiff now *a shareholder*, and was he a shareholder at the time of the wrong? Does the plaintiff *fairly and adequately represent* the interests of the other shareholders?

Note that any defense that would have been available if the corporation had brought the suit is available in a derivative suit.

Since the cause of action belongs to the corporation, so does any *recovery or settlement.* At this point, you will want to consider whether the plaintiff-shareholder is entitled to *reimbursement* for expenses and whether officers and directors are entitled to *indemnification.* Many courts order reimbursement of a victorious plaintiff's expenses if the suit has resulted in a substantial benefit to the corporation. Every state permits the corporation to reimburse the expenses of officers or directors who win on the merits. However, where a director or officer settles or loses a suit, he may be reimbursed for litigation expenses only, indemnified for the settlement, or denied protection altogether depending upon (i) the state statute and (ii) whether he acted in good faith, with reasonable care, and believed he was acting in the best interests of the corporation.

A. VOTING RIGHTS

1. **Right to Vote—In General:** [§485]   Subject to certain exceptions for close corporations (*supra,* §§169-185), shareholders generally have no right to exercise direct management or control over ordinary corporate affairs. However, they may control the corporation *indirectly* to some extent through their voting rights. Shareholders generally have the right to vote (i) for the *election and removal of directors;* (ii) to *amend the articles or bylaws*; and (iii) on *"major corporate action"* or *"fundamental changes"* (*e.g.,* sale of all the assets, merger, consolidation, and dissolution).

   a. **Who may vote:** [§486]   The right to vote is held by the shareholders of record (of shares having voting rights) as of the date of the notice of the shareholders' meeting, unless the articles or bylaws require (as they frequently do) that shareholders be "of record" on some designated date prior to the meeting in order to vote. [Del. Gen. Corp. Law §213(a)—"record date" cannot be more than 60 days, nor less than 10 days, prior to shareholders' meeting]

      (1) **Sale of shares after record date:** [§487]   The corporation must permit the owner of the shares as of the record date to vote, even if he no longer owns the shares at the time of the shareholders' meeting. But the new owner can protect himself by requiring the record owner to give him a *proxy* (*see infra,* §511). In any event, a record owner who votes in a way that injures the new owner may be liable to the new owner for damages. [*In re* Giant Portland Cement Co., 21 A.2d 697 (Del. 1941)]

   b. **Restrictions on right:** [§488]   Voting rights are not "inherent" in any class of stock. Generally, shares may be either voting or nonvoting, or may have multiple votes per share. [Del. Gen. Corp. Law §151(a)] A few statutes have been interpreted to preclude nonvoting stock. [C.A. Davendes Sociedad Financiera v. Florida National Banks, 565 F. Supp. 254 (M.D. Fla. 1982)]

      (1) **Maximum votes per shareholder:** [§489]   A limit on the number of votes that any shareholder may have, regardless of the number of shares he owns, has been upheld. [Providence & Worcester Co. v. Baker, 378 A.2d 121 (Del. 1977)]

(2) **Publicly issued common stock:** [§490]   A number of state regulatory agencies prohibit the issuance of common stock without voting rights or with unequal voting rights. In addition, the major national stock exchanges forbid listed companies from reducing the voting rights of existing common stock (but do permit issuance of *new* common stock with restricted voting rights).

2. **Shareholders' Meetings:** [§491]   Whereas some informality is accepted as to actions by directors (*see supra*, §204), this is not generally true as to actions by the shareholders. In most states, shareholders can act only at meetings duly called and noticed, at which a quorum (usually a majority unless otherwise provided in the articles) is present, by resolution passed by a specified percentage of those present (usually a majority, but a greater percentage may be required for certain shareholder resolutions).

a. **Timing of meeting:** [§492]   Statutes usually require an *annual meeting* of the shareholders for the election of directors. In addition, *special meetings* are authorized whenever called by a designated corporate officer, by the holders of some designated percentage of the voting shares (*e.g.*, 10%), or by "such other persons as may be provided in the articles or bylaws." [Del. Gen. Corp. Law §211]

b. **Notice:** [§493]   Written notice must generally be given some period in advance—*e.g.*, not less than 10 nor more than 60 days before the shareholder meeting. The notice must specify the place, date, and hour of the meeting, and the general nature of the business to be transacted. [Del. Gen. Corp. Law §222]

c. **Withdrawal of quorum:** [§494]   Courts are divided on the question of whether a shareholder meeting that begins with a quorum present may validly continue to transact business after shareholders withdraw, leaving less than a quorum remaining. [*Compare* Levisa Oil Corp. v. Quigley, 234 S.E.2d 257 (Va. 1977)—meeting may not continue when majority shareholders withdraw to protect their interests; *with* Duffy v. Loft, Inc., 151 A. 223 (Del. 1930)—meeting may continue despite withdrawal of person holding proxies for shares necessary for a quorum]

(1) **Statutory view:** [§495]   Some statutes provide that the meeting may continue notwithstanding the withdrawal of shareholders necessary for a quorum. [Cal. Corp. Code §602(b)]

d. **Informal action:** [§496]   Statutes permit shareholder action to be taken without a meeting, upon the unanimous *written consent* of all shareholders entitled to vote or simply upon the written consent of the number of shareholders (*e.g.*, majority) required to take the action. But in the case of non-unanimous consents, prompt notice must be given to *all* shareholders of whatever action was approved. [*See* Del. Gen. Corp. Law §228]

3. **Shareholder Voting**

a. **Straight voting:** [§497]   Unless the articles otherwise provide, in all matters other than the election of directors, a shareholder who is entitled to vote has *one vote* for each share held. The shareholder vote is determined by counting the number of votes for or against each proposition. Anything over 50% of the votes thus controls in the absence of some greater requirement in the articles. (*See infra*, §574.)

   (1) **Compare—statutory provisions:** [§498] However, to effect certain fundamental changes in the corporate structure (*e.g.*, dissolution, merger, certain amendments of articles), statutes frequently require a higher percentage of shareholder approval. (*See infra*, §§1028, 1061, 1069, 1086.)

b. **Cumulative voting for directors:** [§499] Straight voting allows the holders of a bare majority of the shares complete control over the minority (except where statutes require a higher percentage of shareholder approval). To assure some representation on the board for a minority holding some significant percentage of the shares, shareholders may be granted the right to vote *cumulatively* for directors. [Cal. Corp. Code §708]

   (1) **Mechanics:** [§500] Each share is given one vote for each director to be elected. Thus, if a shareholder owns 10 voting shares, and there are five directors to be elected, the shareholder has 10 votes for each director, or a total of 50 votes. She may then "cumulate" her votes—meaning that she can cast them all for one director, some for one and some for another, or any other way she chooses.

     (a) **Effect:** Where five directors are to be elected, a shareholder holding approximately 17% of the shares can insure the election (and prevent the removal) of one director on the board by casting all her votes for a single director.

     (b) **Formula:** The number of shares needed to assure representation on the board varies with the number of shares outstanding and the number of directors to be elected. The following formula can be used:

$$X > \frac{Y \text{ (no. of directors wanted)} \times Z \text{ (no. of shares voting)}}{1 + T \text{ (total no. of directors being elected)}}$$

     (c) **Example:** If a minority shareholder wishes to assure election of two members on a five-person board, and there are 600 shares outstanding, she needs at least—

$$X > \frac{2 \times 600}{1 + 5} \qquad X = 201 \text{ shares}$$

   (2) **Right to cumulative voting**

     (a) **Mandatory:** [§501] Cumulative voting is mandatory in some states; *i.e.*, it exists whether or not provided for in the articles, it cannot be refused in any election, and any provision to the contrary in the articles or bylaws is void. [Cal. Corp. Code §708; *but see* Cal. Corp. Code §301.5(a)—exempts corporations listed on national securities exchanges]

(b) **Permissive:** [§502]   In most states, however, cumulative voting is only permissive; *i.e.*, the statutes allow, ***but do not require***, cumulative voting for directors. Some of these statutes provide that cumulative voting exists in all corporations except where specifically denied in the articles. [*See* Pa. Bus. Corp. Law §1505] Most, however, provide that it exists only if expressly granted in the articles. [Del. Gen. Corp. Law §214; RMBCA §7.28]

   1) **Note:** If cumulative voting exists only where provided for in the articles (or bylaws), it can always be eliminated by whatever percentage vote is required to amend the articles (or bylaws)—often a simple majority of shareholders. [Maddock v. Vorclone Corp., 147A. 255 (Del. 1929)]

(3) **Devices to avoid cumulative voting:** [§503]   The majority may attempt to curtail the minority's right to representation on the board in a number of ways, only some of which are valid.

   (a) **Staggering terms of directors:** [§504]   The fewer directors being elected at any one time, the greater the number of shares needed to assure representation (*see* formula above). Consequently, the majority may seek to amend the articles or bylaws to stagger the terms of directors (*e.g.*, only three members of nine-person board elected each year for three-year term), in order to cut down the impact of the minority's cumulative voting rights.

      1) **Statutory prohibition:** [§505]   To prevent this, staggering of elections is prohibited by statute in some states where cumulative voting is mandatory. All directors must be elected each year. [Cal. Corp. Code §301]

      2) **Compare—case law:** [§506]   Absent such statutes, the cases are split. [Bohannan v. Corporation Commission, 313 P.2d 379 (Ariz. 1957); Humphrey v. Winous Co., 133 N.E.2d 780 (Ohio 1956)—permitting staggered terms; Wolfson v. Avery, 126 N.E.2d 701 (Ill. 1955)—statute authorizing staggered terms violated state constitutional requirement of cumulative voting]

   (b) **Removal of directors elected by minority:** [§507]   If the majority shareholders could remove the directors elected by the minority, the benefits of cumulative voting would be eliminated.

      1) **Statutory limitation:** [§508]   To prevent this, many statutes provide that the majority shareholders may remove the entire board, but that no individual director can be removed during his term if the votes against his removal would be sufficient to elect him through cumulative voting. [N.Y. Bus. Corp. Law §706(c)]

         a) **Compare:** Some such statutes provide that this limitation on the shareholders' power to remove a director applies only to removing an individual director ***without cause***. [Del. Gen. Corp. Law §141(k)]

2) **Removal for cause:** [§509]   In any event, some states provide that individual directors can be *removed by court action for cause* (*e.g.*, breach of fiduciary duty to the corporation), regardless of shareholder votes for retention. Some statutes authorize such action on motion of a state official or a designated percentage of the shareholders. [N.Y. Bus. Corp. Law §706(d)]

(c) **Reducing size of the board:** [§510]   Reducing the number of board members may decrease minority representation. As the above formula indicates, the fewer directors being elected, the more shares will be needed by the minority to assure a seat on the board. For example, if there are five directors, the shareholder holding 17% of the outstanding shares may obtain representation. However, if the number of directors is reduced to three, that shareholder has no assurance of representation (since this would take more than 25%).

4. Voting by Proxy

a. **Definition:** [§511]   A "proxy" is a power granted by a shareholder to another person to exercise the shareholder's voting rights. The term "proxy" is also sometimes applied to the person to whom the power is given, but such a person will be referred to herein as a "proxy holder." The proxy holder is normally an agent of the shareholder, although in some cases the proxy holder has an independent interest in the subject matter of the proxy. (*See infra*, §515.)

b. **Formalities:** [§512]   A proxy normally must be in writing. Typically, the effective period of a proxy is limited by statute. [*See, e.g.*, Del. Gen. Corp. Law §212—three years; RMBCA §7.22—eleven months, unless proxy is validly irrevocable (*see infra*, §515)]

c. **Revocability:** [§513]   Like most other agency powers, a proxy is normally revocable at any time by the shareholder. A shareholder may revoke the proxy by notifying the proxy holder, by giving a new proxy to someone else, or by personally attending the meeting and voting the shares.

(1) **Shareholder's death or incapacity:** [§514]   The death or incapacity of a shareholder ordinarily does not revoke a proxy, unless written notice is given to the corporation before the vote is counted. [RMBCA §7.22; Cal. Corp. Code §705(c)]

(2) **Irrevocable proxies:** [§515]   A proxy may be made irrevocable if, but only if, it *expressly* so states and it is *"coupled with an interest"*—*i.e.*, the proxy holder has an independent interest in the subject matter of the proxy.

(a) **Interest in shares themselves:** [§516]   The general common law rule is that the interest required to make a proxy irrevocable must be an interest in the *shares* themselves, not in the corporation. [*In re* Chilson, 168 A. 82 (Del. 1933); *but see* Deibler v. Chas. H. Elliott Co., 81 A.2d 557 (Pa. 1951)]

1) **Example:** Shareholder S borrows money from L. S pledges her shares to L as security for repayment, and gives L an irrevocable proxy to vote her shares until the loan is repaid. [150

A.L.R. 308] The interest of L in the shares qualifies to make the proxy irrevocable.

2) **Example:** Shareholder S agrees to sell her shares to P. S gives P an irrevocable proxy to vote her shares, pending a transfer of the shares on the corporation's books. The interest of P in the shares qualifies to make the proxy irrevocable.

(b) **Interest in corporation:** [§517]   Statutes in many states provide that certain types of interest in the corporation, rather than in the shares that are the subject of the proxy, can support an irrevocable proxy. These include the interests of persons who have extended credit to the corporation, partly in consideration of the proxy; persons who have agreed to serve as corporate employees on condition that they receive a proxy; and parties to shareholder voting agreements. [RMBCA §7.23]

(c) **Termination of interest:** [§518]   Even when a proxy is irrevocable because coupled with an interest, it becomes revocable when the interest supporting the proxy terminates (*e.g.*, when a loan that supports the proxy is repaid). [RMBCA §7.23]

d. **Proxy solicitation:** [§519]   In publicly held corporations, almost all shareholders vote by proxy. Typically, the management of a publicly held corporation solicits proxies from the shareholders, both for reelection of directors and to approve various types of actions that require shareholder approval. Occasionally, insurgent groups attempt to obtain control of the corporation through a proxy solicitation.

(1) **State regulation:** [§520]   Prior to the 1930s, state courts sometimes invalidated proxy solicitations, and set aside corporate elections pursuant thereto, when the solicitations misrepresented material facts or were found grossly inadequate in disclosing relevant information. Generally, however, state regulation of proxy solicitation was inadequate. This led to federal regulation, in the form of section 14(a) of the Securities Exchange Act of 1934 and the federal proxy rules (*see* below). Recently, state law has also improved in this area. The Delaware courts, for example, now hold that in self-interested transactions involving a controlling shareholder, the controlling shareholder has a duty to disclose all material facts. [Lynch v. Vickers Energy Corp., 383 A.2d 278 (Del. 1977); Weinberger v. UOP, Inc., 457 A.2d 701 (Del. 1983)]

(2) **Federal proxy rules:** [§521]   Section 14(a) of the 1934 Act provides that it is unlawful for any person, in contravention of SEC rules and regulations, to solicit any proxy with respect to any security registered under section 12 of the 1934 Act. Acting under section 14(a), the SEC has adopted the proxy rules, which regulate the solicitation of proxies. [Exchange Act Rules 14a-1 *et seq.*]

(a) **Securities covered:** [§522]   The federal proxy rules apply to any solicitation of proxies, oral or written, in connection with any security registered under section 12 of the 1934 Act. Section 12 requires registration of securities traded on national securities exchanges or equity securities that are held by at least 500 persons and issued by a corporation having total assets in excess of $5 million (*see supra*, §338).

1) **Nonmanagement solicitation of ten or fewer shareholders:** [§523]   The proxy rules do not apply to a solicitation of 10 or fewer shareholders made on behalf of persons other than management. [Exchange Act Rule 14a-2]

(b) **"Proxy" and "solicitation" defined:** [§524]   The definitions of "proxy" and "solicitation" are extremely broad. "Proxy" means "every proxy, consent, or authorization within the meaning of section 14a of the Act. The consent or authorization may take the form of failure to object or to dissent." [Exchange Act Rule 14a-1(f)] "Solicitation" includes: (i) a request for a proxy; (ii) a request to execute, not to execute, or to revoke a proxy; or (iii) furnishing of a form of proxy or other communication to shareholders under circumstances reasonably calculated to result in procuring, withholding, or revoking a proxy. [Exchange Act Rule 14a-1(*l*)]

1) **Continuous plan:** [§525]   These definitions have been given a very expansive interpretation that goes well beyond a formal request for a proxy. For example, a letter sent to shareholders seeking authorization to inspect the corporation's shareholder list constituted a solicitation of proxies under the proxy rules, because it was part of "a continuous plan" intended to end in a solicitation of proxies and to prepare the way for success in that solicitation. [Studebaker Corp. v. Gittlin, 360 F.2d 692 (2d Cir. 1966)]

2) **1992 amendments:** [§526]   In 1992, the SEC radically revised the proxy rules, principally to make it easier for shareholders—especially institutional shareholders—to communicate with each other. A great number of revisions were made; among the most significant are the following:

a) **Safe harbor for certain communications between shareholders:** [§527]   The amended rules create a safe harbor that excludes from the definition of "solicitation" communications between shareholders, if the communications do not solicit proxy voting authority and are sent by persons who have no material interest in the solicitation, other than their interest as shareholders. [Exchange Act Rule 14a-2(b)(1)]

b) **Broadcast or published communications:** [§528]   A person who has filed a definitive proxy statement with the SEC can broadcast or publish communications in advertisements, speeches, or columns without having first sent copies of the definitive proxy statement to those to whom the communications are distributed. [Exchange Act Rule 14a-3(f)]

    c) **Relaxed preliminary filing requirements:** [§529] The amended rules eliminated the requirement of a preliminary filing of soliciting materials, except for the proxy and the proxy statement. This allows newspaper ads and similar materials to be published without prior review by the SEC. [Exchange Act Rule 14a-6]

    d) **Communications about proxy voting:** [§530] The most important of the revisions were those that freed shareholders—and particularly institutional investors—to communicate with each other about proxy voting without the risk that those communications would be deemed a solicitation under the sweeping definition of that term in the proxy rules. [*See* Securities Exchange Act Release No. 34-31326 (1992)]

(c) **Requirement of full disclosure:** [§531] The proxy rules are very complex and require disclosure of a great deal of information. They set forth detailed requirements concerning the "form of proxy" (the written authorization to vote) and the "proxy statement" (the written statement of explanation that must accompany a solicitation). The form of proxy and the proxy statement, taken together, comprise the "proxy materials." Among other things, the proxy rules:

    (i) *Forbid misstatements or omissions* of material facts in proxy solicitations;

    (ii) *Require all persons* soliciting proxies—management or insurgents—to set forth, fully and completely, in the proxy statement, *all material facts* regarding the matters to be voted upon and the identity of all participants in a proxy contest;

    (iii) *Require disclosure* in the proxy statement of the *compensation paid* to the chief executive officer and the four highest paid executive officers other than the chief executive officer, and conflict-of-interest transactions involving more than $60,000; and

    (iv) *Require* that solicitations by management contain or be preceded by an *annual report*, if directors are to be elected at the meeting.

[Exchange Act Rules 14a-3, 14a-9]

(d) **Form of proxy:** [§532] A form of proxy providing for the election of directors must set forth the names of persons nominated for directors. The form of proxy must also clearly provide the means for a shareholder to withhold authority to vote for each nominee. A proxy executed by the shareholder in such a way as not to withhold authority to vote for the election of any nominee will be deemed to grant such authority, provided that the proxy so states in boldface type. [Exchange Act Rule 14a-4]

(e) **Shareholder proposals:** [§533] The corporation must include shareholder proposals in the corporate proxy materials, provided certain conditions are met. [Exchange Act Rule 14a-8] To be eligible under rule 14a-8, the proponent must be a record or beneficial owner of at least 1% or $1,000 in market value of securities entitled to be voted on the proposal. The proposal and its supporting statement may not exceed 500 words.

1) **Exceptions:** [§534] The corporation is not required to include a shareholder proposal under the following circumstances:

   a) **Not proper subject of shareholder action:** [§535] If, under the laws of the state in which the corporation is incorporated, the proposal is not a proper subject for action by shareholders, the corporation is not required to include the shareholder proposal. Whether a proposal is a proper subject for action by shareholders will depend on the applicable state law. A proposal that mandates certain action by the board of directors may not be a proper subject matter for shareholder action, while a proposal recommending or requesting such action may be a proper subject. [Exchange Act Rule 14a-8(c)(1)]

   b) **Violation of law:** [§536] If the shareholder proposal would require the corporation to violate state or federal law or the law of a foreign jurisdiction to which the corporation is subject, the corporation need not include it. [Exchange Act Rule 14a-8(c)(2)]

   c) **False or misleading statement:** [§537] If the shareholder proposal or supporting statement is false or misleading, the corporation does not have to include it. [Exchange Act Rule 14a-8(c)(3)]

   d) **Redress of personal claim or grievance:** [§538] If the shareholder proposal concerns the redress of a personal claim or grievance against the corporation or any other person, or is designed to result in a benefit to the shareholder or to further a personal interest that is not shared with the other shareholders at large, the corporation need not include it. [Exchange Act Rule 14a-8(c)(4)]

   e) **Relates to operations accounting for less than five percent of assets or business:** [§539] The proposal relates to operations that account for less than 5% of the corporation's total assets and less than 5% of its net earnings and gross sales, and is not otherwise significantly related to the registrant's business. [Exchange Act Rule 14a-8(c)(5)] *Note*: In adopting the 5% standard, the SEC stated that shareholder proposals must be included in the proxy statement, notwithstanding their failure to reach the 5% threshold, "if a significant relationship to the issuer's business is demonstrated on the face of the resolution or supporting statement." [Exchange Act Release No. 19,135 (1982)] Thus, the meaning of "significantly related" is not limited to economic significance.

1/ **Example:** A shareholder submitted a proposal calling on the board to appoint a committee to report to the shareholders on whether the production methods of a supplier of pate de foie gras caused undue distress, pain, or suffering to the animals involved and, if so, whether further distribution of the product should be discontinued until a more humane production method was developed. The corporation had annual revenues of $141 million, annual profits of $6 million, and assets of $78 million. Its sales of pate de foie gras were $79,000, gave rise to a net loss of $3,121, and the corporation had only $34,000 in assets related to pate. Thus, none of the company's net earnings, and less than .05% of its assets, were implicated by the shareholder proposal. The court held, however, that in light of the ethical and social significance of the shareholder proposal, and the fact that it implicated significant levels of sales, the shareholder had shown a likelihood of prevailing on the merits with regard to the issue of whether the proposal was "otherwise significantly related" to the corporation's business. [Lovenheim v. Iroquois Brands, Inc., 618 F. Supp. 554 (D.D.C. 1985)]

f) **Other exceptions:** [§540]   The corporation need not include a shareholder proposal in its proxy statement if:

(i) The proposal deals with a *matter beyond the registrant's power* to effectuate;

(ii) The proposal deals with a matter relating to the *conduct of ordinary business operations*;

(iii) The proposal relates to an *election to office*;

(iv) The proposal is *counter to a proposal to be submitted by the corporation* at the same meeting;

(v) The proposal has been rendered *moot*;

(vi) The proposal is substantially *duplicative* of a proposal submitted to the corporation by another shareholder that will be included in the corporation's proxy material for the meeting;

(vii) The proposal relates to *specific amounts of cash or stock dividends*; or

(viii) The proposal deals with substantially the *same subject matter as a prior proposal* that was submitted *within the previous five years* if the proposal was *last submitted within three years* and: (i) the proposal was submitted at only one meeting during the five years and received less than 3% of the votes, or (ii) the proposal was submitted at two meetings during the preceding five years and received at the time of its second submission less than 6% of votes, or (iii) the proposal was submitted at three or more meetings during the previous five years and received at the time of its last submission less than 10% of votes.

[Exchange Act Rule 14a-8(c)(6) - (13)]

2) **Private right of action:** [§541]   A shareholder whose proposal is rejected by a corporation on the ground that the proposal can be excluded under one of the exceptions to rule 14a-8 can bring a private right of action against the corporation to contest the corporation's rejection.

(f) **Providing shareholder lists or mailing communications:** [§542] A shareholder who wishes to communicate with the other shareholders is entitled either (i) to be supplied with a list of shareholders, or (ii) to have his communication included with the corporate proxy materials if the shareholder pays the cost. (With very limited exceptions, the choice between (i) and (ii) is the corporation's, not the shareholder's.) [Exchange Act Rule 14a-7]

(g) **Remedies for violation of proxy rules**

1) **Administrative remedies:** [§543]   The SEC may institute suit for violation of section 14(a) or the proxy rules (*e.g.*, to enjoin the solicitation, to bar a party from voting improperly obtained proxies, or to order a new election).

2) **Private suits:** [§544]   The proxy rules also create an implied private right of action in the individual investor. [J.I. Case Co. v. Borak, 377 U.S. 426 (1964)] Typically, such actions are brought under rule 14a-9, which prohibits solicitation by means of any proxy statement, form of proxy, notice of meeting, or other communication, written or oral, containing any statement that is false or misleading with respect to any material fact, or which omits to state any material fact necessary to make the statements therein not false or misleading.

a) **Materiality:** [§545]   To establish materiality for purposes of a rule 14a-9 action, there must be "a showing of a substantial likelihood that, under all the circumstances, the omitted fact would have assumed actual significance in the deliberations of the reasonable shareholder"—or, to put it differently, a showing of "a substantial likelihood that the disclosure of the omitted fact would have been viewed by the reasonable investor as having significantly altered the 'total mix' of information made available." [TSC Industries, Inc. v. Northway, Inc., 426 U.S. 438 (1976)]

1/ **Note:** It is not enough simply to show that the information "might" have been considered important by a reasonable shareholder, because such a standard could force management to disclose so much trivial data that the real issues in the proxy solicitation could be obscured. [TSC Industries, Inc. v. Northway, Inc., *supra*]

2/ **Example:** The board of C Corp. solicits proxies from C's shareholders for approval of a proposed merger with D Corp. The fact that C's directors, who were recommending approval of the merger, were nominees of D, would be material, because reasonable shareholders would likely take such fact into consideration in deciding whether to follow the directors' recommendation. [Mills v. Electric Auto-Lite Co., 396 U.S. 375 (1970)]

3/ **Compare:** Where full disclosure has been made concerning the extent of a parent corporation's voting control over a subsidiary, mere failure to disclose that officers of the parent are also serving as officers of the subsidiary is not necessarily material, because in light of the disclosures made as to the parent's voting control, the officers' status is not necessarily a matter that a reasonable shareholder would have considered important in voting on the proposed merger. [TSC Industries, Inc. v. Northway, Inc., *supra*]

b) **Neutralization of misleading statements:** [§546] A materially misleading statement concerning an issue may be neutralized, for liability purposes, by correct statements about the issue elsewhere in the proxy statement. However, this will not invariably be the case. "[N]ot every mixture with the true will neutralize the deceptive. If it would take a financial analyst to spot the tension between the one and the other, whatever is misleading will remain materially so, and liability should follow." [Virginia Bankshares v. Sandberg, 501 U.S. 1083 (1991)]

c) **Statements of reasons and beliefs:** [§547] Knowingly false statements of reasons, opinions, or beliefs in a proxy statement—such as a knowingly false statement that the board believes a proposed transaction is fair—can be made the basis of liability under the proxy rules (including private actions), even though the statements are made in conclusory terms. [Virginia Bankshares, Inc. v. Sandberg, *supra*] Of course, the statements must be material, but statements concerning the views of the board on a proposed transaction will normally be material.

1/ **Qualification:** [§548] A knowingly false statement of reasons, opinions, or beliefs is actionable only when, in addition to being a false or misleading description of the true views of the person who makes the statement, the statement is objectively false or misleading. For example, if a proxy statement says that the board believes a proposed transaction to be fair, and the board does not have that subjective belief, but the transaction *is objectively fair*, the statement, although false, would not be actionable. The reason for this qualification is a concern that "to recognize liability on mere disbelief or undisclosed motive without any demonstration that the proxy statement was false or misleading about its subject could lead to strike suits and frivolous litigation."

a/ **Note:** This qualification on the basic holding of *Virginia Bankshares* is unlikely to have much practical significance, because it would be rare to find a case with evidence solely of disbelief or undisclosed motivation without further proof that the statement was defective as to its subject matter.

d) **Causation:** [§549] A false or misleading statement in a proxy statement will not give rise to a private action unless it is the cause of a shareholder vote that the proxy statement solicits. However, a showing of materiality satisfies the causation requirement. Accordingly, where a shareholder seeks to set aside or enjoin a transaction on the ground that shareholder approval was solicited by a proxy statement that involved misstatements or omissions, she need do nothing more to prove causation than to prove materiality. [Mills v. Electric Auto-Lite Co., *supra*, §545; Gaines v. Haughton, 645 F.2d 761 (9th Cir. 1981), *cert. denied*, 454 U.S. 1145 (1982)]

1/ **Where management or parent controls majority of stock:** [§550] If the management or a parent owns or controls a majority of the stock, so that it can cause shareholder approval of the relevant transaction without any votes from the minority, false or misleading statements in a proxy statement will not normally give rise to liability in a private action by the minority shareholders. The theory is that the false statements could not have caused a loss to the minority, because the transaction would have been approved even without their votes. [Virginia Bankshares, Inc. v. Sandberg, *supra*, §547]

a/ **Exception:** [§551] In the *Virginia Bankshares* case, *supra*, the Supreme Court left open whether minority shareholders would have a cause of action, when their votes were not necessary for a transaction, if the false or misleading statements in the proxy statement led the minority shareholders to lose a state remedy (*e.g.*, led them to forgo the exercise of appraisal rights). In *Wilson v. Great American Industries, Inc.*, 979 F.2d 924 (2d Cir. 1992), the court held that minority shareholders did have a right of action in such cases. [*See also* Howing Co. v. Nationwide Corp., 972 F.2d 700 (6th Cir. 1992), *cert. denied*, 113 S. Ct. 1645 (1993)]

e) **Standing:** [§552] Even a shareholder who did not grant a proxy on the basis of a misleading solicitation has standing to challenge the solicitation. The injury that a shareholder suffers from corporate action pursuant to a deceptive proxy solicitation flows from the damage done to the corporation, rather than from the damage inflicted directly upon the shareholder. The damage suffered results not from the deceit practiced on the shareholder alone, but rather from the deceit practiced on the shareholders as a group. [Cowin v. Bresler, 741 F.2d 410 (D.C. Cir. 1984); Stahl v. Gibralter Financial Corp., 967 F.2d 335 (9th Cir. 1992)]

f) **Fault required:** [§553] Under rule 10b-5, scienter is required, so that mere negligence will not suffice as the basis of a private action to impose liability. [Ernst & Ernst v. Hochfelder, *supra*, §346] It is unclear whether mere negligence is sufficient to impose liability in an action for violation of the proxy rules. In *Shidler v. All American Life & Financial Corp.*, 775 F.2d 917 (8th Cir. 1985), the Eighth Circuit held that the plaintiff in a private action under section 14(a) had to establish **some fault**—*i.e.*, section 14(a) does not create strict liability for misrepresentations or misleading statements. In *Gould v. American-Hawaiian Steamship Co.*, 535 F.2d 761 (3d Cir. 1976), the Third Circuit held that negligence is sufficient, on the ground that the language of section 14(a) of the 1934 Act does not suggest a scienter requirement. [*See also* Gerstle v. Gamble-Skogmo, Inc., 478 F.2d 1281 (2d Cir. 1973)] However, in *Adams v. Standard Knitting Mills, Inc.,* 623 F.2d 422 (6th Cir. 1980), the Sixth Circuit held that scienter must be established in a suit against accountants under rule 14a-9, and strongly intimated that it would apply a scienter requirement in all rule 14a-9 suits.

g) **Fairness no defense:** [§554] A materially misleading solicitation entitles the complainant to relief regardless of whether the matter acted upon was fair to the corporation and its shareholders. Otherwise, a judicial finding of fairness could be used to bypass the shareholders' right to make an informed choice after full disclosure. [Mills v. Electric Auto-Lite Co. *supra*, §549]

h) **Nature of relief available:** [§555] The federal courts are empowered to award whatever relief will effectuate the purposes of the statute, which may include both prospective and retroactive remedies. [J.I. Case Co. v. Borak, *supra*, §544]

1/ **Rescission:** [§556] If necessary and otherwise equitable, a court may rescind an action that was approved by the shareholders as a result of a misleading proxy solicitation (*e.g.*, by setting aside a corporate merger). [J.I. Case Co. v. Borak, *supra*]

2/ **Monetary damages:** [§557] Monetary damages are also recoverable if they can be shown. [Mills v. Electric Auto-Lite Co., *supra*]

(h) **Jurisdiction:** [§558] Federal courts have exclusive jurisdiction in any suit for violation of the proxy rules. Any related claim for violation of state law may be joined with the federal claim under the doctrine of pendent jurisdiction.

e. **Expenses incurred in proxy contest:** [§559] Since the expenses involved in a large-scale proxy fight may be enormous, the question of whether corporate funds may be used to reimburse those expenses is extremely important.

(1) **Reimbursement of management's expenses:** [§560] The corporation may properly pay the normal expense of preparing and soliciting proxies to obtain a quorum for the annual meeting. In the event of a proxy contest, the corporation may also properly reimburse reasonable amounts expended by management, as long as the matter in controversy is one of corporate policy, rather than one of personnel (*i.e.*, one in which management seeks simply to retain its office). [Steinberg v. Adams, 90 F. Supp. 604 (S.D.N.Y. 1950)] Management may use corporate funds to fully inform the shareholders concerning the relevant issues and to protect the corporation against a "raid" by wealthy insurgents. [Rosenfeld v. Fairchild Engine & Airplane Corp., 309 N.Y. 168 (1955); 51 A.L.R.2d 860]

(2) **Insurgents' expenses:** [§561] Unlike management, insurgents do not have a right to reimbursement of their proxy expenses, even if they win. However, the corporation can voluntarily reimburse the reasonable expenses of insurgents who win a proxy contest involving policy (rather than personnel), on the ground that they have conferred a benefit on the corporation, at least if the shareholders ratify the reimbursement. [Rosenfeld v. Fairchild Engine & Airplane Corp., *supra*]

5. **Other Methods to Combine Votes for Control—Close Corporations:** [§562] Various voting devices may be used by shareholders (particularly in close corporations) to assure control of corporate policies.

    a. **Shareholder voting agreements:** [§563] Shareholders (often those owning a majority of the stock) may agree with other shareholders to vote in a specified way for a specified period of time. They may agree for a variety of reasons—*e.g.*, as a condition of the other shareholders investing in the corporation. Such agreements usually concern voting for the election of certain directors, but may also cover other matters subject to shareholder vote (amendment of the articles, dissolution, etc.).

        (1) **Pooling agreements:** [§564] A "pooling agreement" is a particular kind of voting agreement whereby shareholders (none of whom usually owns a majority of the stock) agree to vote their shares together in a specified way (or as the majority of them decides) for a specified period.

        (2) **Validity of shareholder voting agreements:** [§565] Early cases often refused to enforce shareholder voting agreements (particularly if all shareholders were not parties thereto), on the ground that shareholders could not irrevocably separate their voting rights from their ownership rights. However, shareholder voting agreements are generally upheld today, as long as they are made for a proper purpose and work no fraud upon creditors or other stockholders. [E.K. Buck Retail Stores v. Harkert, 62 N.W.2d 288 (Neb. 1954)]

            (a) **Purpose of agreement:** [§566] Shareholders generally may vote their shares as they please, and are permitted to combine their votes to serve certain of their own purposes, *e.g.*, to elect themselves as directors.

            (b) **Consideration:** [§567] Pooling agreements have sometimes been challenged for lack of consideration. [Roberts v. Whitson, 188 S.W.2d 875 (Tex. 1945)] Most courts, however, find sufficient consideration in the shareholders' exchange of mutual promises to vote their shares in a specified way.

                1) **Compare:** Alternatively, pooling agreements have been upheld on the theory that the combining of votes for control gives each shareholder a sufficient "interest" in the shares of the other that their agreement is enforceable as a grant of an *irrevocable proxy* (*supra*, §§515-518). [Abercrombie v. Davies, 130 A.2d 338 (Del. 1957)]

            (c) **Statutory authority:** [§568] Statutes today frequently authorize shareholders to enter into agreements respecting the voting of their shares. [Cal. Corp. Code §706(a)—applicable to close corporations only; N.Y. Bus. Corp. Law §620(a)] Some statutes limit the duration of such agreements. [Del. Gen. Corp. Law §218(c)—10 years, unless renewed]

            (d) **Agreements limited to shareholder action:** [§569] The agreements under discussion concern only shareholder action (*e.g.*, voting for directors, amendment of articles, etc.). The validity of shareholder agreements insofar as they seek to bind the parties in voting as directors is considered below (*see infra*, §§576-581).

(3) **Self-executing agreements:** [§570]   Sometimes, the parties to a pooling agreement may attempt to make it "self-executing" by requiring each shareholder to execute and deposit a *proxy* with an agent to vote the shares.

   (a) **But note:** This self-executing plan may not work if any of the shareholders decides to revoke her proxy. Even though she may have expressly agreed not to revoke, her proxy may be held revocable because it is not coupled with "an interest." (Some courts have not regarded a pooling agreement as creating a sufficient "interest" in each other's shares to render the proxy irrevocable [*In re* Chilson, *supra,* §516], but this approach has been modified by statute in a number of states (*see supra*, §517).) Consequently, the other shareholders will have to sue for enforcement of the pooling agreement; they cannot rely on the proxy.

   (b) **And note:** Even where the proxies are held irrevocable, the self-executing arrangement may be viewed as a *voting trust*, in which event it must comply with special requirements (below). [Abercrombie v. Davies, *supra*, §567] Statutes in some states will prevent this result. [*See, e.g.,* Cal. Corp. Code §706(c)—shareholders' voting agreements shall not constitute voting trusts]

(4) **Remedy for breach:** [§571]   If the voting agreement is enforceable, the remedy usually sought in the event of breach is *specific performance*, *i.e.*, a court order compelling the shareholder to vote her shares as agreed. Equitable relief would appear to be justified on the ground that the legal remedy (damages) is usually inadequate.

   (a) **Statutes:** [§572]   Some statutes expressly authorize specific performance of shareholder voting agreements [*See, e.g.,* Cal. Corp. Code §706(a)]

   (b) **When fewer than all shareholders participate:** [§573]   Absent statutory authorization, however, some courts have refrained from granting specific performance of pooling agreements to which *fewer than all* of the shareholders were parties. [Ringling Bros.-Barnum & Bailey Combined Shows, Inc. v. Ringling, 53 A.2d 441 (Del. 1947); *but see* Weil v. Berseth, 220 A.2d 456 (Conn. 1966)—contra]

b. **Agreements requiring greater-than-majority approval:** [§574]   Minority shareholders in a close corporation may seek to achieve a certain degree of control (or, more precisely, a veto power) by obtaining the agreement of the other shareholders (in a contract, or through a charter or bylaw provision) that no shareholder action may be taken without a unanimous (or some percentage greater than majority) vote.

   (1) **Modern trend:** [§575]   The modern trend of judicial decisions permits such devices. [*See, e.g.,* Katcher v. Ohsman, 97 A.2d 180 (N.J. 1953)]

Many statutes now expressly authorize greater-than-majority voting requirements if provided for in the articles of incorporation. [N.Y. Bus. Corp. Law §616—*reversing* Benintendi v. Kenton Hotel, Inc., 294 N.Y. 112 (1945); RMBCA §7.27]

c. **Shareholder agreements binding votes as directors:** [§576] In addition to agreeing how they will vote as shareholders, the shareholders of a close corporation may seek to control more detailed matters of corporate policy, *e.g.*, who will be the corporate officers, what will be the salaries, how much will be paid in dividends. These are "management" questions, traditionally committed to the board of directors (*supra,* §159).

(1) **Less-than-unanimous agreements:** [§577] When fewer than all the shareholders are parties to agreements seeking to bind the directors, most courts have held them ***unenforceable***, reasoning that corporate directors are charged with fiduciary duties to the corporation and any agreement that seeks to restrict or limit their actions as directors is therefore void. It is contrary to public policy to have "passive board." [McQuade v. Stoneham & McGraw, *supra,* §171]

   (a) **But note:** Some more recent decisions, recognizing the special nature and needs of close corporations, have upheld such non-unanimous agreements—at least where no nonparty shareholder claimed prejudice to herself as a result. [Galler v. Galler, *supra,* §172; Glazer v. Glazer, 374 F.2d 390 (5th Cir. 1967)]

(2) **Unanimous agreements:** [§578] When all the shareholders are parties to such agreements, courts have been quicker to uphold them—at least when no damage to creditors or the public has been shown. [Clark v. Dodge, *supra,* §171] But even unanimous agreements have been held unenforceable if they involve "substantial impingements" on the discretion of the board. [Long Park, Inc. v. Trenton-New Brunswick Theatres Co., *supra,* §171]

(3) **Statutes:** [§579] In recent years, a number of special statutes applicable to close corporations have validated shareholder agreements that bind the discretion of directors. Some require that such agreements be unanimous [N.Y. Bus. Corp. Law §620(b)], while others do not [Del. Gen. Corp. Law §§350, 354].

   (a) **Notice:** [§580] A number of these statutes require that these agreements be included in a provision of the articles of incorporation. [*See, e.g.*, N.Y. Bus. Corp. Law §620(b)] Some go further and require that the provision be noted conspicuously on all share certificates. [N.Y. Bus. Corp. Law §620(g)]

      1) **Estoppel:** [§581] It has been held that a shareholder who promised, but failed, to fulfill these statutory requirements is estopped from denying the validity of a shareholder agreement to which he was a party. [Zion v. Kurtz, 50 N.Y.2d 92 (1980)]

d. **Voting trusts:** [§582] A voting trust is another device employed by shareholders to assure control. Each shareholder transfers ***legal title*** of her shares to a trustee, in return for a transferable "voting trust certificate" that evidences her equitable ownership of the shares involved and carries the right to dividends and other distributions of assets. Since the right to vote follows legal title, the trustee has the voting right for the shares involved for the life of the trust.

(1) **Formalities:** [§583] Statutes in most states require such trust agreements to be in writing, filed with the corporation, and open to inspection by all shareholders and owners of voting trust certificates. [Del. Gen. Corp. Law §218(a)]

    (a) **Failure to comply with statutory requirements:** [§584] Although some courts have invalidated voting trusts that do not comply with the statute, others have nonetheless enforced voting trust agreements when the policy of the voting trust statute has been fulfilled. [Oceanic Exploration Co. v. Grynberg, 428 A.2d 1 (Del. 1980)—all shareholders had notice of voting trust agreement even though it was not filed with corporation]

(2) **Duration:** [§585] Statutes generally limit the period for which such trusts may be created (the usual term being 10 years). However, voting trusts set up for a longer term are valid for whatever period is authorized by the statute. [RMBCA §7.30(b)]

    (a) **Extensions:** [§586] Some statutes permit a voting trust to be extended for additional terms—usually on condition that only the assenting shareholders shall be so bound. [RMBCA §7.30(c)]

(3) **Authority of voting trustees:** [§587] The scope of the trustees' authority to vote depends on the terms of the voting trust agreement. This almost always extends to voting for the election of directors. But absent explicit authority in the voting trust agreement, most courts hesitate to allow the trustees to vote on such extraordinary matters as sale of all the corporation's assets, dissolution of the corporation, or termination or extension of the voting trust. [Brown v. McLanahan, 148 F.2d 703 (4th Cir. 1945); *compare* Clarke Memorial College v. Monaghan Land Co., 257 A.2d 234 (Del. 1969)]

    (a) **Fiduciary duty:** [§588] In any event, voting trustees are held to a fiduciary duty to the beneficiaries of the trust in exercising their authority. [Brown v. McLanahan, *supra*]

(4) **Rights of holder of voting trust certificate:** [§589] Other than voting, the shareholder's rights generally remain intact. The shareholder is still entitled to receive dividends, inspect corporate records, etc., and even bring a representative suit (*infra*).

B.   RESTRICTIONS ON TRANSFER OF SHARES

1.   **Restrictions Imposed by Articles, Bylaws, or Shareholder Agreement:** [§590] Stock transfer restrictions are frequently used in close corporations to limit the total number of shareholders (often to enable the corporation to retain statutory benefits

as a "close corporation"; *see supra*, §§172-175), to prevent the entry of unwanted shareholders, or to avoid a major shift in control. Larger corporations on occasion may also limit the transferability of a certain class of shares—*e.g.*, to restrict ownership to a certain group, such as employees. Usually, stock transfer restrictions will be in the corporation's articles or bylaws. Sometimes, however, they are contained in a separate agreement among the shareholders.

a. **Types of restrictions:** [§591]   The two most common types of restrictions on transferability of shares are the right of first refusal and the mandatory buy-sell provision.

    (1) **Right of first refusal:** [§592]   A right of first refusal is a provision giving the corporation or the other shareholders (or both) a first option to buy the stock before any shareholder may sell or otherwise transfer shares to a third party.

    (2) **Mandatory buy-sell:** [§593]   A mandatory buy-sell provision stipulates that on the occurrence of a designated event (*e.g.*, death of a shareholder, termination of employment), the corporation or surviving shareholders *must* buy the stock, and the shareholder (or the shareholder's estate) *must* sell to the corporation or other shareholders.

b. **Validity of restrictions**

    (1) **Common law—reasonableness requirement:** [§594]   The right to transfer is deemed an inherent right of property ownership, and at common law total restraints or effective prohibitions on the transferability of shares were usually held invalid. To be valid at common law, a restriction on transfer must be "reasonable" in view of the needs of the particular corporation and shareholders involved. [Allen v. Biltmore Tissue Corp., 2 N.Y.2d 534 (1957)]

        (a) **"Consent" restrictions:** [§595]   Thus, at common law, a provision that "these shares are nontransferable," or "nontransferable without the consent of each other shareholder," was usually held invalid as unreasonable restraints on alienation. [Rafe v. Hindin, 29 A.D.2d 481 (1968)]

           1) **Special circumstances:** [§596]   Provisions requiring the consent of other shareholders or directors may be upheld under special circumstances. [Penthouse Properties, Inc. v. 1158 Fifth Ave., Inc., 256 A.D. 685 (1939)—corporation owned cooperative apartment house in which shareholders were tenants; restriction requiring shareholders' consent to stock transfer upheld because right of occupancy went with it]

           2) **Modern decisions:** [§597]   Some recent decisions have shown a greater tolerance for consent restrictions and upheld them when not an unreasonable method of limiting corporate control to particular individuals. [Gray v. Harris Land & Cattle Co., 737 P.2d 475 (Mont. 1987)]

(b) **Restrictions as to whom shares may be transferred:** [§598] Restrictions limiting the type of persons to whom the shares may be transferred will be upheld if the restriction is reasonable under the circumstances (*e.g.*, provisions against selling shares to persons engaged in businesses that compete with the corporation).

(c) **Right of first refusal:** [§599] A right of first refusal (option) for a limited period of time in favor of the corporation or other shareholders (or both) will almost always be upheld as a reasonable restraint. (*Example*: "No sale of these shares to a nonshareholder shall be made until the holder first offers them to the corporation on the same terms and conditions as offered to the nonshareholder; and the corporation shall have 30 days thereafter within which to purchase same on such terms.")

(d) **Options to purchase:** [§600] Similarly, provisions giving the corporation an option to purchase the shares in question at a fixed price or book value are usually upheld—even where the shares are now worth much more than the price. More than a large disparity between the option price and current market value must be shown to render an option agreement unreasonable. [Evangelista v. Holland, 537 N.E.2d 589 (Mass. 1989); Concord Auto Auction, Inc. v. Rustin, 627 F. Supp. 1526 (D. Mass. 1986)]

1) **Termination of employment:** [§601] Contractual provisions giving the corporation the right to repurchase the shares of an employee at a designated price upon termination of employment "at-will" have been enforced—even when the purpose for the firing was to acquire the stock at a low price. *Rationale:* Employees who agree both (i) to their being fired at will and (ii) to a particular buy-back formula are held to their bargain. [Ingle v. Glamore Motor Sales, 73 N.Y.2d 183 (1989)]

a) **But note:** Other courts have reasoned that employment at will may *not* be terminated for "any reason at all." The contractual relation implies that the employee will not be fired for *opportunistic* reasons rather than for reasons related to job performance. [Jordan v. Duff & Phelps, Inc., 815 F.2d 429 (7th Cir. 1987)]

(2) **Statutes:** [§602] Today, a large number of states have statutes dealing with the validity of stock transfer restrictions.

(a) **"Reasonable" restrictions:** [§603] Some statutes simply codify the common law, authorizing "reasonable" restrictions on the transfer of shares. [Cal. Corp. Code §204(b)]

(b) **Detailed restrictions:** [§604] Others deal with such restrictions in more detail. For example, the Delaware statute authorizes the following types of stock transfer restrictions, which may appear in the articles, bylaws, or separate shareholder agreements: (i) provisions giving the corporation or other shareholders a right of first refusal for a reasonable time; (ii) provisions giving the corporation or other shareholders the right to consent to a proposed transfer; (iii) mandatory buy-sell provisions; (iv) restrictions on transfer to designated classes of persons "unless manifestly unreasonable"; and (v) "any other lawful restriction on transfer." [Del. Gen. Corp. Law §202]

1) **And note:** Even if the stock transfer restriction is held not to be authorized by statute, the corporation nevertheless is given the *option* to acquire whenever shares are sought to be transferred at a "fair price" to be determined by agreement of the parties or by the court. [Del. Gen. Corp. Law §349]

(3) **Limitation—proper fund available for repurchase:** [§605]   Even if the stock transfer restriction is otherwise valid, where the corporation seeks to repurchase its own shares pursuant to such restriction, most states require that the corporation have available funds from a proper source (*e.g.*, surplus) with which to make the repurchase (*see infra*, §§983-986). [Van Kampen v. Detroit Bank & Trust Co., 199 N.W.2d 470 (Mich. 1972); *but see* Lewis v. Powell, 203 So. 2d 504 (Fla. 1967)—contra]

c. **Shares subject to restriction**

(1) **Common law:** [§606]   Courts at common law have split on whether stock transfer restrictions can be enforced with respect to shares *already issued* at the time the restrictions were adopted. Some hold that the corporation has the power, through amendment of its articles or bylaws (*see infra*, §§1068 *et seq.*), to alter existing shareholder rights—even where the shareholder neither knew nor consented to the restriction. [Tu-Vu Drive-In Corp. v. Ashkins, 61 Cal. 2d 283 (1964); *but see* B&H Warehouse, Inc. v. Atlas Van Lines, Inc., 490 F.2d 818 (5th Cir. 1974)—contra]

(a) **Removal of restriction:** [§607]   There is a similar split on whether stock transfer restrictions can be removed over the objection of dissenting stockholders. [Silva v. Coastal Plywood & Timber Co., 124 Cal. App. 2d 276 (1954)—upholding bylaw retroactively removing stock transfer restrictions; *but see* Bechtold v. Coleman Realty Co., 79 A.2d 661 (Pa. 1951)—contra]

(2) **Statutes:** [§608]   Some modern statutes provide that stock transfer restrictions can be enforced only against shares issued *subsequent* to adoption of the restriction. Such restrictions cannot be enforced against the transfer of shares already issued, unless the owner consents. [Cal. Corp. Code §204(b); Del. Gen. Corp. Law §202(b)]

d. **Transactions subject to restriction:** [§609]   Since restrictions on alienation of property are disfavored as a matter of public policy, stock transfer restrictions may be *strictly construed*. Provisions that contain only general restraints (*e.g.*, covering "all sales or transfers") are often interpreted as applying only to *voluntary* sales. Therefore, in the absence of specific language, the restriction may be held inapplicable to transfers on death [Vogel v. Melish, 196 N.E.2d

402 (Ill. 1964)], to a sale of shares in bankruptcy, or to pledges of shares as security for loan (no transfer of title).

e. **Notice requirement:** [§610]   Unless "noted conspicuously" on the ***certificate itself***, a lawful stock transfer restriction is of no effect against a person who otherwise had no knowledge of the restriction at the time of transfer. [RMBCA §6.27(b); U.C.C. §8-204]

(1) **Actual knowledge:** [§611]   This applies, of course, only to "innocent" persons. One who has ***actual*** knowledge of a stock transfer restriction is bound by it, even if it is not "conspicuously noted" on the face of the certificate. [RMBCA §6.27(b); U.C.C. §8-204]

(2) **"Noted conspicuously":** [§612]   The requirement that the restriction be "noted conspicuously" on the certificate means only that it reasonably appear from the face of the certificate that the shares are subject to some sort of transfer restriction. The restriction itself need not be set forth in full text. [Ling & Co. v. Trinity Savings & Loan Association, 482 S.W.2d 841 (Tex. 1972)]

(3) **"Innocent" transferee:** [§613]   Without such notice, an innocent transferee of the certificate (whether a donee or purchaser) is entitled to have the shares transferred into his name on the books of the corporation and thereafter to receive dividends, vote the shares, etc. Moreover, he takes free and clear of the stock transfer restriction—so he can thereafter resell his shares to another without regard to the restriction.

C. SHAREHOLDERS' INFORMATIONAL RIGHTS

1. **Types of Books and Records:** [§614]   The books and records of a corporation fall into several basic categories—shareholder lists; minutes of board meetings, shareholders' meetings, board committees, and officer committees; financial records, such as books of account and monthly, quarterly, and annual period summaries; and business documents, such as contracts, correspondence, and office memoranda.

2. **Common Law:** [§615]   At common law, a shareholder acting for a proper purpose has a right to "inspect" (examine) the corporate books and records at reasonable times. The shareholder has the burden of alleging and proving a proper purpose for inspection. [Albee v. Lamson & Hubbard Corp., 69 N.E.2d 811 (Mass. 1946)]

3. **Statutes:** [§616]   In most states today, shareholder inspection rights are granted by statutes. Many of these statutes apply only to certain kinds of shareholders, such as those who are record holders of at least 5% of the corporation's stock, or who have been record holders for at least six months. [N.Y. Bus. Corp. Law §624] The statutes are normally interpreted to preserve the proper-purpose test, but to place on the corporation the burden of proving that the shareholder's purpose is improper. [Crane Co. v. Anaconda Co., 39 N.Y.2d 14 (1976)] Those statutes that are limited to only certain kinds of shareholders, or only certain books and records, are usually interpreted to supplement the common law, so that a suit for inspection that does not fall within the statute can still be brought under the common law. [Tucson Gas & Electric Co. v. Schantz, 428 P.2d 686 (Ariz. 1967); *but see* Caspary v. Louisiana Land & Exploration Co., 707 F.2d 785 (4th Cir. 1983)]

a. **Kind of books and records sought:** [§617]   The burden of proof under a statute may be affected by the kind of books and records that are sought. For example, the Delaware statute provides that where inspection is sought of shareholder lists, the burden is on the corporation to prove that the information is being sought for an improper purpose. For other corporate records, the burden is on the shareholder to prove proper purpose. [Del. Gen. Corp. Law §220(c)]

4. **Proper vs. Improper Purposes:** [§618]   In determining what constitutes a proper or improper purpose, the basic test is whether the shareholder is seeking inspection to protect her interest as a shareholder, or instead is acting for a non-shareholder purpose, such as furthering her interest as a potential business rival or as a litigant on a personal, non-shareholder claim. [Rosentool v. Bonanza Oil & Mine Corp., 352 P.2d 138 (Or. 1960)]

a. **Recognized purposes:** [§619]   Among the purposes the courts have recognized as **proper** for exercising the inspection right are the following: (i) to determine whether the corporation is being properly managed or whether there has been managerial misconduct, at least if the shareholder alleges some specific concerns [Skouras v. Admiralty Enterprises, Inc., 386 A.2d 674 (Del. 1978)]; (ii) to determine the corporation's financial condition [Riser v. Genuine Parts Co., 258 S.E.2d 184 (Ga. 1979)]; and (iii) to determine the value of the shareholder's stock [Friedman v. Altoona Pipe & Steel Supply Co., 460 F.2d 1212 (3d Cir. 1972)].

b. **Multiple purposes:** [§620]   As long as the primary purpose is a proper one, the fact that the shareholder has an improper secondary purpose usually will not defeat the claim. [General Time Corp. v. Talley Industries, 240 A.2d 755 (Del. 1968)]

c. **Inspection of shareholders list:** [§621]   Most courts are reluctant to deny a shareholder access to the shareholders list, because such access is often vital to the exercise of other shareholder rights and will seldom if ever harm the corporation through disclosure of business secrets.

(1) **Proxy fights:** [§622]   Inspection of a shareholders list to enable a shareholder to make a takeover bid or engage in a proxy contest with management is normally considered a proper purpose, because it is reasonably related to the interest of the shareholder.

(2) **Shareholder litigation:** [§623]   Similarly, it is a proper purpose to inspect the shareholders list as a means to seek the solicitation of other shareholders to participate in shareholder litigation against management or even the corporation. [Compaq Computer Corp. v. Horton, 631 A.2d 1 (Del. 1993)]

(3) **Social or political interests:** [§624]   In *State ex rel. Pillsbury v. Honeywell, Inc.*, 191 N.W.2d 406 (Minn. 1971), Pillsbury was a shareholder of Honeywell, Inc. Pillsbury opposed the Vietnam war, and asked Honeywell to produce its shareholder ledger and all corporate records dealing with weapons and munitions manufacture. Pillsbury admitted that his sole motive in purchasing Honeywell stock was to persuade Honeywell

to cease producing munitions, but argued that the desire to communicate with fellow shareholders was per se a proper purpose. Honeywell argued that a proper purpose contemplates a concern with investment return. The court held for Honeywell, finding that Pillsbury's motivation (to force Honeywell to cease production of bombs) was not a proper purpose germane to his economic interest as a shareholder.

(a) **Note:** The authority of *Honeywell* is questionable. *Honeywell* purported to apply Delaware law. However, in *Credit Bureau Reports, Inc. v. Credit Bureau of St. Paul, Inc.*, 290 A.2d 691 (Del. 1972), the Delaware Supreme Court repudiated the *Pillsbury* case insofar as it applied to requests for shareholders lists. The court reiterated its prior holding that, under the Delaware statute, the desire to solicit proxies for a slate of directors is reasonably related to the shareholder's interest as a shareholder and that any secondary purpose is irrelevant. The court went on to repudiate *Pillsbury* to the extent it is inconsistent with this holding. [*See* General Time Corp. v. Talley Industries, Inc., 240 A.2d 755 (Del. 1968); *and see* The Conservative Caucus Research, Analysis & Education Foundation, Inc. v. Chevron Corp., 525 A.2d 569 (Del. 1987)]

5. **Compare—Mandatory Disclosure of Information:** [§625] In contrast to the law governing the shareholder's inspection right, which puts the initiative on the individual shareholder, various federal and state statutes require corporations to make affirmative disclosure of certain information.

a. **Securities Exchange Act of 1934:** [§626] Extensive disclosure requirements are imposed on corporations whose stock is registered under section 12 of the Securities Exchange Act of 1934.

(1) **Reports:** [§627] Such corporations must file with the SEC, and any securities exchange on which the stock is listed, reports disclosing their financial condition and certain types of material events. These reports are open to inspection by the public. Under section 13 of the Act, and the rules promulgated thereunder, such corporations must file a Form 10-K annually, a Form 10-Q quarterly, and a Form 8-K within 15 days after the occurrence of certain specified events.

(a) **Information included:** [§628] The Form 10-K must include audited financial statements; management's discussion of the corporation's financial condition and results of operations; and disclosure concerning legal proceedings, developments in the corporation's business, executive compensation, conflict-of-interest transactions, and other specified issues. The Form 10-Q must include quarterly financial data prepared in accordance with generally accepted accounting principles; a management report; and disclosure concerning legal proceedings, defaults on senior securities, and other specified issues. Among the matters that trigger an 8-K report are a change in control of the corporation, the acquisition or disposition of a significant amount of assets, and a change of accountants.

(2) **Proxy rules:** [§629] Under the proxy rules (*supra*, §§521-558), corporations whose stock is registered under section 12 must annually disclose

certain information to shareholders, such as the compensation of the chief executive officer, and the four most highly compensated officers other than the CEO unless the compensation of such officer is less than $100,000, details on the operation of stock option and pension plans, and transactions with insiders during the previous year involving amounts in excess of $60,000.

b. **State statutes:** [§630]   State laws vary greatly as to the amount of information that must be provided by corporations incorporated in the jurisdiction.

    (1) **Report to state:** [§631]   Most states require corporations incorporated in the jurisdiction to file an annual report with an appropriate state officer, such as the secretary of state, providing at least certain minimal information, *e.g.*, the names and addresses of its directors and officers, the address of its principal business office, its principal business activity, and the name and address of its agent for the service of process upon the corporation. [RMBCA §16.22]

    (2) **Report to shareholders:** [§632]   In addition, some states require corporations to send an annual report to shareholders containing financial statements. For example, under the Model Act, a corporation must furnish its shareholders with annual financial statements that include a balance sheet, an income statement, and a statement of changes in shareholders' equity. If financial statements are prepared for the corporation on the basis of generally accepted accounting principles, the annual financial statements furnished to the shareholders must also be prepared on that basis. If the annual financial statements are reported upon by a public accountant, the accountant's report must accompany them. If not, the statements must be accompanied by a statement of the president or the person responsible for the corporation's accounting records: (i) stating his reasonable belief whether the statements were prepared on the basis of generally accepted accounting principles and, if not, describing the basis of preparation; and (ii) describing any respects in which the statements were not prepared on the basis of accounting consistent with the statements prepared for the preceding year.

D. FIDUCIARY OBLIGATIONS OF CONTROLLING SHAREHOLDERS

1. **Introduction:** [§633]   Where a controlling shareholder serves as a director or officer, he owes fiduciary obligations to the corporation in those capacities. Even where a controlling shareholder does not serve as a director or officer, he may owe fiduciary obligations to the minority shareholders in exercising his control. A controlling shareholder must refrain from using his control to obtain a special advantage, or to cause the corporation to take an action that unfairly prejudices the minority shareholders. [Pepper v. Litton, 308 U.S. 295 (1930)]

    a. **Business dealings with corporation:** [§634]   Although a controlling majority shareholder may validly contract with the corporation, he cannot exploit the corporation at the expense of the minority. Thus, if the contract is unfair—as where the price terms are not those that would be set in an arm's-length bargain—the controlling shareholder has breached his fiduciary obligation to the minority. [Sinclair Oil Corp. v. Levien, *supra*, §295]

(1) **Parent-subsidiary dealings:** [§635]   The most common cases in which there are dealings between a controlling shareholder and a corporation are those in which the controlling shareholder is a parent and the corporation is a subsidiary with minority ownership. [Sinclair Oil Co. v. Levien, *supra*]

(2) **Burden of proof:** [§636]   When a transaction between a corporation and its controlling shareholder is challenged, as in a derivative suit by minority shareholders, the burden is on the controlling shareholder to prove the transaction's fairness. [Sinclair Oil Corp. v. Levien, *supra*]

(3) **A.L.I. test:** [§637]   The A.L.I.'s Principles of Corporate Governance provide that a controlling shareholder who enters into a transaction with the corporation fulfills the duty of fair dealing to the corporation with respect to the transaction if:

    (i)   The transaction is *fair* to the corporation when entered into; or

    (ii) The transaction is *authorized in advance or ratified* by disinterested shareholders, following disclosure concerning the conflict of interest and the transaction, and does not constitute a waste of corporate assets at the time of the shareholder action.

[A.L.I. Prin. Corp. Gov. §5.10]

    (a) **Burden of proof—general rule:** [§638]   If the transaction was authorized in advance by disinterested directors, or authorized in advance or ratified by disinterested shareholders following disclosure, the party challenging the transaction has the burden of proof. The party challenging the transaction also has the burden of proof if the transaction was ratified by disinterested directors and the failure to obtain advance authorization did not adversely affect the interests of the corporation in a significant way. If the transaction was not so authorized or ratified, the controlling shareholder has the burden of proof, except as provided below. [A.L.I. Prin. Corp. Gov. §5.10]

    (b) **Transactions in the ordinary course of business:** [§639]   If a transaction between a controlling shareholder and the corporation was in the ordinary course of the corporation's business, a party who challenges the transaction has the burden of coming forward with evidence that the transaction was unfair, whether or not the transaction was authorized in advance or ratified by disinterested directors or disinterested shareholders. [A.L.I. Prin. Corp. Gov. §5.10]

b. **Corporate opportunities:** [§640]   A controlling shareholder is subject to the corporate opportunity doctrine. However, the rules that apply to a controlling shareholder in this respect are not as strict as the rules that apply to directors and officers, because controlling shareholders are typically themselves corporations engaged in business and seeking new opportunities.

(1) **A.L.I. approach:** [§641]   The Principles of Corporate Governance provide that a controlling shareholder may not take advantage of a corporate opportunity unless:

      (i)   The taking of the opportunity is *fair* to the corporation; or

     (ii)   The taking of the opportunity is ***authorized in advance or ratified by disinterested shareholders***, following disclosure of the conflict of interest and the corporate opportunity, provided the taking of the opportunity is not equivalent to a waste of corporate assets.

[A.L.I. Prin. Corp. Gov. §5.12]

    (a) **A.L.I. definition of a corporate opportunity:** [§642]   The A.L.I. defines "corporate opportunity" in the controlling shareholder context as any opportunity to engage in a business activity that:

      (i)   Is developed or received by the controlled corporation, or comes to the controlling shareholder primarily by virtue of its relationship to the corporation; or

     (ii)   Is held out to shareholders of the controlled corporation as being a type of business activity that is within the scope of the corporation's business and will not be within the scope of the controlling shareholder's business.

[A.L.I. Prin. Corp. Gov. §5.12]

  c. **Fundamental changes:** [§643]   A controlling shareholder also owes a duty of fairness in causing fundamental changes, such as mergers or amendments of the articles of incorporation, that may promote its own self-interest at the expense of the minority. (*See infra*, §§1107-1129.)

2. **Actions Entirely in Shareholder Capacity—No Corporate Action:** [§644]   The fiduciary obligations owed by a controlling shareholder may apply even where he does not cause the corporation to do anything, where an act he takes in his shareholder capacity benefits himself unduly at the expense of the minority shareholders. [Jones v. H.F. Ahmanson & Co., 1 Cal. 3d 93 (1969)]

  a. **Standard:** In any transaction in which control of the corporation is material, the controlling shareholders must act with "good faith and inherent fairness" toward the minority. [Jones v. H.F. Ahmanson & Co., *supra*]

  b. **Example:** There were relatively few shares of X Corp. outstanding, and they sold at a very high price. Accordingly, the marketability of the shares was highly impaired. The controlling shareholders transferred their shares to Holding Co., which they had formed. Holding Co. then "went public," which allowed the controlling shareholders to cash out part of their investment, and greatly increased the value and marketability of the remainder. In contrast, the minority shareholders in X were stuck with shares that were even less marketable than before. The controlling shareholders of X Corp. violated their fiduciary duties by engaging in a transaction that, with no business justification, increased the marketability of their own shares and decreased the marketability of the minority's shares, without affording the minority an opportunity to participate. [Jones v. H.F. Ahmanson & Co., *supra*]

3. **Obligations of Shareholders in Close Corporations:** [§645]   Shareholders in a close corporation owe each other an even stricter duty than controlling shareholders in publicly held corporations. It has been said that such shareholders owe each other the same duty of utmost good faith and loyalty that is owed by partners to each other. This duty is owed by all shareholders in a close corporation, majority and minority. [Donahue v. Rodd Electrotype Co., 328 N.E.2d 505 (Mass. 1975); Helms v. Duckworth, 249 F.2d 482 (D.C. Cir. 1957)]

    a. **Equal treatment doctrine:** [§646]   Several important cases have suggested that in a close corporation there must be equal treatment of all shareholders, or, at least, all shareholders must be afforded equal opportunities. Thus, in the *Donahue* case, *supra,* the court held that controlling shareholders of a close corporation who cause the corporation to acquire some of their shares must see that minority stockholders have an equal opportunity to sell a proportionate number of shares to the corporation at an identical price.

        (1) **"Equality":** [§647]   What constitutes "equality" for these purposes may not always be clear. In general, it is not unequal to treat actors differently if there is a legitimate differentiation between the actors upon which the different treatment is based. For example, shareholder-employees don't have to be offered the same salaries if one shareholder is a highly skilled executive and the other has no training in business.

        (2) **Minority view:** [§648]   In *Nixon v. Blackwell*, 626 A.2d 1366 (Del. 1993), the Delaware Supreme Court took a contrary view, holding that shareholders did not have to be treated equally for all purposes, and in particular that different categories of shareholders in a close corporation did not have the right to be treated equally in terms of corporate arrangements affecting the liquidity of their stock.

    b. **Legitimate business purpose:** [§649]   The majority shareholders of a close corporation cannot sever a minority shareholder from the corporate payroll, or refuse to reelect him as a salaried officer and director, without a legitimate business purpose. [Wilkes v. Springside Nursing Home, Inc., 353 N.E.2d 657 (Mass. 1976)]

    c. **Obligation of minority shareholders:** [§650]   A minority shareholder in a close corporation cannot use a veto power unreasonably, as by refusing to vote for dividends when the accumulation of undistributed earnings will lead to a foreseeable tax penalty to the corporation. [Smith v. Atlantic Properties, Inc., 422 N.E.2d 798 (Mass. 1981)]

4. **Disclosure:** [§651]   A controlling shareholder must make full disclosure when dealing with the minority shareholders, as when making a tender offer for their shares [Lynch v. Vickers Energy Corp., *supra*, §520], or when causing the corporation to deal with minority shareholders, as when calling redeemable stock [Zahn v. Transamerica Corp., 162 F.2d 36 (3d Cir. 1947)].

5. **Sale of Control:** [§652]   Controlling shareholders may also owe fiduciary duties to other shareholders in transactions involving sale of controlling stock at a premium or the transfer of control in connection with a sale of their stock.

a. **General rule:** [§653]   The general rule is that a controlling shareholder has the right to sell his controlling stock at a premium; *i.e.*, for a price that is not available to other shareholders. [Zetlin v. Hanson Holdings, Inc., 48 N.Y.2d 684 (1979); Clagett v. Hutchison, 583 F.2d 1259 (4th Cir. 1978)] So, for example, a controlling shareholder can sell his stock at a premium over market, even though other shareholders are only able to sell at the market price.

(1) **Rationale:** [§654]   This rule reflects the fact that controlling stock normally sells at a higher price than noncontrolling stock, and serves a policy purpose by facilitating the transfer of control from less efficient to more efficient hands.

(2) **Equal opportunity doctrine:** [§655]   Some commentators have urged that where a purchaser offers to purchase control of a corporation at a premium, the controlling shareholders owe a fiduciary duty to provide all shareholders with an equal opportunity to participate; *i.e.*, the controlling shareholder must arrange that the offer be made to all shareholders on a pro rata basis. [78 Harv. L. Rev. 505]

(a) **Example:** Suppose S owns 51% of C Corp.'s stock. Under the equal opportunity doctrine, if a purchaser offers to buy S's 51% of C Corp.'s stock at a premium above market price, S could not sell his shares alone, but instead would be required to ask the minority shareholders if they wanted to participate in the 51% offer on a pro rata basis.

(b) **Comment:** There is little case support for this doctrine, and it has been specifically rejected in various cases.

(c) **A.L.I. rule:** [§656]   Under the A.L.I. Principles of Corporate Governance, a controlling shareholder has the same right to dispose of voting shares as any other shareholder, including the right to sell those shares for a price that is not made proportionally available to other shareholders. However, the controlling shareholder does not satisfy the duty of fair dealing to the other shareholders if:

(i) The controlling shareholder *does not make disclosure* concerning the transaction to other shareholders with whom the controlling shareholder deals in connection with the transaction; or

(ii) It is apparent from the circumstances that the *purchaser is likely to violate the duty of fair dealing* and obtain a significant financial benefit for the purchaser or an associate.

[A.L.I. Prin. Corp. Gov. §5.16]

(d) **Impact of *Jones v. H.F. Ahmanson & Co.*:** [§657]   In *Jones v. H.F. Ahmanson & Co., supra*, §644, the California Supreme Court held that controlling shareholders were under a duty to act toward minority shareholders with "good faith and inherent fairness . . . in any transaction in which control of the corporation is material." Although that case did not involve a sale of control, the theory on which it was decided could be extended to a sale of control. If so, it might be the equivalent of the equal opportunity doctrine. As of now, however, the doctrine has found little judicial acceptance in straight sale-of-controlling-stock cases.

b. **Exceptions:** [§658]   The general rule, that control can be sold at a premium, is subject to a number of exceptions in cases where there is something more than a straight sale of controlling stock at a premium.

(1) **Bare sale of office:** [§659]   While a sale of control stock at a premium is permissible, a bare sale of directorships or other corporate offices is invalid. Thus, a controlling shareholder cannot transfer control of the board for consideration if the transfer of control of the board is not simply incidental to a transfer of an amount of stock that is sufficient in itself to carry control. Accordingly, if a person (i) controls the board although he owns only a relatively small amount of stock, and (ii) transfers control of the board in connection with a sale of his stock at a premium (by seriatim resignations and simultaneous appointment of the purchaser's nominees), the appointment of the purchaser's nominees is voidable at the suit of a shareholder, and the seller must account for the premium. [Caplan v. Lionel Corp., 20 A.D.2d 301 (1969) *aff'd*, 14 N.Y.2d 679 (1964)—transfer of control of board in connection with sale of only 3% of outstanding shares held a wrongful "sale of office"]

(a) **Damages:** [§660]   In case of a bare sale of office, the amount that the controlling shareholders receive for "control" belongs to the corporation.

(b) **Exception:** [§661]   However, it is not improper for a selling shareholder to arrange for the resignations of existing officers and directors and the appointment of a new board chosen by the purchaser, as part of a sale of controlling stock, if the block of shares sold constitutes either a majority of the outstanding stock or an amount sufficiently large to carry control "as a practical certainty" (so that the purchaser could have forced the changes of office herself, even if the seller had not facilitated the change of office). [Essex Universal Corp. v. Yates, 305 F.2d 572 (2d Cir. 1969); 13 A.L.R.3d 361]

1) **Test:** [§662]   What constitutes control "as a practical certainty" is a question of fact. In a publicly held corporation, less than 51% will usually suffice; *i.e.*, large blocks of shares may carry voting control even though short of a majority. [*See* Essex Universal Corp. v. Yates, *supra*—indicating that 28% of outstanding shares of publicly held corporation may be sufficient]

(2) **Theory of corporate action:** [§663]   Suppose a prospective purchaser, P, wants to acquire complete control of the assets and business of a corporation, C, and proposes to make an offer to C *to buy C's assets*, or have C *merge* with a corporation that P controls. If C's controlling shareholders instead convince P to purchase just their stock, at a premium, the minority shareholders may assert that the controlling shareholders have diverted a corporate opportunity from C to themselves. This is the theory

of "corporate action." It has been successfully employed by minority shareholders in several cases. [Commonwealth Title Insurance & Trust Co. v. Seltzer, 76 A. 77 (Pa. 1910); Dunnett v. Arn, 71 F.2d 912 (10th Cir. 1934); Roby v. Dunnett, 88 F.2d 68 (10th Cir.), *cert. denied*, 301 U.S. 706 (1937)]

(a) **Comment:** The problem with this theory is that a controlling shareholder cannot be compelled to sell his shares at a price he does not accept. A knowledgeable controlling shareholder therefore might be able to avoid the application of this theory by (i) allowing P to make an offer to C, (ii) voting to reject the offer to C, and (iii) then waiting for an offer from P to purchase his controlling shares.

(3) **Sales involving fraud or nondisclosure:** [§664]   A controlling shareholder violates his fiduciary duty to the remaining shareholders if, as part of the sale of stock at a premium, he deals with minority shareholders without disclosing the terms of his sale.

(a) **Example:** In some cases, especially where the buyer wants more stock than the controlling shareholder owns, the premium paid to the controlling shareholder may depend upon the controlling shareholder convincing minority shareholders who are ignorant of the premium to sell their stock to the buyer at a price lower than that paid to the controlling shareholder.

(4) **Sale of control to transferee who plans to deal unfairly with corporation:** [§665]   Controlling shareholders breach their fiduciary duties to the minority shareholders if they transfer their controlling shares to a person or group whom they know or have reason to know will deal unfairly with the corporation.

(a) **Looting:** [§666]   The principal type of case in this category is a sale of controlling shares to a purchaser whom the controlling shareholder *knows or has reason to know* intends to loot the corporation. [Gerdes v. Reynolds, 28 N.Y.S.2d 622 (1941); Insuranshares Corp. v. Northern Fiscal Corp., 35 F. Supp. 22 (E.D. Pa. 1940)]

1) **Knowledge of purchaser's intent:** [§667]   Usually in such cases there is no question, by the time of the trial, that the purchaser did loot. The main problem is whether the controlling shareholder knew or had reason to know of the purchaser's intent at the time of the sale.

a) **Terms of sale may put controlling shareholder on inquiry:** [§668]   Typically, these cases concern a corporation whose assets are highly liquid (*e.g.*, investment companies whose assets consist of readily marketable securities). Since the value of the stock in such a corporation can be determined with a high degree of precision (because liquid assets are easy to value, and there is normally no goodwill attached to the business), payment of a premium significantly above the fair value of the shares may be enough to put the controlling shareholder on notice that the purchaser intends to recover the premium by looting the corporation's assets. [Gerdes v. Reynolds, *supra*, §666]

1/ **Example:** Bank held controlling shares in C Corp. Bank sold its shares to a purchaser whom Bank knew had a long history of business failures, outstanding fraud judgments, and no apparent assets with which to pay for the shares. Under such circumstances, it was reasonably foreseeable that the purchaser would be likely to loot C Corp., which he did. Bank's sale to such a purchaser was a breach of duty to C and the minority shareholders. [De Baun v. First Western Bank & Trust Co., 46 Cal. App. 3d 686 (1975)]

2) **No duty to investigate:** [§669] In the absence of some ground for suspicion, however, a seller of control stock generally does not have an affirmative obligation to investigate the purchaser's plans to determine whether looting or fraud is intended or likely. [Swinney v. Keebler Co., 480 F.2d 573 (4th Cir. 1973); Levy v. American Beverage Corp., 265 A.D. 208 (1942)]

3) **Damages:** [§670] Where the controlling shareholder knows or has reason to know that the purchaser plans to deal unfairly with the corporation, he is accountable to the minority shareholders for the premium he received (*i.e.*, the amount by which the purchase price exceeded the fair value of his stock) and for any damage caused to the corporation by the purchasers. [Gerdes v. Reynolds, *supra*, §668]

4) **Plans to deprive corporation of profits:** [§671] Even if the controlling shareholder has no reason to expect looting, he is accountable where he knows or has reason to know that the purchaser intends to use control to prevent the corporation from realizing profits it otherwise would have obtained.

a) **Example:** In *Perlman v. Feldmann*, 219 F.2d 173 (2d Cir. 1955), the controlling shareholder of a steel company sold his controlling shares to a group of steel consumers. Steel was in short supply, and the purchasers paid a premium for the control of stock in order to obtain the steel company's output at artificially low prices. The court held that the controlling shareholder had breached his fiduciary duties to the minority shareholders, and ordered him to account for that portion of the price that exceeded the fair value of his stock.

E. SHAREHOLDER SUITS

1. **Introduction:** [§672] Actions brought by shareholders fall into two categories: (i) a *direct action* on the shareholder's own behalf (or on behalf of a class of shareholders to which he belongs) for injury to his interest *as a shareholder*; or (ii) a *derivative suit* filed on *behalf of the corporation* for injury done to the corporation for which it has failed to sue.

2. **Direct (Individual) Suits:** [§673]   Where management has abridged a contractual or statutory duty owed directly *to the shareholder* as an individual (*e.g.*, directors refuse to permit shareholder inspection of corporate records), the shareholder may bring a suit on *his own behalf*—*i.e.*, a direct (or individual) suit.

   a. **Class action:** [§674]   If the alleged misconduct affects the rights of a number of shareholders, the suit may be maintained as a class action, in which case the individual shareholder sues as the *representative* of the class of shares that has been damaged. *Examples:* Management denies all shareholders preemptive rights in new stock issuance; or corporate insider fails to disclose material information when purchasing shares from a number of existing shareholders.

3. **Derivative Suits:** [§675]   If management (or a third party) has abridged a duty *owed to the corporation* (*e.g.*, officers loot the corporate treasury, or customer fails to pay for goods purchased from corporation), and the corporation fails to enforce its cause of action, a shareholder may bring a suit on behalf of the corporation—*i.e.*, a derivative suit.

   a. **Nature of action:** [§676]   The derivative suit is a creature of equity. It was conceived to permit a shareholder to redress injuries done directly to the corporation (injuring the shareholder only indirectly or derivatively), where management has refused to enforce the corporate cause of action, usually because recovery is sought against management for breach of fiduciary duty. [Sax v. World Wide Press, Inc., 809 F.2d 610 (9th Cir. 1989)]

     (1) **Who benefits:** [§677]   A derivative suit enforces the corporation's cause of action, and any recovery usually belongs to *the corporation* rather than the plaintiff-shareholder. (But the plaintiff-shareholder may be entitled to reimbursement for expenses in obtaining such recovery; *see infra*, §754.)

     (2) **Distinguishing direct suits from derivative suits:** [§678]   It must be determined initially whether the shareholder's action is properly direct or derivative in nature. (This is significant because derivative suits are subject to certain prerequisites and security-for-expenses statutes (*infra*, §729) that do not apply to direct suits.) While borderline cases may be difficult to classify, the basic test is which party has the cause of action—*i.e.*, whether the injury was suffered by the corporation or directly by the shareholder—and to whom the defendant's *duty* ran.

       (a) **Direct actions:** [§679]   The following kinds of shareholder actions have been held *direct* (individual) rather than derivative in nature, because the immediate injury is to the shareholder rather than the corporation.

         1) **Example:** Directors of XYZ Corp. refuse to declare a dividend, in order to depress the value of the shares. Shareholder action to compel payment of dividend is a direct action (injury to the shareholder), and a class action in such a case would be proper. [Knapp v. Bankers Securities Corp., 230 F.2d 717 (3d Cir. 1956)]

2) **Example:** Shareholder complains of reorganization allegedly diluting his voting influence in the corporation. This is a direct suit (again a class action may be proper). [Eisenberg v. Flying Tiger Line, Inc., 451 F.2d 267 (2d Cir. 1971)]

(b) **"Special duty" cases—still direct actions:** [§680]   Cases occasionally arise in which the corporation has sustained immediate injury, but the action is nevertheless deemed direct because of some "special duty" owed to the plaintiff-shareholder.

1) **Example:** A suit by a shareholder/pledgor against a director/pledgee for dissipating the corporation's assets has been held to be a direct action. Even though the injury was to the corporation, thus giving rise to a derivative action as well, there was a "special duty" owed arising out of the pledge arrangement. [Citibank, N.A. v. Data Lease Financial Corp., 828 F.2d 686 (11th Cir. 1987)]

2) **Example:** A suit by a corporation-shareholder against one of its directors for looting the assets of the corporation's subsidiary has been held to be a direct action. Even though the injury was to the subsidiary corporation, there was a special fiduciary duty owed by the director to the corporation-shareholder. [General Rubber Co. v. Benedict, 215 N.Y. 18 (1915)]

(c) **Close corporation exception:** [§681]   Some courts have held that minority shareholders of a close corporation may bring a direct action against controlling shareholders for breach of fiduciary duty, thus enabling the plaintiffs to avoid the special restrictions and defenses of a derivative suit. [Schumacher v. Schumacher, 469 N.W.2d 793 (N.D. 1990)] The Principles of Corporate Governance approve this exception if it does not (i) unfairly expose the corporation or the defendants to a multiplicity of actions, (ii) materially prejudice the interests of creditors in the corporation, or (iii) interfere with a fair distribution of the recovery among all interested persons. [A.L.I. Prin. Corp. Gov. §7.01(d)] Other courts have adhered to the traditional rule that a shareholder must redress an injury to the corporation through a derivative suit. [Bagdon v. Bridgestone, Firestone, Inc., 916 F.2d 379 (7th Cir. 1990)]

(d) **Securities acts violations—derivative action:** [§682]   A derivative action will lie for violations of the federal securities acts where the violation constitutes a breach of management's duties to the corporation.

1) **Example:** Where a violation of rule 10b-5 results in injury to the corporation (as distinct from its shareholders), a derivative action will lie if the corporation fails to sue. (*See supra*, §675.)

2) **Example:** Under section 16(b), recovery of "short swing profits" by insiders belongs to the corporation. If it fails to sue, the statute authorizes a minority shareholder to sue on its behalf

(*supra*, §449). (*Note*: This is a statutory action, rather than a true derivative suit, and as a consequence, it is not subject to the same procedural limitations, *see infra*, §§716, 739.)

b. **Prerequisite to suit—exhaustion of corporate remedies:** [§683]   Since a derivative suit seeks to enforce a corporate cause of action, the plaintiff must first show that he has exhausted his remedies within the corporate structure. This is an essential element of the plaintiff's cause of action and thus it must be specifically ***pleaded and proven***. [Fed. R. Civ. P. 23.1; Cal. Corp. Code §800(b)(2)]

(1) **Demand on directors:** [§684]   Since only the board of directors is authorized to bring suit on behalf of the corporation, a shareholder, before proceeding with a derivative suit, must make a sincere effort to induce the directors to remedy the wrong complained of. His complaint must "allege with particularity the efforts, if any, made by the plaintiff to obtain the action he desires from the directors or comparable authority . . . and the reasons for his failure to obtain the action or for not making the effort." [Fed. R. Civ. P. 23.1]

(a) **When excused:** [§685]   Demand on the directors is excused when the shareholder demonstrates that it would be "futile," *i.e.*, when all or a majority of the directors are themselves the alleged wrongdoers or under their control, or have failed to exercise reasonable care to prevent the wrong. [Barr v. Wackman, 36 N.Y.2d 371 (1975)]

   1) **Note—majority approval does not excuse demand:** [§686]   Most courts hold that in the absence of negligence, self-interest, or other indication of bias, the fact that a majority of the directors merely ***approved*** the transaction under attack does not itself excuse the demand; *i.e.*, it does ***not*** follow that these directors will refuse to remedy the error of their business judgment when it is brought to their attention. [Kamen v. Kemper Financial Services, Inc., 939 F.2d 458 (7th Cir. 1991); Aronson v. Lewis, 473 A.2d 805 (Del. 1984); Lewis v. Graves, 701 F.2d 245 (2d Cir. 1983)]

   2) **Model statutes:** [§687]   Both model statutes provide that demand should only be excused on a showing that "irreparable injury" to the corporation would result. [A.L.I. Prin. Corp. Gov. §7.03(b); RMBCA §7.42]

   3) **Violations of federal law:** [§688]   If the derivative suit charges a violation of federal law, the scope of the demand requirement is determined by state rule unless this would be inconsistent with the policies underlying the federal law. [Kamen v. Kemper Financial Services, Inc., 500 U.S. 90 (1991)]

(b) **Effect of directors' rejection of demand:** [§689]   If a derivative suit alleges wrongdoing by a majority of the directors (or by persons who control them), the board's decision not to sue will not prevent the derivative suit. [Lewis v. Curtis, 671 F.2d 779 (3d Cir. 1982)]

1) **Note:** Even if a demand is required because a majority of the directors "merely approved" the challenged transaction (*see supra*), some courts have held that it does not necessarily follow that their decision not to sue will end the matter. [Galef v. Alexander, 615 F.2d 51 (2d Cir. 1980)—participation by directors insufficient to excuse a demand may nonetheless disqualify directors from barring derivative suit]

(c) **"Business judgment, honestly exercised":** [§690]   Where the matter complained of does not involve wrongdoing by the directors or by persons who control them (*e.g.*, where plaintiff-shareholder complains that a third party has breached a contract with the corporation, and wants the corporation to bring suit for damages), the board's good faith refusal to sue bars the action. If the directors reasonably conclude that there is no likelihood of recovery, or that the costs of suit would outweigh any recovery, courts may refuse to allow a derivative suit. *Rationale:* A court will not interfere with a good faith exercise of discretion by the board elected to make business judgments for the corporation. [United Copper Securities Co. v. Amalgamated Copper Co., 244 U.S. 261 (1917)]

1) **Reasonable diligence:** [§691]   The derivative suit will not be barred, however, if plaintiff-shareholder's well-pleaded allegations of fact create a reasonable doubt that the board exercised reasonable business judgment in declining to pursue the cause of action. [Levine v. Smith, 591 A.2d 194 (Del. 1991)]

a) **Discovery not permitted:** [§692]   The Delaware Supreme Court, however, has held that a plaintiff-shareholder is not entitled to discovery in connection with showing that demand was wrongfully refused. Rather, plaintiff must rely on public sources of information or on his right to inspect corporate records (*see supra*, §§614-632). [Rales v. Blasband, 634 A.2d 927 (Del. 1993)]

(d) **Derivative suit against directors:** [§693]   Where the derivative suit alleges wrongdoing by a minority of the directors, the suit may be barred if the disinterested director majority makes a good faith business judgment that the suit is not in the corporation's best interests. [Untermeyer v. Fidelity Daily Income Trust, 580 F.2d 22 (1st Cir. 1978)]

1) **Special litigation committee in suits alleging wrongdoing by a majority of directors:** [§694]   A board of directors (a majority of which may be interested) may appoint a special committee of disinterested directors, which may be advised by special counsel, to determine whether the suit would be in the corporation's best interest. Most courts have held that the good faith decision of such committee to terminate the suit is similarly governed by the business judgment rule. [Auerbach v. Bennett, 47 N.Y.2d 619 (1979)]

a) **Limited judicial review:** [§695] The court will determine whether the special committee was truly disinterested and whether its procedures and methodology of investigation were sufficient. [Auerbach v. Bennett, *supra*]

    1/ **Note:** Some courts have explicitly placed the burden of proving independence, good faith, reasonableness of investigation, and reasonable bases for the special committee's conclusions on the corporation seeking to dismiss the derivative suit. [Zapata Corp. v. Maldonado, 430 A.2d 779 (Del. 1981); *and see* RMBCA §7.44(e)—adopts this position]

b) **Compare—court's independent judgment:** [§696] Some decisions further provide that the court *may* also apply its *own* independent business judgment (as well as consider matters of public policy) as to whether termination of the derivative suit is in the corporation's best interest. [Zapata Corp. v. Maldonado, *supra*; Kaplan v. Wyatt, 499 A.2d 1184 (Del. 1985)—emphasizing that this step is within court's discretion]

    1/ **Burden of proof:** [§697] It has been held in cases where a majority of the directors are charged with self-dealing that the court must determine whether the defendant-directors will be able to show that the transaction complained of was fair and reasonable to the corporation (*see supra*, §267). [Alford v. Shaw, 358 S.E.2d 323 (N.C. 1987)]

c) **Compare—vigorous scrutiny only:** [§698] Other decisions hold that courts should abstain from imposing their own business judgments. Rather, the court should consider a variety of factors—the likelihood of a judgment in the plaintiff's favor, the expected recovery as compared to out-of-pocket costs, whether the corporation took corrective action, and whether dismissal would allow any defendant with control to retain a significant improper benefit—and determine whether the special committee's decision is reasonable. [Houle v. Low, 556 N.E.2d 51 (Mass. 1990)]

d) **Minority view:** [§699] It has been held that directors charged with misconduct have no power to select a special litigation committee. Rather, if the derivative suit alleges wrongdoing by a majority of the board, the corporation may request the court to appoint a "special panel" to act in place of the board of directors. [Miller v. Register & Tribune Syndicate, Inc.. 336 N.W.2d 709 (Iowa 1983)] This procedure is also *authorized* by the Model Act. [RMBCA §7.44(f)]

e) **Violations of federal law:** [§700] If the derivative suit charges a violation of federal law, the question of whether a special litigation committee may terminate the suit by deciding that it is not in the corporation's best interest depends on (i) whether the relevant state law allows the board to delegate such decisions to a committee of disinterested directors, and (ii) whether it would be consistent with the federal law allegedly violated. [Burks v. Lasker, 441 U.S. 471 (1979)]

1/ **Section 10(b):** [§701]   Neither the policies underlying rule 10b-5 nor the disclosure requirements of the federal proxy rules are offended by permitting a special litigation committee to terminate a derivative suit alleging a violation of section 10(b) or of section 14(a) of the Securities Exchange Act of 1934. [Lewis v. Anderson, 615 F.2d 778 (9th Cir. 1979)]

(2) **Demand on shareholders:** [§702]   In most states, the plaintiff in a derivative suit must also make a demand on the shareholders—although this is often qualified by some phrase such as "if necessary." [Fed. R. Civ. P. 23.1] (California and New York require only that demand be made on the directors. [Cal. Corp. Code §800(b)(2); N.Y. Bus. Corp. Law §626; *and see* RMBCA §7.42])

(a) **When excused:** [§703]   Demand on the shareholders is usually excused if the alleged wrongdoing is beyond the power of the shareholders to "ratify." [Continental Securities Co. v. Belmont, 206 N.Y. 7 (1912)]

1) **Fraud:** [§704]   Courts are split on whether a majority of the disinterested shareholders may "ratify" an alleged fraud on the corporation by its directors. [Claman v. Robertson, 128 N.E.2d 429 (Ohio 1955)—fraud ratifiable; Mayer v. Adams, 141 A.2d 458 (Del. 1958)—contra]

2) **Illegal acts:** [§705]   It has been held that shareholders have no power to ratify illegal acts by the directors that cause injury to the corporation (*e.g.*, antitrust violations), and hence no demand need be made prior to a derivative suit. [Rogers v. American Can Co., 305 F.2d 297 (3d Cir. 1962)]

3) **Negligence, unreasonable business judgment:** [§706]   Shareholders do have power to ratify alleged negligence or unreasonable business judgment by the directors. Hence, the demand is not excused under those circumstances. [Smith v. Brown-Borhek Co., 200 A.2d 398 (Pa. 1964)]

4) **Lack of prior authorization:** [§707]   Similarly, shareholders may ratify actions by the board that are voidable due to lack of prior authorization (*e.g.,* no shareholder approval). [Continental Securities Co. v. Belmont, *supra*, §703]

5) **Nonratifiable wrongs:** [§708]   Even if the wrongdoing is not ratifiable, some courts still require a demand on shareholders

so as to inform them and give them an opportunity to take appropriate action—such as removing the directors, electing new ones who will cause the corporation to sue, or determining that the suit is not in the corporation's best interest. [Bell v. Arnold, 487 P.2d 545 (Colo. 1971)]

6) **Cost of demand as excuse:** [§709]   Courts are split on the question of whether a shareholder demand should be excused when the shareholders are so numerous and widespread as to make the cost of such demand extremely expensive. [Levitt v. Johnson, 334 F.2d 815 (1st Cir. 1964)—demand excused; Saigh v. Busch, 403 S.W.2d 559 (Mo. 1966)—contra]

(b) **Effect of shareholders' refusal to sue:** [§710]   If a demand on the shareholders is required (*i.e.*, if the alleged wrongdoing is subject to ratification by the shareholders, or if the jurisdiction requires that the shareholders be informed of the suit) and the majority of disinterested shareholders make a good faith decision not to sue, the derivative suit ordinarily may not be maintained. [S. Solomont & Sons Trust, Inc. v. New England Theatres Operating Corp., 93 N.E.2d 241 (Mass. 1950)]

1) **Rationale:** The shareholder body has power to determine what is in the best interests of the corporation.

2) **Limitation:** [§711]   Of course, the ratification or refusal to sue must be by a *disinterested* majority—not by shareholders who were the direct or indirect wrongdoers or beneficiaries of the allegedly wrongful transaction.

c. **Qualifications of plaintiff**

(1) **Shareholder status:** [§712]   A few states require that the plaintiff be a "registered" shareholder or shareholder "of record" in order to bring a derivative suit. [Wash. Bus. Corp. Act §23A.08.460] However, most also permit suit to be initiated by a "beneficial" or "equitable" owner of shares—*e.g.*, the holder of a voting trust certificate, or the purchaser of shares who has not yet been recorded on the corporation's books. [Theodora Holding Corp. v. Henderson, 257 A.2d 398 (Del. 1969); Cal. Corp. Code §800(b)(1)]

(a) **Convertible bondholders:** [§713]   Some classes of creditors have the right to exchange their debt for shares (*e.g.*, owners of bonds that are convertible into stock). Courts are split on whether such creditors are "equitable" owners of shares. [*Compare* Harff v. Kerkorian, 324 A.2d 215 (Del. 1974)—debtholder until conversion takes place; *with* Hoff v. Sprayregan, 52 F.R.D. 243 (S.D.N.Y. 1971)—Securities Exchange Act includes convertible bonds within definition of "equity security"]

(2) **Contemporaneous ownership:** [§714]   Most states require that plaintiff must have been a shareholder at the time of the alleged wrongdoing.

Shareholders cannot complain of wrongs that occurred *before* they purchased their shares. [Fed. R. Civ. P. 23.1; RMBCA §7.40(a); Cal. Corp. Code §800(b)(1)]

(a) **Rationale:** One historic purpose is to prevent so-called "strike suits"—actions stirred up by persons who search out corporate irregularities, buy a few shares, and file suit to secure a private settlement, rather than to obtain recovery for the corporation. (The current rule, however, requires that any amount received in settlement be paid over to the corporation; *see infra*, §746.) Another reason for the rule is that one not a shareholder at the time of the alleged wrongdoing suffers no injury and thus should not be permitted to sue. [Home Fire Insurance Co. v. Barber, 93 N.W. 1024 (Neb. 1903)]

(b) **Exceptions**

1) **"Operation of law":** [§715] The contemporaneous ownership requirement generally does not apply if the plaintiff acquires her shares "by operation of law from a holder who was a holder at the time of the transaction" complained of (*e.g.*, by inheritance). [Cal. Corp. Code §800(b)(1)]

2) **Securities Exchange Act section 16(b):** [§716] The contemporaneous ownership requirement is expressly inapplicable to shareholder suits for short-swing profits under section 16(b), which really are not true derivative suits. [Dottenheim v. Murchison, *supra*, §449]

3) **Injustice:** [§717] A few state statutes also waive the rule of contemporaneous ownership if it is shown "that there is a strong prima facie case in favor of the claim asserted on behalf of the corporation" and that without such suit serious injustice will result. [Pa. Bus. Corp. Law §1782(b); Cal. Corp. Code §800(b)(1)]

4) **Continuing wrongs:** [§718] Where the wrong is continuing in nature, plaintiff need not have owned the shares at the inception thereof. [Palmer v. Morris, 316 F.2d 649 (5th Cir. 1963)—corporation sold assets to defendant at unduly low price before plaintiff became shareholder but received payments therefor after plaintiff was shareholder]

(c) **Corporation may be barred where controlling shareholder disqualified—"piercing corporate veil":** [§719] Where the controlling shareholder acquired the shares *after* the alleged wrongdoing, the shareholder is clearly barred by the contemporaneous shareholder requirement from maintaining a derivative suit against the former management. And in such cases, equitable considerations may require that the *corporation itself* also be barred. [Bangor Punta Operations, Inc. v. Bangor & Aristook Railroad, 417 U.S. 703 (1974)]

1) **Example:** A purchases all of the stock of XYZ Corp. from B for a fair price. A cannot maintain a derivative suit charging B

with mismanagement during the time B owned the controlling shares. Nor will A be permitted to cause XYZ Corp. to file a suit against B under these circumstances. *Rationale*: Equity will not permit a controlling shareholder to use the corporate veil to obtain indirectly that which he could not recover directly. Since he bargained for and received the controlling shares for a fair price, the seller's prior acts of corporate mismanagement caused the purchaser no injury. To allow the corporation to recover would in effect allow the purchaser to recoup what he voluntarily paid for the shares. [Bangor Punta Operations, Inc. v. Bangor & Aristook Railroad, *supra*]

a) **"Unfair" price:** This rationale does not apply, however, if the price paid did not reflect the earlier wrongdoing by the seller. [Rifkin v. Steel Platt, 824 P.2d 32 (Colo. 1991)—corporation may recover for seller's breach of fiduciary duty prior to sale]

(3) **Motive in bringing suit:** [§720]   At least under the Federal Rules [Fed. R. Civ. P.23.1], it must appear that the plaintiff-shareholder "fairly and adequately" represents the interests of the shareholders generally in enforcing the rights of the corporation. [Hornreich v. Plant Industries, Inc., 535 F.2d 550 (9th Cir. 1976)—action dismissed where it appeared motive of plaintiff-shareholder was to force corporation to settle direct suit by plaintiff against it]

(4) **Compare—action by former shareholders:** [§721]   One who is no longer a shareholder normally cannot maintain either a direct or a derivative suit. However, where he sold his shares *without knowledge* of management's wrongdoing, and the wrong would otherwise go *unremedied*, a former shareholder may be allowed a *direct* action against the wrongdoers to compensate for the loss in value of the shares sold. [Watson v. Button, 235 F.2d 235 (9th Cir. 1956)]

(a) **Example:** A and B were the sole shareholders of XYZ Corp. A looted the corporate treasury, unbeknownst to B. Then, A and B sold their shares to C. Later, B discovered A's wrongdoing, and realized that she received less for her shares because of it.

1) **No derivative action possible:** B cannot maintain a derivative suit on behalf of XYZ because she is no longer a shareholder of record. Nor can C maintain such an action, because of the contemporaneous ownership requirement. Furthermore, because the sole shareholder, C, is barred from suing on behalf of the corporation, the corporation itself is barred. [Kirk v. First National Bank, 439 F. Supp. 1141 (M.D. Ga. 1977)]

2) **Direct action permitted:** Under these circumstances, courts permit the innocent former shareholder (B) to bring a direct action against the wrongdoer (A) for the amount by which the fraud or mismanagement reduced the value of the shares sold because the wrong would otherwise go unremedied. [Watson v. Button, *supra*]

(5) **Multiple derivative suits:** [§722]   The shareholder of a parent corporation has a sufficient economic interest in a subsidiary of the parent to bring a derivative suit on the subsidiary's cause of action. [Blasband v. Rales, 971 F.2d 1034 (3d Cir. 1992)]

(6) **Compare—action after merger or dissolution:** [§723]   The Principles of Corporate Governance permit a person who has ceased to be a shareholder because of a merger or dissolution to bring a derivative suit on behalf of the terminated corporation if no others are eligible to assert the claim. [A.L.I. Prin. Corp. Gov. §7.02(a)(2); *compare* Pessin v. Chris-Craft Industries, Inc., 586 N.Y.S.2d 584 (1992)—when plaintiff's corporation (ABC) has been merged into XYZ and plaintiff has received XYZ stock in exchange for ABC stock, plaintiff cannot bring a derivative suit asserting a claim on behalf of ABC that arose before the merger; plaintiff was not an XYZ shareholder at the time of the alleged wrongdoing and his XYZ stock was not acquired by "operation of law" (*see supra*, §715)]

d. **Procedural issues in derivative suits**

(1) **Pleadings:** [§724]   Under most statutes, the plaintiff-shareholder's complaint must allege a qualification to sue (contemporaneous share ownership), exhaustion of corporate remedies (demand on directors and shareholders, if necessary), and the wrong or injury to the corporation [Fed. R. Civ. P. 23.1]

   (a) **Verify pleadings:** Although plaintiff is required, under the Federal Rules, to verify the pleadings, he need not personally understand the allegations. He may properly rely on the judgment of another person (*i.e.*, his attorney). [Surowitz v. Hilton Hotels Corp, 383 U.S. 363 (1966)]

(2) **Legal representation—conflict of interest problem:** [§725]   Although the corporation is joined as a defendant as an indispensable party, the action is still brought on its behalf; its interests are ordinarily adverse to the other defendants (especially where its officers and directors are charged with wrongdoing). Thus, most courts hold that it is improper for the corporation attorney, or any other lawyer, to represent **both** the corporation and the real defendants. They must retain separate counsel. [Cannon v. U.S. Acoustics Corp., 398 F. Supp. 209 (N.D. Ill. 1975); *and see* Legal Ethics Summary]

   (a) **Attorney-client privilege:** [§726]   The corporation is a "client" of its attorney; thus, communications between the corporation's lawyer and either the corporation's control group of managers or its lower level executives are privileged. [Upjohn Co. v. United States, 449 U.S. 383 (1981)]

(3) **Right to jury trial**

   (a) **General rule:** [§727]   Since a derivative suit is an equitable action, a jury trial often is **not** available in state courts. [Rankin v. Frebank Co., 47 Cal. App. 3d 75 (1975)] But some states do provide a right to a jury trial. [Finance, Investment & Rediscount Co. v. Wells, 409 So. 2d 1341 (Ala. 1981)]

(b) **Federal actions:** [§728]   In federal actions, the Seventh Amendment right to a jury trial has been held to apply to those issues upon which the *corporation* would have had a right to a jury trial had it brought the action. Thus, for example, where the issue is the corporation's right to recover damages for fraud, plaintiff is entitled to a jury trial. [Ross v. Bernhard, 396 U.S. 531 (1970)—decision applicable to federal litigation only, as Seventh Amendment is not binding on states]

e. **Security for expenses:** [§729]   To discourage "strike suits" (*supra*, §714), a number of states have statutes that require the plaintiff-shareholder in a derivative suit, under certain circumstances, to *post a bond* or other security to indemnify the corporation against certain of its litigation expenses in the event the plaintiff loses the suit.

(1) **When plaintiff must post security:** [§730]   Statutes vary considerably as to when security is required.

(a) **Mandatory posting of security:** [§731]   Under some statutes, the plaintiff is required to post security if he owns less than a specified percentage of outstanding shares (*e.g.*, 5%); or less than a specified dollar amount of the corporation's stock (*e.g.*, $25,000 or $50,000). [N.Y. Bus. Corp. Law §627]

1) **May aggregate holdings:** [§732]   In these states, if several shareholders join in bringing the action (or join after the action is filed), their holdings may be aggregated to avoid the security requirement. [Baker v. MacFadden Publications, Inc., 300 N.Y. 325 (1950)]

2) **Acquiring shares after action is filed:** [§733]   It is unclear whether a plaintiff may avoid the security requirement by acquiring the specified percentage or dollar amount after suit is filed. [Haberman v. Tobin, 626 F.2d 1101 (2d Cir. 1980)—suit dismissed, but plaintiff repeatedly disregarded judge's orders]

(b) **Discretionary posting of security:** [§734]   Other statutes make the posting of security discretionary with the court. For example, they may provide that the trial judge is authorized to order the plaintiff to deposit security if it appears "that there is no reasonable possibility that the action will benefit the corporation or its shareholders." [Cal. Corp. Code §800(c)]

1) **Compare:** One statute authorizes the court to deny a request for security if plaintiff can show that it would "impose undue hardship . . . and serious injustice would result." [Pa. Bus. Corp. Law §1782(c)]

(2) **Who is entitled to security:** [§735]   Under most statutes, only the *corporation* is entitled to move for the posting of security; and the bond or other security posted runs only in its favor. [N.Y. Bus. Corp. Law §627]

(a) **But note:** A few statutes also permit officers or directors who are defendants in the action to demand security. [Cal. Corp. Code §800(c)]

(3) **Expenses to be covered:** [§736]   Most statutes require the security to cover all expenses reasonably incurred by the corporation as the result of the derivative suit, including *attorneys' fees*—plus whatever litigation expenses the corporation may be legally or contractually required to pay by way of *indemnification* to its officers or directors as defendants therein (*infra*, §§760-774). [Cal. Corp. Code §800(d)]

(a) **Limitation:** Some states limit the total amount of security that may be required. [*See, e.g.,* Cal. Corp. Code §800(d)—$50,000]

(4) **When liability or security matures:** [§737]   Under some statutes, it is enough that the plaintiff-shareholder loses the derivative suit, *i.e.*, the defendant corporation is *automatically* entitled to recourse against the bond or other security, although the amounts are to be determined by the court. [Ariz. Gen. Corp. Law §49(C)]

(a) **Compare:** Other statutes are more restrictive, allowing recourse against the plaintiff only if the court finds that the derivative suit was brought "without reasonable cause." [Tex. Bus. Corp. Act §5.14]

(5) **Applicability of state statutes to derivative suits in federal court**

(a) **In diversity cases:** [§738]   State security-for-expenses statutes are deemed "substantive" for purposes of the *Erie* doctrine. Thus, in federal derivative suits based on diversity of citizenship jurisdiction, the federal court must apply whatever security statute is applied in the local state courts. [Cohen v. Beneficial Industrial Loan Corp., 337 U.S. 541 (1949)]

(b) **In cases under federal securities act:** [§739]   However, state security-for-expenses statutes do not apply where the derivative suit is based on violation of the Securities Act of 1934. Here, the federal court is exercising federal question jurisdiction, and the Act has been held to reflect a congressional intent that shareholders be afforded access to federal tribunals without the constraint of such state statutes. [McClure v. Borne Chemical Co., 292 F.2d 824 (3d Cir. 1961)]

(6) **Compare—liability for court costs:** [§740]   Quite apart from security-for-expenses statutes, a plaintiff-shareholder who loses is liable for the court costs incurred by the prevailing parties—the same as any other litigant. (*See* Civil Procedure Summary.)

(a) **No attorneys' fees:** [§741]   In most states, however, recoverable court costs do not include attorneys' fees. (Some states are contra.) Under the Model Act and the Principles of Corporate Governance, the court may order payment of reasonable attorneys' fees incurred by defendants if it finds that a derivative action was brought "without reasonable cause." [RMBCA §7.46(2); A.L.I. Prin. Corp. Gov.

§7.04(d); *see also* Fed. R. Civ. Proc. 11, discussed in Civil Procedure Summary]

f. **Defenses:** [§742]   In general, any defense that could have been asserted had the corporation brought the action (*e.g.*, statute of limitations) can also be asserted in the plaintiff-shareholder's derivative suit—plus certain equitable defenses assertable only against the plaintiff personally.

    (1) **Personal defenses:** [§743]   A derivative suit is a proceeding in equity, and laches, unclean hands, pari delicto, and other so-called equitable defenses may therefore be asserted to bar the plaintiff's action.

        (a) **Example:** Thus, a shareholder who *participated* or *acquiesced* in the wrong complained of cannot maintain a derivative suit on behalf of the corporation. Her conduct would be viewed as "unclean hands," precluding equitable relief. [*But see* Kullgren v. Navy Gas & Supply Co., 149 P.2d 653 (Colo. 1934)—contra]

g. **Res judicata:** [§744]   Judgment on the merits or a court-approved settlement in a derivative suit is res judicata to the claims asserted therein. Since the suit was maintained on behalf of the corporation, judgment on the merits *for or against* the defendants bars any further suits for the same wrong—either by the corporation itself, or by any other shareholders in derivative suits.

h. **Settlement and recovery:** [§745]   Since the cause of action belongs to the corporation, so does any settlement or judgment (except in the "unusual circumstances" noted below). The plaintiff-shareholder benefits only indirectly, through any increase in the value of stock.

    (1) **Private settlements barred:** [§746]   If a plaintiff-shareholder personally receives any consideration to discontinue the action, it is held in trust for the corporation and must be paid over. [Clarke v. Greenberg, 296 N.Y. 146 (1947)]

    (2) **Procedural requirements:** [§747]   Most states require that settlement or dismissal of derivative suits be subject to *court approval* after some form of notice to all shareholders. [Fed. R. Civ. P. 23.1; RMBCA §7.45]

        (a) **Without notice and court approval:** [§748]   Absent such notice and approval, the settlement or dismissal will not be given res judicata effect; *i.e.*, other shareholders or the corporation may be permitted to sue again. [Papilsky v. Berndt, 466 F.2d 251 (2d Cir. 1972)]

        (b) **Judicial approach to approval:** [§749]   A proposed settlement must be fair and reasonable to the corporation. Among the circumstances that courts consider are: (i) the validity of the claims, (ii) the difficulties in enforcing the claims, (iii) the amount of proposed settlement, (iv) the collectibility of any judgment, (v) the expense of litigation, and (vi) the views of all parties involved. [Polk v. Good, 507 A.2d 531 (Del. 1986)]

    1) **Burden of proof:** [§750] Proponents of the settlement bear the burden of proof that the settlement is in the best interests of the corporation. [*In re* General Tire & Rubber Co. Securities Litigation, 726 F.2d 1074 (6th Cir. 1984)]

(3) **Under "unusual circumstances," recovery may go to shareholders rather than corporation:** [§751] Under special circumstances, recovery in a derivative suit may be ordered paid directly to certain shareholders rather than to the corporate treasury.

    (a) **Corporation dissolved:** [§752] If the corporation has been dissolved and *all creditors paid*, no purpose would be served by ordering it paid to the corporation, and therefore the court may properly order any recovery paid to the shareholders.

    (b) **Corporate recovery would benefit those not entitled:** [§753] Where a corporate recovery would benefit certain shareholders not entitled to it, the court may order the money paid to other shareholders. For example, in *Perlman v. Feldmann* (*supra*, §671), a shareholder sold "control" of the corporation to a buyer who made it a captive supplier and thereby deprived the corporation of profits it otherwise would have made. The former controlling shareholder was ordered to account for the improper profits he made on the sale. However, these profits were ordered paid to the remaining shareholders rather than to the corporation to prevent the buyer (new controlling shareholder) from participating therein.

    (c) **Comment:** This kind of "bypass" of the corporate treasury is tantamount to the court's declaring a dividend from the corporation to the innocent shareholders. It will ordinarily be done only when the rights of creditors are not prejudiced.

i. **Reimbursement to plaintiff for litigation expenses:** [§754] If victorious, the plaintiff-shareholder may be entitled to reimbursement from the corporation for litigation expenses, including reasonable attorneys' fees.

(1) **Common fund doctrine:** [§755] At least where the derivative suit results in a monetary recovery to the corporation, such reimbursement is based on the equitable doctrine that one who has obtained a "common fund" for the benefit of others (here, the other shareholders) is entitled to reimbursement. [Fletcher v. A.J. Industries Inc., 266 Cal. App. 2d 313 (1968)]

(2) **"Substantial benefit" to corporation:** [§756] Even in the absence of a monetary recovery, many courts order reimbursement to a successful plaintiff if the derivative suit has resulted in a *substantial benefit* to the corporation. [Bosch v. Meeker Cooperative Light & Power Association, 101 N.W.2d 423 (Minn. 1960)—election of directors held illegal; Mills v. Electric Auto-Lite Co., *supra*, §545—management's proxy statement held violative of proxy rules]

    (a) **Derivative suit not required:** [§757] It has been held that a plaintiff may obtain reimbursement for litigation expenses in any suit (including an individual action) that results in a substantial benefit to the corporation. A derivative suit (or a class action) is not required. [Tandycrafts, Inc. v. Initio Partners, 562 A.2d 1162 (Del. 1989)]

(3) **Amount of fee:** [§758]   Courts have used two basic approaches in determining the amount of the fee to be awarded. Some courts award a percentage of the amount recovered for the corporation ("salvage value" approach). [*In re* Oracle Securities Litigation, 131 F.R.D. 688 (N.D. Cal. 1990)] However, the majority approach today focuses on the time counsel spent on the case, adjusted to reflect the quality of the work done and the risk assumed by the lawyer ("lodestar" approach). [Lindy Bros. Builders v. American Radiator & Standard Sanitary Corp., 487 F.2d 161 (3d Cir. 1973)]

   (a) **Middle position:** [§759]   The Principles of Corporate Governance *permit* either the salvage value or lodestar approaches, but sets a percentage of recovery as a ceiling on the maximum fee allowable. [A.L.I. Prin. Corp. Gov. §7.17]

j. **Indemnification of officers and directors:** [§760]   Statutes in all states govern the extent to which the corporation may properly indemnify its directors or officers (or other employees or agents) for expenses incurred in defending suits against them for conduct undertaken in their official capacity. These statutes apply not only to derivative suits, but also to direct actions by the corporation, its shareholders, or third parties (*e.g.*, the state for a criminal violation; or an injured party for a tort).

(1) **Statute as exclusive basis for indemnification:** [§761]   In some states, such statutes constitute the exclusive basis upon which indemnification is permitted. Any broader provision in the corporation's articles or bylaws is void as contrary to public policy. [RMBCA §8.58]

   (a) **Compare:** Other states permit the subject to be governed by the articles or bylaws, shareholder agreements, or votes of the shareholders or directors. [Cal. Corp. Code §317(g); Del. Gen. Corp. Law §145(f); N.Y. Bus. Corp. Law §721]

(2) **"Official capacity":** [§762]   Courts have been generous in construing the scope of coverage afforded by indemnification statutes. Not only are directors and officers entitled to indemnification when sued for breach of duty to the corporation or for a wrong committed on behalf of the corporation, but also for actions that are more tangential to their official roles. [Heffernan v. Pacific Dunlop GNB Corp., 965 F.2d 369 (7th Cir. 1992)—director failed to disclose information to buyer when selling his shares in corporation]

(3) **Where defendant wins:** [§763]   As long as the director or officer accused of wrongdoing *wins on the merits*, there is generally no problem. Every state permits the corporation to reimburse him for his litigation expenses, including attorneys' fees, in defending the action.

(a) **Rationale:** Public policy favors indemnification where the director or officer is vindicated. Indemnification encourages capable directors and officers to seek and retain corporate office and to resist unfounded charges against them. Moreover, it discourages minority shareholders from filing frivolous derivative suits, knowing that the defendants will contest such suits vigorously because their expenses will be paid by the corporation if they win. [Solimine v. Hollander, 19 A.2d 344 (N.J. 1941)]

(b) **Indemnification as discretionary or mandatory:** [§764]   In some states, reimbursement is discretionary with the board. But under many statutes, the corporation is required to indemnify a director or officer where successful on the merits (some add "or otherwise") in defense of a derivative suit or direct action against her in her capacity as director or officer. [Cal. Corp. Code §317(d); N.Y. Bus. Corp. Law §724; Del. Gen. Corp. Law §145]

1) **"Or otherwise":** [§765]   A director or officer is considered to have successfully defended, and thus entitled to indemnification, even if the suit is dismissed because of a "technical" defense—*e.g.*, statute of limitations, improper service of process. [Waltuch v. ContiCommodity Services, Inc., 833 F. Supp. 302 (S.D.N.Y. 1993)]

(4) **Where defendant settles or loses:** [§766]   The statutes vary significantly on the extent to which the indemnification is permissible where the officer or director loses the lawsuit or the suit is settled. Many statutes distinguish between third-party suits and derivative suits:

(a) **Third-party suits:** [§767]   Where the suit against the director or officer is by an outsider (*e.g.*, state in criminal action; injured party in tort action), statutes generally permit indemnification for both litigation expenses and whatever civil or criminal liabilities are incurred (money paid out in settlement, judgment or fines) provided that the disinterested directors or shareholders (or independent legal counsel) determine that the defendant director or officer acted in *good faith* for a purpose reasonably believed to be in the best interests of the corporation and (where a criminal action was involved) there was no reason to believe that the action involved was unlawful. [N.Y. Bus. Corp. Law §722(b); Del. Gen. Corp. Law §145(a); *and see* Cal. Corp. Code §317(b)]

(b) **Derivative suits:** [§768]   However, where the suit against the director or officer is a derivative action charging him with wrongdoing toward the corporation, the statutes in most states are much stricter.

1) **Suit settled:** [§769]   If the derivative suit is settled prior to judgment, most statutes permit indemnification of the officer or director for his *litigation expenses*, including attorneys' fees, provided (i) the settlement was made with court approval, and (ii) the defendant is determined to have acted in good faith, with reasonable care, and with the belief that he was acting in

the best interest of the corporation, such determination being made by a majority of the disinterested directors or shareholders, or by the court. [Cal. Corp. Code §317(c), (e)]

a) **Amount paid in settlement:** [§770] If the above (or similar) conditions are met, some states also permit the corporation to indemnify the director or officer for amounts paid in settlement. [N.Y. Bus. Corp. Law §722(c)]

b) **Public policy:** [§771] Even if the statute is not the exclusive basis for indemnification, and even if a bylaw requires the corporation to reimburse all litigation expenses regardless of the good faith of the director or officer, it has been held that public policy places limits on the corporation's ability to pay. [Waltuch v. ContiCommodity Services, Inc., *supra*—denying reimbursement under these circumstances]

2) **Judgment against defendant:** [§772] When a director or officer in a derivative suit is adjudged to have acted dishonestly, or in bad faith, or to have obtained an improper personal gain, some statutes *prohibit* indemnification by the corporation, and this applies to both his litigation expenses and any liability imposed upon the director or officer. [N.Y. Bus. Corp. Law §721; *and see* Cal. Corp. Code §317(g)—prohibiting indemnification if director acts in "reckless disregard" of duty]

a) **Rationale:** It would destroy the purpose of the derivative suit if the corporation could make the errant director or officer "whole" for the consequences of this breach of duty to the corporation.

b) **Compare:** Other statutes allow the corporation to indemnify the errant director or officer for his litigation expenses including attorneys' fees (but not the damages assessed against him) in the derivative suit—if the court finds "such person is fairly and reasonably entitled to such indemnity." [Del Gen. Corp. Law §145; Cal. Corp. Code §317(c)(1); N.Y. Bus. Corp. Law §722]

(5) **Advancing expenses:** [§773] Most statutes also authorize the corporation to advance expenses in defending these suits prior to final disposition of the matter, as long as the directors and officers agree to repay the advance if it is ultimately determined that they are not entitled to it under the indemnification statute or properly authorized bylaws. [RMBCA §8.53] Thus, the corporation may agree to *advance* expenses even though the eventual result in the suit (*e.g.*, director found guilty of wrongdoing) would bar the corporation from *paying* the expenses. [Citadel Holding Corp. v. Roven, 603 A.2d 818 (Del. 1992)]

(a) **Security not required:** [§774] Most statutes provide that the director's undertaking to repay need not be secured and may be accepted without reference to financial ability to repay. [RMBCA §8.53(b)]

k. **Insurance against derivative suit liability:** [§775]   Most states have statutes that authorize a corporation to purchase and maintain insurance to protect the corporation against liability to its directors and officers for indemnification as authorized by law, and to protect the directors and officers against *any liability* arising out of their service to the corporation and against the expense of defending suits asserting such liability. (Sometimes, but not always, the directors and officers pay a portion of the insurance premium to reflect the cost of their coverage.)

   (1) **Statutes:** [§776]   Some statutes are quite permissive and authorize the corporation to maintain such insurance against any liability or expense incurred by a director or officer acting in an official capacity whether or not the corporation has power to indemnify the director or officer for the alleged misconduct. [Del. Gen. Corp. Law §145(g); Cal. Corp. Code §317(i); RMBCA §8.56]

      (a) **Compare:** Other statutes prohibit a corporation's insuring its officers or directors against liability for acts involving deliberate dishonesty or where the wrongdoer "personally gained a financial profit or other advantage to which he was not legally entitled." [N.Y. Bus. Corp. Law §726(b); *and see* A.L.I. Prin. Corp. Gov. §7.20(a)(2)]

      (b) **Comment:** To the extent that such insurance is permitted, it may enable a corporation to do indirectly (by paying insurance premiums) that which it could not do directly (indemnifying officers and directors against liability for breach of duty to corporation).

      (c) **Public policy:** [§777]   Merely insuring against liability for acts of negligence is no doubt permissible. But if the insurance purports to insure against liability for intentional dishonesty or self-dealing by directors, it may be unenforceable as contrary to public policy.

4. **Compare—Suits by Directors or Officers:** [§778]   Some state statutes permit directors or officers to bring suits on behalf of the corporation. These are generally subject to fewer restrictions than shareholders' derivative suits (*e.g.*, no prior demand on the board of directors or shareholders is required). [N.Y. Bus. Corp. Law §720(b)]

VIII. CAPITALIZATION OF THE CORPORATION

chapter approach

This chapter concerns the capitalization of the corporation through the issuance of shares, and the regulations incident thereto. Some important areas for exam purposes are as follows:

1. **Stock Subscriptions:** Subscriptions are agreements to purchase shares from the corporation. If such an agreement appears on your exam, first determine whether the agreement was entered into before or after formation of the corporation. *Post-incorporation* agreements are binding contracts; *pre-incorporation* agreements, however, vary in enforceability. A pre-incorporation agreement may be found to be merely a continuing offer and, thus, unenforceable. Most statutes eliminate the problem by making pre-incorporation subscriptions irrevocable for a designated period (*e.g.*, six months) in the absence of a contrary agreement.

2. **Consideration Required To Be Paid for Shares:** Statutes generally regulate the form and the amount of consideration the corporation must receive for its shares.

    a. **Form:** Remember that "money paid, labor done, or property actually acquired" is valid consideration, while an executory promise generally is not. More modern statutes do, however, permit issuing shares for a promise of future payment or services.

    b. **Amount:** A corporation must receive full payment for its shares. To determine whether shares have been paid for in full, start by checking to see whether the shares are par or no-par value shares. Remember that, ordinarily, par value shares must be sold for at least par value, or they are considered "watered." Watch out for stock that has either been sold for *less than par value* (discount shares) or issued in exchange for *overvalued property or services*. *No-par* value stock eliminates the watered stock problem because it may be sold at whatever price is deemed *reasonable* by the board.

3. **Fiduciary Duties of Promoters:** If an exam question concerns a promoter selling property to the corporation, note that the promoter has a fiduciary duty of *full disclosure*. If the promoter fails to make a full disclosure with respect to his dealings with the corporation, the corporation may sue for either rescission or damages.

4. **Preemptive Rights:** Ordinarily, a shareholder has a right to subscribe to the number of shares in a *new* issuance that will preserve his proportionate interest in the corporation. Remember that, when recognized, preemptive rights can be enforced by specific performance to compel issuance to plaintiff, damages, or an injunction against the issuance of shares in violation of preemptive rights.

5. **Statutes Regulating Issuance of Shares:** State statutes regulating the issuance of shares are known as "blue sky" laws. Some impose civil or criminal penalties for fraud in connection with the issuance of shares. All require that persons who sell securities be licensed. The most comprehensive blue sky laws require that the stock be registered with the appropriate state official.

    Probably more important for exam purposes are the *federal securities laws*. The Securities Act of 1933 establishes the framework for federal regulation. The most important thing to remember is that no interstate facilities or mails may be used to offer to sell a security unless a *registration statement* has been filed with the SEC. You should also know that *written* offers to sell must always satisfy the requirements for a statutory prospectus (*i.e.*, set forth the key information from the registration statement), and actual sales or deliveries of securities may be made only after the effective date of the registration statement and a prospectus must accompany or precede the delivery of any security.

Be aware, however, that certain securities and transactions are *exempt from the registration requirements*. In particular, watch for the following *exempt transactions*: (i) ordinary trading transactions between individual investors in securities that have already been issued, (ii) transactions by a securities broker, provided she is not acting as an underwriter and the time for initial distribution of the securities has passed, (iii) transactions by an issuer not involving a public offering (*i.e.*, private placements), and (iv) offerings made entirely to residents of the issuer's state.

Finally, note that a question may ask you to consider the remedies for a violation of the securities laws. If so, first ask yourself whether the securities are required to be registered. If so, and if the registration statement contains a misstatement or omits a material fact, recall that *any person* acquiring the securities without knowledge thereof has an action for damages against those connected with the issuance of shares or the registration statement (*e.g.*, the corporation, directors, underwriters, experts, etc.). Note that the corporation is absolutely liable, but the others may defend on the ground that they exercised due diligence. If the securities are exempt, only the original purchaser is entitled to recover and only the issuer or other sellers may be held liable. Also, the purchaser has a cause of action against a seller for failure to comply with the federal requirements (*e.g.*, registration, delivery of prospectus, etc.).

A. SHARES—IN GENERAL [§779]

A "share" represents the stockholder's proprietary interest in the corporation. It arises from acceptance by the corporation of the consideration offered by the subscriber.

1. **What a Share Represents:** [§780]   Specifically, a share represents the right to receive dividends as declared by the board, the right to receive a portion of the corporate assets on liquidation and, if voting shares are involved, the right to vote.

2. **What a Share Does Not Represent:** [§781]   Ownership of a share does *not* entitle the holder to any specific asset of the corporation or any interest in its assets as a whole. Title to corporate assets is in the corporation and cannot be conveyed by the shareholders.

B. CLASSES OF SHARES—PREFERENCES

1. **Introduction:** [§782]   Shares of one or more classes may be authorized in the articles. All shares have equal rights except as otherwise provided in the articles.

2. **Common:** [§783]   Common stock represents the residual ownership of the corporation. The common stockholders are entitled to pro rata dividends, without priority or preference over any other stock. Normally, the common stockholders have voting rights and are entitled to share in the distribution of assets on liquidation.

a. **Classes:** [§784]   A corporation may have more than one class of common stock (*e.g.*, "Common A" and "Common B"), with one class having certain rights that the other does not, or with one class entitled to certain priorities over the other. In such cases, the stock with the rights or priorities is, in effect, "preferred stock" (below).

3. **Preferred:** [§785]   Preferred stock is a class of stock having some sort of preference over other classes of stock—generally as to dividends or liquidation rights.

a. **Classes or series:** [§786]   There may be several classes or series of preferred (*e.g.*, "Preferred A" and "Preferred B")—one with distinct priorities over the other, and both with priority over the common stock.

b. **Redemption rights:** [§787]   Preferred stockholders may be given the right to compel the corporation to repurchase the shares if it has legally available funds to do so. (*See infra*, §§979-980.) This is known as a right of redemption. Frequently, the articles will require the corporation to maintain a *sinking fund* for this purpose (*i.e.*, accumulations of earnings not available for dividend distribution).

c. **Particular preferences:** [§788]   The following are the special rights or priorities (preferences) most often given to preferred stock. As indicated above, these rights exist only where expressly conferred by the articles.

(1) **Preference in receipt of dividends:** [§789]   The most frequent preference (and the most important) is to give preferred stock the right to receipt of dividends—*i.e.*, dividends must be paid to it at a specified rate (*e.g.*, 5% of par value or $5 per share) before dividends are paid to the holders of common stock. Whether the right to dividends is cumulative or noncumulative depends on what is provided in the articles.

(a) **Cumulative:** [§790]   Holders of cumulative preferred shares have the right to receive payment of the designated dividend each year, whether or not there are sufficient earnings to pay it. Nonpayment in a given year does not destroy the right; the dividends "cumulate" until paid. Although there is ordinarily no method of forcing the corporation to pay (absent abuse of discretion by the directors, below), no amounts may be paid as dividends on inferior classes of stock until the current dividend and all arrears are paid on the cumulative preferred shares.

(b) **Noncumulative:** [§791]   The general view is that where dividends are determined to be "noncumulative," the shareholder is entitled to dividends only if and when declared by the board. The right does not accumulate and is completely lost as to any year in which a dividend is not declared. This is true even though there are earnings available from which to pay such dividends. Absent an abuse of discretion, the shareholder cannot force the directors to declare dividends. [Guttman v. Illinois Central Railroad, 189 F.2d 927 (2d Cir. 1951)]

(2) **Participation rights:** [§792]   In addition to preference in receipt of dividends, holders of preferred shares are sometimes given the right to participate with the common shares in any remaining funds available for distribution after the preferred dividend has been paid. Again, the terms and extent of such participation (whether pro rata, or different amounts for each class) are as fixed in the articles.

C. AUTHORIZATION AND ISSUANCE OF SHARES [§793]

This portion of the summary deals primarily with so-called "primary" stock sales; *i.e.*, the *original issuance* of shares by a corporation, as distinguished from later resale of the shares by the issuee.

1. **Authorization:** [§794]   Whatever shares are issued must be *authorized* by the articles or charter of the corporation (*e.g.* "This corporation shall be authorized to issue 1,000 shares of capital stock, each share shall have a par value of $100, and the par value of all shares authorized shall be $100,000"). [RMBCA §2.02]

    a. **When all authorized shares issued:** [§795]   If all of the shares authorized under the articles have already been issued, no further shares can be issued until there is an *amendment* to the articles (*infra*, §§1068 *et seq.*) authorizing a larger number of shares.

2. **Issuance:** [§796]   Issuance is the process by which all or part of the corporation's authorized shares are sold. Issuance requires action by the board of directors accepting an offer to subscribe for shares of the corporation, and directing the secretary to issue appropriate share certificates upon receipt of the specified consideration.

    a. **Legislative control:** [§797]   The sale and issuance of shares by a corporation is subject to detailed regulation under federal and state statutes. (*See* discussion below.)

    b. **Shares outstanding:** [§798]   Once shares have been issued, they are referred to as "outstanding."

    c. **Repurchase of shares outstanding:** [§799]   Under certain circumstances, the corporation may be authorized to repurchase its shares. (*See infra*, §§981-997.) If it does so, it may either:

        (1) *Cancel the shares* (in which case the shares would no longer be issued, thereby increasing the number of shares the corporation could thereafter issue within its authorized capital); or

        (2) *Simply hold repurchased shares as treasury stock*. Such stock is no longer outstanding, but the shares are still considered to be issued. Treasury stock may, however, be resold by the corporation subject to rules different from those for the sale of unissued shares. The Model Act eliminates treasury stock. Reacquired stock is automatically canceled. [RMBCA §6.31]

D. STOCK SUBSCRIPTIONS

1. **Definition:** [§800]   Stock subscriptions are agreements by subscribers to purchase stock or other securities to be issued by the corporation. Such agreements

may be made prior to incorporation (it is often one of the functions of a promoter to obtain such subscriptions); or they may be made after formation as the corporation seeks to obtain or increase its capital.

2. **Offer and Acceptance Problems**

 a. **Post-incorporation subscriptions:** [§801]   Where a subscription agreement is made between a subscriber and a corporation already in existence, it plainly constitutes a binding contract obligating the subscriber to purchase (and the corporation to issue and sell) the securities in question. Ordinary contract principles of offer and acceptance apply.

 b. **Pre-incorporation subscriptions:** [§802]   Whether a subscription for shares in a corporation yet to be formed constitutes an enforceable contract is less clear.

 (1) **Majority view—subscription as "continuing offer":** [§803]   Most courts at common law held that a pre-incorporation subscription is *not* an enforceable agreement on the theory that since the corporation is not yet in existence (and the promoters have no power to bind the corporation, *see supra*, §§109-115), there is no contract. Thus, a pre-incorporation subscription is considered a mere "continuing offer" by the subscriber to purchase shares of the corporation—when, as, and if it comes into existence—which may be revoked by the subscriber before acceptance by the corporation.

 (2) **Minority view—subscription irrevocable as contract among subscribers:** [§804]   To avoid that result, some courts held that a pre-incorporation subscription has a dual character. In addition to being an offer to the corporation (above), it is deemed to be a *contract among the subscribers* based on their mutual promises to become shareholders upon formation of the corporation and acceptance of their offers. As such, it is binding and irrevocable at the outset.

 (3) **Statutes:** [§805]   Statutes in most states today eliminate the problem by making pre-incorporation subscriptions irrevocable for a designated period of time in the absence of contrary agreement. [*See, e.g.*, Del. Gen. Corp. Law §165—six months; RMBCA §6.20(a)—same]

E. CONSIDERATION REQUIRED TO BE PAID FOR SHARES

Statutes in most states regulate both the *form* and *amount* of consideration that the corporation must receive on issuance of its shares.

1. **Form of Consideration:** [§806]   Most states continue to have statutory restrictions on the kinds of consideration for which shares may be issued. Typically, shares may be issued only for "*money paid, labor done, or property actually acquired*."

 a. **Executory consideration:** [§807]   Executory promises generally are *not* legal consideration for the issuance of shares. Thus, *unsecured promissory notes* (executory promises to pay in the future) and executory promises to transfer assets or render services in the future are not lawful consideration.

(1) **Rationale:** The reason executory promises are not legal consideration is to assure that a corporation's capital consists of substantial assets and to prevent the issuance of stock as "fully paid" when the corporation has not actually acquired that which was promised. [Sohland v. Baker, 141 A. 277 (Del. 1927)]

(2) **Compare—secured obligations:** [§808]   An adequately secured promissory note is generally regarded as legal consideration for share issuance, the *collateral* being regarded as "property actually acquired." [General Bonding & Casualty Insurance Co. v. Moseley, 222 S.W. 961 (Tex. 1920)]

(3) **Exceptions:** [§809]   More modern statutes permit issuing shares in exchange for a promise of future payment or services. [RMBCA §6.21(b); *but see* RMBCA §16.21—requiring notice to shareholders when this occurs]

2. **Amount of Consideration:** [§810]   The price that the corporation must receive for shares issued as "fully paid" depends on whether the shares have a par value.

a. **Par value shares:** [§811]   Most statutes require that par value shares be sold *at least at par*. [Del. Gen. Corp. Law §153(a)]

(1) **Exception—to remedy impairment of capital:** [§812]   Some courts hold that a going concern (as distinguished from one just beginning business) whose *capital is impaired* may sell its shares at "the best price obtainable"—even for less than par—for the purpose of recuperating itself. [Handley v. Stutz, 139 U.S. 417 (1891)]

(2) **"Watered stock" liability:** [§813]   Except in the circumstance just noted, par value shares sold for less than par are *not* "fully paid" (regardless of what the share certificate itself may state). Such stock is said to be "watered."

(a) **Types of "watering":** [§814]   Par value shares may be "watered" in either of two ways:

1) **Discount or bonus shares:** [§815]   Shares may be issued for *consideration that is not even nominally equivalent* to their par value (*e.g.*, shares having par value of $1,000 issued for $500). These shares are often called "discount shares," and if no consideration at all is paid the shares may be referred to as "bonus shares."

2) **Property or services overvalued:** [§816]   Shares may be issued in exchange for property or services that are nominally equivalent to par value but only because the property or services are overvalued (*e.g.*, shares having par value of $1,000 issued for property or services actually worth $500). This is the classic situation of "watered stock."

(b) **Remedies for creditors:** [§817]   If the corporation becomes insolvent, its creditors may be able to recover from the shareholders the amount by which their shares were "watered."

1) **Which creditors may sue:** [§818] The courts are split on whether all corporate creditors may impose such liability, or only those who extended credit *after* the shares were issued; *i.e.*, the issue is whether prior creditors can be said to have been prejudiced by the issuance of watered stock. The answer depends on which theory of liability the court adopts:

   a) **Misrepresentation theory—subsequent creditors:** [§819] Most courts regard the issuance of stock as an implied representation to its creditors that the corporation has received assets equivalent in value to the par value of the shares issued. Under this approach, only those creditors who extended credit after the shares were issued are entitled to complain of watered stock. These subsequent creditors are presumed to have extended credit *in reliance* on the corporation having received par value for its shares. However, the defendant-shareholder may prove that the subsequent creditor did not rely. [Hospes v. Northwestern Manufacturing & Car Co., 50 N.W. 1117 (Minn. 1892)]

   b) **Trust fund theory—all creditors:** [§820] A minority view imposes liability for stock watering on the theory that the capital stock of the corporation constitutes a trust fund for all of its creditors. Under this theory, a shareholder who has received shares having a par value in excess of the assets transferred to the corporation is liable to *any creditor*—prior or subsequent—with or without notice, and irrespective of reliance. [Wood v. Dummer, 30 F. Cas. 435 (C.C.D. Me. 1824)]

   c) **Statutory obligation:** [§821] A few statutes have been interpreted as codifying the trust fund theory. [Del. Gen. Corp. Law §162; Hanewald v. Bryan's Inc., 429 N.W.2d 414 (N.D. 1988)]

2) **Extent of liability—determining value of consideration:** [§822] Most courts held that if the parties in good faith believed that the value of the property or services given to the corporation was equal to the par value of the shares issued, the stock was not watered. The effect is that watered stock liability exists only where there is *intentional overvaluation* of the assets being received by the corporation.

   a) **Note:** Most states today have statutes embodying this rule. For example, the Delaware statute provides, "In the absence of actual fraud in the transaction, the judgment of the directors as to the value of such consideration shall be *conclusive*." [Del. Gen. Corp. Law §152]

b. **No-par value shares:** [§823] All states today authorize the issuance of no-par value stock. One purpose of no-par stock is to permit a corporation to issue stock in return for assets that have a small or doubtful value at present, but a high speculative return. In other words, no-par was developed to *eliminate* the problem of watered stock liability. No-par shares may be sold at *whatever price* is determined to be *reasonable* by the board of directors.

(1) **Effect of statutes requiring stated value:** [§824]   Most statutes require that the directors (or shareholders) determine (or state) the value of the consideration to be received by the corporation for no-par shares. [Del. Gen. Corp. Law §153]   In such event, no-par shares cannot be issued unless the assets are in fact worth their stated value; otherwise, the shares are "watered" and all the rules and consequences discussed above apply. [G. Loewus & Co. v. Highland Queen Packing Co., 6 A.2d 545 (N.J. 1939)]

c. **Actual situation today:** [§825]   Watered stock liability suits are much less frequent today than in the past. One reason is that many states have some sort of regulatory statute ("blue sky" laws, *infra*, §§857-863) controlling the form and amount of consideration for which shares may be issued. The result is that shares are rarely issued for less than a fair and adequate consideration to the corporation.

d. **Model Act and California rule:** [§826]   The Model Act and California have *eliminated* the designations of par and no-par. Shares may be sold at *whatever price* the board of directors determines in good faith to be their value. [RMBCA §6.21; Cal. Corp. Code §409(a)]

F.   FIDUCIARY DUTIES OF PROMOTERS

1. **Duty to Corporation:** [§827]   Promoters also owe a fiduciary duty to the corporation they form. Problems typically arise when, after formation, a promoter sells property that he owns to the corporation (for cash or for shares).

a. **Duty of disclosure:** [§828]   A promoter owes the corporation a fiduciary duty of *full disclosure* as to any dealings with it in which he has a personal interest. This requires a full revelation of the promoter's interest in the property being sold to the corporation, and *all material facts* that might affect the corporation's decision to purchase—perhaps including the extent of the promoter's profit on the transaction.

b. **Effect of promoters taking all the stock with no plan to issue additional shares:** [§829]   Where the promoters become the *sole* shareholders of the corporation, and there is no plan to issue shares to others as part of the original capitalization, a failure to disclose their adverse financial interest is not deemed a violation of their fiduciary duty to the corporation at common law—on the theory that they cannot conceal something from themselves.

c. **Effect of plan to issue additional shares:** [§830]   The result may be different where, although the promoters were the only stockholders at the outset, a *further issue* to innocent subscribers was contemplated as *part of the original capitalization*. Initially, there was a split of authority on whether the *corporation* (under a new board of directors or through a derivative suit) can maintain an action against the original shareholders (promoters) for nondisclosure.

(1) **Massachusetts rule:** [§831]   Most courts follow the "Massachusetts rule," which permits the corporation to maintain such an action. [Old Dominion Copper Mining & Smelting Co. v. Bigelow, 89 N.E. 193 (Mass. 1909)]

    (a) **Rationale:** The original capitalization of the corporation is viewed as a single transaction even though the shares are issued in stages, and sale to innocent subscribers is viewed to have been intended as part thereof, so that the promoters' sale of their assets will not be deemed to have been approved by *all* the shareholders absent full disclosure to them. [Northridge Cooperative Section No. 1, Inc. v. 32nd Avenue Construction Corp., 2 N.Y.2d 514 (1957)]

(2) **Federal rule:** [§832]   The federal courts formerly held that no action could be maintained by the corporation. [Old Dominion Copper Mining & Smelting Co. v. Lewisohn, 210 U.S. 206 (1908)]

    (a) **Rationale:** The corporation was considered a legal entity whose status could not be affected by a subsequent enlargement of its membership. Since the corporation could not sue before the innocent shareholders came in, it could not sue afterwards.

2. **Effect of Securities Laws:** [§833]   The whole problem of promoters' fiduciary duties to a corporation organized by them is now also governed by state and federal laws regulating the issuance of corporate securities. (*See* full discussion *infra*, §§856 *et seq.*) In general, these laws make *mandatory* full disclosure of all material facts affecting the value of property received by the corporation in consideration for issuance of its shares. In particular, the Securities Act of 1933 requires disclosure of any shares issued or amounts paid to promoters within the previous two years and the consideration given by the promoter therefor. Furthermore, some state laws stipulate that the corporation *must* receive a *fair and adequate consideration* for each issuance.

    a. **Result of violation:** [§834]   Violation of such laws may result in penal sanctions against the promoters. Civil remedies are also available to the corporation and/or the innocent shareholders allowing them to recover the amount by which they have been damaged.

G. PREEMPTIVE RIGHTS

1. **Definition:** [§835]   A shareholder's preemptive right is the right to subscribe to that amount of shares in a new issuance that will preserve his existing proportionate interest in the corporation. In this way, preemptive rights protect the shareholder's voting percentage and proportionate interest in the net worth of the corporation.

    a. **Common law:** [§836]   At common law, preemptive rights were *inherent*— they existed even if not provided for in the articles or bylaws. [Stokes v. Continental Trust Co., 78 N.E. 1090 (N.Y. 1906)]

    b. **Statutes:** [§837]   Today, statutes in practically every state regulate preemptive rights.

      (1) **Implied:** [§838]   Some statutes reflect policies favoring preemptive rights, and thus provide that such rights exist unless expressly denied in the articles. [N.Y. Bus. Corp. Law §622]

      (2) **Expressly granted:** [§839]   Other statutes are aimed at restricting preemptive rights because preemptive rights hinder financing, and accordingly the statutes provide that no shares shall have preemptive rights unless expressly granted in the articles. [Del. Gen. Corp. Law §102(b); RMBCA §6.30(a)]

      (3) **Close corporations:** [§840]   Preemptive rights are more important in the case of small, closely held corporations. Where close corporations are treated separately by statute, preemptive rights are almost always provided.

2. **When More Than One Class of Shares Exists:** [§841]   If a corporation has more than one class of shares (*e.g.*, common and preferred) and each class has different rights as to voting, dividends, and liquidation, it may be impossible to preserve the proportionate interest of each class exactly when a new class of shares possessing such rights is issued.

    a. **Statutes:** [§842]   Some statutes simply allow this problem to be resolved in the articles. [Del. Gen. Corp. Law §102(b)] Others authorize the board to apportion the new issues so as to "preserve as nearly as practicable" the relative rights of the different classes—and make the board's apportionment final absent fraud or bad faith. [N.Y. Bus. Corp. Law §622(d)]

3. **Authorized But Unissued Shares:** [§843]   The general rule at common law was that preemptive rights applied only to new issues resulting from an ***increase in the authorized capital*** of the corporation. Thus, where the shares involved had been previously authorized but were not issued at the time of the original stock issuance, preemptive rights were denied—on the theory that the proportionate interest of each shareholder should be calculated in terms of the number of shares originally authorized.

    a. **Statutes:** [§844]   Some statutes resolve the problem by providing that, unless otherwise stated in the articles, there are no preemptive rights in shares sold within six months of their original authorization. Thereafter, preemptive rights apply. [RMBCA §6.30(b)(iii)]

4. **Shares Sold for Consideration Other Than Cash:** [§845]   Most courts hold that preemptive rights apply only to shares issued for cash, and not to shares issued in exchange for property or personal services rendered to the corporation or shares issued to accomplish a merger. *Rationale:* It is more important to allow the corporation to obtain unique property or services by issuing its shares than to protect minority shareholders against dilution.

    a. **Statutes:** [§846]   Of those statutes that deal with the problem at all, most deny preemptive rights in shares issued for noncash consideration unless otherwise provided in the articles. [RMBCA §6.30(b)(3)(iv)]

5. **Remedies:** [§847]   When recognized, preemptive rights can be enforced either by: (i) suit for ***specific performance*** to compel issuance to the plaintiff of authorized

shares in an amount necessary to retain his proportionate interest; (ii) *damages* computed on the basis of the difference between the subscription price of that amount of newly issued shares and their market value (on the theory that plaintiff can then acquire the shares on the market); or (iii) a court of equity *enjoining* the corporation from issuing shares in violation of the preemptive rights. [Stokes v. Continental Trust Co., *supra*, §836]

6. **Equitable Limitations on Issuance of New Shares:** [§848]   Regardless of whether preemptive rights are recognized, courts have recognized "quasi-preemptive rights," thereby forbidding majority shareholders or directors from causing an *unfair dilution* of the minority's interest by issuing shares to themselves at less than fair value. [Bennett v. Breuil Petroleum Corp., 99 A.2d 236 (Del. 1953)]

   a. **Example:** X Corp. has 600 shares outstanding, owned equally by A, B, and C. The value of the shares is $10 each. A and B (also directors) cause X Corp. to issue to them 600 new shares for $5 each. C's interest is diminished in value from $2,000 to approximately $1,500.

   b. **Fiduciary obligation:** [§849]   Other courts have simply held that the majority (as directors and as shareholders) owe a fiduciary duty to the minority, and that their issuing shares to themselves for less than fair value, or to obtain or perpetuate control is a "fraud" upon the minority shareholder. Under this approach, a court of equity may *set aside the unfair issuance* even if there were preemptive rights, which the minority failed to exercise. [Katzowitz v. Sidler, 24 N.Y.2d 512 (1969)—new shares issued at $100 per share, when book value was $1,800; but minority shareholder lacked funds to exercise his preemptive rights]

      (1) **Breach of duty:** [§850]   Thus, it is a breach of fiduciary duty, irrespective of the existence of preemptive rights, for directors to obtain control by issuing shares to themselves or their associates, even at a fair price, unless the directors can show a bona fide corporate purpose for such issuance, which purpose could not have been accomplished substantially as effectively by alternative means. [Schwartz v. Marien, 34 N.Y.2d 487 (1975)] (For further discussion of fiduciary duties owed by majority shareholders to minority, *see supra*, §§633 *et seq.*)

   c. **Significance of rule 10b-5:** [§851]   Apart from common law "equitable limitations," it is a violation of rule 10b-5 for directors to cause the corporation to issue stock to themselves or their associates at an unfairly low price or for the purpose of obtaining or perpetuating control. Such an issuance is a "fraud" on the corporation within the meaning of rule 10b-5, and if the corporation fails to sue, a derivative action may be filed by a minority shareholder against the directors involved. (*See supra*, §682.)

H.   UNDERWRITING

1. **Defined:** [§852]   Underwriting is the process whereby a securities dealer takes stock from a corporate issuer and arranges for its sale to the public.

2. **"Firm Commitment" Underwriting:** [§853]   In a "firm commitment" underwriting, the underwriters insure the sale of the entire issue by purchasing it outright from the corporation. The underwriters then seek to market the stock to the public.

3. **"Best Efforts" Underwriting:** [§854]   In a "best efforts" underwriting, the underwriters are bound only to use their special skills and efforts to attempt sale of the issue, and are not responsible for any unsold stock.

4. **Statutory Regulation:** [§855]   Underwriters are subject to strict regulation under both federal and state laws, which (among other things) generally require full disclosure of the compensation arrangements with the issuer and subject the underwriter to the same anti-fraud prohibitions applicable to the issuer (below).

I.   STATUTES REGULATING ISSUANCE OF SHARES

1. **In General:** [§856]   Both state and federal laws have been enacted regulating the issuance of securities. Since federal laws expressly do **not** preempt the field [Securities Act of 1933 §18], a corporate issuer must often comply with **both** state and federal regulations.

2. **State Regulation—"Blue Sky" Laws:** [§857]   State statutes regulating the issuance of securities are known as "blue sky" laws (their constitutionality resting on the legitimate state interest in preventing "schemes which have no more basis than so many feet of blue sky"). [Hall v. Geiger-Jones Co., 242 U.S. 539 (1917)] Every state has some type of blue sky law; many have special regulatory bodies charged with administration and enforcement of these laws. There are three basic types of blue sky laws (states combining the features of more than one type):

   a. **Fraud type:** [§858]   Some laws simply impose civil or criminal sanctions for fraud in connection with the issuance of securities. No permit or registration is required to issue securities, and there is generally no special administrative agency charged with enforcement of the statute. No state uses this method alone.

   b. **License type:** [§859]   All states have laws requiring that various persons who sell securities—brokers, dealers and agents of corporate issuers—register with the state and submit certain information.

   c. **Securities registration type:** [§860]   The most comprehensive type of blue sky law requires that stock be registered (or "qualified") with an appropriate state officer or agent prior to issuance.

      (1) **Registration by notification:** [§861]   Some of these laws require a complete description of the issuer and shares to be issued, and the shares must be sold as described. The purpose of such laws is simply disclosure; *i.e.*, there is generally no discretion in the state to deny permission to issue the stock.

      (2) **Registration by qualification:** [§862]   However, other laws of this type provide for *substantive review* of the proposed issuance by a state official who can prevent issuance if it fails to meet statutory requirements, *e.g.*, that it is "fair, just, and equitable."

      (3) **Registration by coordination:** [§863]   Some states provide that securities registered under the federal scheme may be issued by submitting to the state official essentially the same information as is required under the Securities Act of 1933.

3. **Federal Regulation:** [§864]   The *Securities Act of 1933* [15 U.S.C. §77] establishes the basic framework for federal regulation of the public distribution of securities through use of interstate commerce or the mails. It provides for a *registration-type* system of regulation, the purpose of which is to assure *full disclosure* of all pertinent facts to any prospective investor. The agency charged with enforcement is the Securities and Exchange Commission ("SEC"). Note that the SEC has no power to disapprove a proposed issuance; its only power is to compel *disclosure* of all pertinent details.

   a. **Registration statement:** [§865]   Basically, the 1933 Act forbids the use of interstate facilities or the mails to offer to sell a security, unless a registration statement has been filed with the SEC. [Securities Act §5(c)]

      (1) **Waiting period:** [§866]   During the time between filing the registration statement and the date that it becomes "effective" (a time known as the "waiting period"), no *written* offer to sell a security may be made through interstate facilities or the mails unless it satisfies the requirements for a "statutory prospectus." (This rule on written offers also applies after the effective date.) [Securities Act §5(b)(1)]

      (2) **After effective date:** [§867]   Actual sales of securities, or deliveries after sale, through interstate facilities or the mails may only be made after the "effective date" [Securities Act §5(a)]—and a prospectus must either accompany or precede the delivery of any security [Securities Act §5(b)(2)].

   b. **Integrated disclosure:** [§868]   Corporations subject to the reporting requirements of the Securities Exchange Act of 1934 whose shares are actively traded (as defined) may incorporate by reference their 1934 Act filings in their 1933 Act registration statements. [Securities Act Release No. 6331 (1981)]

      (1) **"Shelf" registration:** [§869]   Corporations may also offer securities over a two-year period after the effective date of a registration statement that automatically incorporates by reference subsequently filed 1934 Act reports. [Securities Act Rule 415]   This permits these corporations to sell securities "off the shelf" when they feel market conditions are favorable.

   c. **Relevant terms**

      (1) **"Offer to sell":** [§870]   This term includes "every attempt or offer to dispose of, or solicitation of an offer to buy, a security or interest in a security, for value." [Securities Act §2(3)] It has been broadly interpreted to include all activities which, under the circumstances, are designed to stir public interest in a security. [*In re* Carl M. Loeb, Rhoades & Co., 38 S.E.C. 843 (1959)—publicity in advance of a proposed issuance]

      (2) **"Security":** [§871]   This includes not only stock, bonds, and most promissory notes, but also any offering that constitutes an investment contract or certificate of interest or participation in any profit-sharing agreement, regardless of form. [Securities Act §2(1)]

(a) **Test:** [§872]   The test is "whether the scheme involves an investment of money in a common enterprise with profits to come *solely* from the efforts of others." [SEC v. W.J. Howey Co., 328 U.S. 29 (1946)] Some courts have expanded this to include profit schemes wherein "the efforts made by those other than the investor are the undeniably significant ones." [SEC v. Glenn W. Turner Enterprises, Inc., 474 F.2d 476 (9th Cir. 1973)]

(b) **Application:** [§873]   The term "security" has thus been applied to a wide variety of interests—*e.g.*, fractional interests in oil royalties or mineral leases, percentages of patent rights or fruit orchards, and interests in limited partnerships, mortgages or deeds of trust. But it has been held not to apply to an employer-financed pension plan because the employee made no monetary investment and the fund's income came mainly from employer contributions rather than the efforts of the fund's managers. [International Brotherhood of Teamsters v. Daniel, 439 U.S. 551 (1979)]

1) **Sale of business:** [§874]   Sale of all the stock of a company *is* the sale of "securities." Even though the sale is simply a method to transfer ownership of a business, the stock has all the traditional characteristics of a security. [Landreth Timber Co. v. Landreth, 471 U.S. 681 (1985)]

2) **Promissory notes:** [§875]   Some promissory notes are not subject to the federal securities acts. A four-factor test is used to determine whether the note bears a "strong family resemblance" to a "noninvestment" type of financial instrument. The note *is* a "security" if: (i) the *purchasers*, or (ii) other *reasonable persons* conceive of it as an investment, (iii) the notes are *commonly traded* as investments, and (iv) the note is *not subject to some other federal regulation*. [Reves v. Ernst & Young, 494 U.S. 56 (1990)]

(3) **"Registration statement":** [§876]   A registration statement is a detailed statement of all matters pertaining to the proposed issuance. The form is designed to force *disclosure* of all factors that may affect the fairness of the issue and the financial status of the corporation. Full details must be provided as to the issuer's property and business; the identity and background of all corporate officers and directors; the compensation they receive; the nature of the security being offered; sales costs, underwriting commission and discounts; and the like. [Securities Act §7]

(4) **"Statutory prospectus":** [§877]   A statutory prospectus is a document, filed with the registration statement, that sets forth the key information contained in the statement. [Securities Act §10] As noted above, a copy of the prospectus (but not the registration statement) must be given to every buyer of securities covered by the registration statement.

(5) **"Effective date":** [§878]   The registration statement becomes effective 20 days after filing unless the SEC agrees to an earlier date. If the SEC requires further information, it notifies the corporation that amendments

to the registration statement are necessary. Such amendments start the 20-day period again, unless the SEC consents to an acceleration of the effective date. [Securities Act §8]

d. **Exempt securities:** [§879]   The Act lists a number of types of securities that are exempt from the Act's registration requirements, *e.g.*, certain short-term commercial paper, securities issued by governmental bodies or charitable institutions, and securities subject to other government regulation (such as bank securities or insurance policies). [Securities Act §3(a)]

   (1) **But note:** Even exempt securities are subject to the Act's *anti-fraud* rules. (*See infra*, §931.)

e. **Exempt transactions:** [§880]   The following types of transactions are exempted from the registration requirements of the 1933 Act. (*Note:* The *anti-fraud rules* of the Act may still apply; *see infra*, §931.)

   (1) **Ordinary trading transactions ("casual sales" exemption):** [§881] The Act exempts "*transactions* by any person *other than* an issuer, underwriter, or dealer." [Securities Act §4(1)] This covers ordinary trading transactions between individual investors in securities that have already been issued—in contrast to sales by issuers and others participating in transactions connected with the initial distribution of securities. [SEC v. Chinese Consolidated Benevolent Association, 120 F.2d 738 (2d Cir. 1941)]

      (a) **Not applicable to secondary distributions:** [§882]   The exemption does *not* cover public offerings by a person who acquired the shares from an issuer in a "private placement" (below) if that person took the shares with a *view to public distribution*. Such persons are considered underwriters regardless of whether they are otherwise engaged in the securities business. [Securities Act §2(11); Gilligan, Will & Co. v. SEC, 267 F.2d 461 (2d Cir. 1959)]

      (b) **Not applicable to sales by control persons:** [§883]   The exemption also does not cover public offerings by persons who have a *control relationship* with the issuer. As to such offerings, the control persons are themselves considered issuers under the Act; and those who distribute the securities for them are underwriters. [*In re* Ira Haupt & Co., 23 S.E.C. 589 (1946)]

         1) **"Casual sales" by control persons:** [§884]   However, *rule 144* under the Securities Act exempts sales to the public by control persons of small amounts of securities within designated time periods. (For details on rule 144, *see infra*, §§891-896.)

   (2) **Dealer sales:** [§885]   Transactions by a dealer (securities broker) are exempt, except where (i) she is acting as an underwriter of the securities, or (ii) during the initial distribution of the securities (first 40 days following registration). [Securities Act §4(3)]

(3) **Private placements:** [§886]   Transactions by an issuer "not involving any public offering" are exempt. [Securities Act §4(2)] This applies to an offering to a relatively small number of private subscribers who are *sufficiently experienced or informed* that the disclosure requirements are not necessary for their protection (*i.e.*, they are "able to fend for themselves") and who are acquiring the shares *as an investment* rather than for resale to the public. [SEC v. Ralston-Purina Co., 346 U.S. 119 (1953)]

(a) **Requirement of available information:** [§887]   A high degree of business or legal sophistication by the offerees is not enough to gain the private placement exemption. The offerees *must* have either (i) *full disclosure* of the information that a registration statement would have provided, or (ii) *access* to such information (through an employment or family relationship or by economic bargaining power). [Doran v. Petroleum Management Corp., 545 F.2d 893 (5th Cir. 1977)]

   1) **Note—number of offerees not decisive:** The number of offerees is *not* decisive. Depending on the availability of information, an offering to a few persons may be public and an offering to many persons may be private. In addition, the *size of the offering is* a significant factor. [Doran v. Petroleum Management Corp., *supra*]

   2) **And note:** Under rule 506, an issuer may sell an *unlimited* amount of securities to "accredited investors" (defined *infra*, §888) and up to 35 other purchasers, but the issuer must reasonably believe that these other purchasers (or their purchaser representatives) have such knowledge and experience that they are capable of evaluating the offering *and* they must be furnished detailed information (as defined).

(b) **Small offerings under regulation D:** [§888]   During any 12-month period, an issuer may, without providing *any* information, sell securities:

   1) Up to $1 million to *any number* of purchasers [Securities Act Rule 504]; or

   2) Up to $5 million to *accredited investors*. [Securities Act §4(6)] "Accredited investors" include financial institutions, business development companies, large charitable or educational institutions, the issuer's directors and executive officers, and wealthy individuals (as defined). [Securities Act Rules 501, 505] In addition to accredited investors, the issuer may add up to *35 ordinary purchasers* if it provides detailed information (as defined) to all purchasers. [Securities Act Rule 505]

(c) **Investment intent:** [§889]   Each purchaser in a private offering or one under rule 506 or regulation D must acquire the securities as an investment, and not for resale or distribution to the public. Ordinarily, each purchaser is required to sign a letter of intent to this effect so that shares issued pursuant to this exemption are commonly known as "letter stock" or "restricted securities."

1) **Legal imprint:** [§890]   To assure that the purchasers take the shares for investment, many corporations print a notice on the face of the share certificates to the effect that "these shares have been issued pursuant to an exemption from registration, and may not be freely traded until registered, or further exemption established," and instruct their transfer agents not to transfer shares bearing such imprint.

2) **Resale of restricted securities—rule 144:** [§891]   Such legend imprint renders shares issued under a private offering exemption nonmarketable until registered, or until some further exemption from registration is established. Rule 144 creates an exemption for resale of such shares (and shares owned by control persons; *supra*, §884) if the following requirements are met:

   a) **Public information:** [§892]   There must be specified current public information concerning the issuer.

   b) **Holding period:** [§893]   No resales at all of restricted securities are generally permitted within the first two years following issuance of the shares.

   c) **Limitation on amount sold:** [§894]   Thereafter, purchasers who are control persons can sell during each **three-month** period shares equal to as much as 1% of the total shares outstanding in the same class (or 1% of the average weekly volume of shares traded on national securities exchanges or automated quotation systems during the preceding four weeks, whichever is greater).

   d) **Notice requirement:** [§895]   If more than 500 shares are to be sold, or if the sales price exceeds $10,000, the shareholder must file with the SEC a signed notice of intent to sell the securities concurrently with placing the sale order with the broker. The purpose is to allow the SEC to monitor the marketing of such securities.

   e) **Sales by noncontrol persons:** [§896]   Purchasers who are not control persons may sell *any* amount if: (i) they have owned the securities for three years and they are listed on a national exchange or quoted through an approved automated system, or (ii) they have owned the securities for four years and the issuer has provided specified current public information.

3) **Resale of restricted securities in another private placement:** [§897]   If shares issued under a private offering exemption are resold in a transaction that would have initially

qualified as a private offering (*e.g.*, sale to a sophisticated investor), there has been no public distribution. Thus, the person who resold the shares is not an underwriter. [Ackerberg v. Johnson, 892 F.2d 1328 (8th Cir. 1989)]

    a) **Resale to institutional buyers:** [§898] Under rule 144A, unregistered shares of a class not publicly traded may be sold at any time to an institution that has investments of over $100 million.

(4) **Intrastate offerings:** [§899] Where the offering and sale is made *entirely* to residents of the same state in which the issuer resides and is doing business, the issue is exempt from registration. (A corporation is said to "reside" in the state of incorporation.) [Securities Act §3(a)(11)]

    (a) **Note:** The exemption is strictly construed. Thus, it is lost where securities are inadvertently offered to an out-of-state resident, even if no sale is ever made to that person. Good faith reliance on the offeree's representation of residence is apparently no defense if it proves to be false. [Securities Act Rule 147]

(5) **Other exemptions:** [§900] The 1933 Act also authorizes the SEC to exempt other issuances where the SEC finds that registration is not necessary by reason of the small amount involved or the *limited character of the offering*. [Securities Act §3(b)]

    (a) **Regulation A:** [§901] For a public offering not exceeding *$5 million* in any 12-month period, the SEC permits an *abbreviated offering circular* containing basic information about the stock and its issuer, in lieu of the more detailed registration statement otherwise required. After review by the SEC, the offering circular must be distributed to prospective purchasers of the stock.

    (b) **Rule 145:** [§902] Another provision provides *limited registration* requirements for securities issued pursuant to certain transactions *formally approved by the shareholders* of the issuer, pursuant to statute or the articles—*e.g.*, certain mergers, acquisitions, transfers of assets and reclassification of shares (*see infra*, §§1027, 1061, 1070).

    (c) **Small business issues:** [§903] Another regulation permits the offering through a simplified system of an unlimited dollar amount of securities by a "small business issuer"—defined as one with: (i) under $25 million in revenue in the last fiscal year and (ii) no more than $25 million outstanding securities with the public. [Securities Act Regulation S-B]

f. **Remedies—anti-fraud provisions:** [§904] The 1933 Act provides both civil and criminal sanctions for violation of its registration requirements or any fraud in connection with the issuance of the securities or the filing of the registration statement.

(1) **False registration statement—section 11:** [§905] If the registration statement, when it becomes effective, contains a *misstatement or*

omission of material fact, any person acquiring the securities without knowledge thereof has an action for damages (the amount she lost on the investment) against various persons connected with the issuance.

(a) **Who may sue:** [§906]   This remedy is granted to *any person who has acquired* the securities—not just the original issuee. But a person cannot sue if she *knew* of the misstatement or omission when she acquired the securities. [Securities Act §11(a)]

   1) **Privity not required:** [§907]   No privity is required between the plaintiff and the parties sought to be held liable.

   2) **Must prove shares were part of that offering:** [§908]   If plaintiff acquired her shares in the market *subsequent to distribution* of the registered offering, she must prove that the shares she acquired were *part of that offering*, rather than shares issued at some other time.

(b) **Elements of plaintiff's action:** [§909]   Plaintiff need not prove fraud in the tort sense, or even any intentional wrongdoing. Subject to certain defenses (*see* below), plaintiff need only show that *some material fact was omitted or misrepresented* in the registration statement.

   1) **Materiality:** [§910]   "Material" covers all matters that an average prudent investor needs to know before being able to make an intelligent, informed decision on whether to buy the security.

   2) **Reliance and causation need not be shown:** [§911]   It is *not* necessary for plaintiff to prove that she *relied* on the misrepresentation or omission, or that it *caused* the loss in value of the security. The fact that it was "material" (above) is enough for liability.

      a) **Exception:** [§912]   If plaintiff acquires her shares *after* the corporation publishes an earnings statement for the 12-month period following the effective date of registration, the plaintiff must prove reliance, *i.e.*, that the falsity in the registration statement *caused* her to purchase. [Securities Act §11(a)] (Even here, however, plaintiff need not prove she personally *read* the statement—she could have been relying on investment advice given her by others who had.)

(c) **Who may be held liable:** [§913]   Liability may extend to the *corporation*, its *directors* and persons who are named as being or about to become its directors, all persons who *sign* the registration statement, the *underwriter*, and *experts*—such as accountants, engineers, and other professionals (including *lawyers*)—who are identified as having prepared or certified the registration statement or any report or valuation in connection therewith. [Securities Act §11(a)]

1) **Liability of experts:** [§914]   The responsibility of lawyers, accountants, and other experts is normally limited to those parts of the registration statements *made on their authority*. [Securities Act §11(a)]

(d) **Defenses**

1) **Corporation:** [§915]   The issuer is *absolutely liable* for any material misstatement or omission in the registration statement. [Securities Act §11(b)] The only possible issuer defense is that plaintiff *knew* of the untruth or omission at the time she acquired the shares (*see* above).

2) **Others—"due diligence" defense:** [§916]   All other persons to whom liability extends under section 11 (above) may avoid liability by *proving* that they exercised *due diligence* with respect to the information in that part of the registration statement for which they are sought to be held liable.

a) **Signers, directors, underwriters, etc.:** [§917]   Generally, these persons must prove that, after reasonable investigation, they had reasonable ground to believe that the statements were true and complete as required. [Securities Act §11(b)(3)(A)] Again, the standard of "reasonableness" is that required of a prudent person in the management of her own property. [Securities Act §11(c)]

1/ **Personal investigation required:** [§918]   It is *no defense* that these persons had no knowledge of the misstatements or omissions or that they had been associated with the issuer for only a limited time. They must show not merely that they made inquiry of responsible corporate officers or employees, but also that they *reasonably investigated* the corporation's affairs *personally*. The defendant cannot escape liability by taking management's representations at face value. [Escott v. Barchris Construction Corp., 283 F. Supp. 643 (S.D.N.Y. 1968)]

2/ **Compare—portions made on authority of expert:** [§919]   However, as to those portions of a registration statement made on the authority of an *expert* (*e.g.*, financial statements certified by accountant or valuations certified by appraiser), "due diligence" is established as long as the party-defendant had no reasonable ground to disbelieve the expert's statement. [Securities Act §11(b)(3)(C)]

b) **Experts:** [§920]   As to those parts of the registration statement made on their authority, experts must prove that, after reasonable investigation, they had reasonable ground to believe such parts were true and complete. [Securities Act §11(b)(3)(B)]

(e) **Measure of recovery:** [§921]   The plaintiff is entitled to *actual damages*. This is considered to be purchase price minus resale price, but if she has not sold by the time she sues, damages may not exceed the difference between purchase price and the market value of the security at the time suit is brought. [Securities Act §11(e)]

   1) **Reduction of damages:** [§922]   A defendant may reduce liability by proving that the plaintiff's damages were not attributable to the part of the registration statement as to which the liability is asserted. [Securities Act §11(e)]

(2) **General civil liability—section 12:** [§923]   The 1933 Act expressly imposes civil liability on any person who *offers or sells* a security: (i) in violation of section 5 (requiring registration, delivery of a prospectus, etc.) [Securities Act §12(1)], or (ii) through means of interstate commerce or the mails by use of material misstatements or omissions (*i.e.*, not limited to the registration statement) [Securities Act §12(2)].

   (a) **Scope:** [§924]   Liability for misstatements or omissions under section 12 arises only in connection with a public offering. It does not extend to statements in a private sales contract. [Gustafson v. Alloyd Co., 115 S. Ct. 1061 (1995)]

   (b) **Who may sue:** [§925]   This right of action is afforded only to the original purchaser. There must be a showing of *privity* with the seller.

      1) **Compare:** Under section 11, above (misrepresentation or omissions in the registration statement), *any* holder is entitled to sue; no privity is required.

   (c) **Who may be held liable:** [§926]   By its terms, section 12 applies only to "persons who offer or sell" a security so that only the *issuer and other sellers* apparently can be held liable thereunder.

      1) **Compare:** Under section 11, liability can be imposed on *any person* connected with the registration statement; thus, liability extends to officers, directors, lawyers, accountants, etc.

   (d) **Defenses:** [§927]   Liability under section 12(2) for misstatements or omissions is conditioned on the plaintiff's proving that she did not know of them. Also there is no liability if the defendant proves that he did not and, in the exercise of reasonable care, could not know of them.

   (e) **Measure of recovery:** [§928]   Plaintiff may sue to rescind or, if she no longer owns the security, to recover damages (the amount she lost on the investment).

(3) **Implied civil liability; criminal liability—section 17:** [§929]   The 1933 Act also makes it unlawful for *any* person to offer or sell securities through the mails or in interstate commerce by means of "any device or

scheme to defraud" or "by means of any misstatement or omission" of material fact. [Securities Act §17]

(a) **Right of action implied:** [§930]   Unlike sections 11 and 12, which expressly create a civil cause of action for violation, section 17 simply provides that the acts are "unlawful" (*i.e.*, criminal liability). However, some courts have *implied* a civil remedy against persons who violate section 17, although the scope of this remedy remains unclear.

(4) **Remedies applicable to exempt securities:** [§931]   Note that the anti-fraud provisions of sections 12 and 17 apply to the "offer or sale" of securities *whether or not* the securities are required to be registered. Thus, they cover transactions and securities that are *exempt from the registration* requirements of the 1933 Act (*supra*, §§880-903) and therefore beyond the reach of section 11 (which applies only to omission and falsity in the registration statement; *see* above).

(5) **Indemnification agreements—enforceability:** [§932]   Frequently, persons outside the issuing company who play some role in connection with a stock issuance (particularly underwriters) may bargain for an indemnification agreement—whereby the company and/or its controlling shareholders agree to hold the underwriters harmless from any liability they incur for Securities Act violations.

(a) **Willful violations:** [§933]   If the underwriter (or other indemnified party) has *knowledge* of the violations, the indemnification agreement is *unenforceable* as a matter of law. *Rationale:* One cannot insure himself against his own willful wrongdoing, and to allow indemnity in such cases would encourage flaunting of the Act. [Globus v. Law Research Service, Inc., 418 F.2d 1276 (2d Cir. 1969)]

(6) **Compare to rule 10b-5:** [§934]   As discussed *supra* (§§339 *et seq.*), none of the anti-fraud provisions of the 1933 Act are as broad as section 10(b) of the 1934 Act and rule 10b-5 thereunder.

(a) **Scope:** [§935]   Rule 10b-5 protects *sellers* as well as buyers.

(b) **Procedure:** [§936]   Even as to buyers, an action under rule 10b-5 has certain *procedural advantages* over sections 11 and 12; *e.g.*, it *may* avoid the strictures on damages under the latter (*supra*, §§921, 928) as well as their short statute of limitations, *infra*.

(c) **Costs:** [§937]   Moreover, under sections 11 and 12, a court may assess *unsuccessful* plaintiffs with the *costs of suit* (including attorneys' fees) and may require plaintiffs to post advance *security* for such costs.

(d) **Scienter:** [§938]   Thus, despite the fact that sections 11 and 12 eliminate plaintiffs' need to prove scienter, most purchaser-plaintiffs prefer to maintain a civil action under rule 10b-5, rather than under the anti-fraud provisions of the 1933 Act.

IX. DISTRIBUTIONS TO SHAREHOLDERS

chapter approach

The subjects of this chapter, dividends and the redemption or repurchase of shares, are more likely to arise as subissues rather than as major exam topics. Nevertheless, it is important for you to know at least the following rules:

1. **Dividends:** In discussing issues concerning dividends, keep in mind that shareholders do not have a right to dividends; payment of dividends is within the business judgment of the directors. When a cash or property dividend has been declared, investigate the *source* of the dividend. In most states, these dividends may be paid only out of a surplus of net assets over stated capital. Check the surplus account from which the dividend is to be paid. Some states restrict the use of certain accounts, and most states prohibit the use of reappraisal surplus for dividends. Be aware that *all* states prohibit dividends when the corporation is insolvent or the payment of the dividend would render it insolvent.

   If the directors have declared an illegal dividend, recall that they are personally liable to the corporation to the extent of the injury to creditors and preferred shareholders. As for shareholder liability, if the corporation is solvent, shareholders who receive an illegal dividend without knowledge of its illegality are entitled to keep it, but if the corporation is insolvent, the shareholders who receive an illegal dividend are *absolutely* liable to return it.

2. **Redemption and Repurchase of Shares**

   a. **Redemption:** If a corporation wishes to retire certain shares (usually a preferred class) for the benefit of the common shares, consider redemption, by which the corporation pays the stipulated redemption price and the shareholders must relinquish their shares. Redeemed shares are canceled and stated capital reduced accordingly. Note that a corporation can redeem out of *any available funds* (surplus or stated capital). Most importantly, check to see that the corporation has the power to redeem—*i.e.*, is that power *expressly provided in the articles or bylaws*?

   b. **Repurchase:** All states have statutes authorizing corporations to *repurchase* their own shares. A provision in the articles or bylaws is *not* required. Repurchased shares are not automatically canceled; they remain issued as "treasury stock," with full rights to dividends, voting, etc., when resold. Unlike redemption, a repurchase may be made only under the same conditions that a cash or property dividend may be paid; *i.e.*, only when there is a surplus and only out of certain surplus accounts.

   c. **Limitations:** When faced with a redemption or repurchase problem, ask whether the corporation is *insolvent* or whether the redemption or repurchase will render it insolvent. If so, redemption and repurchase are not permitted. Then ask whether the redemption or repurchase will leave the corporation with *sufficient assets to cover liquidation preferences* of outstanding shares. If not, the redemption or repurchase generally will not be permitted. Finally, ask whether a discretionary redemption or repurchase serves a *bona fide corporate purpose*, rather than the personal interests of directors or insiders. Note that the remedies for unlawful redemption or repurchase are generally the same as those available for illegal dividends.

A. DIVIDENDS

1. **Definition:** [§939]   A "dividend" is any distribution of **cash** or **property** paid to shareholders on account of their share ownership.

2. **Right to Dividends:** [§940]   The general rule is that payment of dividends is a matter within the business judgment of the board of directors. The shareholders ordinarily have no right to dividends even if funds are available. The directors alone determine if and when dividends are to be declared, and the amounts thereof. [Gottfried v. Gottfried, 73 N.Y.S.2d 692 (1947)]

   a. **Equitable limitation:** [§941]   If a complaining shareholder can show that the board's refusal to declare dividends is in **bad faith** or so unreasonable as to amount to an **abuse of discretion**, a court of equity may intervene. Thus, if the directors (on behalf of the majority shareholders) are attempting to abuse the minority by refusing to declare dividends notwithstanding huge earned surpluses (and/or generous salaries to the majority), equity may intervene to protect the minority by compelling distribution of some reasonable portion of the available surplus. [Dodge v. Ford Motor Co., *supra*, §134]

      (1) **Caution:** It should be emphasized that equity will not intervene unless there is palpable abuse or bad faith by the directors. The *Dodge* case is one of the few reported decisions where this has been found. [*See also* Miller v. Magline, Inc., 256 N.W.2d 761 (Mich. 1977)]

      (2) **Fiduciary duty in close corporations:** [§942]   The duty that shareholders of a close corporation owe each other (*supra*, §645) may affect the power to declare dividends held by the majority shareholders (or a minority that has a veto power). [Smith v. Atlantic Properties, Inc., 422 N.E.2d 798 (Mass. 1981)—court may order declaration of dividends to avoid federal tax penalty for undue accumulation of earnings]

3. **Source of Lawful Dividends:** [§943]   The problem most frequently encountered with regard to payment of cash or property dividends is whether **funds of the proper type** are available for distribution. Statutes in virtually all states restrict the **sources** from which cash or property dividends may be paid. These restrictions seek to protect corporate creditors and, often, preferred shareholders. Violation of the restrictions may result in personal liability for the directors who authorize the dividends and the shareholders who receive them.

   a. **Restriction on dividends when capital account impaired**

      (1) **Majority view:** [§944]   Under traditional dividend statutes, cash or property dividends are payable only when the corporation has a surplus—an excess of net assets (total assets minus total liabilities) over stated capital. In these states, dividends cannot be paid out of the corporation's stated capital. [*See, e.g.,* N.Y. Bus. Corp. Law §510(b)]

         (a) **Rationale:** Traditionally, a corporation's stated capital represented amounts contributed by the shareholders to allow the corporation to operate. Creditors were entitled to rely on such amounts for payment of debts incurred by the corporation (*supra*, §§810-822). Therefore, except under designated special circumstances (*infra*, §§959-962), stated capital could not be returned to the shareholders as dividends—at least while creditors of the corporation remained unpaid.

(b) **"Nimble dividends" prohibited:** [§945] The restriction on paying dividends out of stated capital generally prevents so-called "nimble dividends" (*infra*, §949). If the corporation's capital account has become impaired (by virtue of operating losses, depreciation write-offs, or otherwise), the corporation cannot declare dividends even though it has ***current net profits***. The current profits must be used to "repair" the deficit in the stated capital.

   1) **"Net profits" defined:** [§946] A corporation's "net profits" means its earnings during the accounting period, with adjustments as required by good accounting practice (*e.g.*, appropriate reserves for depreciation, bad debts, etc.).

      a) **Exception—"wasting asset" corporations:** [§947] Many states have special dividend rules for corporations engaged in the exploitation of a "wasting asset," *i.e.*, an asset such as an oil well or patent that is to be consumed over a period of time and not replaced. [Del. Gen. Corp. Law §170(b); N.Y. Bus. Corp. Law §510(b)] Subject to some limitations, these statutes permit the corporation's net profits to be computed without a deduction for the depletion (*i.e.*, depreciation) of the value of the wasting asset. In effect, they permit a return of capital to the shareholders in the form of dividends.

(2) **Minority rules:** [§948] Some states have adopted a more liberal policy with respect to payment of dividends, permitting distributions under certain circumstances even though the corporation's stated capital is impaired.

   (a) **"Nimble dividends" permitted in some states:** [§949] Some states permit payment of dividends out of current net profits regardless of impairment of the capital account. Typically, these states broaden the accounting period over which the corporation's net profits are computed for dividend purposes. For example, Delaware permits dividends out of earnings during the current and preceding years (rather than during just the current accounting period). [Del. Gen. Corp. Law §170]

   (b) **California rule:** [§950] California has an even more liberal dividend policy. Broadly, a corporation is permitted to pay cash or property dividends as long as its total assets after such payment are at least equal to 1¼ times its liabilities *and* its current assets are at least equal to its current liabilities. [Cal. Corp. Code §500(b)]

      1) **Effect:** Under this rule, as long as the asset value requirements are met, dividends may be paid even though the corporation has no current profits, and even though the amount contributed as its capital is impaired.

2) **Valuation of assets:** [§951]   The value of corporate assets must be determined in conformity with generally accepted accounting principles. Specifically, the value may include goodwill or capitalized research and development expenses. [Cal. Corp. Code §500(b)]

(c) **Model Act:** [§952]   The Model Act authorizes cash or property dividends as long as the corporation's total assets are at least equal to its total liabilities. [RMBCA §6.40(c)]

1) **Valuation of assets:** [§953]   The value of corporate assets may be based upon any "fair method that is reasonable in the circumstances." [RMBCA §6.40(d)]

(d) **Limitations:** [§954]   Even under these liberal statutes, however, cash or property dividends are never proper where payment thereof would result in the corporation becoming *insolvent* (*infra*, §§967-968), or, in many states, where the payment would endanger *liquidation priorities* of preferred stock. [Cal. Corp. Code §§501-502; Del. Gen. Corp. Law §170; RMBCA §6.40(c); *and see infra*, §§967-969]

(e) **Notice to recipient shareholder:** [§955]   Where dividends are paid out of any source other than earned surplus (below), many states also provide that the corporation must notify the receiving shareholders as to the source of the funds distributed. [Cal. Corp. Code §507; N.Y. Bus. Corp. Law §510(c)]

b. **Restrictions as to type of surplus account from which dividends may be paid:** [§956]   Besides the prohibition in many states on any dividend payment while capital is impaired, there are statutory restrictions on payment of cash or property dividends from certain kinds of surplus accounts.

(1) **Earned surplus:** [§957]   "Earned surplus" is the total net profits retained by the corporation during all of its previous years of operation, *i.e.*, its profits offset by its losses, and further reduced by dividends paid out in previous years.

(a) **Example:** XYZ Corp. has been in business three years. During the first year, it had an operating loss of $5,000. The second year it had profits of $20,000. The third year it broke even and, for the first time, paid a dividend of $10,000. XYZ now has an earned surplus of $5,000 (-$5,000 + $20,000-$10,000).

(b) **As source of dividends:** [§958]   Earned surplus is a proper source of cash and property dividends in all states. Indeed, earned surplus may ordinarily be the only proper source of such dividends in a few states.

(2) **Paid-in surplus:** [§959]   "Paid-in surplus" occurs where par value shares are sold for more than par; where no-par value shares are sold for more than their stated value (so that not all of the consideration received

for no-par shares is allocated to stated capital); or from gifts to the corporation.

(a) **Example:** XYZ Corp. sells 1,000 shares of its $10 par value shares for $12,500. The $2,500 excess over par value is paid-in surplus. Similarly, if XYZ Corp. sells 1,000 shares of its no-par shares for $5,000, the directors designating $1,000 as the stated value of such shares, the $4,000 excess over stated value is paid-in surplus.

(b) **As source of dividends:** [§960] *Most states permit a distribution of dividends out of paid-in surplus.* [N.Y. Bus. Corp. Law §510(b)] Again, it is often required that the corporation notify the shareholders receiving such dividends of their source. [N.Y. Bus. Corp. Law §510(c)] Other states are more restrictive. In some, dividends may not be paid out of paid-in surplus unless the fair value of the remaining assets is at least 25% of the total liabilities. [R.I. Bus. Corp. Act §7-1.1-41]

(3) **Capital reduction surplus:** [§961] Capital reduction surplus arises when the par value or stated value of no-par shares has been reduced by the corporation. There are a variety of methods for reducing capital. In most states, capital may be reduced by amending the articles of incorporation. (*See infra*, §§1068-1084.) In some states, capital reduction can be accomplished only pursuant to special statutory procedures. [Del. Gen. Corp. Law §§242, 244]

(a) **Purpose:** A frequent reason for reducing stated capital is to remedy a capital impairment (*e.g.*, deficits incurred by operating losses in past years). When capital is reduced, the surplus created by the reduction is "capital reduction surplus." Such surplus can be used to offset the prior deficit so that future earnings can be available for dividends, instead of having to be used to "repair" the deficit in the capital account.

(b) **As source of dividend:** [§962] In most states, any capital reduction surplus in excess of that needed to "repair" the capital account may properly be used as a source of cash and property dividends to the shareholders—subject, however, to restrictions similar to those for dividends from paid-in surplus (*supra*, §959).

(c) **Shareholder approval:** [§963] If the capital reduction is accomplished by amending the articles of incorporation, shareholder approval is required. Some states require such approval for **all** methods of capital reduction. Other states allow the board of directors to reduce capital without shareholder approval, *e.g.*, by canceling stock that has been reacquired. [N.Y. Bus. Corp. Law §515]

(d) **Appraisal rights:** [§964] Some statutes give preferred shareholders appraisal rights if a capital reduction adversely affects their interests (*e.g.*, preference on liquidation). [N.Y. Bus. Corp. Law §806(b)(6)]

(4) **Reappraisal (revaluation) surplus:** [§965]   Surplus may also be created by a corporation revaluing assets that have appreciated in value over acquisition cost.

(a) **Example:** XYZ Corp.'s home office is located on land that cost the corporation $100,000 but now has a fair market value of $500,000. By changing the balance sheet value of the land, a "revaluation" surplus of $400,000 is created.

(b) **As source of dividend:** [§966]   Surplus created by unrealized appreciation in asset value is not a proper source of dividends in some states. Other states allow surplus from reappraisal of assets to be used like paid-in surplus or capital reduction surplus. [Randall v. Bailey, 23 N.Y.S.2d 173 (1940)]

c. **Insolvency as restriction on dividends:** [§967]   Virtually all states forbid dividends of any type where the corporation is in fact insolvent, or where payment of the dividend would render the corporation insolvent. [N.Y. Bus. Corp. Law §510(a)]

(1) **"Insolvency" defined:** [§968]   "Insolvency" is defined in two ways. In the bankruptcy sense, a corporation is insolvent when its *liabilities exceed its assets*. In the equity sense, a corporation is insolvent if it is unable to meet its debts as they mature, *i.e.*, *insufficient cash* to pay its bills, regardless of the value of its assets. [N.Y. Bus. Corp. Law §102(a)(8)] If a corporation is insolvent—or a dividend payment would render it insolvent—in either sense, it may not legally pay a dividend.

d. **Protection of preferred stock as restriction on dividends:** [§969]   Holders of preferred shares are generally entitled to payment upon liquidation before any distribution to holders of common stock (*see infra*, §1102). In some states, a corporation cannot pay a cash or property dividend from any source where the payment would endanger the liquidation preference of shares having such a preference (*i.e.*, where net assets after the payment would be less than the liquidation preference) unless the dividend is paid to that class of shares alone. [Cal. Corp. Code §502]

e. **Contractual restrictions on dividends:** [§970]   Especially because of the ease in creating capital reduction surplus to "repair" deficits from previous operating losses (*see supra*, §§961-962), dividend statutes provide relatively little protection to creditors as long as the corporation is not insolvent (*see supra*, §§967-968). As a consequence, institutions that make large, long-term loans may place protective covenants in the loan agreement limiting dividends that might jeopardize repayment of the loan. Similar provisions may be required by underwriters in connection with the public issuance of bonds or preferred stock.

4. Remedies for Illegal Dividends

a. **Personal liability of directors:** [§971]   Directors who declare a dividend from an unlawful source (or under other conditions rendering payment illegal) are jointly and severally liable to the corporation for the benefit of creditors or preferred shareholders affected thereby.

(1) **Defenses:** [§972]   Early cases held that the directors' liability was absolute. But modern statutes and cases recognize a number of defenses. Usually directors are not liable if they voted against the distribution, were absent from the meeting, or relied in good faith (*i.e.*, after making inquiries reasonable under the circumstances) on financial statements showing the availability of a proper source of funds for the payment. [Del. Gen. Corp. Law §§172, 174; N.Y. Bus. Corp. Law §§717, 719]

(2) **Amount of liability:** [§973]   Some statutes allow the corporation to recover the full amount of the unlawful dividend. [RMBCA §8.33] Most, however, limit the recovery to the amount of injury suffered by the creditors and preferred shareholders, *e.g.*, the amount of liabilities owed to the creditors, and the amount by which the dividend impaired liquidation preferences of the preferred shares. [N.Y. Bus. Corp. Law §719]

(3) **Contribution among directors:** [§974]   Any director held liable for unlawful dividends is normally entitled to compel contribution from other directors who could also be held liable (*i.e.*, those with no defense). [RMBCA §8.33; Del. Gen. Corp. Law §174(b)]

    (a) **Contribution from shareholders:** [§975]   Most statutes also permit directors held liable to compel contribution from shareholders who received the unlawful dividend *with knowledge* of the illegality. [RMBCA §8.33(b); N.Y. Bus. Corp. Law §719(d)]

b. **Personal liability of shareholders**

(1) **Where corporation insolvent:** [§976]   If the corporation is insolvent (or is rendered insolvent by the dividend distribution), the shareholders who receive the illegal dividend are often held *absolutely* liable to return it to the corporation for the benefit of the creditors or preferred shareholders affected thereby. *Rationale:* The distribution by an insolvent corporation constitutes a *fraudulent conveyance* (no consideration given by the shareholder), and such a conveyance is void against creditors or those entitled to priority. [Wood v. National City Bank, 24 F.2d 661 (2d Cir. 1928)]

    (a) **Direct action possible:** [§977]   Creditors (or preferred shareholders) affected thereby can bring a direct action against the shareholders receiving the illegal dividend. [Unif. Fraud. Transfer Act §7]

(2) **Where corporation solvent:** [§978]   Where the corporation's solvency is not affected by the distribution, shareholders who receive the payments *innocently*—not knowing the dividend is from an improper source or under illegal conditions—are generally held entitled to retain them. [McDonald v. Williams, 174 U.S. 397 (1899)]

B.   REDEMPTION AND REPURCHASE OF SHARES

1. **Redemption:** [§979]   A "redemption" involves the corporation's acquisition of some or all of a class of its outstanding shares by paying a stipulated redemption price (usually something in excess of par or stated value) to the shareholders, who must then surrender their certificates. Redeemed shares are usually canceled, and

stated capital (shares outstanding) reduced accordingly. The chief purpose of redemption is usually to retire shares with dividend preferences, for the benefit of the common shares.

a. **Source of funds to redeem:** [§980]   In most states, a corporation is permitted to redeem out of *any available funds*, *i.e.*, any kind of surplus or even stated capital. [N.Y. Bus. Corp. Law §513(c)]

(1) **Rationale:** Having conferred upon the corporation the power to redeem, the shareholders are deemed to consent even to the impairment of capital if required for this purpose. Similarly, since redemption must be expressly authorized in the articles or bylaws, creditors are deemed to have notice of the possibility that capital will be reduced thereby.

2. **Repurchase of Shares:** [§981]   A "repurchase" of shares by the corporation is distinguished from a "redemption" in that a repurchase is not effected pursuant to a provision in the articles, and most statutes do not provide that the shares are automatically canceled. The shares remain issued (hence no effect on stated capital), although held by the corporation as "treasury stock" (*supra*, §799) with the full right to dividends, voting, etc., when resold. [*Compare* Cal. Corp. Code §510(a); RMBCA §6.31(a)—shares that have been repurchased are canceled and revert to the status of authorized but unissued stock]

a. **Power to repurchase:** [§982]   Whereas the power to redeem shares must be expressly reserved in the articles, at common law, a corporation generally was deemed to have the inherent right to repurchase its own shares, providing it acted in good faith. (*See infra*, §993.) All states now have statutes authorizing the corporation to repurchase its own shares.

b. **Source of funds for repurchase:** [§983]   Most statutes permit a corporation to repurchase its shares under the same conditions that they permit payment of a cash or property dividend, *i.e.*, only if the corporation has a surplus. [N.Y. Bus. Corp. Law §513(a)]

(1) **Type of surplus account:** [§984]   Just as most states today permit cash or property dividends to be paid out of either earned, paid-in, or capital reduction surplus accounts (*supra*, §§958, 959, 962), any of these accounts generally may be used for the repurchase of outstanding shares.

(a) **California and Model Act rules:** [§985]   Under the California and Model Act rules, repurchase or redemption of shares is conditioned on the valuation of remaining assets, just as with payment of cash or property dividends (*supra*, §§950-951).

(2) **Exceptions—repurchases out of stated capital:** [§986]   Generally, repurchases cannot be made where there is no surplus. However, many statutes authorize a corporation to repurchase its own shares out of stated capital for the following limited purposes:

(i) To collect or compromise a *debt, claim, or controversy with a shareholder*;

(ii) To pay dissenting shareholders for *appraisal rights* in merger proceedings (*infra*, §§999-1020); or

(iii) To *eliminate fractional shares*.

[N.Y. Bus. Corp. Law §513(b)]

3. **Further Limitations on Repurchase and Redemption:** [§987] A repurchase or redemption of shares has the same effect as a dividend—*i.e.*, distributing assets of the corporation to shareholders, thereby putting them beyond the reach of creditors and, often, of senior shareholders. Thus, limitations similar to those imposed on dividend distributions (*supra*, §§943-969) are imposed on redemptions and repurchases of shares.

   a. **Insolvency limitation:** [§988] No redemption or repurchase is permitted where the corporation is insolvent, or where the effect of the redemption or repurchase would be to render the corporation insolvent in either the bankruptcy or equity sense. [N.Y. Bus. Corp. Law §513(a)]

      (1) **Time of valuation:** [§989] The corporation's solvency has usually been determined at the time that payment on the redemption or repurchase is made, rather than at the time the corporation bound itself to redeem or repurchase. Thus, even if the corporation was solvent when it entered into an agreement to repurchase certain shares in the future, the agreement is unenforceable if at the time payment is due, the corporation has become insolvent. [Neimark v. Mel Kramer Sales, Inc., 306 N.W.2d 278 (Wis. 1981)]

         (a) **Promissory note:** [§990] Pursuant to this rule, most courts have held that if a solvent corporation gives a promissory note in repurchasing its shares, the note can be enforced only as long as the corporation remains solvent. If the corporation becomes insolvent, further payments are unenforceable. [McConnell v. Estate of Butler, 402 F.2d 362 (9th Cir. 1968)—on bankruptcy of corporation, holder of note issued to repurchase shares was subordinated to claims of other corporate creditors; *but see* Williams v. Nevelow, 513 S.W.2d 535 (Tex. 1974)—contra]

           1) **Statutes:** [§991] Some statutes have adopted the contrary view. If the promissory note was given when the corporation could properly repurchase its shares, the note may subsequently be enforced as an ordinary debt of the corporation. [Del. Gen. Corp. Law §160; RMBCA §6.40(e)]

         (b) **Surplus requirement:** [§992] In addition to the rule that a repurchase agreement cannot be enforced at a time when the corporation is insolvent, some courts have also held that the corporation must meet the *surplus test* when each payment is made. [Mountain State Steel Foundries, Inc. v. Commissioner, 284 F.2d 737 (4th Cir. 1960); *but see* Neimark v. Mel Kramer Sales, Inc., *supra*—contra]

   b. **Bona fide corporate purposes—equitable limitations:** [§993] In addition to the foregoing restrictions, courts have held that any discretionary redemption or repurchase must serve some bona fide *corporate purpose* (such as to eliminate dissident shareholders)—rather than merely to serve the *personal interests* of the directors or "insiders."

(1) **Repurchase or redemption favoring "inside" shareholders prohibited:** [§994]   A repurchase or redemption cannot be used to favor "inside" shareholders at the expense of others (*e.g.*, buying out the shares of "insiders" when the outlook for the corporation is bleak, or conversely, buying out "outsiders" when prospects for the corporation are bright). [Zahn v. Transamerica Corp., *supra*, §651]

(2) **Protection from corporate "raider":** [§995]   A corporate purpose must be shown when a corporation purchases the shares of a "corporate raider" to prevent his obtaining control, *e.g.*, when directors cause the corporation to purchase shares from a shareholder who otherwise threatens to seize control; or the directors cause the corporation to purchase shares of other shareholders to prevent the "raider" from obtaining them. If the purchases are made solely for the purpose of perpetuating the officers and directors in their jobs, this is not a bona fide corporate purpose. But if there is reason to believe that the corporate takeover by the "raider" would jeopardize the interests of the corporation generally, the repurchase may be justified. [Cheff v. Mathes, 199 A.2d 548 (Del. 1964)]

(a) **Compare—rule 10b-5:** [§996]   Where directors cause the corporation to repurchase or redeem shares for the personal benefit of the directors rather than for bona fide corporate purpose, the corporation as purchaser of the shares is deemed "defrauded," and is entitled to maintain an action against the directors under rule 10b-5. (*See* detailed discussion *supra*, §§339-437.)

4. **Remedies for Unlawful Redemption or Repurchase:** [§997]   Generally, the same remedies available for illegal dividends are available against directors and shareholders for unlawful redemptions or repurchases of shares. (*See* detailed discussion *supra*, §§971-978.)

X. FUNDAMENTAL CHANGES IN CORPORATE STRUCTURE

chapter approach

This chapter concerns fundamental corporate changes (principally, mergers, sales of substantially all assets, amendments of the articles (certificate) of incorporation, and dissolution), and the shareholder rights they trigger. The most important areas for exam purposes are as follows:

1. **Appraisal Rights of Shareholders:** Whenever you encounter a fundamental corporate change on an exam, consider whether the dissenting shareholders have appraisal rights requiring the corporation to buy their shares at "fair value" (or sometimes "fair market value"). Keep in mind that the exercise of appraisal rights often involves an elaborate procedure, such as notice by the shareholder of intent to demand payment, notice by the corporation that the proposed action was authorized, demand for payment by the dissenters, and payment by the corporation of the amount it determines to be the fair value of the shares. If the dissenting shareholders reject the corporation's estimate of fair value, the court determines fair value. Also, appraisal rights are sometimes exclusive— *i.e.*, a shareholder who is entitled to appraisal may not be able to seek other forms of relief.

2. **Statutory Merger:** A statutory merger occurs when one corporation is absorbed into another. This is normally accomplished by the "surviving" corporation issuing its shares to the shareholders of the "disappearing" corporation. In a merger case, consider whether the merger requires approval by the shareholders of each corporation and whether dissenting shareholders have appraisal rights. Generally, a merger must first be approved by the board. Thereafter, it must be submitted to the shareholders of each corporation, who must usually approve it by a majority of the outstanding shares. (Sometimes two-thirds of the outstanding shares is required.) Dissenters are usually entitled to appraisal rights. However, in "short-form" mergers, neither corporation's shareholders are entitled to vote on the plan, and only the subsidiary's shareholders have appraisal rights. Furthermore, under many statutes, only the shareholders of the disappearing corporation in a "small-scale" merger have approval and appraisal rights. Also, some statutes deny appraisal rights if the corporation's stock is listed on a national securities exchange or is held by over 2,000 shareholders.

3. **De Facto Mergers:** Watch for a question where a corporation attempts to circumvent the approval and appraisal rights of shareholders by (i) acquiring substantially all of a corporation's assets in exchange for stock or (ii) acquiring a majority of a corporation's stock in exchange for stock. Remember that many courts have held that a transaction that has the *effect* of a merger is deemed to be a merger for purposes of voting and appraisal rights.

4. **Sale of Substantially All Assets:** A sale, not in the ordinary course of business, of substantially all of the corporation's assets requires the approval of both the board and a majority (sometimes two-thirds) of outstanding shares. Most statutes also grant appraisal rights for shareholders dissenting to a sale of substantially all of the corporate assets.

5. **Amendment of Articles:** Generally, amendments to the articles of incorporation must be approved by the board and a majority (or two-thirds) of the outstanding shares. If the change will particularly affect a certain class, the approval of that class may also be required. Many states and the Model Act give appraisal rights to dissenters where, for example, the amendment adversely alters or abolishes a preferential right; excludes or limits a right to vote; alters or abolishes a preemptive right; or creates, alters, or abolishes a redemption right. Remember, however, that some states do not provide appraisal rights for any article amendments.

6. **Dissolution and Liquidation:** *Dissolution* terminates the corporation's status as a legal entity; *liquidation* terminates the corporation's business. For voluntary dissolution, approval by the board and a majority of the outstanding shares is normally required. Shareholders usually may bring an action for involuntary dissolution when, for example, the directors are deadlocked and irreparable injury is threatened; the directors are acting in an illegal, oppressive, or fraudulent manner; the shareholders are deadlocked; or the corporate assets are being misapplied or wasted. Most statutes also allow the state to institute dissolution proceedings on specified grounds (*e.g.*, fraud in obtaining the certificate of incorporation).

   After dissolution, the corporation must "liquidate" or "wind up" its affairs by paying its debts and distributing the remaining assets. On liquidation, creditors are paid first. Known creditors must be given notice of dissolution. A creditor who is on notice must present its claim within a given time period, or the claim will be barred. After the creditors are paid, every shareholder is generally entitled to a pro rata portion of the net assets remaining. However, preferred shares usually have a liquidation preference, which entitles their holders to payment before any distribution to holders of common stock.

7. **Limitations on Power of Controlling Shareholders:** Fundamental changes that increase the ownership or change the rights of controlling shareholders, directors, or officers are subject to judicial review for fairness. Such changes may, for example, provide a way for controlling shareholders to "freeze out" minority shareholders through a sale of substantially all assets, a cash-out merger, or a reverse stock split. Many courts require that a freeze-out serve a legitimate business purpose; other courts do not require a business purpose, but do require that the transaction meet the standard of entire fairness. "Going private" transactions, either through freeze-outs or self-tenders (tender offers by corporation for minority shares), are subject to extensive federal regulation, which includes disclosure provisions and an anti-fraud provision similar to rule 10b-5.

8. **Tender Offers:** In a tender offer, a bidder makes an offer to the shareholders of a target corporation to tender their shares for cash or securities. Since a tender offer addresses the shareholders in their individual capacities, it is not a corporate transaction from the target's perspective, and gives rise to neither shareholder voting nor appraisal rights in the target's shareholders in the absence of special statutes. Similarly, a tender offer generally does not require approval by the bidder's shareholders or give rise to appraisal rights in those shareholders, unless consummation of the tender offer would amount to a de facto merger.

   Keep in mind that tender offers are regulated in many ways by federal securities laws. For example, a person (or group) who acquires more than 5% of a corporation's securities that are registered under the Securities Exchange Act must file a schedule 13D disclosure form. Similarly, anyone making a tender offer for registered securities must file a schedule 14D disclosure form. Furthermore, the Exchange Act regulates the terms of such tender offers—*e.g.*, to whom they must be offered or the period they must remain open—and requires the target corporation's management to (i) recommend acceptance or rejection of the offer to the shareholders, (ii) remain neutral, or (iii) state that it is unable to take a position.

Remember too that section 14(e) of the Exchange Act prohibits material misstatements or omissions and fraudulent or manipulative acts in connection with a tender offer or a solicitation favoring or opposing a tender offer. Since this section was designed to protect the shareholders of the target, neither the bidder nor the target corporations may sue for damages under section 14(e), although they may seek injunctive relief. Target shareholders who tender their shares based on misleading information may sue for both damages and injunctive relief; nontendering shareholders may also be able to sue, provided they can show damages.

Because state statutes also regulate tender offers, your exam question may also require you to discuss the effect of such a statute. If a state statute is applicable, you should discuss whether the statute violates either the U.S. Constitution's Supremacy Clause (by conflicting with the federal regulation of tender offers) or the Commerce Clause (by regulating interstate commerce or imposing an excessive burden on interstate commerce).

A. INTRODUCTION [§998]

Fundamental changes in a corporation's structure are subject to special statutory requirements. The major fundamental changes are mergers, sales of substantially all assets, amendment of the articles (certificate) of incorporation, and dissolution. Tender offers are also subject to special rules.

B. APPRAISAL RIGHTS

1. **In General:** [§999]   Statutes in most states provide that shareholders who "dissent" from mergers or certain other kinds of fundamental corporate changes may require the corporation to purchase their shares at the "fair value" or "fair market value" of the shares—usually excluding any element of appreciation or depreciation resulting from anticipation or execution of the merger or other change. [Del. Gen. Corp. Law §262; RMBCA §§13.01-13.03, 13.20-13.28, 13.30-13.31; Cal. Corp. Code §§1300 *et seq.*]

2. **Valuation:** [§1000]   Most statutes provide that a dissenting shareholder has the right to be paid the "fair value" of his stock. Some statutes provide that a shareholder has the right to be paid the "fair market value" of his stock.

    a. **"Fair value" statutes:** [§1001]   Under statutes that provide that a dissenter must be paid the fair value of his shares, the two leading methods of valuation are the "Delaware block method" and the methods of modern finance.

       (1) **Delaware block method:** [§1002]   Traditionally, fair value was determined by applying the so-called "Delaware block method" of valuation. Under this method, the court separately determines the value of a corporation's stock under different bases of valuation (usually market

value, earnings value, and asset value, and sometimes, dividend value) and then assigns a weight to each valuation. The value of the stock is then calculated as the weighted average of the applicable valuations. For example, in *Piemonte v. New Boston Garden Corp.*, 387 N.E.2d 1145 (Mass. 1987), the Massachusetts Supreme Court approved the following weighting by the lower court:

Market Value	-	10%
Earnings Value	-	40%
Asset Value	-	50%

(a) **Market value:** [§1003]   The market value is the price at which the corporation's shares were being traded on the market just prior to announcement of the transaction. The weight given to market value will depend in part on how deep the market was, *i.e.*, whether there was extensive or only limited trading in the corporation's stock.

(b) **"Investment" or "earnings" value:** [§1004] "Investment" or "earnings" value is usually measured by determining the corporation's average annual earnings during some number of years (usually five) before the event that triggers appraisal rights, and then capitalizing (*i.e.*, multiplying) that average by a selected multiplier. [Tri-Continental Corp. v. Battye, 74 A.2d 71 (Del. 1950); Francis I. duPont & Co. v. Universal City Studios, Inc., 312 A.2d 344 (1973), *aff'd*, 334 A.2d 216 (Del. 1975)]

(c) **Asset value:** [§1005]   Asset value is normally based on the liquidation value of the corporation's assets. [Poole v. N.V. Deli Maatschappij, 243 A.2d 67 (Del. 1968)]

(d) **Dividend value:** [§1006]   Dividend value is sometimes taken into account, but often no separate weight is given to this element on the ground that it largely reflects the same value as earnings. [Francis I. duPont & Co. v. Universal City Studios, Inc., *supra*]

(2) **Modern financial methods:** [§1007]   A more modern approach to the valuation of stock for appraisal purposes is to allow proof of value to be made by any technique or method that is generally considered acceptable in the financial community and otherwise admissible in court. This approach was adopted by Delaware in *Weinberger v. UOP, Inc., supra*, §520, and is also adopted in New York by statute [N.Y. Bus. Corp. Law §623(h)(4)]. However, non-Delaware courts that have used the Delaware block method in the past may continue to do so. [*See* Leader v. Hycor, Inc., 479 N.E.2d 173 (Mass. 1985)]

b. **"Fair market value" statutes:** [§1008]   Some statutes provide that a dissenter should be paid "fair market value" (rather than "fair value"). Under such statutes, market price may be determinative unless the market is very thin or reflects aberrational factors.

c. **Minority and marketability discounts:** [§1009]   After the value of the corporation has been determined for appraisal purposes, some courts reduce the value of dissenting shares by applying minority discounts, marketability discounts, or both. In effect, minority and marketability discounts are second-step adjustments. In the first step, the court values the entire corporation and then assigns a pro rata share of that value to each share of stock. In the second step (if there is one), the court discounts (reduces) the pro rata value by a certain percentage.

(1) **Minority discounts:** [§1010]   The theory of a minority discount is that because a minority shareholder lacks corporate decisionmaking power, the pro rata value of a minority share is less than its pro rata share of corporate value.

(2) **Marketability discounts:** [§1011]   As a separate issue, some courts apply a marketability discount to minority shares in close corporations, on the ground that because shares in such corporations are not easily marketable, the fair value of such a share is less than the pro rata share of the corporation's value than the share represents.

(3) **Acceptance:** [§1012]   Some courts apply minority discounts, marketability discounts, or both, outside the mandatory buyout context, to determine the value of shares that are owned by shareholders who have dissented from a fundamental change, such as a merger. Generally speaking, though, the courts seem more ready to accept marketability discounts than to accept minority discounts. A few courts accept both. Two leading cases, *Cavalier Oil Corp. v. Harnett*, 564 A.2d 1137 (Del. 1989) and *In re Valuation of Common Stock of Mcloon Oil Co.*, 565 A.2d 997 (Me. 1989), reject both.

(4) **Exception—mandatory buyouts:** [§1013]   Most courts have held that a minority discount should not be applied when a corporation elects to buy out a shareholder who petitions for dissolution under a statutory mandatory buyout provision. (*See infra*, §1093.) In part, this position rests on the theory that if the minority shareholder had proved her case in the dissolution proceeding, and the corporation had been dissolved, each shareholder would have been entitled to the same amount per share. No consideration would be given, in dissolution, to whether the shares were controlling or noncontrolling. A mandatory buyout pursuant to a dissolution proceeding should be treated the same way. Furthermore, if a minority discount were applied in such cases, an unscrupulous controlling shareholder could engage in misconduct and unfairness to pressure minority shareholders to seek dissolution, and then buy the minority out at a depressed price.

3. **Procedure:** [§1014]   To qualify as a "shareholder" for purposes of the appraisal statutes, a shareholder must often follow an elaborate statutory procedure. The corporation must also follow an elaborate procedure in response. Details vary from state to state, but the procedure stated in the Model Act is typical:

a. **Notice to the corporation:** [§1015]   First, the shareholder must deliver to the corporation, before the vote is taken, written notice of her intent to demand payment for her shares if the proposed action is effectuated, and must not vote her shares in favor of the proposed action. [RMBCA §13.21(a)]

b. **Notice by the corporation:** [§1016]   If the proposed corporate action is authorized at a shareholders' meeting, the corporation must deliver a written notice to all shareholders who gave the notice of intent to demand payment and did not vote in favor of the transaction. The notice to dissenters must be sent no later than 10 days after the corporate action was taken, and must:

   (i)   State the *address* to which a demand for payment must be sent, and where and when stock certificates must be deposited;

   (ii)   Inform shareholders *to what extent transfer of their shares will be restricted* after their demand for payment is received;

   (iii)   Supply a *form* for demanding payment;

   (iv)   *Set a date* by which the demand for payment must be made, which may not be less than 30 nor more than 60 days after the date the notice to the shareholder is delivered; and

   (v)   Be accompanied by a copy of the *relevant statutory provisions*.

   [RMBCA §13.22]

c. **Duty to demand payment:** [§1017]   After receiving this notice, the shareholder must then demand payment from the corporation and deposit her stock certificates with the corporation. [RMBCA §13.23]

d. **Corporate response:** [§1018]   As soon as the proposed corporate action is taken, or upon receipt of a demand for payment, the corporation must pay each dissenter who has complied with the procedural requirements the amount the corporation estimates to be the fair value of the shares, plus accrued interest. The payment must be accompanied by:

   (i)   Designated *financial statements and income statements*;

   (ii)   A statement of the corporation's estimate of the *fair value* of the shares;

   (iii)   An explanation of *how the accrued interest was calculated*;

   (iv)   A statement of the *dissenter's rights*; and

   (v)   A copy of the *relevant statutory provisions*.

   [RMBCA §13.25]

e. **Appraisal proceedings:** [§1019]   If a dissenting shareholder is unwilling to accept the corporation's estimate of fair value, the corporation must petition the court to determine fair value. All dissenters whose demands remain unsettled must be made parties to the proceeding. The court may appoint one or more appraisers to receive evidence and recommend a decision on the question of fair value. The dissenters are entitled to the same discovery rights as parties in other civil proceedings. [RMBCA §13.30]

f. **Costs:** [§1020]   The costs of an appraisal proceeding, other than counsel and expert fees, are assessed against the corporation, except that the court may assess these costs against all or some of the dissenters, in amounts the court finds equitable, to the extent the court finds the dissenters acted arbitrarily, vexatiously, or not in good faith. The court may also assess counsel and expert fees, in amounts the court finds equitable, against the corporation if the court finds the corporation did not substantially comply with the statutory requirements, or against either the corporation or a dissenter if the court finds that the party acted arbitrarily, vexatiously, or not in good faith. [RMBCA §13.31]

C. STATUTORY MERGERS

1. **In General:** [§1021]   A statutory merger is a corporate combination in which one corporation is legally absorbed into another. To accomplish a statutory merger the corporation that will survive the merger (the "survivor") issues shares of its stock or other securities to shareholders of the other constituent corporation (the "disappearing corporation"). Under the statute, the disappearing corporation is thereby absorbed into the survivor, and the disappearing corporation's shareholders become shareholders in the survivor. [Del. Gen. Corp. Law §251(a)(e); RMBCA §§11.01, 11.03, 11.05, 11.06]

    a. **Consolidation:** [§1022]   A consolidation is similar to a merger, except that in a consolidation two or more existing corporations combine to form a wholly new corporation. Since the requirements for merger and consolidation are virtually identical, and the consolidation technique is rarely employed, the balance of this section will focus on mergers.

2. **Effect of Merger:** [§1023]   When a merger becomes effective, the disappearing corporation ceases to exist. The survivor succeeds, by operation of law, to all of the disappearing corporation's rights, assets, and liabilities. [Del. Gen. Corp. Law §259; RMBCA §11.06; Cal. Corp. Code §1107(a)]

    a. **Effect on corporate contracts:** [§1024]   Because the survivor succeeds to the disappearing corporation's rights, assets, and liabilities by operation of law, the disappearing corporation's contracts—even contracts that are not ordinarily assignable and indeed, even contracts that are not assignable by their terms—are generally taken over by the survivor by operation of law.

       (1) **Exception:** [§1025]   A contract may specifically provide that it is not assignable in a merger. Furthermore, a court may imply such a term in an appropriate case.

3. **Board Approval:** [§1026]   A merger is begun when the board of directors of each constituent corporation adopts a plan or agreement of merger. Normally, this plan or agreement must set forth:

   (i) The *terms and conditions* of the merger, including the manner of converting shares of the constituents into shares of the survivor;

   (ii) The *mode* of putting these terms into effect;

   (iii) A statement of *any amendments to the survivor's articles* (certificate) of incorporation to be effected by the merger; and

(iv) Any *other terms* agreed upon.

[Del. Gen. Corp. Law §251(b); RMBCA §11.01; Cal. Corp. Code §1101]

4. **Shareholder Approval:** [§1027]   After the merger plan or agreement is adopted by the board, it normally must be submitted to the shareholders of each constituent corporation for their approval.

a. **Percentage of approval required:** [§1028]   Because of the importance of mergers, most statutes require approval by a majority of the outstanding stock—not simply a majority of the shares present at a meeting. [Del. Gen. Corp. Law §251(c); RMBCA §11.03] Some statutes require that a merger be approved by two-thirds of the outstanding stock of each corporation.

b. **Class voting:** [§1029]   A number of statutes require that under certain conditions a merger be approved not only by a majority or two-thirds of the outstanding stock, but also by a designated percentage of each class of shareholders, whether or not otherwise entitled to vote. [RMBCA §11.03; Cal. Corp. Code §1201—approval of each class required, except that no approval by nonvoting preferred shareholders is necessary if no change in the rights, privileges, or preferences of the class]

c. **Appraisal rights:** [§1030]   Shareholders who dissent from a merger, and follow certain procedures, normally have a right to be paid the fair value of their shares. (*See supra,* §§999-1020.)

d. **Mergers that do not require shareholder approval:** [§1031]   There are two kinds of cases in which approval of one or both corporations' shareholders may not be required for a merger—"short-form" mergers and "small-scale" mergers.

(1) **Short-form mergers:** [§1032]   Many statutes provide special rules for the approval of a merger between a parent and a subsidiary in which the parent owns a designated percentage of the stock—normally 90%. [Del. Gen. Corp. Law §253; RMBCA §11.04; Cal. Corp. Code §1110(b)] Such mergers are known as "short-form" mergers.

(a) **Merger effected by boards of directors:** [§1033]   Typically, under these statutes, a short-form merger does not require the approval of either the parent's or the subsidiary's shareholders. Instead, the merger can be effected simply by the boards of the parent and the subsidiary, or, under some statutes, by the board of the parent alone.

1) **Rationale:** Since the parent owns almost all the subsidiary's stock, approval of the subsidiary's shareholders would be a foregone conclusion.

(b) **Appraisal rights:** [§1034]   Although the subsidiary's shareholders do not have the right to vote on a short-form merger, they do have appraisal rights. However, the parent's shareholders have neither voting nor appraisal rights.

(2) **Small-scale mergers:** [§1035]   Some statutes provide that approval by the shareholders of the *survivor* corporation is not required if:

(i) The voting stock of the survivor issued to effect the merger does not constitute more than a certain percentage—usually one-sixth—of the outstanding shares of voting stock immediately after the merger, and

(ii) The merger does not make any change in the survivor's articles (certificate) of incorporation.

[Del. Gen. Corp. Law §251(f); RMBCA §11.03(g); Cal. Corp. Code §1201(b)]

(a) **Rationale:** Such mergers are not economically or legally significant to the survivor and its shareholders.

(b) **Appraisal rights:** [§1036] Following this same rationale, in such cases the survivor's shareholders have no appraisal rights.

(c) **Shareholders of disappearing corporation:** [§1037] The small-scale merger statutes affect only the survivor corporation. Approval by the shareholders of the disappearing corporation is still required, because the merger is economically significant to that corporation. These shareholders also have appraisal rights.

e. **Mergers that do not trigger appraisal rights:** [§1038] Some statutes deny appraisal rights for certain mergers even though the merger requires shareholder approval.

(1) **Exceptions based on nature of merger:** [§1039] As noted above, in a short-form merger, the minority shareholders of the subsidiary have appraisal rights, but the parent's shareholders do not. (*See supra*, §1034.) Likewise, in a small-scale merger, the shareholders of the disappearing corporation have appraisal rights, but the shareholders of the survivor do not. (*See supra*, §1036.)

(2) **Exceptions based on nature of stock**

(a) **Stock listed on national exchange:** [§1040] Some statutes provide that a merger does not give rise to appraisal rights in the case of a corporation whose stock is listed on a national securities exchange.

1) **Rationale:** The theory of this exception is that in such cases the shareholder has an assured market for the stock, and therefore does not need an appraisal right to be able to get out of the corporation when it undergoes a fundamental change. Moreover, it is thought that where stock is traded on an organized market, it is unlikely that the appraisal valuation would differ significantly from the market price of the stock.

(b) **Stock held by over 2,000 shareholders:** [§1041] Some statutes also eliminate appraisal rights in the case of any corporation with 2,000 or more shareholders, whether or not the stock is listed on a securities exchange. [Del. Gen. Corp. Law §262(k)]

          1)   **Rationale:** With that many stockholders, the market is likely to be about as deep as it is on some stock exchanges.

     (c)   **Carve-out from exception:** [§1042] The California statute eliminates appraisal rights as to shares traded on the New York or American Stock Exchange, and as to certain over-the-counter stocks, *except* where the appraisal is demanded by shareholders holding 5% or more of the outstanding shares. [Cal. Corp. Code §1300(b)]

          1)   **Rationale:** If a block of shares this large entered the market, it would sell at a distress price, even in a well-organized market. Furthermore, the fact that so many shareholders prefer appraisal rights to selling their stock on the market provides a good indication that appraisal is not being sought merely as a nuisance tactic.

  f.   **Exclusivity of appraisal rights:** [§1043] Under some statutes, dissenting shareholders who have an appraisal right may not be permitted to invoke another remedy to challenge or upset the merger. (*See infra,* §1126.)

D. DE FACTO MERGERS

1. **Introduction:** [§1044] The explicit statutory rules that govern voting and appraisal rights in mergers often differ considerably from the explicit statutory rules that govern voting and appraisal rights for other kinds of corporate combinations, such as acquisitions by one corporation of the stock or assets of another. For example, a merger normally requires shareholder approval. In contrast, under the literal terms of most statutes, an acquisition of assets or stock normally does not. A merger normally triggers appraisal rights. In contrast, under the literal terms of most statutes, an acquisition of stock or assets normally does not. Under a few statutes, including Delaware, even a sale of substantially all assets does not trigger appraisal rights. Accordingly, there are certain gaps in the statutes, in that if only the explicit rules are considered, corporate combinations that are virtually identical in substance give rise to radically different shareholder rights, depending solely on the form in which management chooses to cast the combination. This difference in treatment sometimes seems anomalous, because a transaction that is cast in the form of an acquisition by one corporation of another corporation's assets or stock may have the practical effect of a merger. To help fill these gaps, the courts have created the de facto merger doctrine.

2. **Acquisition of Substantially All Assets in Exchange for Stock:** [§1045] Suppose one corporation acquires substantially all the assets of another in exchange, not for cash, but for its own stock. As part of the agreement the acquiring corporation assumes the transferor's liabilities, and the transferor agrees to dissolve and liquidate. In that case, the two corporations are combined, as in a merger: the liabilities of the assets of the two corporations are combined, as in a merger; the transferor corporation disappears, as in a merger; and the shareholder groups of the two corporations are combined, as in a merger. [Farris v. Glen Alden Corp., 143 A.2d 25 (Pa. 1958); Rath v. Rath Packing Co., 136 N.W.2d 410 (Iowa 1965)]

  a.   **Comment:** It is true that in an acquisition of assets, stock in the acquiring corporation is issued to the transferor corporation, while in a merger, stock in the survivor corporation is issued directly to the transferor corporation's shareholders. However, if the agreement requires the transferor corporation to immediately liquidate and distribute the stock to its shareholders, this difference is only one of form.

3. **Acquisition of Majority Stock in Exchange for Stock:** [§1046] Alternatively, suppose an acquiring corporation acquires a majority of the stock of another corporation in exchange for its own stock. From the perspective of the acquiring corporation's shareholders, the transaction is functionally equivalent to a merger, at least where the acquired corporation is then dissolved. The assets and liabilities of the two corporations are combined, as in a merger; one corporation disappears, as in a merger; and the two shareholder groups are combined, as in a merger. [Applestein v. United Board & Carton Corp., 159 A.2d 146 (1960), *aff'd*, 161 A.2d 474 (N.J. 1960)]

4. **De Facto Merger Doctrine:** [§1047] To protect the rights of shareholders in such stock-for-assets and stock-for-stock combinations, many courts hold that a transaction that has the effect of a merger is deemed to be a merger for purposes of voting and appraisal rights. Under this de facto merger doctrine, if one corporation acquires substantially all of another corporation's assets and assumes its liabilities in exchange for stock of the acquiror that is distributed to the transferor corporation's shareholders, the transaction will require the approval of the acquiring corporation's shareholders and will trigger appraisal rights for those shareholders. The same rule would apply to an acquisition of a majority of another corporation's stock in exchange for the acquiring corporation's stock. The test is whether the transaction has "all the characteristics and consequences," or the "indicia," of a merger. [Farris v. Glen Alden Corp., *supra*, §1045; Applestein v. United Board & Carton Corp., *supra*; Rath v. Rath Packing Co., *supra*, §1045]

5. **"Equal Dignity" Rule:** [§1048] Some courts have rejected the de facto merger doctrine. In particular, the Delaware courts say that the various forms for combinations all have "equal dignity," and the requirements of one form are irrelevant to others. Under this view, the form and label that management attaches to a corporate combination determines whether the transaction requires shareholder approval and triggers appraisal rights. [Hariton v. Arco Electronics, Inc., 188 A.2d 123 (Del. 1963); Heilbrunn v. Sun Chemical Corp., 150 A.2d 755 (Del. 1959)]

6. **Statutes:** [§1049] Several states have statutes that effectively eliminate the de facto merger problem by treating corporate combinations on the basis of substance rather than form.

   a. **California:** [§1050] The California statute illustrates this approach.

      (1) **Reorganizations:** [§1051] The statute creates a new category of corporate combinations, called "reorganizations." [Cal. Corp. Code §§181, 1200] The following are all considered "reorganizations" under the California statute:

        (i) *Merger reorganization*—A merger other than a short-form merger.

        (ii) *Exchange reorganization*—An acquisition by one corporation of more than 50% of the stock in another, wholly or partly in exchange for shares of the acquiring corporation.

(iii) *Sale-of-assets reorganization*—An acquisition by one corporation of substantially all of the assets of another, wholly or partly in exchange either for the acquiring corporation's shares or for debt securities that are not adequately secured and have a maturity greater than five years.

(2) **Shareholder rights:** [§1052] If a combination is a reorganization, as defined above, shareholders have the following voting and appraisal rights under the California statute:

(a) **Shareholder approval required:** [§1053] A merger or sale-of-assets reorganization must be approved by a majority of the shareholders of both constituent corporations. [Cal. Corp. Code §§15, 117] An exchange reorganization must be approved by shareholders of the acquiring corporation. [Cal. Corp. Code §§1200, 1201(a)]

1) **Exception—small-scale acquisitions:** [§1054] Approval by the shareholders of the acquiring or surviving corporation is not required if the persons who were shareholders immediately before the reorganization (or the corporation itself) end up owning at least five-sixths of the stock of the acquiring or surviving corporation, provided the reorganization does not require amendment of the corporation's articles.

(b) **Appraisal rights:** [§1055] If a reorganization requires approval by a corporation's shareholders under the California statute, the shareholders of that corporation are also given appraisal rights if they dissent from the proposed reorganization (subject to the California exceptions for securities traded on national exchanges (*supra*, §1042)). [Cal. Corp. Code §1300(a), (b)]

7. **New York Stock Exchange Rules:** [§1056] The rules of the New York Stock Exchange, like the California statute, require shareholder approval of certain corporate combinations regardless of form. Under these rules, securities to be issued by a company listed on the Exchange in connection with the direct or indirect acquisition of a business, a company, tangible or intangible assets, or property or securities representing any such interests cannot be listed on the exchange unless the acquisition is approved by the shareholders, if the issuance of common stock used to effect the acquisition could result in an increase in outstanding common shares of 18.5% or more, or has a fair value of 18.5% or more of the market value of the outstanding common shares of the issuing corporation. The American Stock Exchange has a comparable rule.

E. TRIANGULAR MERGERS [§1057]

Triangular mergers are a recent development in the merger area. There are two types of triangular mergers—conventional and reverse.

1. **Conventional Triangular Merger:** [§1058] A conventional (or "forward") triangular merger works like this: Assume that Corporations A and X want to engage in a merger in which A will be the survivor, and X's shareholders will end up with 100,000 shares of A. In a traditional merger, this would be accomplished by having A issue 100,000 shares to X's shareholders. In a conventional triangular merger, A

instead begins by creating a new subsidiary, B. A then transfers 100,000 shares of its own stock to B, in exchange for all of B's stock. X is then merged into B. However, instead of issuing its own stock to X's shareholders, B issues its 100,000 shares of A stock. The net result is that X's business is owned by A indirectly—through B, its wholly owned subsidiary—rather than directly by A itself, as in a traditional merger. X's shareholders end up with 100,000 shares of A stock, just as they would in a traditional merger with A itself.

a. **Purpose:** A major purpose for using this technique is that A may want to avoid assuming X's liabilities. In a traditional merger between A and X, A would succeed to X's liabilities by operation of law. By using a triangular merger, A may be able to insulate itself from direct responsibility for X's liabilities, because X is merged into B, not into A.

2. **Reverse Triangular Merger:** [§1059]   A reverse triangular merger begins like a conventional triangular merger. A creates a subsidiary, B, and transfers 100,000 shares of A stock to B in exchange for all of B's stock. In a conventional triangular merger, X would then be merged into B. In a reverse triangular merger, however, B is merged into X. The merger agreement provides that all previously outstanding X shares are automatically converted into the 100,000 shares of A held by B. All shares in B are automatically converted into shares in X. As a result, B disappears, because it is merged into X. X becomes a wholly owned subsidiary of A, because A owned all the shares of B and all the shares in B are converted into shares in X. X's shareholders own 100,000 shares of A stock, because all shares in X are converted into shares in A.

a. **Purpose:** Like a conventional triangular merger, a reverse triangular merger may insulate A from X's liabilities, because X ends up as a subsidiary of A, rather than merging into A. In addition, however, X's legal status as a corporation is preserved. This could be important where X has valuable rights under contracts, leases, licenses, or franchises that might be lost in a merger in which it was not the survivor.

3. **Voting and Appraisal Rights in Triangular Mergers:** [§1060]   Triangular mergers may be used to erode voting and appraisal rights. For example, in a merger of B into X, the subsidiary (B) rather than the parent (A) is a party to the merger. Literally, therefore, only B's shareholders have voting and appraisal rights. Because B's only shareholder is A, and because A obviously will vote its stock in B in favor of the merger, A's shareholders would not have voting or appraisal rights. In *Terry v. Penn Central Corp.*, 668 F.2d 188 (3d Cir. 1981), it was argued that such a merger is a de facto merger as to A. However, the court rejected this argument, at least under the Pennsylvania statute that governed the transaction, which had earlier been amended with the apparent purpose of rejecting the de facto merger theory.

F. SALE OF SUBSTANTIALLY ALL ASSETS

1. **Shareholder Approval**

a. **Approval normally required:** [§1061]   At common law, a sale of substantially all assets normally required unanimous shareholder approval, on the theory that it violated an implied contract among the shareholders to maintain the corporation in business. Today, virtually every state has a statute authorizing such a sale upon approval by the board and a requisite percentage of the shareholders. In most states, a majority of the outstanding shares is required. [Del. Gen. Corp. Law §271; RMBCA §§12.01, 12.02, 13.02; Cal. Corp. Code §1001(a)] In some states, approval by two-thirds of the outstanding shares is required.

b. **Exception for sales made in ordinary course of business:** [§1062] Some statutes explicitly exclude sales in the ordinary course of business from the requirement of shareholder approval. [RMBCA §12.01; Cal. Corp. Code §1001(a)(2)] Under such a statute, if for example, a corporation was organized to build and sell a single office building, the sale of the building would not require shareholder approval. Even where the statute does not explicitly so provide, courts have treated sales in the ordinary course of business as outside the statutory requirement of shareholder approval, on the theory that even at common law, where unanimous shareholder approval was required, sales made in the ordinary course of business were excepted, because they were deemed to be in furtherance (rather than in breach) of the implied contract among the shareholders. [Jeppi v. Brockman Holding Co., 34 Cal. 2d 11 (1949)]

c. **Exception for corporations in failing circumstances:** [§1063] There is a split of authority on whether the requirement of shareholder approval applies when a corporation is insolvent or in failing circumstances or financial distress. [*See* Teller v. W.A. Griswold Co., 87 F.2d 603 (6th Cir. 1937)—statute inapplicable; Michigan Wolverine Student Cooperative v. William Goodyear & Co., 22 N.W.2d 884 (Mich. 1946)—contra]

d. **Exception for mortgages, pledges, etc.:** [§1064] Most statutes do not require shareholder approval for the corporation's execution of a mortgage or other lien on corporate assets for the purpose of securing a corporate obligation. [RMBCA §12.01; Cal. Corp. Code §1000]

2. **Appraisal Rights:** [§1065] Where a sale of substantially all assets requires shareholder approval, most statutes also provide dissenting shareholders with appraisal rights.

a. **Exceptions:** [§1066] A few statutes do not confer appraisal rights in connection with the sale of assets. [*See* Del. Gen. Corp. Law §262] Furthermore, some statutes that confer appraisal rights generally make exceptions for certain kinds of sales. [Cal. Corp. Code §§181, 1300—no appraisal rights where corporate assets are sold entirely for cash or for adequately secured short-term debt securities]

3. **What Constitutes "Substantially All Assets":** [§1067] In determining whether a sale of assets includes "substantially all assets" for purposes of the statute, the question is not simply the percentage of assets sold, but whether the assets sold constitute substantially all of the corporation's operating assets, account for most of the corporation's revenues, or are vital to the operation of the corporation's business. [Katz v. Bregman, 431 A.2d 1974, *appeal denied*, 435 A.2d 1044 (Del. 1981)]

G. AMENDMENT OF ARTICLES

1. **In General:** [§1068] Fundamental changes in the corporation may be effected through amendment of the corporate articles. Some amendments may be pure formalities (*e.g.*, changing the name of the corporation). Others may substantially

change or impair the rights of the shareholders (*e.g.*, making cumulative preferred shares noncumulative). Still others may substantially affect the corporation itself (*e.g.*, changing the corporation's business purpose).

2. **Vote Required:** [§1069]   An amendment of the corporation's articles normally must be approved by (i) the board and (ii) a majority or (under some statutes) two-thirds of the outstanding shares.

   a. **Class voting:** [§1070]   Under many statutes, amendments that would have certain designated effects on the shares of a given class must be approved not only by the shareholders as a whole, but also by the class voting separately—whether or not stock of the class is otherwise entitled to vote. For example, under the Model Act an amendment to the articles of incorporation requires the approval of each class of shareholders—even those classes not entitled to vote under the articles of incorporation—if it would increase or decrease the authorized shares of the class; limit or deny a preemptive right; change shares of the class into a different number of shares of the same class; change the rights, preferences, or limitations of the class; create a new class of shares having superior or substantially equal financial rights or preferences; or increase the rights, preferences, or number of shares of any class that have superior or substantially equal financial rights or preferences. [RMBCA §§10.04, 11.03(f)(1)]

   b. **Special provisions:** [§1071]   Statutes may also contain special provisions placing limitations on certain kinds of articles amendments. For example, under the Delaware statute, an amendment restricting transferability of shares is not binding on shares already issued, unless approved by the holders of the shares in question. [Del. Gen. Corp. Law §202(b)] Under the California statute, an amendment reducing the number of directors to less than five cannot be adopted over the opposition of more than $16\,^2/3\%$ of the outstanding shares. [Cal. Corp. Code §212(a)]

   c. **Effect of provision in articles requiring higher percentage:** [§1072]   Under most statutes, the articles may validly require a higher (but not a lower) percentage of shareholder approval for any proposed amendment than would otherwise be required by the statute. [Del. Gen. Corp. Law §§216, 242(b)(1); RMBCA §727; Cal. Corp. Code §904(a)(5)] Similarly, most courts will enforce shareholder agreements requiring a higher percentage of shareholder approval than would otherwise be required by statute. (*See supra*, §574.)

3. **Appraisal Rights:** [§1073]   Many states give appraisal rights in connection with certain kinds of article amendments. For example, under the Model Act, shareholders have a right to be paid the fair value of their shares if they dissent from an amendment that materially and adversely alters or abolishes a preferential right; excludes or limits the right to vote on any matter; alters or abolishes a preemptive right; or creates, alters, or abolishes a right of redemption. [RMBCA §13.02(a)(4)] However, many statutes do not provide appraisal rights in connection with article amendments.

4. **Constitutional Issues**

   a. **Contract between state and corporation:** [§1074]   The Supreme Court early held that, for purposes of constitutional law, a certificate of incorporation is a contract between the incorporating state and the corporation, and therefore is within the Contract Clause, which prohibits states from impairing the obligation of contracts. [Trustees of Dartmouth College v. Woodward, 17 U.S. 518 (1819); U.S. Const. art. I, §10]

b. **Contract among shareholders:** [§1075]   Subsequently, the Supreme Court held that the certificate of incorporation was also a contract among the shareholders, and therefore, it could not be changed without their unanimous consent. [Geddes v. Anaconda Copper Mining Co., 254 U.S. 590 (1921)]

c. **Result—limited state power:** [§1076]   The result was to set limits on the power of a state to regulate corporations organized under its laws and also on the power of the shareholders—absent unanimity—to amend the articles of incorporation or make any fundamental change in the corporation that could be regarded as a change in their "contract."

d. **Reserved power clauses:** [§1077]   In response, the states amended their general corporation laws to include "reserved power clauses," *i.e.*, provisions reserving to the state the power to alter, amend, or repeal its corporation laws as regards corporations incorporated after the adoption of such provisions. These reserved power clauses are deemed to be part of the "contract" between the state and the corporation and are therefore given effect by the courts.

e. **Shareholder amendment:** [§1078]   State corporations laws were also amended to permit the shareholders of corporations organized thereunder to amend the articles of incorporation or adopt other fundamental changes with less-than-unanimous consent. These provisions were also given effect.

f. **Today:** [§1079]   Most existing corporations have been either organized or reorganized under statutes that contain reserved-power and shareholder-amendment provisions. Since the granting of any corporate charter is subject to these provisions, the incorporators are deemed to have consented to them. Therefore, the problem whether an amendment to the articles of incorporation constitutes an impairment of contract is relatively minor today.

g. **Remaining problems:** [§1080]   The remaining problems are (i) whether there are any constitutional or implied contractual limitations on the power of the state to amend its laws in a way that affects corporations incorporated prior to the adoption of a reserved power clause, and (ii) whether there are any limits on the power of a state to regulate, or on the power of shareholders to amend the articles of, corporations incorporated after adoption of a reserved power clause.

   (1) **Limitations on powers of state**

      (a) **Changes affecting corporation's business:** [§1081]   In the case of general laws that apply only to the corporation's business activities, as opposed to the rights and duties of shareholders, it is clear today that the state's power to change the law is not limited by *Dartmouth College* (*see supra*, §1074). For example, the state may enact general laws restricting or prohibiting certain businesses even though such businesses were proper at the time the corporation was originally organized, and even though the law affects a corporation incorporated prior to the adoption of a reserved power clause.

(b) **Changes affecting persons:** [§1082]   On the other hand, there may still be some limitations on the state power to regulate the rights of shareholders, director, officers, or corporate creditors, as such, even where reserved power clauses are in effect. Specifically, a state cannot eliminate "vested property rights" or "impair the obligations of contract of third persons." [Coombes v. Getz, 285 U.S. 434 (1932)] In *Coombes*, creditors of a corporation filed an action against its directors under a provision of state law that made directors liable for corporate funds embezzled or misappropriated by officers. While the action was pending, the relevant state law provision was repealed. The Supreme Court held that the repeal was ineffective as to the plaintiff-creditors because it would not be permitted to affect their "vested" rights against the directors.

  1) **Rationale:** The rationale of *Coombes v. Getz* was that the exercise of a state's reserved powers is still subject to the limitations of the United States Constitution. Such state action may constitute a taking without compensation in violation of the Due Process Clause.

(2) **Limitations on shareholders' power**

  (a) **"Vested property rights" theory:** [§1083]   In the past, the vested-property-rights theory also constituted a significant limitation on shareholder power to amend the certificate. Many cases struck down certain kinds of amendments that seriously altered shareholder rights—particularly the rights of preferred shareholders to receive accrued but unpaid dividends—where the type of amendment in question was not explicitly authorized by the statute in force at the time the corporation was organized. [Keller v. Wilson & Co., 190 A. 115 (Del. 1936)] However, other courts rejected this approach [McNulty v. W. & J. Sloane, 34 A.D.2d 284 (1945)], and even those courts that accepted this approach allowed equivalent results to be reached through other techniques, such as mergers. [Federal United Corp. v. Havender, 11 A.2d 331 (Del. 1940)] This problem is largely historical, because most existing corporations have been organized or reorganized under statutes that explicitly authorize almost every conceivable type of shareholder amendment, and because modern courts are generally unsympathetic to the vested-rights theory.

  (b) **Fairness:** [§1084]   A much more significant limitation is that of fairness. Where a controlling shareholder causes a corporation to amend its articles in a manner that arguably benefits that shareholder, a minority shareholder can complain that the amendment is fraudulent or unfair. [Bove v. The Community Hotel Corp., 249 A.2d 89 (R.I. 1969)] The fairness issue frequently arises in attempts to recapitalize a corporation in a manner that adversely affects the rights, preferences, or privileges of a certain class of shareholders—

e.g., reducing the dividend rate on preferred shares, making the dividends noncumulative instead of cumulative, or issuing a new class of preferred with priorities senior to the class already outstanding.

H. DISSOLUTION AND LIQUIDATION

1. **Introduction:** [§1085] Dissolution involves the termination of a corporation's status as a *legal entity*. Dissolution falls into two basic categories, voluntary and involuntary. Voluntary dissolution occurs as a result of a decision of the corporation, acting through appropriate corporate organs. Involuntary dissolution is forced upon the corporation by the courts. To be distinguished from dissolution is the related process of liquidation, which involves termination of the corporation's business.

2. **Voluntary Dissolution:** [§1086] For voluntary dissolution, the statutes typically require a vote of the board recommending a plan of dissolution to the shareholders, and approval of the plan by a majority of the outstanding shares. [RMBCA §14.03] Some statutes have much different requirements. For example, in California board approval is not required, and 50% shareholder approval is sufficient. [Cal. Corp. Code §1900]

3. **Involuntary Dissolution:** [§1087] Involuntary dissolution may be precipitated by shareholders, the state, or, under some statutes, the directors.

   a. **Action by shareholders or directors**

      (1) **Nonstatutory involuntary dissolution:** [§1088] The original rule at common law was that, absent statutory authority, courts had no jurisdiction to grant dissolution at the request of a minority shareholder. [Leventhal v. Atlantic Finance Corp., 55 N.E.2d 20 (Mass. 1944)] Eventually, however, most (although not all) courts took the position that they could grant dissolution for fraud, dissension, deadlock, abuse to minority shareholders, or gross mismanagement, even in the absence of a statute providing for dissolution on those grounds. [Miner v. Belle Isle Ice Co., 53 N.W. 218 (Mich. 1892); Lichens Co. v. Standard Commercial Tobacco Co., 40 A.2d 447 (Del. 1944)] However, nonstatutory dissolution is rarely granted.

      (2) **Involuntary dissolution under statute:** [§1089] Today, statutes in most states set forth grounds under which shareholders can bring judicial proceedings to force dissolution.

         (a) **Grounds:** [§1090] These statutes vary widely as to the grounds for involuntary dissolution. However, the Model Act includes many of the typical grounds. It provides that a court can dissolve a corporation in a proceeding by a shareholder if any of the following grounds are established:

            (i) The *directors are deadlocked* in the management of the corporate affairs, the shareholders are unable to break the deadlock, and because of the deadlock irreparable injury to the corporation is threatened or being suffered, or the business and affairs of the corporation can no longer be conducted to the advantage of the shareholders generally;

(ii) The directors or those in control of the corporation have acted, are acting, or will act in a manner that is *illegal, oppressive, or fraudulent*;

(iii) The *shareholders are deadlocked* in voting power and have failed, for a period that includes at least two consecutive annual meeting dates, to elect successors to directors whose terms have expired; or

(iv) The corporate *assets* are being *misapplied or wasted*.

[RMBCA §14.30(2)]

(b) **Application to close corporations:** [§1091] As a practical matter, involuntary dissolution is highly unlikely to be ordered except in closely held corporations. In such corporations, however, dissolution is a very important remedy, especially for oppression by those in control. The statutes are gradually increasing the grounds for involuntary dissolution to include oppression and like grounds, and the courts are increasingly giving the statutes an expansive reading and are readier than in the past to order dissolution. Although some cases focus on the wrongfulness of the conduct of those who are in control [Baker v. Commercial Body Builders, Inc., 507 P.2d 387 (Or. 1973)], the trend is to focus on whether the conduct of those in control frustrates the reasonable expectations of those not in control [*In re* Kemp & Beatley, Inc., 64 N.Y.2d 63 (1984); Meiselman v. Meiselman, 307 S.E.2d 551 (N.C. 1983)].

(c) **Who can bring action:** [§1092] Under some statutes, there is a limitation on shareholder standing to sue for involuntary dissolution. Under the California statute, for example, a shareholder petition for dissolution can be filed only by one of the following:

(i) *One-third of the shareholders* (other than those alleged to have participated personally in management wrongdoing, where that is the ground on which dissolution is sought);

(ii) *Any shareholder of a statutory close corporation*;

(iii) *Any shareholder* of any corporation, where the ground for dissolution is *expiration of the period* for which the corporation was formed; or

(iv) *Any other person authorized in the articles* to bring such an action.

[Cal. Corp. Code §1800(a)]

(d) **Mandatory buyout:** [§1093] Under some statutes, noncomplaining shareholders may avoid involuntary dissolution by purchasing (or causing the corporation to purchase) the shares of the complaining shareholders at their fair cash value as determined by the court. [Cal. Corp. Code §2000] Normally, under these statutes, if the other shareholders or the corporation make an election to buy out the complaining shareholder, the latter must sell her shares.

1) **Compare—voluntary dissolution:** [§1094]   A similar mandatory buyout right exists under the California statute where voluntary dissolution is initiated by 50% of the shareholders. The other 50% of the shareholders have the option to prevent dissolution by purchasing the shares of those who want to dissolve. [Cal. Corp. Code §2000]

4. **Dissolution Under Shareholder Agreement:** [§1095]   Courts may also order dissolution to effect a preexisting agreement among the shareholders. For example, close-corporation agreements sometimes provide that upon the happening of certain defined events (*e.g.*, completion of a certain project), each shareholder (or certain designated shareholders) will have the option to require dissolution of the corporation. Such agreements are valid and will be given effect, even if not specifically authorized by statute. [Leventhal v. Atlantic Finance Corp., *supra*, §1088]

5. **Action by Directors:** [§1096]   Some statutes permit directors to petition for involuntary dissolution on specified grounds. [Cal. Corp. Code §1800(a)—one-half of the directors can petition for dissolution on the same grounds as shareholders]

6. **Action by State:** [§1097]   Most statutes also allow designated state officials to institute dissolution proceedings on specified grounds. For example, the Model Act authorizes dissolution in a proceeding by the attorney general, if it is established that the corporation obtained its articles of incorporation through fraud or the corporation has continued to exceed or abuse the authority conferred upon it by law. [RMBCA §14.30] The Model Act authorizes the secretary of state to begin proceedings for administrative dissolution if a corporation does not pay any franchise tax within 60 days after it is due, or does not deliver its annual report to the secretary of state within 60 days after it is due. The corporation then has 60 days to correct the problem; if it fails to do so, the secretary can cause administrative dissolution of the corporation. [RMBCA §§14.20-14.21]

7. **Liquidation**

   a. **Nature of liquidation:** [§1098]   Dissolution does not in itself terminate the corporate business. After dissolution, the corporation must still "liquidate" or "wind up" its affairs, pay or make provision for payment of its debts, and distribute its remaining assets or sell the remaining assets and distribute the proceeds. Under the Model Act, for example, a dissolved corporation continues its corporate existence, and may carry on any business that is appropriate to wind up and liquidate its business affairs, including: (i) collecting its assets; (ii) disposing of properties that will not be distributed in kind to its shareholders; (iii) discharging or making provision for discharging its liabilities; (iv) distributing its remaining property among its shareholders according to their interests; and (v) doing every other act necessary to wind up and liquidate its business and affairs. However, the corporation may not carry on any business that is not necessary to wind up and liquidate its business affairs. [RMBCA §14.05]

   b. **Management:** [§1099]   During the liquidation or winding-up process, the corporation continues under the management of the board. However, if the directors continue to operate the business of the corporation after dissolution beyond the period reasonably required for the winding-up process, they may be held personally liable for the corporation's debts. [*Borbein, Young & Co. v. Cirese*, 401 S.W.2d 940 (Mo. 1966)]

c. **Rights of shareholders on dissolution**

(1) **Where corporation has only common stock:** [§1100]   Where a corporation has only common stock, the general rule is that on liquidation every shareholder is entitled to a pro rata portion of the net assets remaining after the claims of creditors have been paid or provided for.

(a) **Form of distribution:** [§1101]   Under most statutes, liquidating distributions to the holders of common stock normally can be made either in cash or (if practicable) in property. [Cal. Corp. Code §2006] In the absence of unanimous consent, the corporation ordinarily cannot discriminate among shareholders by adopting a plan of distribution under which unique property is distributed to certain designated shareholders, while cash is distributed to others (*e.g.*, giving cash to minority shareholders, while giving irreplaceable corporate assets (patents, etc.) to majority shareholders). [*In re* San Joaquin Light & Power Co., 52 Cal. App. 2d 814 (1942)]

(2) **Where corporation has preferred stock:** [§1102]   If there is a class of preferred stock outstanding, the certificate of incorporation will usually provide that shares of that class are entitled to a liquidation preference. This means that the net assets remaining after creditors have been paid must be applied to payment of the preferred stock's liquidation preference before any distribution is made to holders of common stock.

d. **Rights of creditors**

(1) **Notice:** [§1103]   A corporation remains liable on its debts after dissolution. In winding up, the first priority is to pay these debts. To expedite liquidation, however, some statutes create a time limit within which a creditor who has been given proper notice of the dissolution must file a claim in the dissolution proceedings. Creditors who are on notice and do not file a claim within this period are thereafter barred from bringing suit on their claims.

(a) **Disposition by written notice:** [§1104]   The Model Act provides that a dissolved corporation may give known claimants written notice of dissolution. The notice must state a deadline, at least 120 days after the date of the notice, by which the dissolved corporation must receive a claim. The notice must state that the claim will be barred if not received by the deadline. If a claimant who was given such notice does not present the claim to the dissolved corporation by the deadline, the claim is barred. The claim is also barred if a claimant whose claim was presented and rejected does not begin a proceeding to enforce the claim within 90 days from the effective date of the rejection notice. [RMBCA §14.06]

(b) **Disposition by publication:** [§1105] The Model Act also provides that a dissolved corporation may publish notice of its dissolution in a newspaper of general circulation in the county and request that persons with claims against the corporation present them in accordance with the notice. The notice must describe the information that has to be included in a claim, provide a mailing address where the claim may be sent, and state that a claim will be barred unless a proceeding to enforce it is begun within five years after the publication of the notice. All claims against the dissolved corporation, including unknown claims, contingent claims, and known claims that were not the subject of individual written notice, are then barred unless a proceeding to enforce the claim is brought within five years after the newspaper notice. [RMBCA §14.07]

(2) **Right to trace corporate assets:** [§1106] If the corporation's assets are distributed prior to satisfaction of creditors' claims, an unpaid creditor who is not barred by the failure to present a timely claim may recover from the transferee shareholders.

I. LIMITATIONS ON POWER OF CONTROLLING SHAREHOLDERS TO EFFECT FUNDAMENTAL CHANGES IN CORPORATE STRUCTURE

1. **Fiduciary Duties Owed by Controlling Shareholders to Minority—Fairness:** [§1107] Recall that controlling shareholders owe a broad fiduciary duty to minority shareholders with respect to the exercise of corporate control (*supra*, §633). This duty is particularly relevant to fundamental changes in which the controlling shareholders are self-interested (*e.g.*, a merger between Corporation C in which S owns a majority of stock, and Corporation D, which is wholly owned by S). Such transactions are subject to a requirement of fairness and can be set aside if unfair. [Sterling v. Mayflower Hotel Corp., 93 A.2d 107 (Del. 1952)]

   a. **Arm's-length combinations:** [§1108] A long line of Delaware cases hold that even an arm's-length corporate combination is subject to judicial review for fairness of consideration. However, in such cases, the burden of proof is on the plaintiff to show that there is such a gross disparity between the value of the assets sold and the consideration received "as will raise an inference of improper motives or reckless indifference to or intentional disregard of stockholders' interests." [Gimbel v. Signal Companies, 316 A.2d 599 (1974), *aff'd*, 316 A.2d 619 (Del. 1974)]

2. **Freeze-outs:** [§1109] Often a controlling shareholder wishes to eliminate ("freeze out") minority shareholders from any further participation in the corporate enterprise. Among the techniques sometimes used to effect a freeze-out of minority shareholders are the following:

   a. **Sale of substantially all assets:** [§1110] A sale of substantially all assets may be used to freeze out minority shareholders by causing the corporation, C, to sell its assets to a controlling shareholder, S, or to a corporation that S controls, for cash. The minority shareholders in C end up with stock in a corporation that holds only cash (and which is normally dissolved), while S ends up with 100% ownership of the corporate business. [Theis v. Spokane Falls Gaslight Co., 74 P. 1004 (Wash. 1904); Matteson v. Ziebarth, 242 P.2d 1025 (Wash. 1952)]

b. **Mergers:** [§1111]   Most merger statutes now permit the surviving corporation in a merger to issue cash, rather than stock, in exchange for stock of the disappearing corporation. This creates another freeze-out technique: Assume that S is shareholder of Corporation C and owns all the stock of Corporation D. S then arranges a "cash-out merger" of C into D, in which D issues cash rather than stock to C's minority shareholders. Here again, the minority shareholders in C end up with stock in a corporation that holds only cash, and S ends up with all of the corporate business. [Weinberger v. UOP, Inc., *supra*, §1007] (Much the same result can be achieved if D issues debentures or redeemable preferred instead of cash.)

c. **Reverse stock splits:** [§1112]   Most statutes empower a corporation to involuntarily eliminate fractional shares (*i.e.*, shareholdings representing less than one full share) by paying any holder of fractional shares the value of the fractional shares in cash. This gives rise to another freeze-out technique. Under this technique, the corporation effects a reverse stock split by amending its articles to drastically reduce the number of outstanding shares, and then pays off (and thereby ousts) shareholders who own fractional shares as a result of the reverse split.

   (1) **Example:** Corporation C amends its certificate to cause every 1,000 existing shares to become one share. Each person holding less than 1,000 shares thus ends up owning a fractional share, and then is frozen out when C exercises its right to eliminate fractional shares.

d. **Two kinds of freeze-out:** [§1113]   Freeze-outs can be placed into two categories. In some cases, a freeze-out is effected by a combination of two preexisting business *enterprises* (not simply two preexisting corporate *entities*). In other cases (*e.g.*, a reverse stock split or a cash-out merger into a shell corporation), there is no change in the business enterprise, but only a change in the corporate entity, its ownership, or both.

e. **Permissibility of freeze-outs:** [§1114]   The courts have taken different lines on whether freeze-outs are permissible.

   (1) **Legitimate business purpose:** [§1115]   Many courts hold that a freeze-out is permissible if, but only if, it is effected for a legitimate business purpose. [Coggins v. New England Patriots Football Club, Inc., 492 N.E.2d 1112 (Mass. 1986)] Normally, the business purpose test requires a showing that eliminating the minority shareholders will increase corporate income or assets, *i.e.*, will make the pie bigger, rather than simply redistributing the value of the enterprise from the minority shareholders to the controlling shareholders.

      (a) **Operating efficiency:** [§1116]   The clearest business purpose for a freeze-out is a combination between two preexisting business enterprises (most typically, a controlling parent and a partially owned subsidiary) that arguably will result in operating efficiencies.

      (b) **Increase corporate income or assets:** [§1117]   Some cases accept a business purpose even in the absence of a combination of two different business enterprises, where it can be shown that elimination of the noncontrolling shareholders will increase corporate income or assets. [Alpert v. 28 Williams St. Corp., 63 N.Y.2d 557 (1984)] At least one case permitted a reverse stock split technique to be used for elimination of a very small minority interest (0.01%) by analogizing the transaction to a short-form merger. [Teschner v. Chicago Title & Trust Co., 322 N.E.2d 54 (Ill. 1974)] In another case, however, it was held that such a transaction was subject to attack if no compelling business purpose was shown. [Clark v. Pattern Analysis & Recognition Corp., 87 Misc. 2d 385 (1976)]

(2) **Entire fairness:** [§1118]   Delaware does not require a business purpose for a freeze-out. However, any self-interested combinations, including freeze-outs, must meet the standard of entire fairness. [Weinberger v. UOP, Inc., *supra*, §1111; Rabkin v. Philip A. Hunt Chemical Corp., 498 A.2d 1099 (Del. 1985)]

3. **Effect of Securities Acts:** [§1119]   In addition to rights under state law—or even when the only right under state law is to ask for appraisal—a shareholder objecting to a merger (or other fundamental change) may be able to bring an action for violation of rule 10b-5 or the federal proxy rules if the controlling shareholder has not made full disclosure of all material facts surrounding the transaction. (*See supra*, §§339-429, 521-558.) However, where there has been full disclosure, a complaining shareholder's remedies, if any, must be found under state law.

4. **Self-Tender:** [§1120]   Another technique for effectively eliminating most or all minority shareholders is to cause the corporation to make a tender offer for the minority shares (a "self-tender"). This is technically not a freeze-out, because it is not involuntary: A shareholder is not legally required to tender her shares in a self-tender. As a practical matter, however, she may have little economic alternative, because the self-tender may have an adverse effect on nontendering shareholders, by drying up the market for their stock, causing delisting of the corporation's stock, etc.

5. **Going-Private Transactions—Rule 13e-3**

a. **In General:** [§1121]   Transactions that eliminate public ownership, whether through a freeze-out or a self-tender, are sometimes known as "going-private" transactions. Rule 13e-3 of the Securities Exchange Act governs going-private transactions involving corporations with equity securities registered under that Act.

b. **Definition:** [§1122]   A "rule 13e-3 transaction" includes:

(1) *A purchase* of any equity security by the issuer (*i.e.*, the corporation);

(2) *A tender offer* for any equity security made by the issuer; and

(3) *A solicitation of proxies* in connection with a merger or similar corporate transaction, a sale of substantially all assets, or a reverse stock split, if the effect of the transaction is (i) to cause any class of the corporation's equity securities registered under the 1934 Act to be held of record by *fewer than 300 persons*, or (ii) to cause any class of the corporation's equity securities that is listed on a national securities exchange to be *delisted*.

c. **Requirement of filing and disseminating information:** [§1123] An issuer that proposes to engage in a rule 13e-3 transaction must file and disseminate a schedule 13e-3. The schedule 13e-3 must include information on alternative means to accomplish the relevant purpose, the reasons for the structure and timing of the transaction, and the benefits and detriments of the transaction to the issuer and minority shareholders (including the federal tax consequences). The schedule 13e-3 must also state "whether the issuer . . . reasonably believes that the rule 13e-3 transaction is fair or unfair to unaffiliated security holders" and must discuss "in reasonable detail the material factors upon which the belief . . . is based." According to an instruction to the schedule, such factors will normally include:

(1) Whether the consideration offered to minority shareholders constitutes *fair value* in relation to current market prices, historical market prices, net book value, going concern value, and liquidation value.

(2) The *purchase price* paid by the issuer for the securities during the preceding two fiscal years.

(3) *Any report, opinion, or appraisal* obtained from outside parties.

(4) *Firm offers* made by an outsider during the preceding 18 months in connection with a proposed combination.

d. **Anti-fraud rule:** [§1124] If a going-private transaction falls under rule 13e-3, the transaction is subject to an anti-fraud rule that is comparable to rule 10b-5, but does not contain the "in connection with the purchase and sale of securities" limitation of rule 10b-5.

6. **Effect of Appraisal Rights:** [§1125] If a transaction triggers appraisal rights, those rights are sometimes deemed exclusive of other remedies. Just when, and to what extent, appraisal rights will be exclusive is a complex question that depends on the terms of the relevant statute, the ground on which the transaction is attacked, and the precise remedy sought.

a. **Statutes that explicitly make appraisal exclusive remedy:** [§1126] Some statutes explicitly make appraisal rights an exclusive remedy. For example, the Pennsylvania statute provides that if a shareholder dissents from a transaction, he is limited to his appraisal rights, and if he does not dissent, he is conclusively presumed to have consented. [Pa. Bus. Corp. Act §1515(B)]

(1) **But note:** Even under this kind of statute, the availability of appraisal rights normally does not preclude an attack based on the grounds that:

(a) The transaction is *not authorized* under the statute;

(b) The *procedural steps* required to effectuate the transaction (*e.g.*, a shareholder vote) were not properly taken; or

(c) Shareholder approval of the transaction was obtained through *misrepresentation* or without disclosure of material facts.

b. **Most statutes do not explicitly make appraisal exclusive remedy**

(1) **Injunctive relief or rescission:** [§1127]   The general rule is that in the absence of explicit statutory language, the mere availability of appraisal rights does not preclude shareholders from seeking injunctive relief or rescission for fraud (using that term in the broad sense to include unfair self-dealing by fiduciaries). However, some cases suggest that the availability of appraisal rights precludes a suit for injunctive relief or rescission even in the absence of explicit statutory language. [Pupecki v. James Madison & Co., 382 N.E.2d 1030 (Mass. 1978); Blumenthal v. Roosevelt Hotel, Inc., 202 Misc. 988 (1952)]

(2) **Monetary damages:** [§1128]   Even statutes that do not explicitly make the appraisal remedy exclusive are often interpreted to preclude a shareholder from bringing a suit based on the transaction in which he asks only for monetary damages measured by the value of his stock. [Adams v. United States Distributing Corp., 34 S.E.2d 244 (Va. 1945)]

(3) **Delaware view:** [§1129]   The Delaware courts recognize that although monetary remedies normally should be confined to an appraisal proceeding, the appraisal remedy may not be adequate in certain cases, particularly where fraud, misrepresentation, self-dealing, deliberate waste of corporate assets, or gross and palpable overreaching are involved. [Weinberger v. UOP, Inc., *supra*, §1118; Rabkin v. Philip A. Hunt Chemical Co., *supra*, §1118]

J.   TENDER OFFERS

1.   Terminology

a.   **Raider:** [§1130]   The term "raider" refers to a person (normally, although not necessarily, a corporation) that makes a tender offer. The term is somewhat invidious; a more accurate term is ***bidder***.

b.   **Target:** [§1131]   The corporation whose shares the bidder seeks to acquire is referred to as the target.

c.   **White knight:** [§1132]   Often the management of a target realizes that it will be taken over, but prefers a takeover by someone other than the original bidder. The management therefore solicits competing tender offers from other corporations. These more friendly corporations are known as "white knights."

d.   **Lock-up:** [§1133]   A "lock-up" is a device that is designed to protect one bidder (normally, a friendly bidder) against competition by other bidders (deemed less friendly). The favored bidder is given an option to acquire selected assets or shares in the target at a favorable price under designated conditions. These conditions usually involve either defeat of the favored bidder's attempt to acquire the corporation, or the occurrence of events that would make that defeat likely.

e.   **Crown jewels:** [§1134]   To defeat or discourage a takeover bid by a disfavored bidder, the target's management may sell or (more usually) give to a white knight a lock-up option that covers the target's most desirable business or, at least, the business most coveted by the disfavored bidder—its "crown jewels."

f. **Standstill:** [§1135] A target may seek an accommodation with a shareholder who has acquired a significant amount of stock, under which the shareholder agrees to limit his future stock purchases—hence, *standstill*. In the typical standstill agreement, the shareholder makes one or more commitments: (i) it will not increase its shares above designated limits for a specified period of time; (ii) it will not sell its shares without giving the corporation a right of first refusal; (iii) it will not engage in a proxy contest; and (iv) it will vote its stock in a designated manner in the election of directors, and perhaps on other issues. In return, the corporation typically agrees to give the shareholder board representation, to register the shareholder's stock under the Securities Act on demand, and not to oppose the shareholder's acquisition of stock up to the specified limit.

g. **Junk bonds:** [§1136] A "junk bond" is a bond that has an usually high risk of default (and is therefore below investment grade), but correspondingly, carries an unusually high yield.

h. **No-shop clauses:** [§1137] A board of a corporation that enters into an agreement for a merger or other corporate combination (whether with a white knight or otherwise) may enter into a "no-shop agreement" that it will not shop around for a more attractive deal.

i. **Greenmail:** [§1138] "Greenmail" is a payment by a potential target to a potential bidder to buy back the shares in the corporation that the bidder already holds, normally at a premium. In exchange, the potential bidder agrees not to pursue a takeover bid. Some persons are suspected of purchasing shares with the object of collecting greenmail from frightened boards.

j. **Fair-price provision:** [§1139] A "fair-price provision" requires that a supermajority (usually 80%) of the voting power of a corporation must approve any merger or similar combination with an acquiror who already owns a specified interest in the corporation (usually 20% of the voting power). The supermajority vote is not required under certain conditions—most notably, if the transaction is approved by a majority of those directors who are not affiliated with the acquiror and were directors at the time the acquiror reached the specified level of ownership of the company, or if certain minimum-price criteria and procedural requirements are satisfied. A fair-price provision discourages purchasers whose objective is to seek control of a corporation at a relatively cheap price, and discourages accumulations of large blocks, since it reduces the options an acquiror has once it reaches the specified level of shares.

k. **Poison pill:** [§1140] A "poison pill" is a device adopted by a potential or actual takeover target to make its stock less attractive to a bidder. Under one kind of pill, the corporation issues a new series of preferred stock, or other rights, that gives existing shareholders the right to redeem the stock at a premium price after certain events, like a takeover. A "flip-in poison pill" allows all existing holders of target company shares, except the acquiror, to buy additional shares at a bargain price. A "flip-over poison pill" allows existing holders to convert into the acquiror's shares at a bargain price in the event of an unwelcome merger. The pill is intended to deter a takeover bid by making a bid very costly.

l. **Leveraged buyout:** [§1141] A "leveraged buyout" is a combination of a management buyout and a high degree of leverage. A *management buyout* ("MBO") is the acquisition for cash or nonconvertible senior securities of the business of a public corporation, by a newly organized corporation in which members of the former management of the public corporation will have a significant equity interest, pursuant to a merger or other form of combination. *Leverage* involves the use of debt to increase the return on equity. The extent of leverage is measured by the ratio of (i) debt to (ii) debt plus equity. The higher the ratio, the greater the leverage (or, to put it differently, the more highly leveraged the corporation is). A *leveraged buyout* ("LBO") is an MBO that is highly leveraged—*i.e.*, in which the newly organized acquiring corporation has a very high amount of debt in relation to its equity. Characteristically, an LBO is arranged by a firm that specializes in such transactions; can find investors to participate (or will itself invest) along with senior management in the purchase of the new corporation's securities; and can arrange for (or help arrange for) placement of the massive amount of debt that the new corporation must issue to finance the acquisition of the old corporation's business.

m. **Two-tier tender offer:** [§1142] A "two-tier tender offer" is a takeover bid in which the bidder makes an offer for less than all the shares at one price (the "first-tier," or "front end" price), and announces that if the first-tier offer is successful, the bidder will acquire the remaining shares through a freeze-out transaction (the "second tier" or "back end"). In some cases, the bidder states that the back-end price will be less than the front-end price. This kind of tender offer is called a "front-loaded" two-tier offer. The effect is to pressure all shareholders to accept the first-tier offer, so as not to get stuck with the lower back-end price.

2. **Tender Offer—In General:** [§1143] A tender offer is an offer by a bidder to shareholders of a target corporation, asking the shareholders to tender their shares in exchange for either cash or securities. A tender offer almost invariably invites the tender of at least a majority of the target's shares, and frequently invites the tender of all of the target's shares.

a. **Conditions:** [§1144] Typically, the terms of a tender offer provide that the bidder will acquire the shares that are tendered only if certain conditions are met. The most important of these conditions is that some specified minimum of shares must be tendered.

b. **Toehold stock acquisitions:** [§1145] A tender offer is often preceded by a preliminary "toehold acquisition" of shares in the target on the open market.

c. **Second-step transactions:** [§1146] If a tender offer by a corporate bidder is successful, the target initially becomes a subsidiary of the bidder. However, a successful tender offer is frequently followed by a "second-step" or "second-tier" transaction, such as a merger, in which the target is merged into or otherwise combined with the bidder. Shares held by nontendering shareholders are often cashed out as part of the second step through a freeze-out transaction. (*See supra*, §§1109-1118.)

d. **Friendly vs. hostile tender offers:** [§1147] Tender offers are classified as friendly or hostile. A friendly tender offer is an offer that is supported by the target's board. A hostile tender offer is an offer that is opposed by the target's board.

e.   **Approval required:** [§1148]   Strictly speaking, neither type of tender offer is a corporate transaction from the target's perspective. Rather, the transaction is an offer to the target's shareholders in their individual capacities. Accordingly, in the absence of a special statute (*see infra*, §§1192-1198) a tender offer does not require a vote by the target's shareholders and does not give rise to appraisal rights in those shareholders. A tender offer also normally does not require the approval of, or give rise to appraisal rights in, the bidder's shareholders, unless it constitutes a de facto merger (*see supra*, §§1044-1056).

f.   **Defensive tactics:** [§1149]   Often, the board of a target company takes some defensive action to ward off a takeover. For example, the board may seek to combine with an alternative corporation (a white knight), or may agree to sell the business to management (a management buyout), or may give a third party or management an option (lock-up) on a key division of the corporation (the crown jewel). The major source of the rules governing defensive measures is a series of Delaware cases. Certain generalizations can be drawn from these cases, but because they are all important and highly fact-specific, a full understanding of the relevant legal rules requires consideration of the facts and holdings of each case.

   (1)   **The *Unocal* test:** [§1150]   In *Unocal Corp. v. Mesa Petroleum Co.*, 493 A.2d 946 (Del. 1985), Mesa made a two-tier front-loaded tender offer for 37% of Unocal's stock at $54. Mesa was controlled by Pickens, who had a reputation as a greenmailer. The back end of the two-tier offer was to involve an exchange of securities that were also nominally worth $54. However, the securities were junk bonds and, therefore, the value at the back end might have been much lower than $54, so that the offer was coercive. Unocal's board defended against the tender offer by making a self-tender for Unocal stock at $72, but excluding stock owned by Mesa from the self-tender. Mesa sued to enjoin Unocal's defensive measure. In deciding the case, the Delaware court laid down the basic rules to be applied in Delaware to defensive measures:

      (a)   **Best interests test:** [§1151]   When a board addresses a pending takeover bid, it has an obligation to determine whether the offer is in the best interests of the corporation and its shareholders. However, because of the "omnipresent specter" that a board may be acting primarily in its own interests, rather than those of the corporation and its shareholders, there is an "enhanced duty," which calls for judicial examination at the threshold, before the protections of the business judgment rule may be conferred. In the face of this inherent conflict, directors must show that they had ***reasonable grounds for believing that a danger to corporate policy and effectiveness*** existed because of the bid. They satisfy that burden by showing good faith and reasonable investigation, and such proof is materially enhanced by the approval of a board comprised of a majority of outside independent directors who have acted in accordance with the foregoing standards.

(b) **Balance:** [§1152] A further aspect of the *Unocal* test is the element of balance. A defensive measure must be reasonable in relation to the threat posed. This entails an analysis by the directors of the nature of the takeover bid and its effect on the corporate enterprise. Examples of such concerns may include: inadequacy of the price offered, nature and timing of the offer, questions of illegality, the impact on "constituencies" other than shareholders (*e.g.*, creditors, customers, employees, and perhaps even the community generally), the risk of nonconsummation, and the quality of securities being offered in the exchange. A board may reasonably consider the basic stockholder interests at stake, including those of the short-term speculators whose actions may have fueled the coercive aspect of the offer at the expense of the long-term investor. In *Unocal* itself, the court held that a threat was posed by a grossly inadequate two-tier coercive tender offer, coupled with a threat of greenmail, and that the board's response to the threat was reasonable.

(c) **Intermediate standard:** [§1153] Although the *Unocal* test has been somewhat elaborated (and a different test, known as the *Revlon* test, *see infra*, is applied in certain cases), the core of the *Unocal* test has been largely preserved. The key elements of the test are "enhanced scrutiny," on the one hand (*i.e.*, enhanced as compared with the ordinary scrutiny given to board action under the business judgment rule), and determining whether the defensive measure is "reasonable in relation to the threat posed," on the other. In effect, the *Unocal* test is an intermediate standard of review, which is somewhat harder for a board to satisfy than the business judgment rule, but somewhat easier for the board to satisfy than a full fairness review.

(d) *Unitrin:* [§1154] In *Unitrin, Inc. v. American General Corp.*, 651 A.2d 1361 (Del. 1995), the Delaware court refined the *Unocal* test. Under the refined test, the court should direct its enhanced scrutiny first to whether the defensive action was "draconian" by being either preclusive or coercive, and second, if the response was not draconian, to whether it was within a range of reasonable responses to the threat posed by the tender offer.

(2) **The *Revlon* test:** [§1155] In *Revlon, Inc. v. MacAndrews & Forbes Holdings, Inc.*, 506 A.2d 173 (Del. 1986), Pantry Pride made a tender offer for the stock of Revlon. In response, Revlon's board adopted a variety of defensive measures. Competing offers for Revlon went back and forth from Pantry Pride and Forstmann, a white knight. Finally, Revlon gave Forstmann a lock-up on key Revlon assets, and agreed to a no-shop provision. The court held that the lock-up and no-shop provisions were improper, because it was clear that the corporation would be sold to either Pantry Pride or to Forstmann. Once it is clear that a corporation will be sold, the court said, defensive measures are no longer judged under the *Unocal* test. Instead, the board's duty is to simply to get the best price. (This has since become known as the *Revlon* standard):

(a) **Entering into negotiations with third party:** [§1156] The Revlon board's authorization permitting management to negotiate a merger or buyout with a third party was a recognition that the company was for sale. The duty of the board had thus changed from the preservation of Revlon as a corporate entity to the maximization of the company's value at a sale for the stockholders' benefit. This significantly altered the board's responsibilities under the *Unocal* standards. It no longer faced threats to corporate policy and effectiveness, or to the stockholders' interests, from a grossly inadequate bid. The whole question of defensive measures became moot. The directors' role changed with getting the best price for the stockholders at a sale of the company.

(b) **Lock-up provision:** [§1157]   As to the lock-up provision, the court said that a lock-up is not per se illegal under Delaware law, because it can entice a new bidder to enter a contest for control of the corporation, creating an auction for the company and thereby maximizing shareholder profit. However, while a lock-up that draws bidders into the battle benefits shareholders, a lock-up that ends an active auction and forecloses further bidding operates to the shareholders' detriment, and is improper.

(c) **No-shop provision:** [§1158]   As to the no-shop provision, the court held that, like a lock-up, a no-shop provision is not per se illegal, but is impermissible under the *Unocal* standard when a board's primary duty becomes that of an auctioneer responsible for selling the company to the highest bidder.

(d) **When directors must seek best value for shareholders:** [§1159] In *Arnold v. Society for Savings Bancorp, Inc.*, 650 A.2d 1270 (Del. 1994), the Delaware Supreme Court stated that the directors of a corporation have the obligation to act reasonably to seek the transaction offering the best value reasonably available to the stockholders when:

   1)   A corporation *initiates an active bidding process* seeking to sell itself or to effect a business reorganization involving a clear break-up of the company;

   2)   In response to a bidder's offer, a *target abandons its long-term strategy and seeks* an alternative transaction involving *the break-up of the company*; or

   3)   Approval of a transaction results in a *sale or change of control*. However, there is no sale or change in control when control of both companies continues to be held by a large, fluid, changeable, and changing market.

(3) ***Paramount v. Time:*** [§1160]   In *Paramount Communications, Inc. v. Time, Inc.*, 571 A.2d 1140 (Del. 1989), Paramount made an all-cash offer for all the shares of Time, Inc. Time then entered into a business combination with Warner Brothers. Although the merger was in part a response to Paramount's takeover bid, it also executed a preexisting strategic plan of Time. Paramount challenged the combination. The Delaware court held

that even an all-cash, all-shares tender offer could constitute a "threat" within the meaning of the *Unocal* test. *Unocal* involved a two-tier, highly coercive tender offer. In such a case, the threat is obvious: shareholders may be compelled to tender to avoid being treated adversely in the second stage of the transaction. However, the court said, Time's board reasonably determined that inadequate value was not the only legally cognizable threat that a tender offer could present. One concern was that Time's shareholders might elect to tender into Paramount's cash offer in ignorance or a mistaken belief of the strategic benefit that a business combination with Warner might produce. Moreover, Time viewed the conditions attached to Paramount's offer as introducing a degree of uncertainty that skewed a comparative analysis. Accordingly, the court said, it could not conclude that the Time board's decision, that Paramount's offer posed a threat to corporate policy and effectiveness, was lacking in good faith or dominated by motives of either entrenchment or self-interest.

(a) **Reasonable and proportionate response:** [§1161]   Even if a tender offer does pose a threat, under the second branch of the *Unocal* test defensive actions that are coercive may be struck down if they are unreasonable and nonproportionate responses to the threat. However, the court concluded, Time's responsive action to Paramount's tender offer was not aimed at cramming down on its shareholders a management-sponsored alternative, but rather had as its goal the carrying forward of a preexisting transaction. Thus, the response was reasonably related to the threat. Furthermore, the business combination with Warner did not preclude Paramount from making an offer for the combined Time-Warner offer. Thus, the response was proportionate.

(4) ***Paramount v. QVC:*** [§1162]   In *Paramount Communications, Inc. v. QVC Network*, 637 A.2d 34 (Del. 1994), Paramount (the spurned suitor in the *Time* case) entered into a merger agreement with Viacom. If the merger went through, control of Paramount would be vested in a new controlling shareholder. The merger agreement contained a no-shop provision, as well as a stock option agreement that gave Viacom an option to purchase almost 20% of Paramount's stock on extremely favorable terms—a variant of a lock-up. QVC then made a takeover bid for Paramount. Although a bidding contest developed, Paramount's board gave favored treatment to Viacom. The Delaware court held that in a sale-of-control context, the directors must focus on one primary objective—to secure the transaction offering the best value reasonably available for the stockholders—and must exercise their fiduciary duties to further that end. When a corporation undertakes a transaction that will cause a change in corporate control or a breakup of the corporate entity, the directors' obligation is to seek the best value reasonably available to the stockholders. Accordingly, an enhanced-scrutiny test was applicable. The court held that although a no-shop provision is not per se invalid, under the facts of this case the no-shop provision was invalid, because it interfered with the duty of Paramount's board to get the highest price for Paramount. The court also held that although a lock-up provision is not per se invalid, the stock option agreement was invalid under the circumstances of the case.

(5) **Poison pill:** [§1163]   In *Moran v. Household International, Inc.*, 500 A.2d 1346 (Del. 1985), the Delaware Supreme Court held that adoption of a poison pill was not per se improper, on the ground that a poison pill might deter coercive or other questionable tender offers, and there are various ways to launch a tender offer even in the face of a poison pill— such as attempting to replace the board and "redeem" the pill (*i.e.*, causing the new board to effectively revoke the pill). The court also stated that in reviewing a preplanned defensive measure, it was even more appropriate to apply the business judgment rule than in reviewing a defensive measure adopted in response to an actual takeover bid.

    (a) **Change in circumstances:** [§1164]   Although *Moran* held that the mere adoption of a pill was not necessarily improper, it did not say that the board had a free hand to leave a pill in place in the face of a tender offer. In the *Unitrin* case, *supra*, the court said that although *adopting* a poison pill in given circumstances might be appropriate, keeping a poison pill *in place* may be inappropriate when the circumstances dramatically change.

3. **Federal Securities Law—The Williams Act:** [§1165]   Tender offers, and the toehold share acquisitions that often precede them, are regulated in a great number of respects by the Williams Act (and its amendments), which added sections 13(d), 14(d), and 14(e) to the Securities Exchange Act of 1934. A discussion of the obligations imposed by these sections follows.

    a. **Notice of five-percent beneficial ownership:** [§1166]   A person who has acquired beneficial ownership of more than 5% of any class of equity securities registered under section 12 of the 1934 Act must file a Schedule 13D within 10 days of the acquisition. [Exchange Act §13(d)]

    (1) **Contents:** [§1167]   The Schedule 13D must include the purchaser's identity and background; the amount and sources of the funds for the purchase; the purpose of the purchase; any plans with respect to extraordinary corporate transactions involving the corporation whose stock has been acquired; and any contracts, arrangements, or understandings with other persons regarding the corporation's securities.

    (2) **Formation of a group:** [§1168]   For this purpose, the term "person" includes a group. Furthermore, merely combining existing shareholdings for the purpose of control, without more, is sufficient to constitute a "group," and trigger the filing requirements, if the members of the newly constituted group own more than 5% of the corporation's stock. [Exchange Act Rule 13-5(b); GAF Corp. v. Milstein, 453 F.2d 709 (2d Cir. 1971)]

    (3) **Remedy:** [§1169]   A target corporation has an implied right of action for a violation of section 13(d). The appropriate remedy for such violation is an injunction to require a corrective amendment to the filing and to prohibit additional purchases until the filing is corrected. Normally, an injunction that prohibits the purchaser from voting the acquired shares, or requires that previously acquired shares be divested, is not an appropriate remedy, at least where the failure is cured by a subsequent filing.

[Rondeau v. Mosinee Paper Corp., 422 U.S. 49 (1975); General Aircraft Corp. v. Lampert, 556 F.2d 90 (1st Cir. 1977)]

b. **Tender offers under Williams Act:** [§1170] The Williams Act also regulates tender offers. What constitutes a "tender offer" within the meaning of the Williams Act is not completely settled.

(1) **Eight-factor test:** [§1171] Some courts have adopted the following eight-factor test to determine whether an offer to buy stock is a tender offer under the Act:

(i) Did the purchaser engage in *active and widespread solicitation* of public shareholders?

(ii) Is the solicitation made for a *substantial percentage* of the issuer's stock?

(iii) Is the offer to purchase made at a *premium* over the prevailing market price?

(iv) Are the terms of the offer *firm* rather than negotiable?

(v) Is the offer *contingent* on the tender of a fixed number of shares?

(vi) Is the offer open only for a *limited period of time*?

(vii) Are the offerees under *pressure* to sell their stock?

(viii) Do *public announcements* of a purchasing program precede or accompany a rapid accumulation of large amounts of the target's securities?

[Wellman v. Dickinson, 475 F. Supp. 783 (S.D.N.Y. 1979), *aff'd on other grounds*, 682 F.2d 355 (2d Cir. 1982), *cert. denied*, 460 U.S. 1069 (1983); SEC v. Carter Hawley Hale Stores, Inc., 750 F.2d 945 (9th Cir. 1985)]

(2) **Alternative test—substantial risk of insufficient information:** [§1172] The Second Circuit has rejected the eight-factor test. It has held instead that the question of whether an offer to buy stock constitutes a tender offer under the Williams Act turns on whether there appears to be a likelihood that unless the Act's rules are followed, there will be a substantial risk that solicitees will lack information needed to make a carefully considered appraisal of the proposal put before them. [Hanson Trust PLC v. SCM Corp., 774 F.2d 47 (2d Cir. 1985)]

(a) **Example:** Applying the above standard, the Second Circuit held in *Hanson* that the transaction before it was not a tender offer because:

(i) The target had 22,800 shareholders and offers were made to only six of the shareholders. This number was deemed *minuscule* compared with the number of shareholders usually involved in public solicitations of the type against which the Williams Act was directed.

(ii) At least five of the six selling shareholders were *highly sophisticated professionals*, knowledgeable in the marketplace and well aware of the essential facts needed to exercise their professional skills and to appraise the offer.

(iii) The sellers were *not pressured to sell* their shares by any conduct that the Williams Act was designed to alleviate, but only by the forces of the marketplace.

(iv) There was *no active or widespread advance publicity* or public solicitation.

(v) The price received by the six sellers was *not at a premium* over the then-market price.

(vi) The purchases were *not made contingent* upon acquiring a fixed minimum number or percentage of the target's outstanding shares.

(vii) There was *no time limit* within which the buyer would purchase the target's stock.

[Hanson Trust PLC v. SCM Corp., *supra*]

(3) **Open-market purchases:** [§1173] Purchases made anonymously on the open market almost certainly do not constitute a tender offer within the meaning of the Act. [Kennecott Copper Corp. v. Curtiss-Wright Corp., 584 F.2d 1195 (2d Cir. 1978); Calumet Industries, Inc. v. MacClure, Fed. Sec. Reg. Rep. (CCH) ¶96,434 (N.D. Ill. 1978)] However, the SEC has not entirely acquiesced in this position.

c. **Information statement by person who makes tender offer:** [§1174] Section 14(d) requires any person who makes a tender offer for a class of registered equity securities, which would result in that person owning more than 5% of the class, to file a schedule 14D containing specific information.

(1) **Contents:** [§1175] The schedule 14D must contain extensive disclosure of such matters as the offer; the identity of the bidder; past dealings between the bidder and the corporation; the bidder's source of funds; the bidder's purposes and plans concerning the corporation; the bidder's contracts and understandings or relationships with respect to securities of the corporation; financial statements of the bidder, if they are material and the bidder is not an individual; and arrangements between the bidder and those holding important positions with the corporation.

d. **Regulation of terms of tender offers:** [§1176] Section 14(d) of the Securities Exchange Act, and rules 14d and 14e, regulate the *terms* of tender offers. Under these provisions:

(1) A tender offer *must be held open for at least 20 days*.

(2) A tender offer must be *open to all security holders of the class* of securities subject to the tender offer (the "all holders rule").

(3) Shareholders *must be permitted to withdraw tendered shares* during the first 15 days of an offer, or after 60 days if the shares have not been purchased by then.

(4) If the tender offer is *oversubscribed*, the *offeror must purchase on a pro rata basis* from among the shares deposited during the first 10 days, or such longer period as the bidder may designate.

(5) If the tender-offer price is *increased*, the higher price must be paid to *all* tendering shareholders—even those who tendered in response to the lower price—and the offer must remain open at least 10 days after notice of the increase is first published.

e. **Obligations of target's management:** [§1177]   Rule 14e-2 requires the target company, no later than 10 business days from the date the tender offer is first published, to give its shareholders a statement disclosing that the target either: (i) *recommends acceptance or rejection* of the tender offer; (ii) *expresses no opinion* and is remaining neutral toward the tender offer; or (iii) is *unable to take a position* with respect to the tender offer. The statement must also include the reason for the position or for the inability to take a position.

f. **Tender offers by issuers:** [§1178]   Corporations that tender for their own stock ("issuer" or "self" tenders) are subject to obligations similar to those imposed on outside bidders under rules 14d and 14e. [Exchange Act Rules 13(e), 13e]

g. **Anti-fraud provision:** [§1179]   Section 14(e) prohibits material misstatements, misleading omissions, and fraudulent or manipulative acts, in connection with a tender offer or any solicitation in favor of or in opposition to a tender offer. Section 14(e) is closely comparable to rule 10b-5, except that it does not contain the limiting language, "in connection with the purchase or sale" of securities, found in rule 10b-5. It is not yet completely clear who may bring an action under section 14(e). A major Supreme Court decision, *Piper v. Chris-Craft Industries, Inc.*, 430 U.S. 1 (1977), lays down some important rules, but leaves a number of gaps.

(1) **Suit by offeror**

(a) **Damages:** [§1180]   Under *Piper v. Chris-Craft Industries, Inc.*, the bidder does not have standing to sue for damages under section 14(e), particularly a suit against the target corporation's management for false statements made in opposition to the tender offer.

1) **Rationale:** The Williams Act was designed to protect shareholders of the target. It is not consistent with the underlying legislative purpose to imply a damages remedy for the bidder, particularly since the target's shareholders might end up bearing the burden of an award based on misrepresentations by the target's management.

(b) **Injunctive relief:** [§1181]   In *Piper v. Chris-Craft Industries, Inc.*, *supra*, the Court left open the question of suits by the bidder under section 14(e) for injunctive relief against the target or its management. Lower courts have held that the target corporation can sue for an injunction against the bidder for violation of section 14(e), since such an injunction will protect the interests of the target's shareholders. [Gearhart Industries, Inc. v. Smith International, Inc., 741 F.2d 707 (5th Cir. 1984); Weeks Dredging & Contracting, Inc. v. American Dredging Co., Fed. Sec. Reg. Rep. (CCH) ¶96,414 (E.D. Pa. 1978)] The bidder can also bring a suit for injunctive relief against competing bidders. [Humana, Inc. v. American Medicorp, Inc., Fed. Sec. L. Rep. (CCH) ¶96,298 (S.D.N.Y. 1978)]

1) **Rationale:** Unlike damages, an injunction does not impose any burden upon the target's shareholders. Furthermore, an injunction prior to the time when the target's shareholders must decide whether to accept the tender offer allows them to make their decision in an environment purged of false and misleading information. [Weeks Dredging & Contracting, Inc. v. American Dredging Co., *supra*]

(2) **Suit by target corporation**

(a) **Damages:** [§1182]   Since *Piper* was based on the conclusion that the Williams Act was designed to protect the target's shareholders, the target corporation itself would not have standing to sue the bidder for damages under rule 14e.

(b) **Injunction:** [§1183]   The target corporation can sue for an injunction against the bidder for violation of section 14(e), since such an injunction will protect the interests of the target's shareholders. [Gearhart Industries, Inc. v. Smith International, Inc., *supra*, §1181]

(3) **Suit by target's shareholders**

(a) **Suit by tendering shareholders:** [§1184]   Based on the Court's interpretation of the Williams Act in *Piper*, shareholders of the target have standing to sue for both damages and injunctive relief if they tender their shares on the basis of false and misleading information. (Under these circumstances, tendering shareholders could also sue under Rule 10b-5.)

(b) **Suit by nontendering shareholders:** [§1185]   The Court in *Piper* did not express a view on suits by nontendering shareholders, but since the statute does not contain the purchaser-seller limitation associated with rule 10b-5, nontendering shareholders can probably sue under section 14(e), provided they can show damage resulting from a violation of that section. [*See* Electronic Specialty Co. v. International Controls Corp., 409 F.2d 937 (2d Cir. 1969)]

4. **State Statutes Regulating Tender Offers:** [§1186]   Many states now have statutes regulating takeover bids.

a. **First-generation statutes:** [§1187]   The so-called first-generation statutes imposed very stringent requirements on takeover bids. In *Edgar v. MITE*

Corp., 457 U.S. 624 (1982), the Supreme Court held one such statute, the Illinois Takeover Act, unconstitutional. The Court considered the following theories:

(1) **Supremacy Clause:** [§1188]   Three of the six justices who passed on the merits of the case held that the Illinois statute was unconstitutional under the Supremacy Clause, on the ground that a major objective of the Williams Act was maintaining a neutral balance between management and the bidder, and the Illinois Act violated this balance. (*See infra*, §§1194-1197.)

(2) **Commerce Clause:** [§1189]   All six justices who addressed the merits held that the Illinois Act violated the Commerce Clause, by:

   (a) *Directly regulating commerce taking place across state lines*, because the Act applied to prevent an offeror from making an offer even to non-Illinois shareholders; and

   (b) *Imposing an excessive burden on interstate commerce*, by permitting the secretary of state to block a nationwide tender offer.

b. **Second-generation statutes:** [§1190]   After the decision in *Edgar v. MITE Corp.*, a number of states adopted "second-generation" takeover statutes. These statutes fall into two major categories: "fair price" statutes and "control share acquisition" statutes.

(1) **Fair price statutes:** [§1191]   Under the fair price statutes, an acquiror must pay all shareholders the "best price" paid to any one shareholder.

(2) **Control share acquisition statutes:** [§1192]   Under control share acquisition statutes, if a designated stock-ownership threshold is crossed by an acquiring shareholder, he cannot vote the acquired shares without the approval of a majority of the disinterested shareholders.

   (a) *CTS case:* [§1193]   In *CTS Corp. v. Dynamics Corp. of America*, 481 U.S. 69 (1987), the Supreme Court upheld a control share acquisition statute adopted by Indiana. The Indiana statute is limited to targets incorporated in Indiana. The statute applies whenever a person acquires "control shares," *i.e.*, whenever a person acquires shares that (but for the operation of the statute) would bring the person's voting power in the corporation to or above any of three thresholds: 20%, $33^{1}/3\%$, or 50%. An acquiror that crosses such a threshold cannot vote the acquired stock unless voting rights are approved by a majority of all disinterested shareholders voting at the next regularly scheduled meeting of the shareholders or at a specially scheduled meeting. The acquiror can require the management of the corporation to hold such a special meeting within 50 days.

      1) **Supremacy Clause:** [§1194]   The Court held that the Indiana statute was not preempted by the Williams Act. The Illinois statute in *Edgar v. MITE Corp.* had three offending features that the Indiana statute did not share.

a) **Communicating with shareholders:** [§1195] The Illinois statute provided for a 20-day precommencement period. During this time, management could disseminate its views on the upcoming tender offer to shareholders, but bidders could not publish their offers. This conflicted with the Williams Act, because Congress had deleted express precommencement notice provisions from the Williams Act. In contrast, the Indiana statute does not give either management or the bidder an advantage in communicating with shareholders about an impending tender offer.

b) **Delay:** [§1196] The Illinois statute provided for a hearing on a tender offer. Because no deadline was set for the hearing, management could indefinitely stymie a takeover. This conflicted with the Williams Act, because Congress anticipated that bidders would be free to go forward without unreasonable delay. In contrast, the Indiana statute does not impose an indefinite delay on tender offers. Nothing in the statute prohibits an offeror from consummating an offer on the 20th business day, the earliest day permitted under applicable federal regulations, and full voting rights will be vested or denied within 50 days after commencement of the tender offer.

c) **Fairness evaluation:** [§1197] The Illinois statute provided for review of the fairness of tender offers by the Illinois Secretary of State. This conflicted with the Williams Act, because Congress intended investors to be free to make their own decisions. In contrast, the Indiana statute does not allow the state government to interpose its views of fairness between willing buyers and sellers of shares of the target company. Rather, the statute allows shareholders to collectively evaluate the fairness of the offer.

2) **Commerce Clause:** [§1198] The Court in *CTS* also concluded that the Indiana statute does not violate the Commerce Clause, because it does not discriminate against interstate commerce and does not subject activities to inconsistent regulation. The statute applies only to Indiana corporations, and a state has authority to regulate domestic corporations, including the authority to define the voting rights of shareholders.

c. **Third-generation statutes:** [§1199] "Third-generation statutes" do not fall into either the control-share-acquisition or fair-price patterns. Many of these third-generation statutes are aimed at preventing a successful bidder from merging with the target or engaging in certain other transactions with the target for a designated period of time unless certain conditions are satisfied. (The theory is that in many cases the bidder expects to finance the bid partly by using assets of the target as collateral. If the bidder cannot merge with the target, that kind of financing is difficult or impossible. In addition, the bidder may have various business and tax reasons for wanting to merge with the target in a freeze-out merger that eliminates the target's minority shareholders, rather than running the target as a partly owned subsidiary. These purposes are also frustrated by third-generation statutes.) The following illustrate the approaches of third-generation statutes:

(1) **New York:** [§1200]   The New York statute provides for a five-year delay between the time a tender offer occurs and the time the target can be merged or otherwise combined with the bidder, unless the transaction was approved by the target's board of directors prior to the date control was acquired. [N.Y. Bus. Corp. Law §912]

(2) **Wisconsin:** [§1201]   The Wisconsin statute provides that, unless the target's board agrees to the transaction in advance of a successful tender offer, a successful bidder must wait three years after buying the target's shares to merge with the target or acquire more than 5% of its assets.

(3) **Delaware:** [§1202]   Delaware allows a merger to occur before the end of the waiting period if the merger is approved by 85% of the shares other than shares held by the bidder, on the one hand, or by management and employee stock plans, on the other. [Del. Gen. Corp. Law §103]

(4) **Constitutionality:** [§1203] In *Amanda Acquisition Corp. v. Universal Foods Corp.*, 877 F.2d 496, *cert. denied*, 493 U.S. 955 (1989), the Seventh Circuit held that the Wisconsin third-generation statute (*supra*)—a particularly strong third-generation statute—was constitutional. The court held that the statute was not preempted by the Williams Act, because it did not prevent takeover bids or alter any of the procedures governed by the Act, but only made such bids less attractive to engage in. The statute was not invalid under the Commerce Clause, because it applied only to the internal affairs of corporations domiciled in Wisconsin, allowed purchasers of stock in Wisconsin corporations to take immediate control of the corporation, and did not regulate or forbid any interstate transaction.

XI.   CONFLICT OF LAWS PRINCIPLES

chapter approach

Conflict of laws issues rarely arise on Corporations exams. However, you should remember that all questions concerning the internal affairs of the corporation are decided according to the law of the state of incorporation. Also keep in mind that a state may refuse to apply that law if it violates local public policy.

A.   GENERAL RULE

1.   **Law of State of Incorporation Applies:** [§1204]   No matter where the litigation occurs, the general choice of law rule is that all questions concerning the organization or internal affairs of a corporation are decided according to the law of the state in which it was incorporated. [RMBCA §15.05(c)]

   a.   **Example:** A corporation organized in state A has its principal office and place of business in state B. In litigation in state B (or elsewhere) involving the corporation's internal affairs, the court will generally refer to and apply the law of state A.

   b.   **Effect:** This is the reason that many businesses choose to incorporate in Delaware, Nevada, or other states having laws deemed favorable to corporate management. As discussed earlier, Delaware law does away with mandatory cumulative voting (_supra,_ §502) and eases the limitations against a corporation indemnifying its officers and directors for liabilities incurred in office (_supra,_ §§766-772).

B.   LIMITATIONS

1.   **Local Public Policy:** [§1205]   Nevertheless, local courts may refuse to apply the law of another state where this would validate some act strongly offensive to local public policy.

   a.   **Example:** A California court has refused to permit a Delaware corporation to solicit shareholder approval for an amendment to its articles of incorporation that would have eliminated cumulative voting for directors. Even though such an amendment would have been permitted under Delaware law, the California court held that California had a legitimate interest in the matter since the corporation's principal business was in California and many of its shareholders resided there. Hence, the court insisted upon applying its own local laws prohibiting the amendment. [Western Air Lines v. Sobieski, 191 Cal. App. 2d 399 (1961)]

2.   **Local Statutes:** [§1206]   A few states now have statutes that subject foreign corporations having substantial local "contacts" to various local regulations intended to protect shareholders and creditors. [Cal. Corp. Code §2115; N.Y. Bus. Corp. Law §§1306, 1317-1320]

a. **"Pseudo-foreign" corporations:** [§1207]   Under the California statute, if more than *half* of the corporation's business (average of its property, payroll, and sales) is done within the state and more than half of its shareholders have California addresses, it is treated as a "pseudo-foreign" corporation. Such corporations are subject to California law with respect to such matters as election and removal of directors, directors' standard of care and liability for unlawful distributions, shareholder rights to cumulative voting and inspection of records, shareholder approval and dissenters' rights in the case of reorganizations, and required corporate records and reports to shareholders. [Cal. Corp. Code §2115(b)]

b. **Constitutionality:** [§1208]   The validity of these statutes under the Full Faith and Credit and Commerce Clauses of the Constitution has been questioned, but not yet authoritatively resolved.

c. **Exemptions:** [§1209]   The "pseudo-foreign" corporation statute does not apply to out-of-state corporations whose shares are listed on national securities exchanges. These exchanges are deemed to have adequate "fairness" rules of their own, and their geographical shareholder-distribution requirements make it unlikely that more than half the shareholders would ever be residents of a single state. [Cal. Corp. Code §2115(e)]

REVIEW QUESTIONS

FILL IN
ANSWER

CHARACTERISTICS OF CORPORATIONS

1. If Smith owns 10% of the outstanding shares of XYZ Corporation, is Smith responsible for 10% of XYZ's debts? _____

2. Do shareholders in a corporation generally have management power and direct control of its affairs? _____

3. A, B, and C are the sole shareholders of ABC Corporation. A dies; B and C sell their shares to D and E, respectively. Does ABC Corporation still exist? _____

4. Are both corporations and partnerships "legal entities"? _____

5. In a limited partnership, does a limited partner have the same right to management and control as a partner in an ordinary partnership? _____

6. Able and Baker formed Acme Corp., a widget manufacturing business. Corporate formalities were observed when Acme Corp. was formed, but since then Able and Baker have neither held any meetings nor maintained any corporate records. Lately, Baker has been paying his household bills from Acme's account, and Able bought his wife a car with an Acme check. May C Corp., an Acme creditor who has not been paid for months, reach Able and Baker's personal assets to satisfy its claim? _____

7. Don, Ed, and Frank formed DEF Trucking Corporation, with investments of $250 each. They are the sole shareholders. They have observed all corporate formalities and have kept DEF's assets separate from their own. They have allowed DEF to run up debts of $100,000 in excess of its assets. Can the creditors "pierce the corporate veil" to reach the assets of Don, Ed, and/or Frank? _____

8. Does the "Deep Rock" doctrine permit the creditors of an insolvent corporation to collect their debts directly from the shareholders? _____

9. Beulah is a major shareholder of the XYZ Corporation. XYZ owes Creditor $10,000. Can XYZ assert, as an offset against its debt, a claim that Beulah has against Creditor? Can XYZ sue in its own name on Beulah's claim? _____

ORGANIZING THE CORPORATION

10. Under typical statutes governing incorporation, must the articles of incorporation state:

    a. The specific business purpose for which the corporation is formed? _____

    b. The number of shares it proposes to issue? _____

11. Under typical statutes governing incorporation, is it required that the incorporators also be permanent directors? _____

12. Under typical statutes governing incorporation, must **both** the articles of incorporation and the bylaws be filed with an appropriate state official in order to create corporate status? _____

13. The incorporators of White Corporation inadvertently filed defective articles of incorporation but thereafter contracted and acted as a corporation. Assuming the statutory requirements had been met, which, if any, of the following parties can attack White's status as a corporation? _____

    (A) Its own shareholders.

    (B) Its creditors.

    (C) The state.

14. The "corporation by estoppel" doctrine operates only against a third party who has dealt with the corporation and only as to the particular dealing. True or false? _____

15. Where statutes provide that corporate status is conclusively presumed from a proper filing of articles of incorporation, may shareholders rely on the "de facto incorporation" doctrine if the articles are **not** properly filed? _____

16. During the promotion stage of Central Corporation, Promoter Perry enters into a contract on behalf of the corporation for the purchase of equipment from Manufacturer. After formation, Central rejects the contract and refuses to proceed with the purchase. Can Manufacturer enforce the contract against Central? _____

17. Same facts as above except that Central, after formation, ratified the promoter's contract. If it subsequently changes its mind, can it be held liable on the contract? _____

18. Can Central enforce the contract against Manufacturer? _____

19. If Central rejects the contract, is Perry liable individually? _____

POWERS AND LIABILITIES OF A CORPORATION

20. Can a corporation exercise powers other than those explicitly enumerated in its articles of incorporation? _____

21. Does a corporation have the **implied** power to enter into a partnership? _____

22. May a corporation validly make an educational or charitable gift that serves **no** direct corporate business purpose? _____

23. Can a **lawful** act ever be an "ultra vires" act? _____

24. If a corporate employee, in the course of employment, commits a tortious act that was within the scope of employment, but was unauthorized, can the corporation use ultra vires as a defense? _____

25. Brown Corporation enters a contract with Bob, a builder. The contract is of a kind that is ultra vires for Brown.

a. If neither side has performed, can Bob enforce the contract if the corporation raises an ultra vires defense? _____

b. If both sides have performed, can Brown rescind? _____

c. If Bob has performed, but Brown has not, can Bob enforce the contract? _____

MANAGEMENT AND CONTROL

26. At their annual meeting, the shareholders of XYZ Corp., a publicly held corporation, voted to fire President and hire Jones as new general manager at $100,000 per annum. Are these resolutions effective? _____

27. Does "statutory close corporation" status depend entirely on the existence of a specified number of shareholders? _____

28. Small Corporation is a statutory close corporation with five shareholders, who are also the five directors.

   a. May the five shareholders make a written agreement concerning distribution of dividends and election of officers? _____

   b. One of the shareholders makes a permissible sale of one-half of his shares to an outsider. The share certificate indicates the existence of a written agreement concerning management. Is the transferee bound by the agreement? _____

29. Is it ever permissible for a corporation to have only one director? _____

30. May the board of directors remove a director? _____

31. In most states, a director must own at least one share in a corporation of which he is a director. True or false? _____

32. Under modern statutes, can the shareholders ever, **without cause**, remove a director before the expiration of her term? _____

33. XYZ Corp. has seven directors, elected annually for one-year terms.

   a. May the board of directors enter into a five-year employment contract with the general manager, thus binding future boards? _____

   b. May the XYZ board delegate interim management decision-making authority to an executive committee composed of three of the directors? _____

   c. May five of the seven directors properly agree in advance as to how they will vote at board meetings? _____

   d. At an unscheduled meeting, four members are present and make a decision by a three-to-one vote. The three absent directors subsequently waive notice and approve the minutes of the meeting. Is the board action valid under most statutes? _____

34. Even without prior agreement, a director is always entitled to reasonable compensation for ordinary services as a director. True or false? _____

35. By majority vote, the directors of Shield Corp., acting in good faith, reduce existing fire insurance coverage without investigating the value of the property insured, even though Shield was not in a position to self-insure. As a result, Shield sustains a major financial loss when the property is destroyed by fire.

   a. Does the "business judgment rule" absolve the directors of liability for the losses? _____

   b. Is each director who voted with the majority personally liable for the losses to Shield? _____

   c. Are those who voted against the decision also liable? _____

   d. If two of the directors were serving without pay, are they nevertheless personally liable? _____

   e. If the directors relied on apparently sound reports by corporate officers (or on the advice of professional experts) that the property was "fireproof," are the directors relieved of liability? _____

36. Under most statutes, corporate officers are elected by the shareholders. True or false? _____

37. The president of Green Corp. hired three new employees as division managers without consulting the board of directors. On finding out, can the board cancel the employment contracts as unauthorized? _____

CONFLICT OF INTEREST IN CORPORATE TRANSACTIONS

38. Acme Corp. has nine directors, but four are absent from a meeting of the board. Director Donald, making full disclosure of all pertinent facts, offers to sell an office building to Acme. Donald's offer is accepted by a three-to-two vote, with Donald voting in favor. Under modern statutes—

   a. Was Donald properly counted toward a quorum? _____

   b. Was Donald's vote properly counted on the sale? _____

39. Same facts as above. Assume Acme buys the building from Donald, after full disclosure to the board, a proper quorum, and a disinterested majority vote of the board.

   a. At a later date, can the corporation rescind simply on the ground that the contract was made with an interested director? _____

   b. If the contract is later challenged as unfair in a shareholders' derivative suit, is the burden of proof on Donald to prove that it was fair to the corporation? _____

   c. If the shareholders *unanimously* ratify the contract, can Acme sue to rescind for unfairness? _____

d. If the contract is ratified by a *majority* of the shareholders, can Acme avoid it? _____

40. On the same facts, *if* the contract had been unfair, and Acme sought damages, could Donald be held liable for more than the difference between the price paid by Acme and the fair market value of the building? _____

41. Red Corp. and Blue Corp. have a majority of directors in common. Is it ever proper for the two corporations to contract with each other? _____

42. Winnie is a director of Textile Corp. The inventor of a new weaving machine, having offered it to Textile, also offers to sell it to Winnie.

   a. May Winnie buy the invention for her own business use while Textile is still considering the offer? _____

   b. If Winnie knows that Textile is financially unable to meet Inventor's price, may she buy the machine? _____

   c. If Textile makes a firm decision to reject the offer, may Winnie buy? _____

   d. If Winnie purchases from Inventor while Textile is still considering the offer, may Textile force Winnie to transfer the machine to Textile *at her cost*? _____

   e. If Winnie is on the boards of two different textile corporations, and Inventor directly approaches Winnie individually, may she choose to which corporation she will transmit the offer? _____

43. Herbert is a director of Blank Corp. and has also served as Blank's secretary for five years.

   a. May Herbert properly vote on the amount of his own salary as secretary? _____

   b. If Herbert's salary is set by the disinterested directors, can it later be challenged in a derivative suit simply on the grounds that it is more than the average salary paid for similar positions in other corporations? _____

   c. If Herbert's salary is based on a percentage of corporate profits, is it automatically subject to challenge as a waste of corporate assets? _____

   d. If a disinterested board votes a substantial, but reasonable, increase in Herbert's salary, retroactive to the beginning of his service as secretary, can the corporation (*e.g.*, under a new board or as a result of a shareholder suit) recover the amount of the retroactive increase? _____

INSIDER TRADING

44. At common law, do directors and officers owe fiduciary obligations to individual shareholders to disclose inside information about the corporation when trading in its stock? _____

45. Do section 10(b) and rule 10b-5 of the 1934 Act apply to securities that are *exempt* from the registration and reporting requirements of the Act? _____

46. Virginia, a promoter of Round Corp., sold to Round, without full disclosure, property worth $20,000 in exchange for its issuance of shares having a par value of $35,000.

    a.   Can Round sue Virginia under rule 10b-5?

    b.   Can a shareholder of Round maintain a derivative suit against Virginia under rule 10b-5?

    c.   If Round had paid Virginia $35,000 in *cash* instead of stock, could Round sue under rule 10b-5?

47. Can a plaintiff suing in state court on a state law claim join with it a 10b-5 claim arising from the same transaction?

48. Edgar, a shareholder of Circle Corp., brings an action seeking rescission of a just-completed merger of Circle into Square Corp., on the ground that Square made a false statement of a material fact in order to induce the shareholders' consent to the merger. Does rule 10b-5 apply?

49. Old Corp. issues a very optimistic press release that intentionally misstates material facts about its earnings. In reliance thereon, Davis buys stock. Also in reliance thereon, Edward, a shareholder, decides *not* to sell his stock. When the true facts are known, the stock falls sharply.

    a.   Can Davis sue Old under rule 10b-5, even though he purchased his shares on the open market and not from Old?

    b.   Can Davis seek either rescission *or* damages?

    c.   Can Edward sue Old?

50. John is a director of New Corp. and knows that New has a new invention that will make its stock rise. Before any public announcement, John buys 1,000 shares directly from Thomas and also advises his neighbor, in confidence, to invest heavily in New stock because of the invention. The neighbor promptly follows John's advice.

    a.   Can Thomas rescind?

    b.   Is the neighbor liable under rule 10b-5?

51. Nondisclosure of a mere *possibility* may give rise to an action under rule 10b-5. True or false?

52. Is a corporate officer liable under rule 10b-5 for a merely negligent omission of a material fact in a corporate report, if a purchaser relies thereon to his detriment?

53. Franklin is vice president of Grand Corp., which is listed on the New York Stock Exchange and has 1,000,000 shares outstanding. In March, he bought 1,000 shares of Grand from Greg at $30. In June of the same year, he sold the shares at $45.

a. Is Franklin liable under section 16(b) of the 1934 Act to disgorge the profit he made?

    _____

b. Can Greg rescind or recover $15,000 from Franklin under section 16(b)?

    _____

c. If Franklin's trading was *not* based on any inside information, does this affect his liability?

    _____

54. Regina is a director of Home Corp. In February, she sold 100 shares of Home at $12; in March, she bought 200 shares at $10; in August, she sold 200 shares at $10. Is Regina liable under section 16(b)?

    _____

55. Stone Corp. has 100,000 shares outstanding. Alice, who is neither an officer nor a director of Stone, sold all of her 25,000 shares in July at $10. In August, she purchased 5,000 shares at $8. Is she liable under section 16(b)?

    _____

56. Robert, the secretary of Wood Corp., is designated by Wood to represent its stock interest (less than 10%) in Rock Corp. by serving as a director of Rock. Can Wood Corp. be held liable for short-swing profits it derives from Rock stock under section 16(b)?

    _____

57. If an insider uses confidential information in *purchasing* stock of his corporation, but does *not* sell any stock in the corporation within six months of the purchase, can he be held liable either by the corporation or by the persons from whom he purchased?

    _____

VOTING BY PROXY

58. If shares are sold between the "record date" and the time of a shareholders' meeting, is the new owner entitled to vote the shares at the meeting?

    _____

59. If 100 shares are eligible to vote and four directors are to be elected by cumulative voting, a shareholder must have one-fourth of the shares (*i.e.*, 25 shares) to be able to elect one director. True or false?

    _____

60. In a corporation with cumulative voting, will reducing the size of the board or providing for staggered terms reduce the effective voting strength of a minority bloc of shares?

    _____

61. Is proxy voting permitted after a shareholder's death?

    _____

62. Shareholder Simon, owner of 10,000 shares, pledges 5,000 to X as security for a loan, and gives X an irrevocable proxy. Simon then gives Y a proxy for his other 5,000 shares. Simon, X, and Y all appear at the meeting to vote.

a. May X vote 5,000 shares?

    _____

b. May Y vote 5,000 shares?

    _____

63. The management of Ace Corp., whose shares are traded on a national exchange, solicits proxies for its annual meeting. Under the federal proxy solicitation rules, which, if any, of the following shareholder proposals is management required to include in the proxy solicitation materials?

    _____

(A)   Nomination of directors with supporting statements.

(B)   A demand that the corporation take a public stand on foreign policy issues.

(C)   A proposal that would bind the board to replace a corporate vice president.

64.   The management of Black Corp. solicited proxies for a vote on a proposed merger. The solicitation included several misstatements of material facts. The merger was approved.

a.   In a shareholder suit to rescind the merger, must the plaintiff-shareholder prove the *materiality* of the misstatements?   _____

b.   Must he prove that the merger approval *resulted* from the misstatements?   _____

c.   If the terms of the merger were fair to the corporation and the shareholders, can plaintiff still obtain relief?   _____

65.   Following a proxy contest involving basic policy decisions of Alpha Corp., management loses in the voting.

a.   Can the corporation reimburse management for its expenses in the proxy contest?   _____

b.   Can the corporation reimburse the victorious insurgents?   _____

SHAREHOLDER AGREEMENTS

66.   Is a pooling agreement among fewer than all shareholders in a close corporation valid?   _____

67.   Will most courts enforce an agreement among shareholders that binds them in their actions as *directors*, if all shareholders are not parties to the agreement?   _____

68.   A, B, and C, three shareholders in a close corporation, create a voting trust, transferring legal title in their shares to Thomas as trustee.

a.   Can A revoke before expiration of the term of the trust?   _____

b.   Does the trust last as long as A, B, and C are shareholders?   _____

c.   Can Thomas vote the shares in *every* shareholder vote?   _____

TRANSFER Of SHARES

69.   Small Corp., a close corporation, has a provision in its articles that no shareholder may sell or transfer her shares without first giving the corporation, and then the other shareholders, a right of first refusal for 30 days.

a.   Is this restriction valid under most modern statutes?   _____

b.   May Small exercise the option if the repurchase would impair its stated capital?   _____

c.   If a shareholder dies, may Small insist on the right to repurchase from her legatee?   _____

d.   If a shareholder, in violation of the restriction, sells her shares to a transferee with notice of the restriction, may Small refuse to recognize the transfer?   _____

70.   Under modern statutes, if a corporation has a lien on shares, is a transferee without notice liable for the amount owed?   _____

SHAREHOLDER'S INFORMATIONAL RIGHTS

71.   At common law, did a shareholder have an *absolute* right to inspect corporate books and records?   _____

72.   Under modern statutes, can the shareholders' right to inspect corporate books and records be eliminated by specific provision in the articles of incorporation?   _____

73.   Is the objective of gaining control of a corporation through a proxy fight a "proper" purpose that justifies obtaining access to the shareholder list by insurgent shareholders?   _____

CONTROLLING SHARES

74.   The majority shareholder of Beta Corp. causes the board of directors to declare an excessive—but lawful—dividend. Does a minority shareholder have standing to object, even though he too will receive the dividend?   _____

75.   Minority shareholders in a close corporation actually owe a stricter fiduciary duty to other shareholders than do controlling shareholders of a publicly held corporation. True or false?   _____

76.   Owen, the owner of 60% of the shares of Omega Corp., sells his Omega stock to Olive at a premium, *i.e.*, a price above market value. Must Owen share the premium with the other shareholders?   _____

77.   If a majority shareholder is selling his stock, may he, as part of the sale transaction, arrange for the incumbent directors to resign so that the purchaser can take immediate control?   _____

78.   Sally, a majority shareholder in Epsilon Corp., sells her Epsilon shares to Louis at a price far above their fair value. Louis subsequently loots the corporate treasury.

a.   Can Sally be held liable to the minority shareholders?   _____

b.   If Sally is liable, is her liability limited to the minority's "share" of the premium she received?   _____

DERIVATIVE SUITS

79.   The test of whether an action should be brought as a direct suit or as a derivative suit is the number of shareholders who claim to have been injured. True or false?   _____

80. The board of directors of Red Corp. has failed to sue for damages on a Red contract with another corporation, which the latter has breached. Jane, a Red shareholder, wishes to bring a derivative suit to enforce Red's cause of action.

    a.   Must Jane first make a demand on the Red board of directors? _____

    b.   If a disinterested Red board rejects Jane's demand, can she still maintain her suit? _____

    c.   Must Jane also make a demand on the Red shareholders? _____

    d.   If a demand on the Red shareholders was required and the shareholders refuse to sue, may Jane maintain her suit? _____

81. Must a derivative suit plaintiff always have been a shareholder at the time of the alleged wrongdoing? _____

82. If a sole shareholder cannot file a derivative suit against former managers because he owned no stock when the wrongful acts occurred, may he instead instigate a suit by the corporation? _____

83. If a corporate director is a defendant in a derivative suit, may the corporation's attorney represent the director? _____

84. Is a corporation a necessary party to a derivative suit brought on its behalf? _____

85. Is a jury trial ever available in a shareholder derivative suit in federal court? _____

86. If a losing derivative suit plaintiff was required to post security for expenses, is the corporation automatically entitled to recover the amount posted? _____

87. If a plaintiff-shareholder proves her derivative suit claim, will the court normally enter judgment in favor of the *corporation*? _____

88. If a plaintiff-shareholder loses in a derivative suit against a third party, may the corporation later sue in its own name on the same claim? _____

89. Plaintiff in a derivative suit recovers a judgment against defendant directors.

    a.   Is the plaintiff entitled to reimbursement from the corporation for his expenses? _____

    b.   Are the losing directors entitled to indemnification by the corporation for damages assessed against them? _____

    c.   If the plaintiff had lost, could the corporation reimburse the defendants for their expenses? _____

90. May a corporation properly provide insurance coverage for its officers and directors to protect them against personal liability or expenses in derivative suits? _____

CLASSES OF STOCK

91. If a corporation's articles authorize "preferred" stock, but fail to state what preferences the stock is entitled to, is it entitled to at least dividend and liquidation preferences? _____

92. The articles of Corporation Y provide for preferred stock with a "5%, cumulative, dividend preference."

   a. Must the directors pay the 5% dividend in a year in which funds are available? _____

   b. If no dividends were paid on the preferred in a given year, do the arrearages have preference over dividends on the common stock in a subsequent year? _____

AUTHORIZATION AND ISSUANCE OF SHARES

93. Once all of the authorized shares have been issued, may the board of directors authorize the issuance of more shares? _____

94. If a corporation repurchases shares and holds them as "treasury stock," does this affect the corporation's authorized or issued capital? _____

STOCK SUBSCRIPTIONS

95. Prior to the formation of Star Corp., A, B, and C each agree to subscribe to 100 shares of stock when issued at an agreed price. If A revokes before Star's incorporation is completed, can Star enforce the agreement against A? _____

CONSIDERATION FOR SHARES

96. Which of the following shares have been lawfully issued by ABC Corp.? _____

   (A) 1,000 shares issued to Politician Paul as a gift?

   (B) 1,000 shares issued to Promoter Pat in exchange for her preincorporation services?

   (C) 1,000 shares issued to Promoter Pamela in exchange for her management services to be performed during the following two years?

97. May par value shares be sold by a corporation—

   a. For *less* than par value? _____

   b. For *more* than par value? _____

98. In April, Union Corp. issued to Arthur 100 shares of $10 par stock—marked "fully paid"—in exchange for property worth only $300. In March, one month before the transaction between Union and Arthur, Creditor Cal extended $1,000 credit to Union. In June, following the transaction between Union and Arthur, Creditor Cora extended $1,000 credit to Union. Union has now become insolvent.

a.   Can Cal sue Arthur for $700?   _____

b.   Can Cora?   _____

99.   Same facts as above. If both Arthur and the directors of Union believed in good faith that Arthur's property *was* worth $1,000 when it was exchanged for stock, is Arthur's liability changed?   _____

PROMOTERS

100.   Promoters Peter and Paul of Acme Corp. sell a warehouse to Acme that they bought for $30,000 and that has a fair market value of $40,000. In exchange for the property, they receive 5,000 shares of $10 par stock. If Peter and Paul have not made full disclosure as to the amount of their profit, may Acme rescind?   _____

101.   Assume the same facts except that Peter and Paul were the *sole shareholders* at the time of the transaction.

a.   If only 5,000 shares have been authorized, does the corporation have a cause of action at common law?   _____

b.   If the corporation has an authorized capital of 10,000 shares, and the issuance of the remaining 5,000 shares is planned as part of the original capitalization, will the corporation have a cause of action after the other shares are issued?   _____

PREEMPTIVE RIGHTS

102.   Did common law preemptive rights protect a stockholder against the dilution of her control by *any* new share issuances?   _____

103.   When a shareholder's preemptive rights have been violated by an issue of shares, his only remedy is to seek damages from the corporation. True or false?   _____

UNDERWRITING

104.   Can underwriters be held subject to the same liabilities as issuers for fraud in the sale of securities under federal law?   _____

STATUTES REGULATING ISSUANCE OF SHARES

105.   Can state blue sky laws validly require disclosure of information in connection with the issuance and sale of securities that is *not* required under applicable federal securities laws?   _____

106.   Can the Securities and Exchange Commission, under the 1933 Act, veto a proposed stock issuance if it is economically unsound?   _____

107.   Which of the following issuances or transfers, if any, are exempt from the registration requirements of the Securities Act of 1933?   _____

(A)   Mr. Smith inherits 100 shares of X stock and sells them to his neighbor.

(B) Y Corp. offers a new issue to only 20 persons, all of whom live in the same state and have financial experience and access to full information about Y.

(C) Same facts as (B), but the 20 persons live in four different states.

(D) Same facts as (B), but two of the offerees are brokers who intend to resell the stock to the public.

108. Can the purchaser of shares issued under a "private offering" exemption ever sell these shares *without registration?* _____

109. Orange Corp. knowingly files a false registration statement containing material misstatements. Ralph, without knowledge of the misstatements, buys 1,000 shares from Orange at the issuing price of $10. The stock goes down to $7 per share. Ralph promptly files suit.

    a. Is Ralph entitled to judgment against Orange, its directors, its underwriter, and the accountant who certified the financial portion of the registration statement? _____

    b. Must Ralph prove the elements of common law fraud? _____

    c. Must Ralph prove reliance on the misstatements? _____

110. Same facts as above except that Ralph, immediately after purchasing the shares, sold them to Cynthia at $10 per share. The price then went down to $7.

    a. Does Cynthia have a cause of action against Orange under section 11? _____

    b. Is Cynthia entitled to either rescission *or* damages from Orange? _____

111. Assume Orange had sold its stock by use of a material misstatement *other than* in its registration statement. Under section 12 of the 1933 Act—

    a. Does Ralph have a cause of action against Orange? _____

    b. Does Cynthia? _____

112. The purchaser of securities that were exempt from the registration requirements of the 1933 Act may nevertheless recover under the Act for material misstatements or omissions in connection with the purchase of such securities. True or false? _____

DIVIDENDS

113. Can common stockholders, by majority vote, compel payment of dividends, *if* sufficient funds are available? _____

114. Under most statutes, may dividends generally be paid out of stated capital if there are current net profits? _____

115. Corporation A sold 100,000 shares of its $20 par stock for $23 per share. Can the $300,000 later be available for dividends in most states? _____

116. Corporation B reduced the par value of its 100,000 shares of common stock from $12 to $10. Can it distribute the $200,000 as dividends in most states? _____

117. Corporation C owned real property with a book value of $200,000 based on its acquisition cost. The property is now worth $500,000. Can Corporation C pay dividends from the $300,000 increased value? _____

118. Can a director who votes for an illegal dividend be held **personally** liable for the amount distributed? _____

119. The directors of Acme Corporation all voted for an unlawful dividend, rendering Acme insolvent. Are the shareholder-recipients liable? _____

REDEMPTION AND REPURCHASES

120. If funds are available, does a corporation always have inherent power to redeem its shares? _____

121. May a corporation **repurchase** its shares on a selective basis (from certain shareholders and not from others)? _____

122. If a corporation contracts to repurchase its shares on an installment payment basis, is it enough that it has adequate funds available from a legal source on the date the contract is made (as distinguished from the dates each installment comes due)? _____

123. The directors of Gold Corp., knowing that shareholder X was planning a fight to unseat them, authorized the repurchase of X's shares at a premium. As long as a lawful source of funds was available, was their action proper? _____

FUNDAMENTAL CHANGES

124. The boards of directors of Red Corp. and Blue Corp. adopt a plan to merge Red into Blue. Neither corporation had any prior relationship with the other. Which, if any, of the following statements is correct under most statutes? _____

   (A)   The merger must be approved by shareholder votes of **both** Red and Blue.

   (B)   The debts and contract obligations of Red are automatically assumed by Blue upon completion of the merger.

   (C)   Red is automatically dissolved upon completion of the merger.

125. Same facts as above. Assume that both Red Corp. and Blue Corp. had dissenting shareholders who complied with all the statutorily required procedures.

   a.   Do the dissenting shareholders of both Red and Blue have appraisal rights? _____

   b.   Can a shareholder who voted for the merger nevertheless exercise appraisal rights? _____

c. Is the "fair value" for a dissenter's shares always the recognized market price at the effective date of the merger? _____

126. Green Corp. owns 90% of the stock of Brown Corp.; two individual shareholders each own 5% of Brown.

   a. If both boards of directors approve a "short-form" merger of Brown into Green, must both corporations' shareholders also approve? _____

   b. Do dissenting shareholders of Green have appraisal rights? _____

   c. Can Green eliminate the two minority shareholders by giving them cash instead of Green stock? _____

127. The board of directors of Gray Corp. contemplates a sale of "substantially all its assets" to Black Corp. for cash. Which of the following statements, if any, is correct under most statutes? _____

   (A) The shareholders of Gray must approve.

   (B) The shareholders of Black must approve.

   (C) In defining "substantially all" of Gray's assets, the determining factor is the percentage of gross assets to be sold.

128. The board of directors of Day Corp. wishes to acquire Night Corp., but fears opposition from a strong minority of its own shareholders. Day offers to buy Night's assets in exchange for Day stock with the proviso that Night will then vote on a plan of dissolution.

   a. Can the minority shareholders of Day object that they had no opportunity to vote on the transaction? _____

   b. If the sale has been consummated, can it be set aside? _____

129. If a board of directors unanimously approves a change in the articles of incorporation, is shareholder approval ordinarily also required? _____

130. May the state bring an action for involuntary dissolution of a corporation for abuse of its corporate authority? _____

131. Is a bankrupt corporation automatically dissolved? _____

132. If, after dissolution, directors conduct further business not reasonably incident to liquidation, can they be held personally liable for corporate debts? _____

133. If the assets of a dissolved corporation have been distributed while a creditor's timely claims are unsatisfied, the creditor can recover from the shareholder-distributees. True or false? _____

134. If controlling shareholders materially misrepresented the facts of a proposed merger so as to advantage themselves, can a dissenting shareholder exercise her appraisal rights under state law *and also* bring an action under federal securities acts? _____

135. Acme Corp. makes a tender offer to buy 60% of the shares of Star Corp. for cash.

    a.   Must the shareholders of both corporations approve?   _____

    b.   After acquiring the Star shares, may Acme dissolve Star?   _____

    c.   Must Acme disclose its plans for Star at the time it makes the tender offer?   _____

ANSWERS TO REVIEW QUESTIONS

1. **NO** — Shareholder liability is usually limited to the amount of the investment, and only the corporation is liable on its debts. [§2]

2. **NO** — Except in extraordinary circumstances, shareholders have **no** power to manage and control; these powers are vested in the board of directors and the officers acting under the board's authority. This is a major difference between corporations and partnerships, because partners do have the right to participate in management. [§§4, 22]

3. **YES** — A corporation is a separate entity, whose existence can be perpetual and is unaffected by changes in the owners of its shares. This is another major difference between a corporation and a partnership. In a partnership, the death, withdrawal, or insolvency of any partner normally terminates the partnership. [§§5, 14-15]

4. **NO** — A corporation is a legal entity, but a partnership is not, even though the law sometimes treats partnerships as if they were legal entities. [§§1, 9]

5. **NO** — A limited partner, whose financial liability is limited to the amount of his investment, **may not** participate in the management of the business. [§§35, 37-40]

6. **YES** — In determining whether to "pierce the corporate veil" (*i.e.*, disregard the corporate entity and impose liability on shareholders for corporate obligations), the commingling of assets (treating corporate assets as if they were the shareholders' own assets) and lack of corporate formalities (no directors' or shareholders' meetings, and no corporate records) are major factors considered by the court. Both suggest the corporation is merely the "alter ego" of the shareholders and should be disregarded. [§§61-63, 67]

7. **DEPENDS** — Although DEF **was** maintained as a separate entity, some courts would permit creditors to disregard corporateness and reach the shareholders because DEF was undercapitalized; *i.e.*, Don, Ed, and Frank should have reasonably anticipated that $750 was inadequate capitalization to meet the obligations of DEF. [§§65, 69]

8. **NO** — When this doctrine is applicable, the corporation's debts to shareholders are **subordinated** to its debts to outside creditors, but no additional personal liability is imposed on shareholders. (In effect, the debt owed to the shareholders is treated as additional investment capital.) [§§73-75]

9. **NO (both questions)** — The rule that the corporate form may be disregarded to avoid injustice is for the benefit of third parties, not the corporation; therefore, a corporation generally may not assert in its own name a claim or defense that belongs to a shareholder. (Note, however, that Beulah could *assign* her claim to XYZ Corp., in which case, it could assert same.) [§72]

10.a. **GENERALLY NO** — Although a few states require a specific statement, most do not, and some statutes (*e.g.*, Delaware) permit a purpose as general as to engage in any lawful activity for which a corporation may be organized. [§§78-81]

b. **NO** — Statutes commonly require the articles of incorporation to indicate the number of shares *authorized*. The number to be issued is usually decided at a post-incorporation meeting of the board of directors. [§§79, 83-84]

11. **NO**   Incorporators file the articles and, if the statute does not provide that the initial directors be named in the articles, the incorporators hold an organizational meeting at which bylaws are adopted and directors are elected to serve until the first shareholders' meeting. [§§82-83]

12. **NO**   The filing of the articles in proper form is required to create the corporation, but bylaws are usually adopted at a post-incorporation organizational meeting. Bylaw provisions may be regulated by statute, however. [§§78, 83-84]

13. **(C)**   On the facts, it appears that White Corp., lacking sufficient compliance for "de jure" status, has met the conditions for "de facto" status—good faith, a colorable attempt to comply with a statute under which the corporation could have been formed, and actual use of corporate powers. Under modern law, the status of a "de facto" corporation can usually be challenged *only* by the state. In contrast, complete compliance with statutory requirements creates a "de jure" corporation, whose corporate status cannot be challenged by anyone. [§§88-93]

14. **FALSE**   Both the shareholders of a nominal corporation, having claimed corporate status in a transaction with a third party, and a third party who has dealt with the enterprise as if it were a corporation may be estopped from denying corporateness. [§§94-96]

15. **DEPENDS**   Jurisdictions with statutes based on the old Model Act have abolished the de facto doctrine. However, under the Revised Model Act, only persons who *knew* there was no incorporation are barred from asserting de facto status. [§§103-104]

16. **NO**   Even under the American rule, the corporation is not liable on promoters' contracts, unless the corporation adopts the contract. [§§110-115]

17. **SPLIT**   Under the English rule, even corporate ratification will not create contractual liability (but the corporation may be liable in quasi-contract for any benefits obtained). Under the American rule, contractual liability *is* created by either express or implied ratification. [§§110-115]

18. **YES**   Under both the English and American rules, Central may choose to enforce the contract. [§116]

19. **DEPENDS**   If Perry had expressly disclaimed individual liability, he cannot be held. Otherwise, most courts will allow Manufacturer to enforce the contract against Perry, who may then have a right to indemnification by Central. [§§117-119]

20. **YES**   Under modern law, courts broadly construe a corporation's implied power to do what is *reasonably necessary to achieve its express purposes*, unless otherwise prohibited. Moreover, modern statutes confer many powers on corporations. [§§128-129]

21. **NO**   Because participation in a partnership involves an impermissible delegation of managerial responsibility, in the past most courts held that a corporation could

not enter into a partnership, absent specific authorization. (Modern statutes now specifically authorize this.) [§132]

22. **YES** Under the modern view, such gifts, if *reasonable*, are permitted even without any showing of a direct benefit to the corporation. [§§133-137]

23. **YES** Any action outside corporate purposes and powers may be "ultra vires," regardless of its legality. [§140]

24. **NO** The corporation cannot rely on a disclaimer of its legal power to commit the particular act to avoid liability. [§§143-144]

25.a. **YES (modern law)** At common law, neither party could enforce an ultra vires executory contract. Under modern statutes, ultra vires is not a defense to an executory *or* executed contract. Under some circumstances, however, a shareholder may seek to *enjoin* performance. [§§146, 151-152]

  b. **NO** The rule is the same at common law and under modern statutes. A fully performed contract, although ultra vires, is not subject to rescission. [§§147, 152]

  c. **NO (modern law)** Under modern law, the ultra vires defense is *disfavored* even when one party has performed, but most statutes permit recovery in quasi-contract from the nonperforming party. At common law, the majority view denied the ultra vires defense to the nonperforming party in such a case. [§§149, 152]

26. **NO** Such management decisions are within the powers of the directors; shareholders have no *direct* control over the management of ordinary corporate affairs including the hiring and firing of corporate officers. (Some statutes, however, permit powers of management and control to be exercised by shareholders in a *close corporation*.) [§§159, 167, 176-178]

27. **NO** Most close corporation statutes impose additional requirements, such as identification as a close corporation in the articles of incorporation and restrictions on the transfer of shares. [§§170, 173-175]

28.a. **YES** Unlike an ordinary corporation, in which such an agreement would be deemed an improper infringement of the powers of the directors, written shareholder management agreements are generally permitted in close corporations. [§177]

  b. **YES** Statutes frequently require a "conspicuous" notation of the existence of the agreement on a share certificate of a close corporation. If such a notation is present, a transferee takes subject to the agreement. [§§180, 185]

29. **YES** Many statutes authorize single-member boards, especially where there is only one shareholder. A few statutes authorize single directors for all corporations. [§187]

30. **DEPENDS** Under common law and the majority view, the board cannot remove a director, with or without cause. However, some modern statutes permit removal for cause. [§197]

31. **FALSE** However, unless prohibited by statute, the articles of incorporation or the bylaws may prescribe any reasonable qualifications for directors—including share ownership. [§188]

32. **YES**   Unlike common law, which permitted removal only for cause, many modern statutes generally permit removal, without cause, by a vote of shareholders. [§§194, 196]

33.a. **YES**   Absent a prohibition in the articles of incorporation, a board may make a contract that extends beyond the directors' term of office. A future XYZ board could remove the general manager, but he would then have a cause of action for breach of contract. [§§193, 244]

  b. **YES**   It is common for a board to authorize day-to-day management by such a committee, although there are limitations on the committee's power to make certain decisions of a fundamental nature (*e.g.*, dividends, mergers, etc.). [§§207-209]

  c. **NO**   Fiduciary duties of directors require that directors be able to exercise free discretion in making corporate decisions. (Exceptions have been created for close corporations.) [§214]

  d. **YES**   Modern statutes reduce required formalities and permit waiver of notice before *or* after an unscheduled meeting. Furthermore, an action taken by a majority of the directors present is binding, *if* there was a quorum. A quorum is ordinarily a majority of the authorized number of directors. [§§200-203]

34. **FALSE**   Generally, a director is not entitled to compensation for ordinary services as a director, unless compensation is provided for by the articles or by board resolution passed *before* services were rendered. However, a director may be entitled to compensation for authorized *extraordinary* services and for services as an officer or employee. [§§215-217]

35.a. **PROBABLY NOT**   The business judgment rule protects a director who has made an erroneous policy decision in good faith *and* in the exercise of diligence. In the majority view, it does not protect a director who has not acted diligently. [§§223-226]

  b. **YES**   Since the directors' action *caused* the loss, they are personally liable, and the liability is joint and several. Note that some statutes permit limitation or elimination of director liability absent bad faith, intentional misconduct, or illegal acts. [§§230-232]

  c. **NO**   If the director has recorded her dissent, then she is not liable. [§231]

  d. **YES**   Lack of compensation is ordinarily no defense. The director's fiduciary duty is not diminished by the fact that service is without pay. [§233]

  e. **YES**   *If* the reliance was reasonable *and if* the report or advice was within the competence of the person providing it, the directors have a defense to liability. [§§235-236]

36. **FALSE**   Under most statutes, the major officers of a corporation are elected by the board, although some statutes permit election of officers by shareholders. [§244]

37. **PROBABLY NOT**   The president of a corporation, by majority view, has *apparent authority* to make decisions and bind the corporation in transactions that are part of the ordinary course of the corporation's business. Hiring division managers is probably within that category. [§§250-254]

38.a.	**YES**	Most states permit an interested director to be counted toward a quorum (although a contrary result would have been reached at common law). [§§258-259]
b.	**NO**	Neither at common law nor under most statutes may an "interested" director's vote be counted on the transaction in which he has a personal interest. [§§258-259, 272]
39.a.	**NO**	Since there was full disclosure, most courts would require a showing of fundamental unfairness to the corporation. However, at common law such a contract was automatically voidable by the corporation. [§§260-265]
b.	**YES**	The burden of proof is generally on the interested director, who must prove the fairness of the transaction. However, the burden may be shifted to the plaintiff in cases where the shareholders have ratified the contract. [§§266, 270-271]
c.	**NO**	Assuming full disclosure, unanimous shareholder ratification will preclude a suit by the corporation. However, if the corporation is insolvent, a creditor's suit may be possible. [§268]
d.	**DEPENDS**	Ratification by a disinterested majority may estop the corporation or at least shift the burden of proof to the plaintiff. Courts are split as to the effectiveness of an attempted ratification by an interested majority of the shareholders. [§§269-276]
40.	**POSSIBLY**	The difference between price and fair market value would be the *usual* measure of damages. However, if Donald had purchased the building in order to resell it to Acme at an excessive price, some courts would penalize him by fixing damages at the difference between Donald's acquisition cost and the amount paid to him by Acme. Some courts may also order the interested director to repay his salary earned during the breach period, and others may assess punitive damages. [§§283-287]
41.	**YES**	Modern statutes generally permit transactions between two corporations with interlocking directorates, *if* the transactions are fair and there is full disclosure. At common law, however, a transaction between Red and Blue was voidable at the option of either. [§§289-292]
42.a.	**NO**	Since Textile was already considering the offer, this would be a clear usurpation of corporate opportunity and a breach of Winnie's fiduciary duty of loyalty. [§§296, 298]
b.	**DEPENDS**	Some courts hold that Textile's inability frees Winnie to take advantage of the opportunity. However, some courts would bar Winnie, on the rationale that her duty is to attempt to find the necessary financing for Textile. [§§302-303]
c.	**YES**	If Textile, fully informed, refuses the opportunity, there is no conflict of interest to prevent Winnie from proceeding. [§305]
d.	**YES**	Textile may compel a transfer of the machine and an accounting for any interim income or profits. If Winnie buys while the offer is a corporate opportunity and then sells the machine to Textile, Textile may recover Winnie's entire profit. [§§307-308]

e. **NO** Winnie may have to transmit the offer to both corporations. If she offers it to only one, she may be liable to the other. [§309]

43.a. **SPLIT** Most states would not permit Herbert's vote to be counted to make up a majority vote, although some statutes provide otherwise. The effect of shareholder ratification would be the same as in any other case of an "interested director" transaction. [§§219, 310-313]

b. **NO** As long as the salary is reasonable, the fact that it is above market value for the services will not preclude application of the business judgment rule to protect both Herbert and the board of directors. The directors may, in good faith, believe that Herbert is worth more than an average secretary. Note that the business judgment rule nearly always precludes finding executive compensation excessive in a publicly held corporation. [§§314-319]

c. **NO** As long as the total compensation bears a reasonable relationship to the value of Herbert's services, there is no "waste." And, note that under such an arrangement, Herbert's interests would be more likely to coincide with Blank's interests than to conflict with them. [§§321, 329-330]

d. **PROBABLY** On general contract principles, past services are not ordinarily a legally sufficient consideration for the payment by Blank. A contrary result might be reached, however, if there was consideration (*e.g.*, the retroactive increase was expressly conditioned upon Herbert's remaining in the position for a specified period); or if it could be shown that the increase fell within the business judgment rule. [§§324-326]

44. **NO** The common law majority view was that no duty was owed. However, exceptions were recognized in many cases where "special facts" compelled disclosure (*e.g.*, in cases involving face-to-face dealing). [§§334-337]

45. **YES** Section 10(b) and rule 10b-5 apply to the purchase and sale of *all* securities. The only jurisdictional limitation to section 10(b) is the requirement that the "purchase or sale" must be effected by an instrumentality of interstate commerce. [§342]

46.a. **YES** Section 10(b) extends to any purchase or sale. "Sale" is construed broadly so as to include an original issuance by a corporation. [§§341-342, 383, 391-395]

b. **YES** If the corporation-seller does not act, a shareholder who meets the relevant procedural requirements can bring a derivative suit under rule 10b-5. [§384]

c. **NO** If there is neither a purchase nor sale of any *security*, the Act does not apply. [§§342, 390-395]

47. **NO** Federal courts have *exclusive* jurisdiction over rule 10b-5 actions. *Compare:* If plaintiff sues in federal court, he may, under the doctrine of supplemental jurisdiction, join his state law claim in the federal action. [§§430-431]

48. **YES** "Purchase or sale" is broadly defined. The term includes the exchange of shares that occurs in connection with a merger. [§393]

49.a.	**YES**	Davis was a purchaser. It is not necessary that the defendant be either a purchaser or a seller. Nor is privity between defendant and the injured purchaser required. [§§344, 365-366, 390, 422]
b.	**NO**	Davis is limited to damages, because the defendant corporation was not the seller. *If* Davis had bought from Old, rescission would be available. [§§365, 421-422]
c.	**NO**	Edward was neither a purchaser nor a seller within the meaning of the Act. "Aborted" sales are not sufficient. [§390]
50.a.	**DEPENDS**	If New Corp. is publicly held, Thomas can recover damages, but probably cannot rescind, since he can replace his stock. However, rescission is permissible if New Corp. is a close corporation. [§§415-420]
b.	**YES**	A tippee who knows or should know that the tipper breached his fiduciary duty to the corporation is liable under rule 10b-5. A tipper breaches that fiduciary duty by communicating inside information for personal gain. Tips to friends are treated as benefiting the tipper because they are the same as trades by the insider followed by gifts of the profits. [§§374-376]
51.	**TRUE**	A possibility may be *material* if the likelihood of the occurrence of the event and its anticipated effect on the corporate business are such that a prospective buyer or seller would attach importance to the information. [§345]
52.	**NO**	Scienter is an element in a 10b-5 action. Mere negligence is an inadequate basis for liability. [§§346-347]
53.a.	**YES**	If a corporation's securities are covered by section 16, an officer is liable for short-swing profits, no matter how few shares he owns. [§§443-444, 452]
b.	**NO**	Greg may do neither under section 16(b), as the liability runs only in favor of the corporation. However, Greg would have an action under rule 10b-5 if Franklin traded on the basis of material inside information. [§§448, 473-475]
c.	**NO**	The language of section 16(b) appears to be absolute and courts hold the defendant liable whether or not he used inside information. [§§444, 473]
54.	**YES**	To find short-swing profits, a court looks at the six-month period after *or before* any purchase or sale. The highest sale price is matched with the lowest purchase price; thus, Regina's liability is $200. [§§445-447]
55.	**NO**	Section 16(b) covers only persons who were more-than-10% beneficial owners at both the time of purchase and the time of sale. However, one who is an officer or a director at *either* purchase *or* sale is liable. [§440]
56.	**YES**	Robert has been *deputized* to act as a director for Wood Corp. However, if Robert had been requested to be a director *by Rock* and was not selected to represent Wood's interest, Wood Corp. would not necessarily be considered an insider of Rock. Even so, Wood might be considered an insider if Robert in fact represents Wood's interest or gives inside information to Wood. [§§453-454]

57. **YES**   He may be liable to the sellers under rule 10b-5, as to which there is no six-month limit. In addition, he also incurs a common law liability to the corporation for his profits, on the ground that he breached a fiduciary duty by converting a corporate asset (inside information) to his own use. However, if the sellers recover a judgment against him, the amount could probably be deducted from any corporate recovery. [§§475-483]

58. **DEPENDS**   On whether the record owner gives the new owner a proxy. The new owner can *compel* record owner to give a proxy, but until he does, record owner alone is entitled to vote. [§§486-487]

59. **FALSE**   Twenty-one shares will be enough to elect one director. $x > \dfrac{1 \times 100}{1 + 4}$ [§500]

60. **YES**   Any device that reduces the number of directors to be elected at one time results in a higher percentage of outstanding shares being needed to elect a director—and thus, ordinarily reduces minority power. [§§504, 510]

61. **YES**   Unless written notice is given to the corporation before the vote is counted. [§514]

62.a. **YES**   Assuming that X's proxy was expressly made irrevocable, Simon's appearance is of no effect, because the proxy was coupled with an interest. When Simon repays the loan, the proxy will become revocable. [§§515-516, 518]

   b. **NO**   Simon may revoke Y's proxy by express notification, by executing a new proxy, or as here, by voting the shares himself. [§513]

63. **NONE**   (A) is incorrect because the rule requiring inclusion of shareholder proposals with management proxy solicitations does not apply to elections of directors. [§540]

     (B) is incorrect because management may exclude proposals that are beyond the corporation's power to effect or are not significantly related to the corporation's business. [§§534, 540]

     (C) is incorrect because a proposal need not be included if it purports to bind the board on a matter that is within their discretion, and not that of the shareholders. A purely advisory proposal, however, would probably be upheld. Note that the burden of proof is on management whenever it excludes a shareholder proposal. [§534]

64.a. **YES**   If misstatements or omissions are not material, there is no violation. A statement is material if the omitted fact would have assumed actual significance in the deliberations of the reasonable shareholder. [§§544-548]

   b. **NO**   If plaintiff proves that the misstatements were material, courts will assume that they may have affected the voting process and outcome, *i.e.,* causation. [§§549-551]

   c. **YES**   Fairness is no defense when shareholders have been misled. Fully informed shareholders might have rejected even a "fair" proposal. [§554]

65.a.	**YES**	Management has the right to recover its reasonable expenses, whether or not it wins, as long as the controversy is over corporate policy, not personnel. [§560]
b.	**PROBABLY**	*If* the insurgents win, some courts have upheld voluntary reimbursement on the ground that a benefit has been conferred on the corporation. [§561]
66.	**YES**	Most modern cases uphold such agreements as valid contracts or as irrevocable proxies. However, some courts will not grant specific enforcement in case of breach unless all shareholders were parties. [§§565, 571]
67.	**NO**	When the agreement is not unanimous, the majority view is that it is unenforceable as an infringement on the discretion of the board. However, recent statutes and case law liberalize this rule for close corporations. [§§576-581]
68.a.	**NO**	A voting trust is usually irrevocable for its life, unless there is unanimous agreement to terminate it. [§§582, 585]
b.	**NO**	Statutes generally limit the duration of voting trusts. Most statutes provide for extensions. [§585]
c.	**NO**	Unless there is explicit authorization in the trust agreement, most courts will not allow the trustee to vote on extraordinary matters such as dissolution of the corporation. [§587]
69.a.	**YES**	Most statutes authorize restrictions on the transfer of shares *if* they are reasonable and are not total restraints on alienability. [§§594, 599]
b.	**NO**	A corporate right of first refusal in connection with a restriction on transfer of shares does not ordinarily alter the limitations on proper sources for repurchase of shares. [§605]
c.	**NO**	Absent a specific provision, restrictions may not be held to apply to involuntary transfers. Generally, stock transfer restrictions are narrowly construed. [§609]
d.	**YES**	A corporation may continue to recognize the transferor as the owner, *if the transferee had notice* (as here). [§§610-612]
70.	**NO**	Under the U.C.C., unless a lien is shown on the face of a share certificate, the corporation cannot enforce it against a bona fide purchaser who lacks notice of any restriction. The corporation must transfer the shares and recognize the new owner. [§§610-613]
71.	**NO**	The right was not absolute. The burden of proof was on the shareholder to show that the inspection was for a proper purpose. (Under most modern statutes, the burden is on the corporation to show an improper purpose.) [§§615-616]
72.	**NO**	Today, shareholder inspection rights are in most cases statutory. Considered fundamental, they cannot be eliminated by the articles. [§616]
73.	**YES**	The purpose is proper because it is related to the shareholder's legitimate interests in the corporation. [§§618-619, 621-622]

74.	**YES**	If the dividend distribution was designed to serve the interests of the majority shareholder and is harmful to the corporation, the controlling shareholder has breached his fiduciary duty to the minority shareholder. [§644]
75.	**TRUE**	*All* shareholders of closely held corporations owe each other the same duty of utmost good faith and loyalty that is owed by partners to each other. [§645]
76.	**NO**	Absent fraud, knowledge of purchaser's plan to loot, or other unfairness in the transaction, the majority view is that sale of control at a premium is not in itself a breach of a fiduciary duty. The seller need not account to the minority for the premium he has received. [§§653-657, 663-666]
77.	**YES**	This practice is permitted as long as the stock interest is large enough to give the purchaser effective control, so that he could have effected the changes immediately himself. However, the "sale" of directorships would be invalid if not connected with the sale of a stock interest large enough to carry effective voting control. [§§659-662]
78.a.	**PROBABLY**	If the seller of controlling shares knows or has reason to know that the transferee plans to deal unfairly with the corporation, the seller has breached her fiduciary duty. A price far above fair value should probably have put Sally on notice of Louis's intent. [§§666-669]
b.	**NO**	A seller who has breached her duty is liable to the minority shareholders either for their portion of the premium *or* for the actual damages caused to the corporation by the buyer, whichever is larger. [§670]
79.	**FALSE**	The critical questions are *who* suffered the injury—*i.e.*, the corporation or the shareholders—and to whom the breached duty ran. [§678]
80.a.	**YES**	A potential derivative suit plaintiff must first exhaust corporate remedies and a demand on the board of directors is an essential element of the cause of action, unless the shareholder can show that such a demand would have been futile. [§§683-685, 687-688]
b.	**NO**	If a disinterested board has, in good faith, refused to act, courts will protect its exercise of business judgment and bar the derivative suit. [§§690-691]
c.	**SPLIT**	Some states require demand only on the board of directors. Others require a demand on the shareholders if the act in question was within their power to ratify, but excuse the demand if such ratification were not possible. [§§702-703]
d.	**PROBABLY NOT**	If disinterested shareholders have refused to sue, they have, in effect, ratified the board's decision. If such ratification was within shareholder power, and was reasonable, the derivative suit is barred. [§710]
81.	**NO**	Contemporaneous share ownership is the *usual* requirement in most states. However, even in these states exceptions exist for a plaintiff who subsequently acquired his shares by operation of law (*e.g.*, inheritance), and some statutes waive the requirement when serious injustice would otherwise result. [§§714-718]

82.	**PROBABLY NOT**	If the sole shareholder is disqualified, equity may also bar suit by the corporation itself. [§719]
83.	**NO**	The director's interest is adverse to that of the corporation, so each must ordinarily have separate counsel. [§725]
84.	**YES**	The corporation *must* be joined as a party. The corporation is a defendant, even though its interests are ordinarily adverse to those of the other defendants. [§725]
85.	**YES**	Even though such suits are equitable in nature, the Seventh Amendment right to trial by jury applies to those issues upon which the corporation, as a plaintiff, would have been entitled to a jury. [§728]
86.	**NO**	Even where statutes provide that the defendant corporation, if it wins, may automatically move against the posted security, the court determines the amount of the award (usually limited to its reasonable costs and attorneys' fees). In some states, the security is available for defendant's costs only if the court finds that the plaintiff acted unreasonably in bringing suit. [§737]
87.	**YES**	Recovery usually goes to the corporation. However, if the corporation has been dissolved or if a corporate recovery would benefit shareholders not entitled to participate in it, the court may award payment directly to the innocent shareholders. [§§745, 751-753]
88.	**NO**	A judgment on the merits in a derivative suit is res judicata as to both the corporation and other shareholders. [§774]
89.a.	**YES**	The corporation must ordinarily reimburse the plaintiff because he has obtained either a "common fund" or some other "substantial benefit" for the corporation. He is entitled to his expenses, including attorneys' fees. [§§754-757]
b.	**NO**	A director who has lost on the merits is not entitled to indemnification for the liability imposed. Otherwise, the recovery by the corporation would merely go right back to the defendant. [§§768-773]
c.	**YES**	In most states, reimbursement of a winning defendant is discretionary with the board, but some statutes require the corporation to reimburse a defendant who wins on the merits in a derivative suit. [§§763-765]
90.	**YES**	Many statutes permit such insurance, but they differ as to whether the coverage may extend to *any* liability or expenses. [§§775-777]
91.	**NO**	Any preferences must be *expressly set forth* in the articles. Otherwise, all classes of shares will be treated alike. [§§782, 788]
92.a.	**NO**	Unless the payment of dividends is expressly made mandatory, payment is within the discretion of the directors. If no dividend is declared on the preferred, however, no dividend may be paid on the common stock. [§§789-790]
b.	**YES**	Since the preferred shares are cumulative, both the current preferred dividend *and* all arrears take precedence over the common stock in any year. [§§789-790]

93.	**NO**	No further shares can be issued unless there is an amendment to the articles of incorporation authorizing a larger number of shares. The board of directors alone cannot amend the articles of incorporation; a shareholder vote is required. [§§795, 1069]
94.	**NO**	Treasury stock is considered as "issued" while in the hands of the corporation. The repurchase by the corporation does not affect the number of shares the corporation is authorized to issue. [§799]
95.	**NO (majority)**	Most courts at common law hold that, until the corporation comes into existence and accepts the subscription, a subscription is no more than a revocable continuing offer. A minority is contra, holding that the subscription is a binding contract among subscribers to become shareholders. [§§803-805]
96.	**(B) ONLY**	(A) is not lawful consideration because most statutes require that shares be issued in exchange only for money paid, property acquired, or labor done. [§806]
		(B) is lawful in most states, although some courts require that the "labor done" be done *after* the corporation is in existence (most, however, do not). [§806]
		(C) is not lawful because executory promises—whether for money, property, or future services—are not legal consideration for the issuance of shares under *most* statutes. [§807]
97.a.	**GENERALLY NO**	Except in special situations, a corporation may generally not sell its shares for less than par value, although the par value price may include underwriting commissions. Shares sold for less than par are "watered." [§§811-813]
b.	**YES**	Corporations frequently issue "low par" stock to provide financial flexibility, to create "paid-in" surplus, and to avoid watered stock problems. [§811]
98.a.	**NO**	At least under the majority view, based on a "misrepresentation" theory, a prior creditor (Cal) could not have been misled by the issuance of watered stock and therefore cannot compel the issuee to make up the difference. Under the minority "trust fund" theory, Arthur is liable to Cal. [§§819-821]
b.	**YES**	Under both the misrepresentation theory and the trust fund theory, Arthur is liable to Cora, who was a subsequent creditor. (Some courts that follow the misrepresentation theory would require Cora to show reliance when she extended the credit.) [§§819-821]
99.	**YES**	Most courts apply a "good faith rule" to preclude watered stock liability when there is no intentional overvaluation of property being exchanged for stock. [§822]
100.	**YES**	Promoters owe a fiduciary duty to the corporation. Hence, if the promoters did not make full disclosure (either to an independent board of directors, *or* to all existing shareholders and to persons known to be planning to become shareholders), rescission is a proper remedy. [§828]
101.a.	**NO**	Where the promoters were the sole shareholders, the common law view was that the corporation had no cause of action, since full "disclosure" had been made to all shareholders. [§769]

b. **YES** — Most courts allow suit by the corporation on the rationale that the later, but planned-for, subscribers are among the stockholders to whom disclosure must be made. [§§830-832]

102. **NO** — Preemptive rights at common law generally do not extend to the issuance of shares for property or services, the reissue of treasury shares, or the issue of previously authorized shares. [§§841-844]

103. **FALSE** — The shareholder may also seek to compel issuance of additional shares to himself. [§847]

104. **YES** — Although underwriters, like issuers, have a "due diligence" defense. [§§916-919] Additionally, full disclosure of arrangements between issuers and underwriters is required by federal and some state laws. [§850]

105. **YES** — The federal securities acts expressly do *not* preempt the field. Therefore, when issuing shares, a corporation must often satisfy both state and federal requirements. [§856]

106. **NO** — The thrust of the 1933 Act is informational—*i.e.*, to compel disclosure, usually through the registration requirements. The SEC neither approves nor disapproves of proposed issuances. [§864]

107. **(A), (B), and (C)** — (A) is exempt under the "casual sale" exemption. [§881]

(B) is exempt under the "private placement" exemption, assuming that each purchaser acquires the stock as an investment and signs a letter of intent to that effect; and possibly under the "intrastate offering" exemption as well. [§§886-899]

(C) is still exempt. The "private placement" exemption and the "intrastate offering" exemption are separate. Failure to qualify for one does not prevent qualification for the other. [§§886-899]

(D) is not exempt. The "private placement" exemption requires an intent by purchasers to acquire the securities *as an investment* (not for resale). [§889]

108. **YES** — Rule 144 now exempts limited resales under specified conditions. [§§892-895, 897-898] Also, the purchaser may resell without registration if he has held the shares for a significant length of time and is a noncontrol person. [§896]

109.a. **DEPENDS** — Only Orange is absolutely liable. The others may avoid liability if they exercised due diligence with respect to those portions of the registration statement for which Ralph seeks to hold them liable. Note that the burden of proof of due diligence is *on the defendants*. [§§915-920]

b. **NO** — Section 11 of the 1933 Act requires only a showing of the materiality of the misstatement; *i.e.*, that it concerned a matter that would influence the decision of an average prudent investor. [§§909-910]

c. **NO** — Ralph need not prove his reliance on the misrepresentation nor that the misrepresentation caused the decline in price of the stock. [§§911-912]

110.a.	**YES**	Under section 11, *anyone* who acquired the securities without knowledge of the misstatement may sue; privity is not required. [§§906-907]
b.	**NO**	Cynthia is entitled only to damages. [§921]
111.a.	**YES**	Issuers and dealers are liable for the use of any material misstatements or omissions, assuming the use of the mails or any means of interstate commerce. [§§923-924, 926]
b.	**NO**	Section 12 liability runs only in favor of the original purchaser, not a transferee. [§925]
112.	**TRUE**	Sections 12 and 17 apply to the offer or sale of *any* securities, whether subject to the registration requirements or not. [§931]
113.	**NO**	Declaration of dividends is within the discretion of the board of directors. Absent an abuse of discretion, the shareholders have no power to compel declaration of a dividend. [§§940-941]
114.	**NO**	If there is no earned surplus (*i.e.*, current net profits are offset by prior losses) and no other available surplus account, payment of a dividend would "impair capital." In most states, the current profit must be used to "repair" capital. Otherwise, the payment of a dividend might jeopardize creditors and preferred shareholders. [§§943-955]
115.	**YES**	The excess over par value is paid-in surplus, which is a lawful source of dividends in most states. Some statutes require that shareholders be notified if the source of a dividend is anything other than earned surplus. [§§959-960]
116.	**YES**	Assuming that it is not needed to repair the capital account, most states would permit dividend payments from capital reduction surplus. [§§961-963]
117.	**NO**	Most states do *not* permit unrealized appreciation in value of assets as a source of dividends. A few states do permit such use of revaluation surplus, especially if the asset is readily marketable (*e.g.*, listed securities). [§§965-966]
118.	**YES**	Unless absolved by good faith reliance on corporate financial statements, the directors are liable—at least up to the amount of injury to shareholders and debts owed to creditors. Liability is joint and several. [§§971-975]
119.	**YES**	When the corporation is insolvent, each shareholder is absolutely liable for the return of the amount of the dividend. *If* the corporation were not insolvent, shareholder liability would depend on notice. [§§976-978]
120.	**NO**	Redemption must always be expressly provided for in the articles of incorporation. In contrast, a corporation generally *does* have an inherent right to repurchase its own shares. [§§980, 982]
121.	**YES**	Unlike a redemption, which usually must be by lot or pro rata, a repurchase can be made selectively, subject only to limitations of fiduciary duty. [§§982, 993-994]

122.	**NO**	The availability of funds is tested by most courts **when the payment** (or each installment) **is due**. Most states permit repurchase out of only those sources of funds then available for a cash or property dividend. [§989]
123.	**NO**	A redemption or repurchase must serve some **bona fide corporate purpose**. Self-perpetuation in office, alone, would not satisfy this requirement. [§993]
124.	**ALL**	(A) is correct because most states require approval by an extraordinary majority—a two-thirds or a majority vote of the outstanding shares, not merely of the shares present at a meeting of both corporations. Further, some statutes require approval by each class of shareholders. [§§1027-1029]
		(B) is correct because the surviving corporation succeeds to the rights and obligations of the transferor by operation of law. No agreement is necessary. [§§1023-1024]
		(C) is correct because no further action is required to dissolve the transferor; it ceases to exist upon the filing of the merger certificate with the state. [§§1021, 1023]
125.a.	**YES**	A merger makes such fundamental changes in both corporations that, under most statutes, shareholders who reject the changes are entitled to force the corporation to buy them out. [§1030]
b.	**NO**	A shareholder must have voted **against** the merger and also have met other procedural requirements in order to qualify for appraisal rights. He cannot vote in favor, assess the effects, and then change his mind. [§§1014-1017]
c.	**NO**	Other factors such as asset value and investment value will be weighed, as will temporary market-price distortions. Further, adjustments will be made for the effect of the merger on the market price. [§§1000-1013]
126.a.	**NO**	Approval is not required from **either** corporation's shareholders. In a "short-form merger" of a subsidiary into a qualifying parent, statutes generally permit simplified procedures. [§§1031, 1033]
b.	**NO**	In a short-form merger, the shareholders of the parent do not have appraisal rights. However, the shareholders of Brown, the subsidiary, would have such rights. [§§1034, 1039]
c.	**YES**	Under most statutes, the surviving corporation may issue cash, securities, or other property to the subsidiary's minority shareholders, even if it results in a freezeout. [§1111]
127.	**(A) only**	(A) is correct; approval is everywhere required, although statutes vary as to the percentage vote needed. Sales made in the regular course of business, however, do not require shareholder approval. [§§1061-1062]
		(B) is wrong because no fundamental change in Black occurs, and hence approval by its shareholders is not required. [§1061]
		(C) is wrong because the test is whether the transaction will essentially terminate the transferor's business. Thus, the controlling factor is the percentage of **operating** assets sold. [§1067]

128.a. **YES**   This is a classic de facto merger. The use of Day's stock for the purchase and the projected dissolution of Night suggests that the ultimate effects are those of a merger. A court may require the same shareholder vote as for a merger. (But note that some courts—principally Delaware—do not recognize the de facto merger doctrine). [§§1044-1047, 1053]

   b. **YES**   The boards of directors may be required to submit the plan as a merger to both sets of shareholders and to recognize appraisal rights of dissenters. [§1047]

129. **YES**   Under most statutes, amendments to the articles must be approved by holders of a majority or two-thirds of the corporation's shares *and* by the board. [§1069]

130. **YES**   However, dissolution is discretionary with the court, which may—depending on the seriousness and persistence of the misconduct—instead either suspend the corporation's powers or enjoin future misconduct. [§§1087, 1097]

131. **NO**   Dissolution requires affirmative action by the corporation itself or by the court. [§1085]

132. **YES**   However, liquidation can be a long and complex process, so that courts may be hesitant to conclude that the business transacted was not incident to the liquidation. [§1099]

133. **TRUE**   A creditor's claim is superior to that of shareholders. Each shareholder is liable up to the amount of assets he received in liquidation. [§§1100, 1103, 1106]

134. **YES**   In this situation, the appraisal rights are not an exclusive remedy. Depending on the nature of the transaction, the 1933 Act and/or the 1934 Act might apply. [§1119]

135.a. **NO**   The Acme Board must authorize the transaction, but its shareholders do not vote unless Acme's articles must be amended. No offer is made to Star, *as a corporation*, and there is therefore no vote. Each Star shareholder, as an individual, may accept or reject the offer. [§1148]

   b. **YES**   As controlling shareholder, Acme may vote to dissolve Star. [§1146]

   c. **PROBABLY**   Various federal and state statutes now require the filing of information statements disclosing contemplated changes in the target corporation should the tender offer be successful. The federal statute (Williams Act) requires filing of such information with the SEC where the target corporation is subject to the reporting requirements of the 1934 Act or its securities are traded on a national securities exchange. [§§1174-1175, 1186-1203]

SAMPLE EXAM QUESTION I

In late 1995, Daniel Dollar, an accountant, and Peter Prop, a salesman, agreed to form a corporation, Wingtip, Inc., to engage in the business of selling private airplanes. The planes would be purchased from a major private airplane manufacturer under credit arrangements whereby Wingtip would pay only a small amount down, and the manufacturer would retain a security interest in the plane. The business would operate out of rented hangar and office space located at a local airport. It would have only one salaried employee, a bookkeeper-secretary. In lieu of salary, Wingtip's salespeople would work on a commission basis. Prop would generally oversee Wingtip's business, would hire the personnel, and would be Wingtip's president, but would not be compensated (except by way of dividends); he would devote only about 20% of his time to Wingtip's affairs. The parties estimated that to operate the business on this basis, Wingtip would need $4,000 in capital. Of this amount, $3,000 would be put up by Dollar and $1,000 by Prop. However, Dollar would take 60% of Wingtip's shares and Prop would take 40%, since Prop was to oversee Wingtip's business while Dollar was to be involved only in important policy decisions.

Wingtip was incorporated on January 2, 1996. Prop and Dollar put up the agreed amounts of cash, and 60 shares were issued to Dollar and 40 to Prop. Dollar then transferred five of his shares to his married daughter, Joan Green. Prop rented the hangar and office space, engaged the necessary personnel, made arrangements with a major private airplane manufacturer, and began Wingtip's business in the contemplated manner. Since Prop and Dollar were able to make major decisions between them, and since they were old friends, no formal board was ever designated, nor were former officer elections ever held. Over the first six months of 1996, Wingtip broke even.

In July 1996, Prop learned that Flyout Corporation, a competitor of Wingtip, was going out of business, and was offering the 15 used planes in its inventory at a very low cash package price. Prop felt this was too good an opportunity to pass up, and signed a contract with Flyout, on Wingtip's behalf, as its president, to purchase the 15 planes for $150,000. Prop realized that Wingtip could not pay this amount, but he was sure he could make the necessary credit arrangements. However, when Dollar learned what Prop had done, he refused to go along with the deal, and informed Flyout that Wingtip would not buy the planes. Flyout then brought an action for breach of contract, naming Wingtip, Prop, Dollar, and Green as defendants.

Assume that Flyout's suit is meritorious and that the judgment will be in the $20,000 range. Discuss the liability of Wingtip, Prop, Dollar, and Green.

SAMPLE EXAM QUESTION II

In 1994, Oliva purchased a new highway ice cream stand for $15,000, the list price of the building and equipment. In the same year, Allen opened a new hot dog stand, at a cost of $15,000, on adjoining property. After four years, Oliva and Allen decided to combine, and to continue personally operating the stands. Without the aid of an attorney, Oliva formed the Cream Dog Corporation with an authorized capital of 50 shares of $1,000 par common stock. Pursuant to statute, she filed articles of incorporation with the secretary of state, but due to inexperience, failed to comply with the statutory requirements of local filing and proper publicity of the incorporation. Oliva told Rollins, one of her suppliers, of everything that she had done. Rollins offered Oliva $30,000 for the ice cream stand. Despite the fact that a number of independent appraisers had just valued Oliva's business at a maximum of $27,000, Oliva refused.

Oliva transferred the ice cream stand to the corporation in exchange for 30 shares of stock marked "fully paid." On behalf of the corporation, she offered Allen 15 shares for the hot dog stand. Oliva stated only that she was entitled to the greater share because her ice cream business had been making the greater profit. On the other hand, Oliva argued, Allen's business was worth no more than its original cost. Allen agreed with Oliva on the value of his business, but disagreed as to the valuation of Oliva's business. As a compromise, Oliva agreed to have the corporation issue 20 shares to Allen, marked "fully paid," in exchange for his hot dog stand. Allen agreed that these shares be recorded on the corporation's books as having been issued in exchange for $15,000 worth of property, and that Oliva handle all of the legal and accounting details. Oliva and Allen both became directors of Cream Dog.

Shortly thereafter, having examined the corporate financial statements, Rollins began to sell supplies to both of the Cream Dog stands. Subsequently, Cream Dog became insolvent, and Rollins obtained a judgment against it for $10,000. He is the sole creditor who remains unsatisfied.

Advise Rollins of his rights against Oliva and Allen.

SAMPLE EXAM QUESTION III

Machine, Inc. was organized in 1991 by Bilker to manufacture small tools. Its authorized stock was as follows: 6% Nonvoting Preferred—1,000 shares at $100 par value; Common—200,000 shares at $1 par value. Bilker then owned some machinery that he had purchased from Abel and Cane in 1990 for $40,000. It had a present market value of about $30,000. Bilker transferred this to Machine in exchange for 40,000 shares of common stock. Several days thereafter, Machine issued 30,000 shares of common stock each to Abel and Cane, who each paid $35,000 cash. A few days later, a half dozen investors bought all the preferred stock for $100 per share.

At the first shareholders' meeting, Bilker, Abel, and Cane were elected as Machine's three directors. They continued to be elected annually as such until December 25, 1996, when Abel died. The next shareholders' meeting is scheduled for January 15, 1997.

Machine's business had not done well from the outset. For several years, Bilker had unsuccessfully attempted to interest some outsiders in buying some of Machine's unissued common stock. Early in 1996, the board became interested in diversifying Machine's business by acquiring control of the Crafts Company, a lawn furniture manufacturer. Crafts had just recently been purchased for $50,000 by Kanine Corporation, all of whose stock was owned jointly by Cane and his wife, Nina. Bilker and Abel were unaware of the identity of Kanine's shareholders.

At a Machine's directors' meeting of April 1, 1996, at which Abel was unable to be present due to illness, the directors voted unanimously to buy Crafts from Kanine in exchange for the 100,000 shares of unissued Machine common stock.

When Abel died, he bequeathed his Machine common stock to his nephew, Doltless. Doltless also owns 100 shares of Machine preferred stock, which he purchased in January 1996 from an original owner.

Doltless wishes to be elected to Machine's board and to redress any legal wrongs done to the corporation. He seeks advice as to what, if anything, can be done toward these ends, and how he should go about doing it. Discuss fully.

SAMPLE EXAM QUESTION IV

Consolidated Orange Products, Inc. ("CO") is a corporation engaged in freezing and canning orange juice and other fruit juices and food products. It has eight plants located nationwide. CO's stock is listed on the New York Stock Exchange. Article IV(3) of CO's certificate provides for cumulative voting.

In connection with CO's forthcoming annual meeting, Donald Deem, a CO shareholder, has submitted the following proposals for inclusion in CO's proxy materials:

1. To amend CO's bylaws to provide that any director may be removed by the shareholders without cause.

2. To amend CO's bylaws to provide that whenever CO proposes to construct a new plant, it shall first prepare an impact statement showing the effects of the proposed plant on the environment (including details on air, water, and thermal pollution, if any), a copy of which statement shall be sent to each of CO's shareholders.

3. To amend CO's bylaws to provide that no new plant shall be constructed without shareholder approval.

Discuss which of these proposals, if any, must be included in CO's proxy materials.

SAMPLE EXAM QUESTION V

Hardback Corporation is engaged in the book publishing business. Hardback has 2,000 shares of common stock issued and outstanding; of these, 1,000 shares are owned by Denise Dure, and 1,000 by Stanley Stray. Dure oversees marketing strategy, and the development and maintenance of author relations; Stray oversees the administrative, financial, and editorial side of the business. Dure and Stray had operated Hardback as a partnership from 1983 to 1996; in 1996 they incorporated for tax reasons. Hardback's board consists of Dure, Stray, and Wright, a senior employee.

Dure has learned that Stray proposes to sell his stock in Hardback to Lawrence Light. Light is a wealthy playboy who has always wanted to have an interest in a publishing house. Dure knows him, does not particularly like him, and thinks very little of his business ability. Although Dure and Stray never entered into a formal shareholders' agreement, Dure feels that a sale of stock by Stray would be contrary to what was understood, even if not made explicit, in the Dure-Stray relationship.

Dure now seeks advice on whether she can prevent Stray from selling to Light, and if not, whether there are any arrangements she can make, or steps she can take, to protect her economic interests against Light's lack of skill and judgment.

(Assume that Dure cannot afford to buy Stray's shares at the price Light is willing to pay.)

SAMPLE EXAM QUESTION VI

Jax, Inc. was incorporated in 1995 with 2,500 shares of common stock at a par value of $100 per share authorized. Of those, 2,200 shares of Jax stock have been issued and are outstanding. From 1989 through 1994, Jax incurred net operating losses totaling $80,000. At the end of 1995, the corporation had net earnings of $25,000 for that year. The Jax board of directors, consisting of A, B, and C, met on February 16, 1996, and unanimously voted to declare a cash dividend of $10 per share on outstanding stock.

Pursuant to a bylaw authorizing the board to appoint officers and committees, at the February meeting A, B, and C also unanimously voted to create an Executive and Finance Committee composed of B, C, and W. W was not a director or officer of Jax, but was a shareholder. The bylaw permitted, and the board resolution provided, that the Committee would have all the powers of the board of directors.

On June 15, 1996, the board authorized the purchase by Jax of 200 shares of Jax stock, held by D, at a price of $95 per share. D had indicated he was ready to sell them at that price to a competitor of Jax.

On July 18, 1996, the Executive and Finance Committee directed Jax to issue 100 shares of previously unissued stock to E, as "fully paid" shares in return for E's promissory note to Jax in the sum of $7,500. Such stock was issued to E for his note as described.

On August 31, 1996, as president of Jax, A wrote to F, a shop superintendent employed by the company who was retiring on his 65th birthday, as follows:

> In light of your years of faithful service to this company since it was established, I have decided that upon your retirement today, Jax will pay you a monthly pension of $300 for the rest of your life, so long as our financial condition warrants it.

X, a Jax shareholder, seeks advice as to the legality of:

1. The declaration of the cash dividend.

2. The appointment of the Executive and Finance Committee.

3. The purchase of shares from D.

4. The issuance of the 100 shares to E.

5. The promise to F to pay him a monthly pension.

Discuss.

ANSWER TO SAMPLE EXAM QUESTION I

1. **Liability of Wingtip:** Wingtip's liability depends on whether Prop had authority to make the contract with Flyout on its behalf. There is nothing to indicate that Prop had *actual* authority. Wingtip's business plan called for the planes to be "purchased from a major private airplane manufacturer under credit arrangements whereby Wingtip would pay only a small amount down. . . ." Prop was to oversee Wingtip's business, but Dollar was to be involved in "important policy decisions." Certainly, a major deviation as to financing, source of supply, and quality of aircraft seems to be an important policy decision, which Prop had no actual authority to make. The issue then is whether Prop had *apparent* authority, or *power of position*.

An initial question in considering apparent authority is whether Prop was president of Wingtip. Although it had been agreed between Prop and Dollar that Prop would be Wingtip's president, he was never formally elected to that office. Nevertheless, Prop should be deemed Wingtip's president, at least as to third parties, and probably even within the corporation. It is characteristic of a close corporation that formalities are not rigorously followed. Prop and Dollar, who owned all but five shares of Wingtip's stock, explicitly agreed to Prop's being a president, and in all probability Green either acquiesced, or was represented in corporate affairs by Dollar.

Assuming that Prop was Wingtip's president as to third persons, he would have a president's *apparent authority* (power of position) as to those persons. There are several competing rules as to a president's apparent authority. An older rule, now discarded for all practical purposes, is that a president has no more authority than any other director, but the two rules that continue to have support are (i) that the president has power to bind the corporation to contracts within the ordinary course of its business; and (ii) that the president has power to bind the corporation even to contracts of an "extraordinary" nature, provided, at least, that the contract is one the board could authorize or ratify. Under the second rule, which is less widely accepted, Wingtip would be bound. Under the first rule, Wingtip's liability is less certain.

Since this situation concerns apparent authority, presumably the issue is whether the transaction would appear to be in the ordinary course when viewed from the perspective of the third party—here, Flyout. The amount involved may very well have indicated to Flyout that the transaction was not in the ordinary course, particularly since Flyout, as a competitor, may have been familiar with Wingtip's business.

On the other hand, Wingtip was engaged in the business of selling airplanes, and it seems reasonable for Flyout to assume that the president of such a corporation would have authority to buy airplanes for resale. Therefore, Wingtip should be held liable on the contract.

2. **Liability of Prop, Dollar, and Green:** Even if Wingtip is liable on the contract, Flyout would also seek to hold Wingtip's shareholders liable (since Flyout will recover a judgment of $20,000, and Wingtip has assets of only $4,000). Normally, of course, a shareholder's liability is limited to his or her investment in the corporation (a shareholder has no individual liability for the corporation's debts).

However, two factors in this case might justify "piercing the corporate veil" and holding the shareholders individually liable. One is the failure to follow normal corporate formalities. Shareholders' and board meetings were not held, and officers were not elected. However, while lack of such formalities is often pointed to in piercing the veil cases, it normally would not suffice to justify individual liability in itself, especially in a close corporation (if only because it is seldom connected with the plaintiff's loss).

A very important factor is the possibility that Wingtip was undercapitalized. It is true that Wingtip was able to break even for six months. Nevertheless, $4,000 does not seem like sufficient capital for engaging in the kind of business Wingtip set up (particularly considering the kind of personal injury liability that might be involved in such a business). Few cases have rested individual liability solely on the ground of undercapitalization, but in this case a lack of formality is present as well.

It is also arguable that a contract creditor is in a weaker position than a tort claimant to base recovery on this theory, since he goes into the situation knowing that he is dealing with a limited liability enterprise, and had a prior opportunity to investigate the enterprise's resources. However, the better view is that even a contract creditor is justified in expecting that the entity with which he deals will be capitalized to absorb the consequences of predictable business events.

Assuming individual liability would be imposed in this case, the next question is which shareholders should be liable? Again, there are conflicting rules. Under one rule, all the shareholders would be liable as partners. Under a second, only the individual who actually conducted the transaction—Prop—would be liable. Under a third rule, which is probably the soundest rule, only the corporation's *active managers* would be liable—Prop and Dollar.

ANSWER TO SAMPLE EXAM QUESTION II

1. Defective Incorporation

The first issue is whether Oliva and Allen are insulated against personal liability despite the defects in the incorporation process (failure to file locally and properly publicize filing). Three questions must be asked:

(a) Was a *de jure corporation* formed despite these failures? The answer to this question is almost certainly no. For a de jure corporation, there must be substantial compliance with the statute. These are more than insignificant defects.

(b) Was a *de facto corporation* formed? Some modern statutes appear to eliminate the de facto doctrine. Assuming that Cream Dog's state of incorporation does not have such a statute, it is a close question whether Cream Dog is a de facto corporation. Clearly there was a good faith actual use of the corporate existence. The issue then is whether there was a good faith, colorable attempt to comply with the statutory requirements for incorporation. Since the defects were due to inexperience, the good faith test is met. Moreover, the most essential step, proper filing of the original articles, was taken.

(c) If, however, the omitted steps are found to be too important for the enterprise to be a de facto corporation, the next question is whether it constitutes a *corporation by estoppel* as against Rollins? (That is, will Cream Dog be treated as a corporation for purposes of transactions with Rollins?) Statutes that put an end to the de facto doctrine may or may not have a comparable effect on the estoppel doctrine.

Assuming the applicable statute does not have such an effect, there is a strong case for applying the doctrine. Rollins dealt with Cream Dog as if it were a corporation. Since he had actual notice of the attempted incorporation, there was no causal relationship between the failure to file and properly publish (both of which may be seen as provisions directed toward giving notice) and the loss resulting to Rollins. All parties were proceeding on the premise that the liability of the owners was limited by due incorporation. Therefore, the doctrine may be applied, and Oliva and Allen may be insulated from personal liability.

(Note that even if Oliva is liable, Allen might argue that he should not be held personally liable, on the ground that he did not participate in organizing the corporation, and the court should hold liable only the person responsible. It seems doubtful that this is a good defense because Allen was also a director and, therefore, responsible for corporate activity. Many courts even impose liability on shareholders where a corporation is defectively formed.)

2. Watered Stock

The second issue concerns watered stock. Most states require that par value shares be sold for at least par. If they are not, creditors can require, upon bankruptcy, a stockholder who has not paid par (at least on an original issue, such as is involved here) to pay the difference between what he originally paid and par. The theory behind the par value rule is that creditors have a right to rely upon the corporation's receiving capital equivalent to the par value. The only creditor (Rollins) examined the balance sheet, and undoubtedly saw that the corporation did not receive par. Thus, in those states that require reliance to be proved by a creditor before he can recover, it seems doubtful that Rollins can prove reliance. (Some states, however, presume creditor reliance, and would put the burden on the defendant to prove that Rollins did not rely.) Other states do not require reliance. They treat the corporation's stated capital as a "trust fund" for creditors, and permit all creditors to recover irrespective of reliance.

Assuming that Rollins can recover if the stock was issued for less than par, was there such an issuance here? From the facts, Allen received $20,000 par value stock for property worth no more than $15,000 (under any theory of value), so Allen owes $5,000. Thus, Rollins may recover the $5,000 from Allen.

Rollins will have a more difficult time arguing that Oliva's stock was watered (*i.e.*, that her property was overvalued), since Rollins himself offered her $30,000 for it. Under the majority rule, watered stock liability exists only for ***intentional*** overvaluation of assets received by the corporation. If, as appears to be the case here, the parties believed in good faith that the property was equal to par value, the stock is not watered.

Therefore, Rollins will be limited to any corporate assets still available and Allen's $5,000 to satisfy the claim.

ANSWER TO SAMPLE EXAM QUESTION III

1. Doltless's ability to be elected to the Machine's board will greatly depend on whether there is cumulative voting. In some states cumulative voting is mandatory; it is permissive in the rest, usually existing only if so provided in the articles or bylaws. Assuming it exists in this case, with 200,000 voting common shares outstanding, Doltless would need 50,001 shares to elect one director:

$$x > \frac{200,000}{3+1} \qquad \frac{200,000}{3+1} = \$50,000 \qquad x > 50,000$$

As things presently stand, Doltless will be unsuccessful because he owns only 30,000 shares. However, there are several routes he might pursue to improve his situation.

Doltless could attempt to assert preemptive rights in the 100,000 shares issued Crafts. Since Abel (Doltless's predecessor in interest) held 30% of the common stock at the time, if Doltless were successful, he would get an additional 30,000 shares. This would give him enough to elect a director. This assumes preemptive rights exist (in some states they exist unless negated by the articles; in other states, the opposite is true).

These 100,000 shares were authorized and issued, and the general rule is that there are no preemptive rights therein (the rationale being all shareholders knew that 200,000 shares were previously authorized and they had no right to rely on more than their percentage of that). But, in this case, five years have passed with the original percentage existing. It might well be argued that after this period of time the original issue had terminated. In fact, in some states, statutes provide a limited time, *e.g.,* six months, for the original issue after which preemptive rights again attach. Furthermore, there is the doctrine that if originally authorized stock is subsequently sold for expansion purposes, rather than just raising additional working capital to be used in the original business, preemptive rights attach. That would seem to be the case here. However, Doltless will fail in this preemptive rights approach because preemptive rights do not apply if the stock is issued for property rather than cash. It should also be clear that preferred stock has no preemptive rights.

Alternatively, Doltless could seek to get the issuance of the 100,000 shares to Crafts rescinded. If he were successful, it would take only 25,001 shares to get a director elected, and his 30,000 shares would be more than sufficient.

At the meeting of April 1, only two directors were present, Bilker and Cane. Cane was clearly an interested director vis-a-vis the Crafts transaction, due to his holdings in Kanine. As a director, he was necessary for a quorum. This alone might make the transaction voidable at common law, as would the fact that he voted for the deal. Under statutes like New York's and California's, the quorum issue is not determinative, nor is Cane's vote, despite the fact that it was a determinative vote. The transaction would not be voidable under modern statutes unless it is unfair. Failure to make full disclosure to an independent board renders the transaction unfair.

If the action to rescind is held to be a derivative suit since it alleges injury to the corporation, most jurisdictions would require Doltless to be a contemporaneous owner. As an owner of preferred (who would have a general interest in the integrity of the corporation's assets), he would meet this requirement. Even as an owner of common, it would seem that he could qualify under the exception for shares devolving by operation of law (here, inheritance). Historically the contemporaneous ownership requirement existed to prevent the buying of lawsuits by strikers (the reason for the rule has no application here).

Some states have statutes that require the plaintiff-shareholder to post security to indemnify the corporation for expenses. If there is a minimum percentage requirement (*e.g.,* 5% in New York), Doltless would be excused. In other states (*e.g.,* California), security rests within the discretion of the court. Doltless's action will benefit the corporation, so here too he would be excused.

Demand on directors, generally required in all states, should be excused here because it would be futile. Cane is interested and that leaves only Bilker. Demand on shareholders (a prerequisite in most states "if necessary") might be required, especially because it would be simple and inexpensive and might result in Bilker's joining the suit and making it more effective. The wrong (voidable board action) might also be considered subject to shareholder ratification. Cane would clearly cast his 130,000 votes against the suit, but since this is an ***interested*** vote, it clearly should not bar suit.

If Bilker casts his 40,000 votes against suit, this arguably could be a decision of a majority of the disinterested shareholders, having full disclosure, that the suit was not in the corporation's best interests. This might be held to be a reasonable judgment given Machine's alleged need for diversification by purchase of Crafts. (But some courts might hold the transaction void and thus incapable of shareholder ratification. *Note:* This might excuse shareholder demand altogether.) Or, some courts might find that there just are not enough disinterested shareholders, since Cane owns 65%; or, because Bilker might be a defendant in another suit by Doltless (*see* below), his vote might be considered interested; or there is the possibility that Bilker can be divested of 10,000 of his shares (*see* below), thus removing his edge over Doltless.

There are other possibilities in respect to the Crafts transaction that would provide redress to the corporation, but would not enhance Doltless's voting position.

It appears clear that Crafts's value was much less than the $100,000 worth of par value stock paid for it. Perhaps it could be argued that it was a reasonable business judgment for the board to believe that the value to Machine was $100,000, but this is unlikely due to Cane's interest in the matter and the recent market valuation of $50,000.

Usually, only creditors can recover for watered stock. However, an occasional case has permitted enforcement by the corporation, when it needs the money (such as the case here). Since this is the corporation's cause of action, the suit would be derivative, thus presenting the issues discussed above.

Apart from the par value rule, Cane's failure to disclose his interest in the transaction would be considered a breach of his fiduciary duty resulting in damages for the corporation (if not rescission, as discussed above). The corporation would at least be entitled to the difference between the value of the stock issued and the value of the assets received. It might even be possible to force Cane to disgorge his entire profit as a penalty and deterrent, for breach of fiduciary duty. This, again, would be a derivative suit.

The nondisclosure by Cane in connection with his "purchase" of stock from Machine, and his consequent breach of fiduciary duty would also appear to give Machine a cause of action under rule 10b-5, assuming some use of the mails or interstate commerce. Doltless could bring a derivative action for this, and this federal action would excuse him from any state security for expense requirements.

There is a possible argument that Cane appropriated Machine's corporate opportunity when he caused Kanine to purchase Crafts. This argument depends on facts not available—was Machine actively seeking diversification at the time? In what capacity did Cane learn about Crafts's availability? To the contrary, the facts appear to indicate that Kanine bought Crafts before Machine decided to diversify. Since Crafts was therefore not even in Machine's "line of business," the argument would seem to fail. But if an action lies, it is derivative since it was the corporation's opportunity.

Finally, there is Bilker's 1991 sale of machinery to the corporation. Again, under either valuation test, Bilker's stock appears to be watered to the extent of $10,000. (The fact that Cane and Abel paid $10,000 over par value would not appear to cure the defect. This would be a premium over par value and was probably so recorded. As such, it would not be so permanently "locked in" for the benefit of the corporation and its creditors.) But, again, most states would hold the corporation estopped from bringing suit since it was a party to the contract. Doltless was not a contemporaneous owner for purposes of a derivative suit, and he might well be barred by a statute of limitations. But if Doltless could counter all these hurdles, he probably would be more benefited by a suit to rescind 10,000 shares. The corporation, however, clearly would be better off if damages were recovered, and, after all, it is the corporation's cause of action.

Bilker was a promoter in 1991. As such, he was obliged to disclose his profits on the transaction. Although he was the sole party in interest at the time, it was clearly contemplated that other shareholders were to be brought in immediately. Under the better rule, disclosure should have been made to them. It may well be that Cane and Abel will be held to have had disclosure because of their prior dealings with Bilker in respect to this very machinery. Thus, Bilker's duty as to them was satisfied. But there is no evidence that the 1991 purchasers of preferred had any knowledge or disclosure of Bilker's profits—and they had a real interest in the integrity of the "cushion" or assets that Machine had.

Thus, as to them, it would appear that Bilker violated his duty of disclosure, thereby affording a common law cause of action to the corporation for his gain (also under rule 10b-5), which was at least $10,000: the difference between what he got, and what he gave up. But the suit is derivative, Doltless is not a contemporaneous owner, and what about the statute of limitations? Even if there is no contemporaneous ownership requirement, Doltless may be barred because he is Able's successor, who may have been estopped because of knowledge.

ANSWER TO SAMPLE EXAM QUESTION IV

Proposal 1: CO is governed by the proxy rules, since its stock is listed on the New York Stock Exchange. Proxy rule 14a-8 provides that management must include a timely filed shareholder proposal in the corporate proxy materials, unless the proposal falls within an exclusion in rule 14a-8. The only exclusion that might be applicable to Proposal 1 is rule 14a-8(c)(1), which allows management to omit a shareholder proposal if "under the laws of the issuer's domicile [it is] not a proper subject for action by security holders."

The issue is whether the proposed bylaw conflicts with CO's certificate. If it does, Proposal 1 would not be a proper subject for shareholder action, since in case of conflict between certificate and bylaw, the certificate prevails. Article IV(3) of CO's certificate provides for cumulative voting. This provision would be undercut by removal without cause, since the majority shareholders could eliminate minority-elected directors seriatim, by removing each one without cause. Then each vacancy could be filled by an election, for a single director, in which the minority could not effectively cumulate its votes.

It is true that under the cases the mere fact that a certificate or bylaw amendment weakens cumulative voting does not render it invalid, but Proposal 1 seems to cross the line—not only weakening cumulative voting, but effectively destroying it. Many statutes bar removal of a director if the votes against removal would be sufficient to elect the director through cumulative voting. On this basis, the proposed bylaw would be invalid if adopted, and the proposal to adopt it would, therefore, not be a proper subject for CO's shareholders.

Proposal 2: Proposal 2 raises several problems under 14a-8. First, it can be argued that Proposal 2 is not a proper subject under state law as infringing on the powers of the board to manage the corporation's business. But Proposal 2 only requires a report. The decision whether or not to build a plant would still be in management's hands. (However, it could be argued that the *manner* in which decisions are made is itself a management function.)

Second, rule 14a-8(c)(7) permits management to omit a proposal if it deals with a matter relating to the conduct of the ordinary business operations of the issuer. Certainly, Proposal 2 deals with the conduct of business operations. Since the addition of a plant would be a major undertaking, it is not clear that it relates to the conduct of "ordinary" business operations, but for this purpose any decision within the general framework of CO's business would probably be regarded as "ordinary." However, the relation of Proposal 2 to business operations is only indirect.

The bylaw would not regulate how management operates the corporation's business; it would not even set parameters for management's decisions; all it would do is direct that when a certain type of decision is proposed, management must send the shareholders information concerning the proposal. While the decision could go either way (since the proposed bylaw would increase the flow of information to shareholders, which is the object of the proxy rules, and since it gives no direction or recommendation concerning how CO's business should be conducted), it should not be deemed to fall within the 14a-8(c)(7) exception.

Finally, the proxy rules allow management to omit a proposal if it deals with a matter that is not significantly related to the issuer's business or is beyond the issuer's power to effectuate. However, Proposal 2 is within the power of CO to effectuate, and it seems to be significantly related to CO's business (since it deals with closely relevant externalities of CO's operations). Proposal 2 must be included in CO's proxy materials.

Proposal 3: Unlike Proposal 2, Proposal 3 directly regulates the allocation of powers over CO's business, by shifting the power to approve new plants from management, where it would normally be located, to the shareholders. Statutes sometimes provide that the business of a corporation shall be managed by the board, unless the certificate otherwise provides. However, Proposal 3 does not call for amendment of the certificate, and the statutory provision vesting management in the board cannot normally be varied (at least outside the context of a close corporation), except insofar as the statute explicitly permits. Proposal 3 may be omitted from CO's proxy materials.

ANSWER TO SAMPLE EXAM QUESTION V

1. **Prevention of Sale:** Corporate stock is normally freely transferable, absent an agreement to the contrary. Dure's major argument for preventing Stray from selling his shares would be based on the fact that such a sale "would be contrary to what was understood, even if not made explicit, in the Dure-Stray relationship." More specifically, Dure would claim that Hardback is really a joint venture, in which the prior "understanding" was preserved, notwithstanding adoption of the corporate form. There is some support in the facts for this position, since Hardback was operated as a partnership from 1983-1996, and was incorporated only for tax reasons. Certainly such an implicit understanding would probably be reasonable in almost any close corporation.

However, it is doubtful that a court would view this kind of implicit understanding as sufficient to override the well-entrenched rule that corporate stock is freely transferable, particularly where the circumstances do not indicate that the sale violates any fiduciary obligation that Stray might owe Dure. Thus, Dure probably could not restrain Stray from selling his stock to Light.

2. **Protection of Dure's Interest:** Whether there are any arrangements Dure can make, or steps she can take, to protect her economic interests against Light's lack of skill and judgment, the first point is to note that Dure's position is not as bad as she might think. The mere

fact that Light holds stock will not, in itself, give Light any voice in corporate management, since the power to manage the corporation's business is in the board, not the shareholders. Light's holding would, of course, give him a voice in *shareholder* matters, but that would probably not be very significant as to the corporation's day-to-day affairs. In any event, with only a 50% interest Light would not be able to take any effective action as a shareholder, unless Dure concurs.

The immediate question, then, is whether Light could get a seat on the board. Since the directors are elected by the shareholders, and since Dure holds 50% of the stock, again the answer seems to be no (at least for the short range). Assuming Light could not cumulate his votes, the most votes he could give any one candidate, including himself, is 1,000. Dure could also cast 1,000 votes for any one candidate, and therefore if Dure does not vote her shares for Light, the result of any election would be a tie. In that case, a new (also futile) election would have to be called, and the old directors would hold over. The old directors, of course, are Dure and Wright. Assuming Wright stayed on the board and did not side with Light, Dure would have a quorum for board action and probably could get the board to vote as she wished. Thus, at least for the short term, Dure probably has no great reason for alarm.

In the long run, however, such a posture might not be viable. Several statutes provide for the appointment of a provisional director if the directors are divided, but these would be inapplicable because Hardback's *directors* would not be divided. However, under the hypothesized facts, Light might be able to obtain involuntary dissolution on the ground of deadlock at the shareholder level (although some courts are unwilling or reluctant to grant this remedy in the case of a prosperous corporation, particularly where the deadlock does not threaten the prosperity). But while dissolution might be undesirable to Dure, it would probably be even more undesirable to Light, who could not carry on a similar business, as could Dure. (Alternatively, Dure might seek dissolution herself, on the theory that she could effectively take over Hardback's business on the dissolution sale, since Light would be in no position to do so. However, if Dure sought dissolution herself, she would be accountable to Light for Light's share of the prospective business opportunity, if she purchased the business, and probably this would also be true in a custodial dissolution as well.)

Taking into account the bargaining power of each party, Dure is probably in a position to strike a bargain with Light under which Light would get some, but limited, participation in business decisions of Hardback. Such limited participation might satisfy Light, since he is, after all, only a dilettante. Since Hardback is a close corporation, such an agreement would probably be valid at common law, and if Hardback is incorporated in a state with special close corporation legislation, the articles could be amended to qualify it as a statutory close corporation, and ensure the enforceability of such an agreement.

ANSWER TO SAMPLE EXAM QUESTION VI

1. **Cash Dividend:** In most states, Jax would not be legally permitted to declare a cash dividend. As of the end of 1994, Jax's capital was impaired in an amount of $80,000 (its accumulated operating losses). The $25,000 net earnings in 1995 is ordinarily not available for dividends, but must instead be used to repair the impairment of capital. As of the end of 1995, Jax has no surplus (assets in excess of liabilities and stated capital), which is usually required for the payment of dividends. Rather, it still has a deficit of $55,000. Creditors are entitled to rely on the fact that, before dividends are paid to shareholders, the corporation's assets must exceed its liabilities and capital.

Some states, however, permit the payment of "nimble dividends." Under this rule, dividends may be paid to the extent of current net profits (profits during the preceding year or two), even though capital is impaired (*i.e.,* even if there is no surplus). Under this rule, Jax could pay its declared $22,000 dividend.

In California, Jax could pay the dividend as long as after such payment its total assets were at least 1¼ times its total liabilities, and its current assets were at least equal to its current liabilities. Since the figures are not available in respect to these matters, one cannot say whether Jax's dividend would be permissible in California.

In any event, even in California or a nimble dividend state, Jax could not legally pay the dividend if it were insolvent or would thereby become insolvent. Jax is obviously not insolvent in the bankruptcy sense, *i.e.,* its liabilities do not exceed its assets, since it has capital of $165,000. However, insolvency includes inability to meet debts as they mature, and as to this the facts are incomplete.

2. **Appointment of Committee:** Virtually every statute contains provisions allowing the board to create committees, and delegate thereto certain of the board's powers. However, the composition and powers of the Jax Executive and Finance Committee conflict with those statutory provisions in two respects. First, the statutes typically limit committee membership to directors, and W is not a director. Second, the statutes typically carve out certain powers that cannot be delegated, and here the Jax board delegated all its powers. It can therefore be argued that the Jax Executive and Finance Committee was not validly created and constituted, and its actions are void.

As to the first point, however, unless the relevant statute provided that executive or finance committees consist of at least three directors, the Jax committee could have been constituted of only B and C. Therefore, any action (such as the issuance of stock in this case) in which B and C concurred, might be deemed valid notwithstanding W's participation. Similarly, as to the second point, the fact that the Jax committee was vested with more powers than was legally permissible should not necessarily make invalid the exercise of a power that could be legally delegated, and the issuance of stock is a power that can be delegated to an executive committee under most statutes.

3. **Purchase of Shares:** Under both common law and statute, corporations are empowered to repurchase their own shares. However, the general rule is that the same conditions that are prerequisite to the payment of dividends must also be met before a corporation may repurchase its own shares (*i.e.,* the corporation must have a surplus at least equal to the amount of the repurchase). Here, the repurchase amount is $19,000. Jax has no surplus whatever. Even in a "nimble dividend" jurisdiction, there is only $3,000 of current net profits remaining after the February 16 dividend declaration. As for the "California rule," the facts are not known, as indicated above. Thus, it would seem that Jax cannot legally repurchase from D.

Many states do make certain exceptions to this rule and permit a corporation to repurchase its shares out of capital, under designated circumstances. Here, D will sell to a competitor if not to Jax, but this is not within the exceptions to the general rule.

4. **Issuance of Shares:** The issuance may be illegal on two separate grounds. First, most states require that par value shares be originally issued by the corporation for at least par value. Here, Jax issued previously authorized, but unissued stock, at $75 per share, despite the fact that it was $100 par. Unless the jurisdiction has special procedures for such issuance at less than par, this issuance is illegal.

Even though the shares were improperly issued for less than par, the general rule is that neither the corporation, nor a shareholder in a derivative suit, can sue E for the balance up to par. Jax, having issued the shares as "fully paid" in an arm's length transaction, is ordinarily estopped to claim otherwise. However, if Jax were to become insolvent, certain of its creditors may be able to sue E for the difference between par and what E paid for the stock.

Second, most states have constitutional or statutory provisions that a corporation may issue its shares only for "money paid, labor done, or property actually acquired." E's unsecured promissory note (assuming it is not secured by adequate collateral), is *not* lawful consideration for these purposes. Unless this is a minority jurisdiction that follows the modern view permitting a corporation to issue its shares in exchange for a promise to pay in the future, the issuance to E may be considered void and subject to cancellation by Jax.

5. Pension for F: It would appear that A, as president of Jax, has authority to compensate corporate employees, like F, in the usual and regular course of the business. Further, since there is no indication that there is any conflict of interest in respect to this transaction, A cannot be held liable for this promised pension, as long as the payment involves a matter of reasonable business judgment. Nonetheless, neither officers nor directors may "give away" or "waste" corporate assets, absent unanimous shareholder approval. Pursuant to this doctrine, it has often been held that agreements by the corporation to pay for past services is a waste of corporate assets on the ground that the corporation has received nothing in exchange. Furthermore, since F has given no consideration for the pension, F cannot enforce this promise against Jax.

On the other hand, some courts have held that a corporation may pay reasonable bonuses or pensions to employees for past services, if approved by a majority of the shareholders. (But there is no evidence of shareholder approval here.) In addition, some states have statutes that specifically authorize the board to provide pensions in recognition of past services. (But the pension here was promised by Jax's president and not by the board. Thus, unless this is a jurisdiction that grants the president authority to do any act that the board could authorize, the pension cannot be sustained on this approach.)

TABLE OF CASES

A.P. Smith Manufacturing Co. v. Barlow - §136

A.T. Brod & Co. v. Perlow - §394

Aaron v. SEC - §348

Abbott v. Hapgood - §112

Abercrombie v. Davies - §§567, 570

Ackerberg v. Johnson - §897

Adams v. Smith - §324

Adams v. Standard Knitting Mills - §553

Adams v. United States Distributing Corp. - §1128

Adler v. Klawans - §455

Affiliated Ute Citizens v. United States - §§350, 413

Alabama Farm Bureau Mutual Casualty v. American Fidelity Life Insurance Co. - §389

Albee v. Lamson & Hubbard Corp. - §615

Alexander & Alexander of N.Y., Inc. v. Fritzen - §304

Alford v. Shaw - §697

Allen v. Biltmore Tissue Corp. - §594

Alpert v. 28 Williams St. Corp. - §1117

Amanda Acquisition Corp. v. Universal Foods Corp. - §1203

American Timber & Trading Co. v. Niedermeyer - §285

Anderson v. K.G. Moore, Inc. - §204

Applestein v. United Board & Carton Corp. - §1047

Arnold v. Phillips - §76

Arnold v. Society for Savings Bancorp, Inc. - §1159

Aronson v. Lewis - §686

Ashbury Railway Carriage & Iron Co. v. Riche - §146

Auer v. Dressel - §§167, 195

Auerbach v. Bennett - §§694, 695

B&H Warehouse, Inc. v. Atlas Van Lines, Inc. - §606

Backman v. Polaroid Corp. - §§369, 370

Bagdon v. Bridgestone - §681

Baker v. Bates-Street Shirt Co. - §101

Baker v. Commercial Body Builders, Inc. - §1091

Baker v. MacFadden Publications, Inc. - §732

Baldwin v. Canfield - §204

Bangor Punta Operations, Inc. v. Bangor & Aristook Railroad - §719

Barnes v. Andrews - §230

Barr v. Wackman - §685

Basic, Inc. v. Levinson - §§345, 351, 366

Bateman Eichler, Hill Richards, Inc. v. Berner - §399

Bates v. Dresser - §229

Beard v. Elster - §329

Bechtold v. Coleman Realty Co. - §607

Bell v. Arnold - §708

Benintendi v. Kenton Hotel, Inc. - §575

Bennett v. Breuil Petroleum Corp. - §848

Blackie v. Barrack - §422

Blasband v. Rales - §722

Blau v. Lehman - §454

Blue Chip Stamps v. Manor Drug Stores - §§384, 390, 391, 396

Blumenthal v. Roosevelt Hotel, Inc. - §1127

Bohannan v. Corporation Commission - §506

Borbein, Young & Co. v. Cirese - §1099

Bosch v. Meeker Cooperative Light & Power Association - §756

Bove v. The Community Hotel Corp. - §1084

Brane v. Roth - §226

Brinson Railway v. Exchange Bank - §135

Brophy v. Cities Service Co. - §476

Brown v. McLanahan - §§587, 588

Brown v. North Ventura Road Development Co. - §198

Bruch v. National Guarantee Credit Corp. - §197

Bryan, United States v. - §362

Builders' Duntile Co. v. W.E. Dunn Manufacturing - §116

Burg v. Horn - §§299, 300

Burks v. Lasker - §700

Burns v. Gonzalez - §26

C.A. Davendes Sociedad Financiera v. Florida National Banks - §488

CTS Corp. v. Dynamics Corp. of America - §§1193, 1198

Cady, Roberts & Co. - §§340, 355

Calumet Industries, Inc. v. MacClure - §1173

Campbell v. Loew's, Inc. - §195

Cannon v. U.S. Acoustics Corp. - §725

Cantor v. Sunshine Greenery - §§92, 104

Caplan v. Lionel Corp. - §659

Carl M. Loeb, Rhodes & Co., In re - §870

Carpenter, United States v. - §363

Caspary v. Louisiana Land & Exploration Co. - §616

Cavalier Oil Corp. v. Harnett - §1012

Cede & Co. v. Technicolor, Inc. - §230

Central Bank of Denver v. First Interstate Bank of Denver - §381

Central Transportation Co. v. Pullman's Palace Car Co. - §150

Chambers v. Beaver-Advance Corp. - §326

Charlestown Boot & Shoe Co. v. Dunsmore - §§4, 159

Chartrand v. Barney's Club, Inc. - §114

Chasins v. Smith, Barney & Co. - §414

Chelrob, Inc. v. Barrett - §288

Chemical Bank v. Arthur Andersen & Co. - §395

Chiarella v. United States - §§354, 355, 357, 358, 374

Chilson, *In re* - §§516, 570

Citadel Holding Corp. v. Roven - §773

Citibank, N.A. v. Data Lease Financial Corp. - §680

Clagett v. Hutchison - §653

Claman v. Robertson - §704

Clark v. Dodge - §§171, 578

Clark v. Pattern Analysis & Recognition Corp. - §1117

Clarke v. Greenberg - §746

Clarke Memorial College v. Monaghan Land Co. - §587

Coggins v. New England Patriots Football Club, Inc. - §1115

Cohen v. Ayers - §271

Cohen v. Beneficial Industrial Loan Corp. - §738

Cohen v. Cocoline Products, Inc. - §221

Commonwealth Title Insurance & Trust Co. v. Seltzer - §663

Compaq Computer Corp. v. Horton - §623

Concord Auto Auction, Inc. v. Rustin - §600

Conservative Caucus Research, Analysis & Education Foundation, Inc. v. Chevron Corp. - §624

Continental Securities Co. v. Belmont - §§703, 707

Cookies Food Products, Inc. v. Lakes Warehouse Distributing, Inc. - §266

Coombes v. Getz - §1082

Corning Glass Works v. Lucase - §135

Costello v. Fazio - §76

Cowin v. Bresler - §552

Crane v. Anaconda Co. - §616

Cranson v. IBM - §§97, 104

Credit Bureau Reports, Inc. v. Credit Bureau of St. Paul, Inc. - §624

Crowley v. Communications for Hospitals, Inc. - §318

D.A. McArthur v. Times Printing Co. - §114

David v. Southern Import Wine Co. - §115

DeBaun v. First Western Bank & Trust Co. - §668

Deibler v. Chas. H. Elliott Co. - §516

Diamond v. Oreamuno - §476

Dirks v. SEC - §§354, 373, 374, 375, 377, 378, 379, 380

Dodge v. Ford Motor Co. - §§134, 941

Donahue v. Rodd Electrotype Co. - §§645, 646

Doran v. Petroleum Management Corp. - §887

Dottenheim v. Murchison - §§449, 716

Duffy v. Loft, Inc. - §494

Dunnett v. Arn - §663

Dupuy v. Dupuy - §398

Durfee v. Durfee & Canning, Inc. - §266

E.K. Buck Retail Stores v. Harkert - §565

Edgar v. MITE Corp. - §§1187, 1190, 1194

Eisenberg v. Flying Tiger Line, Inc. - §679

Electronic Specialty Co. v. International Controls Corp. - §§368, 1185

Eliasberg v. Standard Oil Co. - §270

Elkind v. Ligget & Meyers, Inc. - §§371, 424, 425

Ernst & Ernst v. Hochfelder - §§346, 347, 367, 553

Erskine v. Chevrolet Motors Co. - §120

Escott v. Barchris Construction Corp. - §918

Essex Universal Corp. v. Yates - §§661, 662

Estate Counseling Service, Inc. v. Merrill Lynch, Pierce, Fenner & Smith, Inc. - §404

Evangelista v. Holland - §600

Everett v. Transnation Development Corp. - §194

Farris v. Glen Alden Corp. - §§1045, 1047

Feder v. Martin Marietta Corp. - §§454, 455

Federal United Corp. v. Havender - §1083

Financial Industrial Fund, Inc. v. McDonnell Douglas Corp. - §368

Financial Investment & Rediscount Co. v. Wells - §727

Flanagan v. Jackson Wholesale Building Supply Co. - §106

Fletcher v. A.J. Industries, Inc. - §755

Fliegler v. Lawrence - §278

Ford, People v. - §§88, 90

Foremost-McKesson, Inc. v. Provident Securities Co. - §§464, 465

Framingham Savings Bank v. Szabo - §112

Francis v. United Jersey Bank - §§223, 226, 231, 233

Francis I. duPont & Co. v. Universal City Studios - §§1004, 1006

Frank v. Anthony - §194

Freeman v. Decio - §476

Fridrich v. Bradford - §424

Friedman v. Altoona Pipe & Steel Supply Co. - §619

GAF Corp. v. Milstein - §1168

G. Loewus & Co. v. Highland Queen Packing Co. - §824

Gaines v. Haughton - §549

Galef v. Alexander - §689

Galler v. Galler - §§172, 214, 577

Gearhart Industries, Inc. v. Smith International, Inc. - §§1181, 1183

Geddes v. Anaconda Copper Mining Co. - §1075

General Aircraft Corp. v. Lampert - §1169

General Bonding & Casualty Insurance Co. v. Moseley - §808

General Rubber Co. v. Benedict - §680

General Time Corp. v. Talley Industries - §§620, 624

General Tire & Rubber Co. Securities Litigation, In re - §750

Gerard v. Empire Square Realty Co. - §204

Gerdes v. Reynolds - §§666, 668, 670

Gerstle v. Gamble-Skogmo, Inc. - §553

Giant Portland Cement Co., In re - §487

Gilligan, Will & Co. v. SEC - §881

Gimbel v. Signal Companies - §1108

Glazer v. Glazer - §577

Globe Woolen Co. v. Utica Gas & Electric Co. - §265

Globus v. Law Research Service, Inc. - §933

Goldberg v. Meridor - §385

Gollust v. Mendel - §450

Goodman v. Ladd Estate Co. - §157

Goodwin v. Aggasiz - §335

Gottfried v. Gottfried - §940

Gould v. American-Hawaiian Steamship Co. - §553

Graham v. Allis-Chalmers Manufacturing Co. - §231

Gratz v. Claughton - §446

Gray v. First Winthrop Corp. - §436

Gray v. Harris Land & Cattle - §597

Green v. Occidental Petroleum - §404

Greenfield v. Heublein, Inc. - §370

Guiricich v. Emtrol Corp. - §213

Gustafson v. Alloyd Co. - §924

Guth v. Loft, Inc. - §301

Guttman v. Illinois Central Railroad - §791

Haberman v. Tobin - §733

Hall v. Geiger-Jones Co. - §857

Hamill v. Davis - §100

Handley v. Stutz - §812

Hanewald v. Bryan's, Inc. - §821

Hanson Trust PLC v. SCM Corp. - §1172

Harff v. Kerkorian - §713

Hariton v. Arco Electronics, Inc. - §1048

Harris v. American Investment Co. - §§413, 417

Hayes Oyster Co., State ex rel. v. Keypoint Oyster Co. - §262

Healey v. Catalyst Recovery of Pennsylvania, Inc. - §388

Heffernan v. Pacific Dunlop GNB Corp. - §762

Heilbrunn v. Sun Chemical Corp. - §1048

Helms v. Duckworth - §645

Henshaw v. American Cement Co. - §221

Hoff v. Sprayregan - §713

Holdsworth v. Strong - §§352, 398

Holy Cross Gold Mining & Milling Co. v. Goodwin - §206

Holzman v. de Escamilla - §38

Home Fire Insurance Co. v. Barber - §714

Hooper v. Mountain States Securities Corp. - §342

Hornreich Plant Industries, In re - §720

Hospes v. Northwestern Manufacturing & Car Co. - §819

Houle v. Low - §698

Howing Co. v. Nationwide Co. - §551

Humana, Inc. v. American Medicorp, Inc. - §1181

Humphrey v. Winous Co. - §506

Hurley v. Ornsteen - §206

In re - see name of party

Ingle v. Glamore Motor Sales - §601

Insuranshares Corp. v. Northern Fiscal Corp. - §666

International Brotherhood of Teamsters v. Daniel - §873

Ira Haupt & Co., In re - §833

Irving Trust Co. v. Deutsch - §§303, 307

J.F. Anderson Lumber Co. v. Myers - §127

J.I. Case Co. v. Borak - §§544, 555, 556

J.W. Butler Paper Co. v. Cleveland - §90

Jacksonville Mayport, Pablo Railway & Navigation Co. v. Hooper - §141

Janigan v. Taylor - §413

Jeppi v. Brockman Holding Co. - §1062
Johnston v. Greene - §§297, 300
Jones v. H.F. Ahmanson & Co. - §§644, 657
Jordan v. Duff & Phelps, Inc. - §601
Joseph Greenspon's Sons Iron & Steel Co. v. Pecos Valley Gas Co. - §253
Joseph Schlitz Brewing Co. v. Missouri Poultry & Game Co. - §149
Joy v. North - §224

Kamen v. Kemper Financial Services, Inc. - §§686, 688
Kaplan v. Wyatt - §696
Kardon v. National Gypsum Co. - §§342, 344
Katcher v. Ohsman - §575
Katz v. Bregman - §1067
Katzowitz v. Sidler - §849
Keller v. Wilson & Co. - §1083
Kelly v. Bell - §136
Kelner v. Baxter - §110
Kemp & Beatley Inc., *In re* - §1091
Kennecott Copper Corp. v. Curtiss-Wright Corp. - §1173
Kennerson v. Burbank Amusement Co. - §210
Kerbs v. California Eastern Airways - §329
Kern County Land Co. v. Occidental Petroleum Corp. - §§470, 471
Kerrigan v. Unity Savings Association - §305
Kidwell *ex rel.* Penfold v. Meikle - §387
King Manufacturing Co. v. Clay - §337
Kirk v. First National Bank - §721
Kirwan v. Parkway Distillery, Inc. - §275
Klinicki v. Lundgren - §303
Knapp v. Bankers Securities Corp. - §679
Kridelbaug v. Aldrehn Theatre Co. - §114
Kullgren v. Navy Gas & Supply Co. - §743

Lampf, Pleva, Lipkind, Prupis & Petrogrow v. Gilbertson - §§433, 435, 436, 437
Landreth Timber Co. v. Landreth - §874
Leader v. Hycor, Inc. - §1007
Lee v. Jenkins Bros. - §254
Leventhal v. Atlantic Finance Co. - §§1088, 1095
Levine v. Smith - §691
Levisa Oil Corp. v. Quigley - §494
Levitt v. Johnson - §709
Levy v. American Beverage Corp. - §669
Lewis v. Anderson - §701
Lewis v. Curtis - §689
Lewis v. Graves - §686
Lewis v. Mellon Bank - §456
Lewis v. Powell - §605

Lewis v. Varnes - §456
Lichens Co. v. Standard Commercial Tobacco Co. - §1088
Lincoln Stores, Inc. v. Grant - §309
Lindy Bros. Builders v. American Radiator & Standard Sanitary Corp. - §758
Ling & Co. v. Trinity Savings & Loan Association - §612
Long v. Georgia Pacific Railway - §147
Long Park, Inc. v. Trenton-New Brunswick Theatres Co. - §§171, 578
Lovenheim v. Iroquois Brands, Inc. - §539
Lynch v. Vickers Energy Corp. - §§520, 651

McCarthy v. Litton Industries, Inc. - §126
McClure v. Borne Chemical Co. - §739
McCrory v. Chambers - §135
McDonald v. Williams - §978
McDonnell v. American Leduc Petroleums, Ltd. - §234
McNulty v. W. & J. Sloan - §1083
McQuade v. Stoneham & McGraw - §§171, 214, 577
Maddock v. Vorclone Corp. - §502
Marciano v. Nakash - §278
Maryland Metals, Inc. v. Metzner - §309
Matteson v. Ziebarth - §1110
Mayer v. Adams - §704
Meiselman v. Meiselman - §1091
Memorial Hospital Association v. Pacific Grape Products Co. - §253
Michigan Wolverine Student Cooperative v. William Goodyear & Co. - §1063
Miller v. American Telephone & Telegraph Co. - §227
Miller v. Magline, Inc. - §941
Miller v. Miller - §302
Miller v. Register & Tribune Syndicate - §699
Mills v. Electric Auto-Lite Co. - §§545, 549, 554, 557, 756
Milwaukee Refrigerated Transit Co., United States v. - §71
Miner v. Belle Isle Ice Co. - §1088
Minton v. Cavaney - §65
Mitchell v. Texas Gulf Sulphur Co. - §§418, 422
Montecito Water Co., People v. - §89
Moran v. Household International Inc. - §§1163, 1164
Moss v. Morgan Stanley, Inc. - §§360, 361

Namerdy v. Generalcar - §105
New York Trust Co. v. American Realty Co. - §288

Newman, United States v. - §§359, 360
Nims v. Mt. Herman Boys' School - §143
Nixon v. Blackwell - §648
Northridge Cooperative Section No. 1, Inc. v. 32nd Avenue Construction Corp. - §831

Oceanic Exploration Co. v. Grynberg - §584
Old Dominion Copper Mining & Smelting Co. v. Bigelow - §831
Old Dominion Copper Mining & Smelting Co. v. Lewisohn - §832
Oracle Securities Litigation, *In re* - §758
Ortiz v. South Bend Lathe - §125
Osborne v. Locke Steel Chain Co. - §325
Owens v. Palos Verdes Monaco - §24

Page v. Page - §15
Palmer v. Morris - §718
Papilsky v. Berndt - §748
Pappas v. Moss - §273
Paramount Communications, Inc. v. QVC Network - §1162
Paramount Communications, Inc. v. Time, Inc. - §1160
Park, United States v. - §243
Pendergrass v. Care Care, Inc. - §127
Penthouse Properties, Inc. v. 1158 Fifth Ave., Inc. - §596
People v. - *see* name of party
Pepper v. Litton - §633
Perlman v. Feldman - §§671, 753
Pessin v. Chris-Craft Industries, Inc. - §723
Piemonte v. New Boston Garden Corp. - §1002
Pillsbury, State *ex rel.* v. Honeywell, Inc. - §624
Pinter v. Dahl - §399
Piper v. Chris-Craft Industries, Inc. - §§1179, 1180, 1181, 1182
Plaut v. Spendthrift Farms - §436
Polk v. Good - §749
Poole v. N.V. Deli Maatschappij - §1005
Providence & Worcester Co. v. Baker - §489
Pupecki v. James Madison & Co. - §1127

Quaker Hill, Inc. v. Parr - §118

REA Express, Inc. v. Interway Corp. - §352
Rabkin v. Phillip A. Hunt Chemical Corp. - §§1118, 1129
Rafe v. Hinden - §595
Rales v. Blasband - §692
Randall v. Bailey - §§414, 966
Rankin v. Frebank Co. - §727

Rapoport v. 55 Perry Co. - §13
Rath v. Rath Packing Co. - §§1045, 1047
Remillard Brick Co. v. Remillard-Dandini Co. - §278
Reves v. Ernst & Young - §875
Revlon, Inc. v. MacAndrews & Forbes Holdings, Inc. - §§1153, 1155
Rifkin v. Steel Platt - §719
Ringling Bros.-Barnum & Bailey Combined Shows, Inc. v. Ringling - §573
Riser v. Genuine Parts Co. - §619
Rivoli Theatre Co. v. Allison - §268
Roberts v. Whitson - §567
Robertson v. Levy - §§103, 105
Robinson v. Cupples Container Co. - §352
Roby v. Dunnett - §663
Rogers v. American Can Co. - §705
Rogers v. Hill - §§330, 332
Rolf v. Blyth, Eastman, Dillon & Co. - §347
Rondeau v. Mosinee Paper Corp. - §1169
Rosenfeld v. Fairchild Engine & Airplane Corp. - §§560, 561
Rosentool v. Bonanza Oil & Mine Corp. - §618
Ross v. Bernhard - §728
Rothberg v. Rosenbloom - §399
Rowen v. LeMars Mutual Insurance Co. of Iowa - §286
Rubin v. United States - §395
Ruetz v. Topping - §331

S. Solomont & Sons Trust, Inc. v. New England Theatres Operating Corp. - §710
Saigh v. Busch - §709
San Joaquin Light & Power Co., *In re* - §1101
Santa Fe Industries, Inc. v. Green - §§382, 383
Sax v. World Wide Press, Inc. - §676
Schein v. Chasen - §476
Schnell v. Chris-Craft Industries, Inc. - §160
Schumacher v. Schumacher - §681
Schwartz v. Marien - §850
Schwartz v. United Merchants & Manufacturers, Inc. - §252
SEC v. Carter Hawley Hale Stores, Inc. - §1171
SEC v. Chinese Consolidated Benevolent Association - §881
SEC v. Glenn W. Turner Enterprises, Inc. - §872
SEC v. MacDonald - §419
SEC v. Materia - §358
SEC v. Maurice Rind - §437
SEC v. Ralston-Purina Co. - §886
SEC v. Texas Gulf Sulphur Co. - §§343, 345, 366, 368, 427

SEC v. W.J. Howey Co. - §872

Shapiro v. Merrill Lynch, Pierce, Fenner & Smith, Inc. - §424

Shidler v. All American Life & Financial Corp. - §553

Shlensky v. South Parkway Building Corp. - §§267, 284

Shlensky v. Wrigley - §§136, 225

Silva v. Coastal Plywood & Timber Co. - §607

Sinclair Oil Corp. v. Levien - §§295, 634, 635, 636

Sisco-Hamilton Co. v. Lennon - §70

Skouras v. Admiralty Enterprises, Inc. - §619

Smith v. Atlantic Properties, Inc. - §§650, 942

Smith v. Brown-Borhek Co. - §706

Smith v. Van Gorkom - §226

Smolowe v. Delendo Corp. - §469

Sohland v. Baker - §807

Solimine v. Hollander - §763

Speedway Realty Co. v. Grasshoff Realty Corp. - §120

Stahl v. Gibralter Financial Corp. - §552

Stanley J. How & Associates v. Boss - §119

State ex rel. - see name of party

State Teachers Retirement Board v. Fluor Corp. - §372

Steinberg v. Adams - §560

Sterling v. Mayflower Hotel Corp. - §§294, 1107

Stokes v. Continental Trust Co. - §§836, 847

Strong v. Repide - §336

Studebaker v. Gittlin - §525

Summers v. Dooley - §22

Sunstrand v. Sun Chemical Corp. - §347

Superintendent of Insurance v. Bankers Life & Casualty Co. - §344

Surowitz v. Hilton Hotels Corp. - §724

Sutton's Hospital Care - §141

Swinney v. Keebler Co. - §669

TSC Industries, Inc. v. Northway, Inc. - §§345, 545

Tandycrafts, Inc. v. Initio Partners - §757

Taylor v. Standard Gas & Electric Co. - §§73, 76

Taylor v. Wright - §336

Teller v. W.A. Griswold Co. - §1063

Terry v. Penn Central Corp. - §1060

Teschner v. Chicago Title & Trust Co. - §1117

Theis v. Spokane Falls Gaslight Co. - §1110

Theodora Holding Corp. v. Henderson - §712

Thompson & Green Machinery Co. v. Music City Lumber Co. - §105

Tift v. Forage King Industries - §§122, 127

Timberline Equipment Co. v. Davenport - §§103, 105, 106

Tri-Continental Corp. v. Battye - §1004

Trustees of Dartmouth College v. Woodward - §§1074, 1081

Tucson Gas & Electric Co. v. Schantz - §616

Tu-Vu Drive-In Corp. v. Ashkins - §606

Union Pacific Railroad v. Trustees, Inc. - §136

United Copper Securities Co. v. Amalgamated Copper Co. - §690

United States v. - see name of party

Unitrin, Inc. v. American General Corp. - §§1154, 1164

Unocal Corp. v. Mesa Petroleum Co. - §§1150, 1152, 1153, 1154, 1156, 1158, 1160, 1161

Untermeyer v. Fidelity Daily Income Trust - §693

Upjohn Co. v. United States - §726

Valuation of Common Stock of Mcloon Oil Co., In re - §1012

Van Kampen v. Detroit Bank & Trust Co. - §605

Veco Corp. v. Babcock - §309

Vincent Drug Co. v. Utah State Tax Commission - §103

Vine v. Beneficial Finance Co. - §393

Virginia Bankshares v. Sandberg - §§546, 547, 548, 550, 551

Vogel v. Melish - §609

Walkovszky v. Carlton - §70

Waltuch v. ContiCommodity Services, Inc. - §§765, 771

Watson v. Button - §721

Webber v. Webber Oil Co. - §198

Weeks Dredging & Contracting, Inc. v. American Dredging Co. - §1181

Weil v. Berseth - §573

Weinberger v. UOP, Inc. - §§520, 1007, 1111, 1118, 1129

Weiss Medical Complex, Ltd. v. Kim - §258

Wellman v. Dickinson - §1171

Western Air Lines v. Sobieski - §1205

Whetstone v. Ottawa University - §135

Wilkes v. Springside Nursing Home, Inc. - §649

Wilson v. Great American Industries, Inc. - §551

Winchell v. Plywood Corp. - §205

Wirtz v. Ocala Gas Co. - §71

Wolfson v. Avery - §506

Wood v. Dummer - §820

Wood v. National City Bank - §976

Zaist v. Olson - §68
Zapata Corp. v. Maldonado - §696
Zetlin v. Hanson Holdings, Inc. - §654

Zion v. Kurtz - §581
Zobrist v. Coal-X, Inc. - §398

INDEX

A

AFFILIATED CORPORATIONS, §70
AGENT
    for service of process, §79
    officer as, §§245-249. *See also* Officers
ALTER EGO THEORY, §67
    See also Piercing corporate veil
AMENDMENT OF ARTICLES, §§1068-1084
    See also Articles of incorporation
ANTI-FRAUD PROVISIONS
    See Securities Act of 1933
APPRAISAL RIGHTS, §§999-1020
    See also Fundamental changes
    amendment of articles, §1073
    de facto mergers, §§1044, 1047-1048, 1052, 1055
    generally, §999
    "going private," §§1125-1129
    mergers, §§999-1022
    procedure, §§1014-1020
        costs, §1020
        defense to demand, §1018
        demand, §1017
        notice, §§1015-1016
        proceedings, §1019
    sale of assets, §§1065-1066
        stock for assets, §1045
    statutory mergers, §§1000-1022, 1030-1043
    triangular mergers, §1060
    valuation, §§1000-1013
        discounts, §§1009-1013
        "fair market value" statutes, §1008
        "fair value" statutes, §§1001-1007
ARTICLES OF INCORPORATION, §§78-81
    amendment, §§1068-1084
    appraisal rights, §1073
        constitutional issues, §§1074-1084
        contracts, §§1074-1076
        limitations on shareholders, §§1083-1084
        limitations on state, §§1081-1082
        reserved power clauses, §1077
        shareholder amendment, §1078
            generally, §1068
            procedures, §§1069-1073
        voting, §§1069-1072
            class, §1070
    authorization of shares, §§793-799
    contents, §§79-81
        mandatory, §79
            agent for service, §79
            authorized shares, §79
            name, §79
        optional, §80
            business purpose, §81
            directors, §80
            par value, §80
    execution, §78
    filing, §78
AUTHORIZATION OF SHARES, §§793-799

B

BLUE SKY LAWS, §§857-863
    issuance of shares, §§857-863
        fraud type, §858
        license type, §859
        registration type, §§860-863
BOARD OF DIRECTORS
    See Directors
BREACH OF CONTRACT
    promoters, §§110-120. *See also* Promoters
    stock subscriptions, §§801-805. *See also* Stock
        subscriptions
BUSINESS ASSOCIATIONS, §9
BUSINESS JUDGMENT RULE, §§225-228, 315-320,
        690-692
BYLAWS
    adoption, §§83-84
    shareholder approval, §168
    transfer restrictions, §590. *See also* Transfer of shares

C

CAPITAL REDUCTION SURPLUS, §§961-964
CAPITALIZATION
    authorization of shares, §§793-799
    inadequate, §65
    issuance of shares, §§797-799. *See also* Issuance of
        shares
    stock subscriptions, §§800-805. *See also* Stock
        subscriptions
CERTIFICATE OF INCORPORATION
    See Articles of incorporation
CHARACTERISTICS, §§1-59
    corporations, §§1-6
        centralized management, §4
        entity status, §1
        limited liability, §2
        perpetual existence, §5
        taxation, §6
        transfer of interest, §3. *See also* Shares
    joint venture, §34
    limited liability companies, §§45-59
    limited liability partnerships, §§41-44
    limited partnerships, §§35-40
    partnerships, §§8-34
CLOSE CORPORATIONS
    alter ego theory, §67
    defined, §170
    formalities, §173
    obligations of shareholders, §§645-650
    shareholder agreements, §§171-172, 177. *See also*
        Voting agreements
        agreements concerning management, §177
        modern trend, §172
        traditional view, §171
    shareholders' rights, §§178-179
        direct management, §§178-179

dividends, §942
  management liabilities, §179
  minority rights, §§645-657
statutory close corporation status, §§173-185
  California statute, §175
  Delaware statute, §§174, 181-184
  Model Close Corporation Supplement, §185
transferees' rights and liabilities, §§180-185
  Delaware statute, §181
  Model Statutory Close Corporation Supplement, §185

COMMON FUND DOCTRINE, §755
COMMON STOCK, §§783-784
  See also Shares
COMPENSATION
  See Conflict of interest; Directors
CONFLICT OF INTEREST, §§256-332
  business dealings with corporation, §§257-288
    participation in meeting, §§258-259
    remedies, §§283-288
      damages, §§284-287
      rescission, §288
    statutes, §§277-282
    voidable transactions, §§260-276
      disclosure requirement, §§262-264, 278
      fairness requirement, §§265-267, 278-279
      ratification, §§268-276
      statutes, §§277-282
  compensation for services, §§310-332
    authorization, §§311-313
    business judgment rule, §§315-320
    future services, §§328-329
    past services, §§324-327
    reasonableness, §§314-332
    value of services, §§330-332
    waste, §§321-332
  competing with corporation, §309
  corporate opportunity doctrine, §§296-308
    and "interested" director, §300
    corporation unable, §§302-304
    corporation unwilling, §305
    defined, §§297-301
    remedies, §§306-308
  duty of loyalty, §256
  insider trading, §§333-484. *See also* Insider trading
  interlocking directorates, §§289-295
CONFLICT OF LAWS, §§1204-1209
CONSIDERATION, §§806-826
  amount, §§810-826
    blue sky laws, §825
    California rule, §826
    no-par value shares, §§823-824
      "stated value," §824
    par value shares, §§811-822
      good faith rule, §822
      watered stock, §§813-822. *See also* Watered stock
  executory, §§807-809
  form, §§806-809
  improper, §§807-808
  secured obligations, §808
CONSOLIDATION, §1022

  See also Mergers
CONTRACTS
  breach. *See* Breach of contract
  promoters'. *See* Promoters
  ultra vires acts, §§145-157. *See also* Ultra vires acts
CONTROL PERSONS
  See Conflict of interest; Directors; Officers
CONTROLLING SHAREHOLDERS
  See Fiduciary duties
CORPORATE OPPORTUNITY DOCTRINE, §§296-308
  See also Conflict of interest
CORPORATE POWERS
  See Powers
CORPORATE PURPOSE
  See Purpose
CORPORATE RECORDS
  See Directors; Shareholders
CORPORATE STRUCTURE, CHANGES
  See Fundamental changes
CORPORATIONS BY ESTOPPEL, §§94-98
  shareholders, §§95, 97
  technical defenses, §96
  tort claims, §98
CREDITORS' RIGHTS
  dissolution, §§1103-1106
  liquidation, §§1103-1106
  suits vs. shareholders. *See* Piercing corporate veil
  watered stock, §§817-822
CRIMINAL ACTIONS
  anti-fraud (1933 Act), §§904-933
  rule 10b-5, §§428, 934-938
  ultra vires, §144
CUMULATIVE VOTING
  See Voting rights

D

DE FACTO CORPORATIONS, §§91-106. *See also* Estoppel, corporations by
  and corporations by estoppel, §94
  liability of, §§97-98, 104-106
  requirements, §92
  statutes eliminating, §§103-104
DE FACTO MERGERS, §§1044-1056
  acquisition of assets for stock, §1045
  acquisition of majority stock, §1046
  doctrine, §1047
  equal dignity rule, §1048
  statutory abolition, §§1049-1056
    California, §§1050-1055
    New York Stock Exchange, §1056
DE JURE CORPORATIONS, §§88-90
  mandatory and directory, §90
  substantial compliance, §89
DEADLOCK, §1090
DEEP ROCK DOCTRINE, §§73-76
DELEGATION OF AUTHORITY BY DIRECTORS
  See Directors
DERIVATIVE SUITS, §§675-778. *See also* Shareholders

contemporaneous ownership, §§714-719
defenses, §§742-743
demand on directors, §§684-701
demand on shareholders, §§702-711
direct suit compared, §§678-682
exhaustion of corporate remedies, §§683-711
former shareholders action, compare, §721
indemnification of control persons, §§760-774. *See also*
    Indemnification
insurance against liability, §§775-777
multiple suits, §722
piercing corporate veil, §719
plaintiff qualifications, §§712-723
procedural issues, §§724-728
   jury trial, §§727-728
   pleadings, §724
reimbursement for litigation costs, §§754-759
   common fund doctrine, §755
   "substantial benefit," §§756-757
res judicata, §744
security for expenses, §§729-741
settlement and recovery, §§745-753
suits by officers compared, §778

DIRECTORS
See also Conflict of interest; Officers
appointment, §§186-190
   number, §187
   qualifications, §188
   vacancies, §§189-190
casual sales, §§880-884
classified boards, §192
compensation. *See also* Conflict of interest
   as director, §215
   as officer, §217
   conflict of interest, §218
   extraordinary services, §216
   waste, §219
conflict of interest, §§256-332. *See also* Conflict of
    interest
duties, statutory, §§239-243
duty of due care, §§223-237
   amount of care, §§224-229
   bank directors, §229
   business judgment rule, §§225-228
   defenses, §§233-237
   liability, §§230-232
duty of loyalty, §238
election of, §162
functioning of board, §§200-214
   delegation of authority, §§207-210
   meetings, §§200-206
   noncompliance, consequences, §§204-206
   provisional directors, §§211-213
   voting agreements, §214
illegal dividends, §§242, 971-975
indemnity. *See* Indemnification
insider trading. *See* Insider trading
insurance against liability. *See* Derivative suits
interested. *See* Officers
meetings, §§200-206
   noncompliance, §§204-206

notice, §201
organizational, §84
quorum, §202
voting, §§203-206
power to bind beyond term, §193
provisional, §§211-213
removal, §§194-199
   by board, §§164, 197
   by court, §§165, 198-199
   by shareholders, §§163, 194-196
right to inspect records, §§220-222
statutory duties, §§239-243
suits by, §778
term, §§191-193
   classified boards, §192
   power to bind beyond, §193
voting agreements, §214

DISREGARD OF CORPORATE ENTITY
"alter ego," §§61, 67
commingling of assets, §62
domination and control by shareholder, §66
fraud, dishonesty, wrong, or injustice requirement, §68
in favor of corporation or shareholders, §72
lack of corporate formalities, §63
piercing corporate wall between affiliated corporations,
   §70
suits by corporate creditors against shareholders,
   §§61-69
undercapitalization, §65
use of corporate form to evade statutory or contract
   obligations, §71

DISSOLUTION, §§1085-1097
involuntary, §§1087-1097
   actions by shareholders or directors, §§1088-1094,
    1096
   close corporations, §1091
   deadlock, §1090
   purchase of plaintiff's shares, §§1093-1094
   shareholder agreement, §1096
   standing, §1092
   state actions, §1097
partnerships, §§15-21, 52-56
   limited liability partnerships, §§52-56
   RUPA disassociation, §§18-21
voluntary, §§1086, 1094

DIVIDENDS, §§939-978
defined, §939
nimble, §§945-947, 949
remedies for illegal, §§971-978
   directors' liability, §§971-975
    contribution, §§974-975
    defenses, §973
   shareholders' liability, §§976-978
right to, §§941-942
source of, §§943-970
   California rule, §§950-951
   capital reduction surplus, §§961-964
   contractual restrictions §970
   earned surplus, §§957-958
   insolvency, §§954, 967-968
   limitation, §954

nimble dividends, §§945-947, 949
notice, §955
paid-in surplus, §§959-960
preferred stock, §969
reappraisal surplus, §§965-966
RMBCA, §§952-955
stated capital, §§944-947
wasting asset corporations, §947
DONATIONS, §§133-139
DUE CARE
   See Directors

E

ENTERPRISE LIABILITY, §70
ENTITY THEORY, §1
EQUAL OPPORTUNITY DOCTRINE, §§655-657
ESTOPPEL, CORPORATIONS BY, §§94-98
   effect of statutes, §105
EVASION OF OBLIGATIONS, §71
EXPERTS
   liability, §§913-914
   reliance on, §236

F

FIDUCIARY DUTIES
   controlling shareholders
      actions in shareholder capacity, §644
      business dealings with corporations, §§634-639
         parent-subsidiary, §635
      close corporations, §§645-650
      corporate opportunities, §§640-642
      disclosure, §651
      fundamental changes
         appraisal rights, §§1125-1126
         fairness, §§1107-1108
         freeze-outs, §§1109-1118
            business purpose, §§1115-1117
            fairness, §1118
            going private, §§1121-1124
            mergers, §1111
         reverse stock splits, §1112
            rule 13e-3, §§1121-1124
            sale of assets, §1110
            securities laws, §1119
            two kinds, §1113
         preemptive rights, §§849-850
         remedies, §§1125-1129
         self-tender, §1120
      sale or transfer of control, §§652-671
         corporate action, §663
         equal opportunity doctrine, §§655-657
         fraud and nondisclosure, §664
         general rule, §§653-657
         sale of office, §§659-662
         to looters, §§665-671
      directors. *See* Conflict of interest; Directors; Insider
        trading

promoters, §§108, 827-834. *See also* Promoters
FRAUD
   anti-fraud provisions. *See* Securities Act of 1933
   blue sky laws, §§857-863
   piercing corporate veil, §68
FREEZE-OUTS, §§1109-1118. *See also* Fiduciary duties
FUNDAMENTAL CHANGES, §§998-1203
   amendment of articles, §§1068-1084. *See also* Articles
      of incorporation
   controlling shareholder power, §§1107-1129. *See also*
      fiduciary duties
   de facto mergers, §§1044-1056
   dissolution, §§1085-1097. *See also* Dissolution
   liquidation, §§1098-1106. *See also* Liquidation
   mergers and consolidations, §§1021-1060. *See also*
      Mergers and consolidations
   sale of substantially all assets, §§1061-1067. *See also*
      Sale of substantially all assets
   tender offers, §§1130-1203. *See* Acquisition of stock

GH

GOING PRIVATE TRANSACTIONS, §§1121-1124
GUARANTEES, §131

I

INDEMNIFICATION
   derivative suits, §§768-777
   directors, §§760-774, 932-933
   insurance for, §§775-777
INSIDER TRADING, §§333-484
   See also Rule 10b-5
   common law duty of disclosure, §§334-337
      "special facts" approach, §336
      to shareholders, §§334-337
   common law liability, §476
      rule 10b-5 compared, §§482-484
      section 16 compared, §§477-481
   remedies, §§400-429
      application, §§409-429
         closely held corporations, §§410-414, 420
         government, §§426-429
         publicly held corporations, §§415-425
      civil penalties, §429
      criminal sanctions, §428
      damages, §§402-408
         benefit of bargain, §403
         out-of-pocket, §§402-404
         restitutionary relief, §§405-408
      injunctive, §427
      rescission, §§406-408
   rule 10b-5, §§339-437. *See also* Rule 10b-5
      defenses, §§397-399
      elements of plaintiff's action, §§344-352
         diligence, §398
         materiality, §345

reliance, §§349-352
scienter, §§346-348
jurisdiction, §§430-431
nondisclosure, §§340, 353-372
persons liable, §§340-341, 353-395
insiders, §§345-348, 353-355, 382-399, 451-456
temporary insiders, §380
non-insiders, §§356-396
aiders and abettors, §§381, 485
pari delicto defense, §§398-399
tippees, tippers §§373-379
purchaser or seller, §§390-396
remedies, §§400-429
application, §§409-429
closely held corp., §§410-414, 420
government, §§426-429
publicly held corp., §§415-425
potential damages, §§401-408
securities covered, §342
standing, §§343-344, 390-396
statute of limitations, §§433-437
section 16, §§440-484
generally, §§440-450
disclosure, §§440-442
liability, §§443-471
objective theory, §469
subjective theory, §§470-471
insiders, §§451-465
beneficial ownership, §§457-465
deputization, §454
director, §§453-454
officer, §452
relatives, §460
time status is determined, §§455-456, 463-465
purchase and sale, §§466-471
"garden variety," §466
unorthodox, §§467-471
rule 10b-5 compared, §§472-475
securities affected, §439
short swing profit, §§445-447
who may recover, §§448-450
Securities Exchange Act of 1934, §338
generally, §338
jurisdiction, §§430-431
rule 10b- 5. *See* Rule 10b-5, above.
section 16. *See* Section 16, above.
statute of limitations, §§433-437
venue and service, §432
INSPECTION OF RECORDS, §§614-632
See also Directors; Shareholders
common law, §615
mandatory disclosure compared, §§625-632
proxy rules, §629
state statutes, §§630-632
proper purposes, §§619-623
litigation, §623
multiple purposes, §620
proxy fights, §622
social or political reasons, §624
statutes, §§616-617
types of records, §614

INSURANCE AGAINST DERIVATIVE SUIT LIABILITY, §§775-777
INTERLOCKING DIRECTORATES, §§289-295
ISSUANCE OF SHARES
See also Preemptive rights
blue sky laws, §§857-863. *See also* Blue sky laws
consideration. *See* Consideration
federal regulation, §§864-938. *See also* Securities Act of 1933
generally, §§797-799
state regulation, §§857-863. *See also* Blue sky laws
stock subscriptions. *See* Stock subscriptions
underwriting, §§852-855

JK

JOINT VENTURE, §19

L

LIABILITY
corporation, §2
directors
criminal, §243
defenses, §§233-237
due care, §§230-232
experts, §§913-914
illegal dividends, §§242, 971-975
insider trading. *See* insider trading
rule 10b-5, §241
Securities Act of 1933, §240
limited liability companies, §§45, 58
limited liability partnership, §42
limited partnership, §§35-40
partnership, §§11, 30-33
promoters. *See* Promoters
shareholders, §§97, 99-101
LIMITATION OF ACTIONS
See Statute of limitations
LIMITED LIABILITY COMPANIES, §§45-59
advantages, §57
close corporation compared, §59
defined, §45
dissolution and withdrawal, §§52-56
distributions, §51
duration, §47
limited partnership compared, §58
management, §50
organization, §46
ownership, §48
transfer of interests, §49
LIMITED PARTNERSHIPS, §§35-40
LIQUIDATION, §§1098-1106
creditors' rights, §§1103-1106
management, §1099
nature of, §1098
shareholders' rights, §§1100-1102

M

MANAGEMENT AND CONTROL, §§159-332
  See also Conflict of Interest
  centralized, §4
  directors. *See* Directors
  limited liability companies, §50
  officers. *See* Officers
  partnerships, §§22-23
  shareholders' rights, §§161-185. *See also* Fiduciary
      duties; Shareholders
  close corporations. *See* Close corporations
  generally, §159
MEETINGS
  directors'. *See also* Conflict of interest
    noncompliance, §§204-206
    notice, §201
    organizational, §§82-84
    quorum, §202
    voting, §203
  shareholders', §§491-496
MERGERS, §§1021-1060
  appraisal rights, §§999-1020
    exceptions, §§1038-1043
    procedure, §§1014-1020
    valuation of shares, §§1000-1013
  consolidations, §1022
  de facto mergers, §§1044-1056. *See also* De Facto
      mergers
  statutory mergers, §§1021-1043
    board approval, §1026
    consolidation, §1022
    effect, §§1023-1025
    generally, §1021
    shareholder approval, §§1027-1043
      appraisal rights, §1030
        exceptions, §§1038-1042
      class voting, §1029
      exclusivity, §1043
      percentage required, §1028
      short form, §§1031-1034
      small scale mergers, §§1035-1037
  triangular mergers, §§1057-1060
    conventional, §1058
    reverse triangular merger, §1059
    voting and appraisal rights, §1060
MINORITY RIGHTS
  See Fiduciary duties; Voting rights

N

NIMBLE DIVIDENDS, §§945-947, 949
  See also Dividends
NO-PAR VALUE STOCK
  See Par value
NOTICE
  directors' meeting, §201
  noncompliance, §§204-206

O

OFFICERS
  See also Control persons; Directors
  authority, §§245-255
    power to bind corporation, §§253-254
    president, §§250-254
    ratification, §249
    types of authority, §§245-249
  casual sales, §§881-884
  conflict of interest. *See* Conflict of interest
  duties, §255
  election, §§83-84, 244
  insider trading. *See* Insider trading
  suits by, §778
ORGANIZATIONAL MEETINGS, §§82-84
  bylaws, §§83-84
  directors, §§83-84
  election of officers, §§83-84
  issuance of shares, §§83-84
  notice, §201
ORGANIZING THE CORPORATION, §§77-106
  articles of incorporation, §§78-81. *See also* Articles of
      incorporation
  corporations by estoppel, §§94-98
  de facto corporations, §§91-93
  de jure corporations, §§88-90
  defective, liability, §§99-106
  organizational meetings, §§82-84. *See also* Organiza-
      tional meetings

P

PAR VALUE, §§811-823. *See also* Shares; Watered stock
  articles of incorporation, §80
PARTNERSHIPS, §§7-44
  authority, §§24-27
  defined, §9
  dissimilarities, §§9-33
  dissolution, §§14-21
    RUPA disassociation, §§18-21
  duration, §14
  governing by agreement, §§22-23
  joint ventures, §34
  liability, §§11, 30-33
  limited liability companies, §§45-59
  limited liability partnership, §§41-44
  limited partnerships, §§35-40
  management and control, §§22-23
  ownership of assets, §§28-29
  participation and corporate power, §132
  transfer of interest, §§12-13
PERPETUAL EXISTENCE, §5
PIERCING CORPORATE VEIL, §§60-72
  between affiliated corporations, §70
  generally, §60
  in favor of corporation or shareholders, §72
  suits by creditors vs. shareholders, §§61-69
    alter ego theory, §67
    commingling, §62

fraud, §68
inadequate capitalization, §65
lack of formalities, §63

POOLING AGREEMENTS, §564. *See also* Voting
agreements

POWERS, §§128-158
express, §128
implied, §128
modern statutes, §129
problem areas, §§130-139
donations, §§133-139
guarantees, §131
participation in partnership, §132
ultra vires acts. *See* Ultra vires acts

PREDECESSOR BUSINESS, OBLIGATIONS OF,
§§121-127
general rule—no liability, §122
exceptions, §§123-127

PREEMPTIVE RIGHTS, §§835-851. *See also* Issuance
of shares
authorized but unissued shares, §§843-844
common law, §836
consideration other than cash, §§845-846
defined, §835
equitable limitations on issuance, §§848-851
fiduciary duty, §§849-850
quasi-preemptive rights, §848
rule 10b-5, §851
more than one class, §§841-842
quasi-preemptive rights, §848
remedies, §847
statutes, §§837-840

PREFERRED SHARES, §§785-792
See also Shares

PRIVATE PLACEMENTS, §§886-898
available information required, §887
holding period, §893
investment intent, §§889-897
legal imprint, §890
noncontrol persons, §896
notice, §895
offerees, §887
restricted securities, §§891-898
small offerings, §888

PROMOTERS
contracts, §§110-120
corporation rights and liabilities, §§110-116
American rule, §§113-116
English rule, §§110-111, 116
Massachusetts rule, §112
quasi-contract, §§111, 115
right to enforce, §116
promoters' rights and liabilities, §§117-120
liability, §§118-119
third parties, §120
defined, §107
fiduciary duties, §§108, 827-834
to corporation, §§827-832
additional shares, §§830-832
disclosure, §828
sole shareholders, §829

to each other, §108
watered stock, §§813-822
creditors' remedies, §§817-822
securities laws, §§833-834

PROXY SOLICITATION, §§519-561
See also Voting rights
expenses of proxy contests, §§559-561
federal proxy rules, §§521-558
disclosure, §531
jurisdiction, §§552, 558
material facts, §§545-546
shareholder proposals, §§533-541
violation of, §§543-558
administrative remedies, §543
causation, §§549-551
"fairness," §§548, 554
private suits, §§544-558
remedies, §§555-557
scienter, §553
generally, §§511-519
securities covered, §§522-530
state regulation, §520

PURPOSE
corporate, §81

Q

QUASI-CONTRACT, §§111, 115
QUORUM, §202
QUO WARRANTO ACTIONS, §§87, 93

R

RATIFICATION
directors' failure to exercise due care, §§237, 913-919
interested director transactions, §§268-276
officers' acts, §249
promoters' contracts, §§110-120

REDEMPTION AND REPURCHASE, §§979-997
limitations on, §§987-996
bona fide purposes, §§993-996
California rule, §985
insolvency, §§987-992
liquidation preferences, §969
rule 10b-5, §996
redemption, §§979-980
source of funds, §980
remedies for unlawful, §997
repurchase, §§981-986
power to repurchase, §982
source of funds, §§983-986
stated capital, §986

REGISTRATION STATEMENT, §§864-938
See also Securities Act of 1933
false, §§904-938

REPURCHASE, §§981-986
See also Redemption and repurchase

REVERSE STOCK SPLITS, §1112. *See also* Freeze-outs
RULE 10b-5, §§339-437, 472-475

See also Insider trading
common law liability, compare, §§482-484
elements, §§344-352
  diligence, §398
  materiality, §345
  reliance, §§349-352
  scienter, §§346-348
insider trading. *See* Insider trading
jurisdiction, §§430-431
nondisclosure, §§340, 353-372
persons liable, §§340-341, 353-395
  aiders and abettors, §§381, 485
  insiders, §§345-348, 353-355, 382-399, 451-456
  temporary insiders, §380
  tippees, tippers, §§373-379
section 16, compared, §§472-475
securities covered, §342
  standing, §§343-344, 390-396
  statute of limitations, §§433-437

S

SALE OF SUBSTANTIALLY ALL ASSETS,
      §§1061-1067
appraisal rights, §§1065-1066
defined, §1067
shareholder approval, §§1061-1064
  failing circumstances, §1063
  mortgages, pledges, §1064
  "ordinary course of business" sales, §1062
SECTION 16
See Insider trading
SECURITIES ACT OF 1933, §§864-938
anti-fraud provisions, §§904-938
  exempt securities, §931
  false registration statement, §§905-922
    damages, §§921-922
    defenses, §§915-920
    elements, §§909-912
    experts, §§919-920
    standing, §§906-908
    who may be liable, §§913-920
  general civil liability, §§923-928
  implied civil liability, §§929-930
  indemnification, §§932-933
  rule 10b-5 compared, §§934-938
disclosure, integrated, §§868-869
effective date, §878
exempt securities, §879
exempt transactions, §§880-903
  casual sales, §§881-885
    control persons, §§883-884
    secondary distributions, §882
  dealer sales, §885
  intrastate offerings, §899
  private placements, §§886-898. *See also* Private
    placements
  regulation A, §901
  rule 145, §902
  small businesses, §903

generally, §864
offer to sell, §870
promoters' fiduciary duties, §§833-834
registration statement, §§865-867, 876, 905-922
  contents, §876
  false, §§905-922
  waiting period, §§866-867
remedies, §§904-938
security defined, §§871-874
shelf registration, §869
statutory prospectus, §877
SECURITIES EXCHANGE ACT OF 1934
See Insider trading; Proxy solicitation; Rule 10b-5;
    Section 16
SHAREHOLDERS
alter ego theory, §67. *See also* Piercing corporate veil
appointment of directors. *See* Directors
bylaws, §168
close corporations, §§169-172, 177-179
Deep Rock doctrine, §§73-76
derivative suits. *See* Derivative suits
dividends. *See* Dividends
election of directors, §162
fiduciary obligations. *See* Fiduciary duties
liability
  corporation by estoppel, §§95, 97-98
  no corporation, §§99-101
  statutes, §§102-105
management and control, §§161-175. *See also*
    Management and control
meetings, §§491-496
organic changes, §161. *See also* Fundamental changes
preemptive rights. *See* Preemptive rights
ratification, §166
redemption and repurchase. *See* Redemption and
    repurchase
removal of directors, §§163, 194-196
right to inspect records, §§614-624. *See also* Inspection,
    right to
  common law, §615
  political and social interests, §624
  proper purpose, §§618-624
    proxy fights, §622
  Securities Exchange Act of 1934, §§626-629
  state disclosure statutes, §§630-632
  statutes, §§616-617
  types of records, §614
subordination of debts, §§73-76. *See also* Piercing
    corporate veil
suits by, §§672-778
  class action, §674
  derivative, §§675-777. *See also* Derivative suits
  direct, §§673-674, 679-682
  directors, officers, compare, §675
  generally, §672
suits by creditors vs., §§61-69. *See also* Piercing
    corporate veil
voting rights, §§485-589. *See also* Voting rights
SHARES
authorization, §§794-795
classes, §§782-792

common, §§783-784
preferred, §§785-792
  cumulative, §790
  noncumulative, §791
  participation, §792
  redemption, §787. *See also* Redemption and
    repurchase
consideration. *See* Consideration
defined, §779
generally, §§779-781
issuance, §§83-84, 796-799. *See also* Issuance of shares
redemption. *See* Redemption and repurchase
transfer. *See* Transfer of shares

SHORT-FORM MERGERS, §§1031-1034, 1039
SHORT SWING PROFITS, §§445-447
See also Insider trading; Section 16
SMALL-SCALE MERGERS, §§1035-1037, 1039
STATUTORY MERGERS, §§1021-1043. *See also*
    Mergers
STOCK
See Shares
STOCK DIVIDENDS
See Dividends
STOCK SUBSCRIPTIONS, §§800-805
offer and acceptance, §§801-805
  pre-incorporation, §§802-805
    separate agreement, §§803-804
      continuing offer, §803
      irrevocable contract, §804
    statutes, §805
STOCK TRANSFERS
See Transfer of shares
STOCKHOLDERS
See Shareholders
SUBORDINATION OF DEBTS, §§73-76
SUBSCRIPTIONS
See Stock subscriptions
SUBSTANTIAL COMPLIANCE, §89. *See also* De jure
    corporations
SURPLUS
See Dividends

T

TENDER OFFERS, §§1130-1203
federal securities law, §§1165-1185
  antifraud provision, §§1179-1185
  information statement, §§1174-1175
  issuers' tender offers, §1178
  notice of ownership, §§1166-1169
  obligations of management, §1177
  regulation of terms, §1176
  tender offer defined, §§1170-1173
    alternative test, §1172
    eight-factor test, §1171
    open market purchases, §1173
generally, §§1143-1164
  approval, §1100
  conditions, §1144
  defensive tactics, §§1149-1164

    balance element, §1152
    best interests test, §1151
    best value, §1159
    lock-up provisions, §1157
    negotiation with third party, §§1155-1156
    no-shop provision, §1158
    poison pill, §§1163-1164
    standards of scrutiny, §1153
  friendly vs. hostile, §1147
  second-step transactions, §1146
  toehold acquisitions, §1145
state law, §§1186-1203
  first generation, §§1187-1189
  second generation, §§1190-1198
  third generation, §§1199-1203
terminology, §§1130-1142
Williams Act, §§1170-1185
  remedies, §§1179-1185
TORTS
ultra vires acts, §101
TRANSFER RESTRICTIONS
See Transfer of shares
TRANSFER OF SHARES
generally, §3
restrictions, §§590-613
  notice, §§610-613
  shares subject to, §§606-608
  transactions subject to, §609
  types, §§591-593
validity, §§594-605
  options, §600
  right of first refusal, §599
  statutes. §§602-604
  termination of employment, §601

U

ULTRA VIRES ACTS, §§140-158
contract actions, §§145-157
  common law, §§145-150
    executory contracts, §146
    federal rule, §150
    fully performed contracts, §147
    partly performed, §§148-150
  statutes, §§151-158
criminal actions, §144
defined, §140
torts, §143
UNDERWRITING, §§852-855
"best efforts," §854
defined, §852
"firm commitment," §853
regulation of, §855

V

VOTING AGREEMENTS
See also Voting rights
close corporations, §§563-581

directors, §214
shareholders. *See* Voting rights
voting trusts, §§510-518
VOTING RIGHTS, §§485-589
close corporations, §§562-589
   voting agreements, §§563-581
   voting trusts, §§582-589
cumulative voting, §§499-510
   avoidance devices, §§503-510
      reducing board size, §510
      removal of minority directors, §§507-509
      staggered terms, §504
generally, §§485-490
proxy, §§511-561
   defined, §511
   expenses of proxy contests, §§559-561
   formalities, §512
   revocability, §§513-518

solicitation, §§519-558. *See also* Proxy solicitation
shareholders' meetings, §§491-496
straight voting, §§497-498
VOTING TRUSTS, §§582-589

WXYZ

WASTE, §§321-332
WATERED STOCK, §§813-822, 825
creditors' remedies, §§817-822
   misrepresentation theory, §819
   trust fund theory, §820
   value of consideration, §822
types, §§814-816
WILLIAMS ACT, §§1165-1185
   See also Acquisition of stock

Notes

Notes